W9-DGM-477

ARCHAEOLOGY AND FERTILITY CULT IN THE ANCIENT MEDITERRANEAN

PAPERS PRESENTED AT THE FIRST INTERNATIONAL CONFERENCE ON ARCHAEOLOGY OF THE ANCIENT MEDITERRANEAN

THE UNIVERSITY OF MALTA
2 – 5 SEPTEMBER 1985

edited by
ANTHONY BONANNO

B.R. Grüner Publishing Co.
Amsterdam

Cataloguing in Publication Data

International Conference on Archaeology of the Ancient Mediterranean (*1st : 1985 : University of Malta*)

Archaeology and Fertility Cult in the Ancient Mediterranean : papers presented at the First International Conference on Archaeology of the Ancient Mediterranean, the University of Malta, 2 – 5 September 1985 / edited by Anthony Bonanno. – Amsterdam : B.R. Grüner, 1985

ISBN 90 6032 288 6

1. Mediterranean region – Ancient history
2. Fertility cults – Ancient world

I. Bonanno, Anthony, 1947 – II. Title

GN845.M415 930.091822

Printed and bound in Malta
by The University of Malta Press
1986

CONTENTS

PREFACE

As convenor of the conference at which these papers were presented, I count it as a further privilege as well as a pleasure to introduce this collection. Most of the contributors are too well known to need commending to the world of scholarship. The others are well-established scholars in their respective fields. All have profited from each other's company during the conference; in the same way, we hope, they will continue to benefit from the same company in this publication.

I would have felt it my duty to sum up the proceedings of the meeting, commenting on the contribution of each paper and, preferably, on the discussions that followed the delivery of the papers. But to do that would have meant extending the length of this foreword beyond the acceptable limits. To discuss only the highlights of the conference, on the other hand, would have involved the risk of offending several speakers by ignoring their valid contributions. One or two comments of a general nature, nonetheless, seem to be quite in order.

We are aware – as we were aware from the very start – that the long stretch of time, from Neolithic to Roman, and the number and diversity of cultures covered by the theme of the conference might possibly involve a somewhat superficial treatment of the subject. Fortunately this was not the case since the speakers succeeded in penetrating the core of the problem while maintaining a broad view of the period in question.

It can be said that for prehistory the field remains divided between two conflicting views, one supporting wholeheartedly the existence of a universal belief in an all-pervading and all-embracing Mother Goddess – of which the fertility cult is just one, albeit important, aspect – and the other questioning the very bases of that theory. But there seems to be a greater disposition for further dialogue and attenuation of entrenched positions. On the other hand, the fertility content in Near Eastern and Classical religions remains indisputable, even from the evidence brought forward in this publication. The conference proved to be also, and not accidentally, of special significance to Maltese archaeology. A further, non-religious, function for Malta's prehistoric temples has been suggested by two speakers – an opinion shared by myself and expressed elsewhere.

The distribution of the papers in this volume differs slightly from that followed in the course of the conference. Instead of leaving all the papers concerned with prehistoric religion in one group, it was judged more appropriate to collect those on Maltese prehistory under a separate heading. Papers related to Greek and Roman religions are grouped together for balance.

No efforts have been spared on the editor's part to standardise the format of the papers and at the same time to see them through the press as quickly as possible. For this purpose a note for contributors was circulated; but to discipline scholars must be one of the most daunting tasks one can possibly face. Hence the delay in delivering the complete text to the printer and the few divergences in the format of some papers. In one or two cases, admittedly, the references in note form seemed convincingly unavoidable, and we are infinitely grateful to those who had to take great pains to comply with our requirements.

One paper presented at the conference and some sections from a couple of others had to be sacrificed for editorial reasons. Regrettably the same lot befell a substantial number of illustrations provided by some authors. The conference members will certainly miss the paper by Marija Gimbutas in this volume. In view of her express wish not to have her article published along with that of another speaker at the same conference I very much regret I had no other choice but to accede.

While renewing my thanks to the individuals and institutions listed in my opening address, in particular UNESCO, the American Centre (Malta) and the Istituto Italiano di Cultura, I wish to express my gratitude to Mid-Med Bank Limited for their contribution, and Mr John Pollacco of Special Interest Travel for his constant moral and practical support during the preparations for the conference. Finally, I would like to thank Dr L. Seychell and Mrs C. Depasquale for their help in proof-reading the French texts and Mr Joe Spiteri for his assistance in the preparation of the plates.

15th October 1986 A. BONANNO

LIST OF MEMBERS, WITH ADDRESSES

ALLPORT Catherine, 156 Sullivan Street, New York, NY10012, U.S.A.

AMBEKAR Jayavant B., Department of Sociology, Shivaji University, Kolhapur, 416004 Maharashtra, India

ANABOLU (USMAN) Mükerrem. E.U. Edebijat Fakultesi, Bornova, Izmir, Turkey

ANATI Emanuel, Centro Comuno di Studi Preistorici, 25044 Capo di Ponte (BS), Italy

ATTARD Carmel, 67 Brared Street, Birkirkara, Malta

BÁNFFY Eszter, Archaeological Institute of the Hungarian Academy of Sciences, Budapest 1, Uri U. 49, H-1250, Hungary

BATTITI-SORLINI G., Department of Classics, State University at Albany, Albany, N.Y., U.S.A.

BIAGGI Christine, 1 Ludlow Lane, Palisades, New York 10964, U.S.A.

BONANNO Anthony, University of Malta, Msida, Malta

BRADSHAW Barbara, 441 So. Arden Blvd., California, U.S.A.

BRU Margarita, Universidad Complutense, Joaquin Maria Lopez 23, 28015 Madrid, Spain

CAMERON Dorothy, 10 Rafferty St., Chapman A.C.T. Z611, Australia

CILIA Joseph L., Margerita Flats No1, Ċensu Busuttil Street, Fgura, Malta

CUTAJAR Dominic, 13 Portobello Court, Col. Savona Street, Sliema, Malta

CYR Donald L., Stonehenge Viewpoint, 2821 De la Vina Street, Santa Barbara, CA 92015, U.S.A.

DARE Virginia, Woods Road, Palisades, NY 10964, U.S.A.

DONTOPOULOS Charoula, 2 Stony Hill Lane, W. Nyack, NY 10994, U.S.A.

DUNLAP Gail E., 2 Stony Hill Lane, W. Nyack, NY 10994, U.S.A.

FERGUSON Ian F.G., Shakespeare School of English, 46 Rue St Pierre, 14300 Caen, France

FRYE Joya G., Box 667, Woods Road, Palisades, NY 10964, U.S.A.

GALLIN Lenore, Department of Anthropology, UCLA, Los Angeles, CA 90024, U.S.A

GIMBUTAS Marija, Institute of Archaeology UCLA, Los Angeles, CA 90024, U.S.A.

GOMEZ-TABANERA José M., C. Pedro Antonio Menendez 2-2°C, Oviedo, Spain

HAYDEN Brian, Department of Archaeology, Simon Fraser University, Burnaby B.C., Canada V5A 1S6

HÖLBL Günther, Hirschengasse 21/36, A-1060 Wien 6, Austria

HVIDBERG-HANSEN, F.O., Institute of Semitic Philology, University of Aarhus, 8000 Aarhus C, Denmark

JOHNSON Buffie, 102 Greene Street, New York, NY 10012, U.S.A.

LAFFINEUR Robert, Chargé de Cours à l'Université de Liège, Drève de Méhagne 8, B-4600 Chaudfontaine, Belgium

LE GLAY Marcel, Institut d'Art et d'Archéologie, 3 Rue Michelet, F-75005, Paris, France
LÉVÊQUE Pierre, Faculté des Lettres et Sciences Humaines, Université de Besançon, 30 Rue Megevand, 25030 Besançon, Cedex, France
LIPINSKI E., Department of Oriental Studies, University of Louvain, Blijde Inkomststraat 21, B-3000 Leuven, Belgium
LOBELL Mimi, Pratt Institute, School of Architecture, 200 Willoughby Avenue, Brooklyn, New York, NY 11205, U.S.A.
MARANGOU Christina, 27 Rue de la Madeleine, 1000 Bruxelles, Belgium
MAYER Marc, Universitat Autonoma de Barcelona, Department d'Art, Facultat de Lletres, Bellaterra, Barcelona
MELI Joseph M., President – Malta Archaeological Society, C/O 329 Saint Paul's Street, Valletta, Malta
MERCIER Anne, 40 Rue J.P. Timbaud, 75011 Paris, France
MESHEL Zev, Department of Archaeology, Tel Aviv University, Tel Aviv, Israel
NOY Tamar, Israel Museum, 91012 Jerusalem, Israel
PAUTREAU Jean-Pierre, Chargé de Recherche au CNRS, Institut du Quaternaire, Université de Bordeaux I, 33405 Talence Cedex, France
REIS Patricia, 5838 Occidental Avenue, Oakland, California 94608, U.S.A.
RENFREW Colin, Department of Archaeology, Downing Street, Cambridge CB2 3DZ, England
ROCCHI Maria, C.N.R., Istituto Studi Micenei, Via G. della Bella 18, 00162 Rome, Italy
RODA' Isabel, Universitat Autonoma de Barcelona, Department d'Art, Facultat de Lletres, Bellaterra, Barcelona
SEGERT Stanislav, Near Eastern Languages and Cultures, University of California. Los Angeles, CA 90024. U.S.A.
TRUMP Bridget, 87 De Freville Avenue, Cambridge, England
TRUMP DAVID, Board of Extra-Mural Studies, University of Cambridge, Cambridge, England
TZACHILI Iris, Chemin des Tigelles 3, 1150 Bruxelles, Belgium
VAN ROOY H.F., Department of Semitic Languages, University of Potchefstroom, Potchefstroom 2520, South Africa
VAN STRAATEN Zak, Office of the Dean, Faculty of Social Science & Humanities, University of Cape Town, Rondebosch 7700, South Africa
VAZQUEZ-HOYS Ana Ma., c/Uruguay 13-7°A, Madrid 28016, Spain
VELLA Horatio C.R., Department of Religious Studies, Classics and Philosophy, University of Zimbabwe, P.O. Box M.P. 167, Mt. Pleasant, Harare, Zimbabwe
WEKERLE C.M., "Xlukkajra", Tas-Silġ Road, Marsaxlokk, Malta
WETTINGER G., 2 Old Mill Street, Mellieħa, Malta
WILSHIRE Donna, 1360 Marlborough Avenue, Plainfield, New Jersey, 1360 Marlborough Avenue, Plainfield, New Jersey 07060, U.S.A.
ZADI Grekou, Maître Assistant, Faculté des Lettres, BPV 34 Abidjan, Côte d'Ivoire

OPENING ADDRESSES

Address of Professor George P. Xuereb, Rector of the University of Malta

I welcome you on behalf of this Athenaeum. I have much pleasure in seeing among you a number of renowned scholars in the field of Archaeology. But I am equally pleased in welcoming younger scholars, some at the beginning of their career, others well on the way of establishing a scientific reputation. A warm welcome to you all. We sincerely hope that all the participants, both local and visiting, will profit from the exchange of ideas in a friendly atmosphere inside and outside this Conference Hall.

The University of Malta has made a late entry in the field of Archaeology. One recalls with much satisfaction that Temi Zammit, the distinguished Maltese archaeologist, was Rector of the University of Malta between 1920 and 1926, that in the years 1938 - 1939 John Ward Perkins, then at the beginning of his brilliant career, was appointed Professor of Archaeology. Furthermore, John Evans's work on the prehistoric antiquities of these islands in the fifties, published in his widely read *Malta* (1959) and his monumental *Survey* (1971), was monitored by a Committee formed to administer a grant made available to this University by the Inter-University Council for Higher Education Overseas and chaired by the Rector, Professor J. Manché. It is against this background that we feel particularly satisfied that this initiative, the organization of this Conference, came from our University.

The University of Malta has been striving in the past two decades to promote Mediterranean studies in all disciplines, whether historical or of immediate, contemporary significance. This Conference thus forms an integral part of this programme.

It is my earnest wish that during your informal discussions you consider the possibility of setting up an organization to promote occasional meetings on other themes of Mediterranean Archaeology and, perhaps, to strengthen the academic standing of Archaeology within this institution. I can assure you, ladies and gentlemen, that you will have my most active support in this matter. This assurance we firmly give; we do so for a number of reasons.

We accept a continuing relevance of the Humanities — we subscribe to Owen Chadwick's view that the humanities have an enduring place in our intellectual culture. Graduates need flexible intellectual skills — the humanities can provide these skills as they provide the values, inherited or formed, necessary for their fruitful application.

The mind has an innate freedom and, of this, the Athenaeum is a guardian — we are the source of nourishment and encouragement — we are to safeguard freedom of the mind so that it follows the argument wherever it leads, so that it studies pertinent questions and provides the answers that further enrich human inheritance.

I wish you success in your workings with the words by which the old Romans used to inaugurate important events: "Quod bonum, faustum, felix, fortunatumque sit".

Address of Dr. A. Bonanno, Conference Convenor

After the Rector's welcome on his own behalf and on behalf of the University I wish to convey to you my own welcome in my capacity as Convenor of this meeting and on behalf of the Conference Organizing Committee.

I feel I should begin this short address with a word of explanation about the theme of the Conference: "Archaeology and Fertility Cult in the Ancient Mediterranean". I must admit that when the proposed title was first sent out to various scholars for their advice, more than two years ago, we were not aware of the complexities involved, but we kept ourselves open to suggestions. In connection with this the Organizing Committee is most grateful to Professors Evans and Renfrew and to Dr Trump for their precious advice on the wording of the title of the Conference and for their encouragement in the initial stages of its organization. We appreciate very much the presence of Colin Renfrew and David Trump among us and we cannot but regret the absence of John Evans in view of the encouragement and help he gave us and of his remarkable contribution to Maltese archaeology.

What do we expect to achieve by this meeting? From the very start it was felt that the whole idea of what I prefer to call 'Fertility Syndrome', rather than 'Fertility Cult', was in an urgent need of a re-appraisal in the light of recent archaeological research and discoveries and without ignoring the useful contributions made by other disciplines, like anthropology. We tried to bring together some of the major authorities on the subject so that they would be able to exchange their views — in some cases diametrically opposed ones — in a congenial environment. If a consensus, however limited, is not reached, the whole problem could perhaps be redefined and placed in a new perspective in the hope of providing a sounder and firmer launching pad for future research and methodology. After Peter Ucko's deadly blow to the theory of *the* Fertility Cult (the idea of a worship of a goddess of fertility diffused throughout the Mediterranean, and beyond), the astounding discoveries of Çatal Hüyük, so pregnant with overt fertility symbolism, short of providing support to the established thesis, must have made the supporters of the anti-thesis — one would expect — a little less sweeping in their condemnation. As chairman of the Conference, however, I feel I should desist from committing myself further on the subject.

Since the Fertility Cult theory owes its origins ultimately to the study of the religions of the proto-historical and Classical civilizations it was judged that these Mediterranean cultures should not be omitted, and authoritive scholars in their respective fields were called on to share with us the results of their researches.

But why Malta? There are several reasons for choosing Malta as the venue for the Conference. But I shall limit myself to three. In the first place, because the idea of holding such a meeting was conceived here. Secondly, because we feel we have got something to give and do not want, therefore, to remain on the receiving end. Thirdly, because the rich artistic repertory of our prehistoric past, which has so often been interpreted in 'fertility' terms, seems to us to be crying out for a serious, objective study. Malta's prehistoric figurines have remained far too enigmatic, and for far too long.

We had several interesting suggestions regarding the format of the programme, to all of which we gave serious consideration. We eventually arrived at the conclusion, that the programme as presented to you this morning was the best one in the circumstances.

The preparations for this meeting have not been easy. There have been obstacles to overcome. As any of you who have ever been involved in the organization of such meetings will know very well, there are moments when one wonders why on earth one gets involved in anything of this sort. But your presence here today is our reward. We are very happy indeed to have you with us, and we shall do our utmost to render the atmosphere as homely and as comfortable as possible. In case of difficulties the members of the Organizing Committee and of the Secretariat will do whatever is in their possibility to help.

In this country we do not have a tradition of State support for the humanities, nor do we have the governmental mechanisms which would enable the State to sponsor a conference of this sort. We do not have the equivalent of a National Research Centre, as you have in France and Italy, for example. We earnestly hope that this embarrassing state of affairs will change, the sooner the better. I am sure that several of my colleagues have at some stage or other been deeply embarrassed, as I have been repeatedly in the past two years, by our inability to reciprocate the sort of generous hospitality which we ourselves so often receive abroad. We are, therefore, very grateful to all those institutions and individuals who have given us financial or practical aid on this occasion. Among these allow me to single out the University of Malta for patronizing the Conference, UNESCO for making a generous grant available, the American Centre (Malta) for meeting the travel expenses of our American guest speaker and other participants hailing from the United States, and the Istituto Italiano di Cultura for doing the same for our Italian guest speaker.

A final word of personal gratitude to the individual members of the Organizing Committee and to the guest speakers for accepting our invitation and for consenting to assume the extra burden of chairing the various sessions.

Organising Committee:

Dr A. Bonanno	Mr J. Pollacco
Mr J. Ciappara	Mr A.M. Schembri
Dr T. Gouder	Dr G. Wettinger
Professor C. Farrugia	Ms F. Craig

SECTION I: PREHISTORY

THE QUESTION OF FERTILITY CULTS

Emmanuel Anati

I. USES AND ABUSES OF THE TERM

The term "Fertility Cult" has been fashionable for the last three generations of anthropologists and archaeologists, and may at times have been used and abused too readily. Also, the term is very general and is open to personal evaluations and interpretations. The word *cult* implies beliefs and rituals or at least performances. When used, the term should be defined both in terms of concepts and of ritualistic behaviour involved.

There is no doubt that both ancient and modern cultures are concerned with human procreation which may be seen either as a positive or as a negative result of sexual relations, or may not be related at all to sexual activities. Another common concern is the fertility of the land and the abundance of hunting and fishing resources. However, specific information on beliefs and practices concerning "Fertility Cults" in the ancient Mediterranean and elsewhere prior to the Bronze Age is scanty and in need of further analysis. Concerns relevant to fertility may be part of more complex conceptions regarding nature and the supernatural.

It has been somehow customary to talk of ' fertility cult" any time a figure is found which stimulates our associations with sexual or erotic themes. The same association may even emerge with a simple female figurine. This attitude was followed by several of the major advocates of a sort of "Universal" prehistoric religion focusing on the cult of the "Mother Goddess" (Crowford 1957; James 1959). Such attitude reaches conclusions which can hardly be proven, and has resulted in the collection of an immense quantity of materials defined as "evidences" of fertility cults, out of which a very small percentage has clearly been determined as having this purpose.

The term "Fertility Cult" implies a ritualistic performance meant to promote fertility of nature or human procreation, and it is quite rare to find archaeological evidence demonstrating that such performances have indeed taken place. Even in such explicit cases where specific representations appear of copulation and pregnancy in anthropomorphic figures, or rain and sun are represented in connection with vegetation, the motivation of the depiction may not necessarily be that of promoting fertility.

Out of the numerous images left behind by prehistoric man which have been related to the fertility cult, indeed only very few are explicit, such as those from the rock art of Camonica Valley, which depict scenes of ploughing a field, associated with acts of copulation (Anati 1982a: 304). These scenes, which belong to the first millennium B.C., depict one man in the act of ploughing, that is, penetrating the earth with the plough, which is carried by two powerful animals, either oxen or horses. Close by, a human being is shoveling the earth while being penetrated from the back by another man. Such scenes describe a clear performance which implies some sort of beliefs connecting an agricultural activity with a sexual performance.

Just one such specific association would be inconclusive, but when the same combination is repeated several times in the same way, on different rock surfaces, then there is a good probability that it describes a concept expressed by a performance meant to stimulate the fertility of the field. On the other hand, a scene of ploughing alone or a scene of copulation alone should not necessarily lead to the same conclusions. Incidentally, the same practice of provoking the fertility of the field by having sexual intercourse on them before or after or during ploughing, is still a widespread habit in India and among other populations with Indo-European roots.

In the same general context, that is, in the rock art of the Camonica Valley from period IV-C, which goes back to the 8th-7th century B.C., several other scenes of erotic character are found. They include sexual intercourse with donkeys and with dogs, scenes of masturbation, and plain scenes of intercourse between two human beings.

There is no doubt that all these depictions illustrate customs or wishes of the persons who produced them. Despite several hypotheses, however, there is no unanimous consent as to the possible relationship between the depicted performances and the ideologies and conceptions of a fertility cult. (Anati 1982a: 301).

II. THE ART OF HUNTERS AND ITS CONTENTS

In all continents, hunting societies have left behind a wealth of art production with specific connotations, particular to their mentality (Anati 1984: 13-56). Usually, animal figures bear an overwhelming role. A few animals are particularly emphasized and must have played a conceptual role far beyond their economic importance. Most of this "hunter's art" has no scenes of descriptive or anecdotal character. The earliest scenes we know are hunting scenes, and they appear, in all continents, only at a late and evolved stage in the sequence of the art of hunters. Previously, figures may be either isolated or related to each other by conceptual associations. Often animal figures are connected with ideograms the significance of which is not as yet fully understood. (Anati 1983a: 91-108). Such overall patterns, which are common in all continents, are typical also of Palaeolithic art in Europe, which is mainly concentrated in France, Spain and Italy, with minor clusters in other countries around the Mediterranean basin and in Central Europe.

Both mobiliary art and rock art in caves and in the open air have revealed vigorous masterpieces which are very appealing to our 20th century taste. Like most groups of such art in other parts of the world, it is evident that one of the conceptual characteristics of hunter's art finds its roots in a dual approach to nature, where masculine and feminine elements meet, combine, and interact to create a harmonious whole (Anati 1981: 200-210). This is paritcularly evident where large panels of many figures allow the study of associations, as emphasized already by André Leroi-Gourhan, Annette Laming and others (Leroi-Gourhan 1965: 114 ff; Laming 1962 289-291).

This art also includes clearly masculine and feminine symbols. In some cases they are naturalistic depictions of *phalli* and *vulvae*. Also animal associations reveal a complex symbology of sexual values and a combination of animals in the same composition may have sexual connotations. At the moment it does not seem possible, however, to determine if these kinds of associations are related to a fertility cult. the current tendency is to view them as expressions of an allegoric mythological world which must have occupied the minds and concerns of their makers (Anati 1983a: 116-118).

The obvious depictions of sexual organs undoubtedly reveal an interest in sexuality, but do not seem to provide direct evidence of a cult. It is worth stressing that erotic concerns do not necessarily concern fertility and procreation. In some cases, like in the cave of Tito Bustillo in nothern Spain, a special corner of the cave decorated with several vulvar figures has been thought to represent an angle reserved to women, and in such case the *vulvae* would simply be the specification of the sex to whom this portion of the cave was reserved. Another corner of the same cave is decorated with depictions of game animals, and it was likely a corner reserved to men.

Similar situations are known in the rock-shelters and caves of

Central Tanzania, which were used by hunting societies for instructing and educating young men and women towards initiation and puberty rites. There, preparing for a full adult life included, among other things, the teaching of sexual behaviour and the interaction and cooperation required for a couple to live in harmony. Some teachings concern procreation and how to avoid it, but there is no evidence of fertility "cults" despite numerous erotic paintings and figurines.

As for the mobiliary art, the Palaeolithic period in Europe has left behind a wealth of incised and painted tablets as well as plastic figurines (Delporte 1979).

Associations between animal figures and symbols reveal the presence of a well defined symbology reflecting the dualistic view of the world, typical of hunting societies, as I have analysed elsewhere (Anati 1981; 1983a; 1983b). Assimilations and connections are particularly evident in two repetitive patterns. One them associates the stick or "batonnet" as a male symbol, to a mouth of certain animals, a feminine symbol. Another pattern is assimilating the bison and the human female. This again, reflects an overall symbology connected with the ideological structure of Palaeolithic hunters. However, attempts to identify in it a cult of fertility are of dubious legimitacy.

Human depictions are more common in mobiliary art than in rock art and more common in the figurines than in the plaquettes (Vialou 1982; Guthrie 1984). While in the plaquettes animal figures are far more numerous than human ones, in the plastic figurines there are more humans than animals. They are of both sexes, with a predominance of feminine figurines which are known in the popular literature as "Venuses". It is questionable however, whether the numerous attempts made at analysing only feminine figurines in terms of a hypothetical cult of a "Mother Goddess" disregarding the human male as well as the animal figurines, are to be taken seriously.

In several instances, authors have referred to them as a proof for a fertility cult but, despite a profusion of theories, yet no one has demonstrated what kind of performance, concept, and ritual would be behind such a "fertility cult". Very few of the female figures are shown to be pregnant. While most of them have prominent breasts and buttocks: this may just reflect no more than the concept of beauty of their time.

From this very quick summary it appears that while sexual awareness and perhaps also sexual problems may emerge from Palaeolithic art, it is hard to find in it any concrete evidence of "fertility cults". In fact this consideration is in harmony with what we know about more recent hunting societies. They may at time have concerns about animal reproduction to assure their subsistence, and there may be evidence of a resort to magic and incantations, such as the depictions of ostrich eggs by the Australian aborigenes meant to stimulate the reproduction of this animal. But there is no evidence of a true fertility cult of animal reproduction.

It has been suggested, for European Upper Palaeolithic, that the so-called "Venuses" may reflect a widely spread reverence for a mythical ancestral "matron". This is not impossible but it cannot be proven as yet. In any case, a hypothetical cult of a "Primordial Mother" would not necessarily imply a fertility cult (Anati 1983a; 102-104).

III. EARLY POST-PALAEOLITHIC EVIDENCE

We have seen that there is no concrete evidence of fertility cults among hunters societies and, in particular, in the Palaeolithic age of Europe and the Mediterranean. The wish to raise the population of the human group seems to be a character of sedentary populations. Likewise, a wish to increase the fertility of the soil can interest only agricultural societies.

As mentioned, Palaeolithic man may have done something to insure the reproduction of wild livestock. Rather than a cult, this may be considered as a sort of practice of magic. It is a part of a much wider and more complex concept expressing the search for a relationship between the human and the animal world, and also the search for a logical and phenomenological frame for natural surroundings. As discussed elsewhere, a view of the cosmological concepts of the Palaeolithic hunters is gradually emerging (Anati 1983a: 116-118).

Mesolithic people relied for their food source primarily on collecting, as well as fishing and hunting small game. We find frequent net-like patterns in their rock art and other graphic productions representing the hunting and fishing artifacts. Their concern seems to be addressed more to the efficiency of the tools they produced than to practices intended to make the forces of nature produce more food. To date in fact there is no direct evidence of performances connected with fertility cults in the European Mesolithic (Harrod 1983: 229-308; Marshack 1983: 111-120).

Another type of culture which in Europe is partially contemporary to that of the Mesolithic, is usually referred to as Epi-

Palaeolithic (Anati 1982). Its art is characterized by a predominance of a figurative art of belated Palaolithic traditions in such areas as the Spanish Levante, the Alpine region, northern Scandinavia and the Central Sahara, producing at times depictions of erotic character (Anati 1982a: 143-151).

Figures describing human copulation in the Alps, sexual intercourse between two animals in northern Norway and Sweden, or depictions indicating a clear connection between sexual performances and successful hunting in the Sahara, may reveal beliefs and practices indicating the concern for virility and fertility as elements favouring the vigour of natural resources and economic prosperity. Scenes of sexual intercourse are common in the rock art of North Africa and of the Near East (Mori 1975; Malhomme 1959; 1961; Anati 1963: 191 ff.). Some of them, like one at Kilwa in northern Arabia, are certainly belonging to Hunting-Gathering societies; others are the production of later pastoral groups.

Figurines from the Natufian culture of Palestine include a copulating couple and a few phallic objects of stone which are certainly an expression of their interest for sex, but provide no explicit evidence for fertility cults. Phallic pestles may indicate a connection between virility and the abundance of food. It is significant that this eroticism of the Natufian culture is uncommon in Early Post-Palaeolithic cultures and is found here at the setting of the beginning of a food producing economy, in a culture which in fact, in economic terms, could be considered Proto-Neolithic rather than Mesolithic (Garrod 1957).

The birth of food production generated new kinds of concerns for the fertility of the land and brought forth a process of raised interest in the augmentation of the size of the group, thus favouring efforts in this direction.

The Epi-Palaeolithic cultures and other cultures usually developing in marginal areas showed concern about sexuality, the Mesolithic cultures, with the exception of the Natufians, seem to be little concerned with sexual representations. The Neolithic period develops a taste and an interest for this kind of depiction, revealing a new and much more sophisticated and "intellectualized" approach to the problems of human reproduction and of fertility of the fields (Frankfort 1958).

IV. THE BIRTH OF AGRICULTURE AND CONNECTED IDEOLOGIES

Early Neolithic in the Mediterranean and surrounding areas has produced a great many art objects and several cult-sites, including temples. Pre-pottery Jericho, the earliest fortified town we know of, had several buildings devoted to worship and cult, and some aspects of their beliefs and rituals have emerged (Kenyon 1970: 1-17). Among other things, skulls modelled and buried in the worship place seem to reflect a special attention to the veneration of ancestors. In another public building, a trinity of mythical beings, including a bearded man, a woman and a child, seem to indicate the concern this people had for family life, to the extent of producing a prototype. Some colleagues have suggested the presence of a fertility cult, but so far the archaeological discoveries are not explicit in this sense.

The important Anatolian sites of Çatal-Hüyük and Hacilar, excavated by James Mellaart, have provided a great wealth of art and cult objects (Mellaart 1967). Among other things the so-called "Lady of the animals" appears as some sort of mythic "matron", which was a reference point for the people who worshipped there. It may have the connotation of an ancestral "Mother of the Tribe", who subjugated the totemic animal, had intercourse with it and gave birth to the archetypal child. She was worshipped in the broader context of a complex myth of origin, which finds other aspects in the beautiful frescoes of Çatal Hüyük. In such context, though he is probably less important, a male ancestor is present as well (Mellaart 1967: 180).

Another interesting aspect at Çatal Hüyük is the presence of a birth-giving lady in the context of an impressive room with series of horned cattle heads. This seems to be one of the earliest known direct examples in the Mediterranean area of a concern for fertility and procreation, idealised in such a way as to offer adequate basis to consider the presence of some sort of cult or worship connected with fertility. The ox and the ox-horns later became clear symbols of fertility, and this may well be a very early example of such association. Incidentally this association, which is particularly evidenced in later cattle-breeding societies, has preserved its core in the etymology of the Hebrew word for "fertility" *pirion* — which derives from ox — *par*. In fact Çatal Hüyük may have been an early site of development of cattle domestication.

Further north, in the Danube valley, another important Early Neolithic site yielded numerous art objects which are likely to be connected with the cult. Lepenski Vir, excavated by Dragoslav Srejovic, had some sort of protecting spirits in the form of stone statues inside the huts (Srejovic 1969: 1975). In each hut the family consumed its meals around the fireplace, in the company of the ancestor spirit. Some of these spirits had peculiar shape: at least one of them has the united characteristics of a fish and a human face. The people of Lepenski Vir lived of fishing in the Danube river and it has been suggested that this ancestral face, half-human, half fish, may synthesize their relationship with the supernatural world and express their concern for maintaining good relationship with their mythic cousins, the fish, who provided them with food. In the same site, another statue has an egg-like form, with a high relief of a vagina. Both concerns for food-getting and human reproduction seem to be evidenced in this Early Neolithic site.

Increasing concern for sexuality as shown by figurines and other art objects, became common in full Neolithic time in various cultures in Israel, in North Africa, as well as in Spain and Italy. Along with it there is evidence for water and the sun taking an increasing place in symbology and concern. The ritual collection of dripping water in the Scaloria cave in Italy and various cases of rock art connected with water sources in the Canary Islands and elsewhere seem to indicate a certain connection between water and life, a concept that has survived into contemporary cults (baptism etc.) (Beltran 1975: 209-220; Radmilli 1975: 175-184; Tiné 1975: 185-190).

While Egypt, Mesopotamia and other early centres of urban and literate civilization were developing sophisticated ideologies and cults, where the frequent erotic connotations may have in some cases been connected with the stimulation of fertility, the general trends seem to be those of commemorating and stimulating natural and supernatural forces of various kinds, mythical patriarchs and matrons. The wealth of archaeological material reveals the search for attaining economic plenty, social security, military strength, beauty, and prestige. The wish to increase procreation may be present occasionally, but looking at the general image provided by the immense material discovered by archaeology as well as at the early literary sources, the fertility cult as an isolated element was apparently not a common trend.

The worship of mythical ancestors, both male and female, is, however common in several incipient and early agricultural societies, as evidenced by the Jericho trinity, by the matron of Çatal-Hüyük, by the fat lady of Malta, and by numerous figurines spread over the entire circum-Mediterranean areas, as elsewhere, in Neolithic times.

Considering the diversities revealed by the documentation from various areas, it is hard to view it as a singular phenomenon. There is a common denominator, as all these examples lead to a common archetypal reference to mythical ancestors, the idealized mothers or fathers of the ethnic group, and this is not just a Mediterranean element, it is a universal element found in many populations of all continents.

In various cases, there is preference for male "patriarchs" or female "matrons". But there are also androgynous or asexual images, which are particularly numerous in clay figurines (Ucko 1968).

The concern for idealizing the prototype of a relationship with mythical or real "dream-time genealogy" seems to be a well known universal pattern, from the book of Genesis to the myths of origin of numerous tribal societies around the world. Ancestral spirits and images are worshipped in tribal societies in all continents, and no doubt this was a pattern common in the ancient Mediterranean as well.

To what extent, however, this pattern was connected to some kind of fertility cult remains an open question. In addition, the association of the ancestral "Mother" of the tribe to "Mother Earth" may have some general denominator common to many food producing societies which acquired local characteristics and diversifications. The available archaeological evidence in the ancient Mediterranean should be analysed in a broader view of recurring patterns and paradigms.

The study of phenomenology may reveal archetypes and universal elements. Considering the known visual material, it is questionable whether we can actually define the characteristics of a so-called "Mediterranean world". Rather, the art works, places of worship and cult objects appear to be expressions of the elementary mental processes of association, filtered through local cultural and conceptual patterns.

V. ARCHETYPES AND PARADIGMS

What are generally called "fertility cults" involve concepts and performances which may be subdivided into two major categories: those concerned with the fertility of the land and those concerned with human fertility. At times, both categories are present together. As we have seen, the quest for success in hunting and fishing activities has only sporadically produced concepts and practices which can be included in the "fertility cult" category.

The concern for the fertility of the land is a universal trend of agricultural societies. Magical or religious rites to stimulate rain, or to increase the production of the fields, take forms which follow some general universal principles.

Most ancient societies, like modern ones, must have been faced with an ambivalent attitude towards sexual relations: the natural biological need of performing coitus on one side, the refrain necessary to avoid undesired offspring on the other. Apparently today this is an almost universal pattern with only a few exceptions usually limited to strongly patriarchal groups of extended families. This appears to affect both agricultural and pastoral societies where the raising of children means increasing labour forces. Besides such specific cases, sterile persons may wish to undertake some special action to provoke the miracle of having children, but they are a small minority.

Three fundamental paradigms seem to emerge: I. All societies today, and certainly all food producing societies in all times, are bound by sexual taboos, limiting and conditioning the sexual life of their peoples through what we usually call "morality". This has always caused some sort or repression which took shape in artistic externalizations, in the visual arts, in poetry, in music and dance. But all this seems to have little to do with fertility cults. Rather it has to do with repressed sexual imperatives, with needs for intimate human relations and for affection, and appears to be a universal paradigm.

II. The quest for understanding the dynamics of nature, the wandering and typically human queries *why*? and *how*? again appears to be a universal characteristic of humankind, ever since man left behind works of art reflecting his need to discover the mysterious laws of nature. This means at least since the appearance of *Homo Sapiens Sapiens*, some 40,000 years ago. Since this time the eternal problems of birth and death have always preoccupied men all over, and this again is a universal paradigm. It is connected with the human need to understand phenomena rather than that of putting into action magic or religious performances to incentivate them. Again, this has little to do with a cult of fertility.

III. The quest for origin is reflected by creation myths in almost every society in the world. The reference to ideal images of mythical ancestors, male or female or both, is another universal paradigm. Also in this third case, there is not necessarily a relation to fertility cults.

While fertility cult practices connected with food production are part of the ideology of several agricultural societies, those focusing on human procreation are more problematic; there are examples, but they are sporadic, and do not seem to reflect general patterns. From this general survey of the problem it would seem that rituals and practices to prevent human fertility may have been, frequently, as widespread as those intended to promote fertility.

A question to be left open is whether most of the evidence that has been attributed so far to fertility cults (minus the few conclusive cases), should not rather, be referred to one of the three universal paradigms just mentioned.

Summary

The term "Fertility Cult" has been very fashionable for many years now, and may at times have been used and abused too readily. Also, the term is very general and is open to personal interpretation. There is no doubt that both ancient and modern cultures are concerned with human procreation and with fertility of the land and the abundance of hunting and fishing resources. However, specific information on beliefs and practices concerning "Fertility Cults" in the ancient Mediterranean and elsewhere prior to the Bronze Age, is scanty and in need of futher analysis. Concerns relevant to fertility may be part of more complex conceptions regarding nature and the supernatural.

The Fertility Cult, as an isolated element, was apparently not a common trend. The worship of mythical ancestors, both male and female is, however, common in many prehistoric and tribal societies. In various cases there is a preference for male "patriarchs" or female "matrons". In addition, the association of the ancestral "mother" of the tribe, and the "mother earth" may have some universal connotations which acquired local characteristics and diversifications. The available archaeological evidence in the ancient Mediterranean should be analysed in a broader view of recurring patterns and paradigms. The study of phenomenology may reveal achetypes and universal elements.

Considering the known visual material, it is questionable whether we can view the ancient Mediterranean as a single cultural unit and whether we can actually define the characteristics of a so called "Mediterranean World". Rather, art work, places of worship and cult objects appear to be expressions of the elementary mental process of association, filtered through local cultural and conceptual patterns.

Bibliography

ANATI, E.
1963 — *Palestine Before the Hebrews*, New York (Alfred A. Knopf) & London (Jonathan Cape).
1968 — *Arte rupestre nelle regioni occidentali della Penisola Iberica*, Capo di Ponte (Edizioni del Centro).
1981 — The Origins of Art, *Museum*, XXXIII/4, pp. 200-210.
1982 — *I Camuni. Alle radici della civiltà europea*, Milano (Jaca Book).
1983a — *Gli elementi fondamentali della cultura*, Milano (Jaca Book).
1983b — Intelletualità dell'uomo preistorico: una visione in prospettiva, *Studi in onore di Dinu Adamesteanu*, pp. 97-109. .
1984 — The State of Research in Rock Art, *BCSP, Bollettino del Centro Camuno di Studi Preistorici*, 21, pp. 13-56.

BELTRAN, A.
1975 — Religion préhispanique aux Canaries: l'apport des gravures rupestres, in E. Anati (ed.) *Les religions de la préhistoire*, pp. 209-226.

BIRDSELL, J.
1979 — Some predictions for the Pleistocene based on Equilibrium Systems among recent Hunter-Gatherers, in R.B. Lee & I. De Vore, *Man the Hunter*, pp. 229 ff.

CROWFORD, O.G.S.
1957 — *The Eye Goddess*, London.

DELPORTE, H.
1979 — *L'image de la femme dans l'art préhistorique*, Paris (Picard).

EVANS, J.D.
1971 — *The Prehistoric Antiquities of the Maltese Islands*, London (Athlone Press).

FRANKFORT, H.
1958 — The Archetype in Analytical Psychology and the History of Religion, *Journal of the Warburg and Courtauld Inst. London*, 21.

FROBENIUS, L.
1963 — *Ekade Ektab*, die Felsbilder Fezzans, Graz (Academische Verlaganstalt).

FROBENIUS L. & OBERMAIER M.
1965 — *Hadschra Maktuba*, Urzeitziche Felsbilder Kleinafrikas, Graz (Akademische Verlag Anstalt).

GARROD, J.
1957 — *The Natufian Culture. The life and economy of a Mesolithic people in the Near East*, London.

GUTHRIE, R.D.
1984 — Ethological Observations from Palaeolithic Art, in H.G. Bandi *et al., La contribution de la zoologie et de l'éthologie à l'interprétation de l'art des peuples chasseurs préhistoriques*, pp. 35-74.

HARROD, J.
1983 — The Bow: An Expression of the Mesolithic Mind, in E. Anati (ed.) *Prehistoric Art and Religion*, pp. 299-308.

JAMES, E.D.
1959 — *The Cult of the Mother Goddess*, London.

KARAGEORGHIS, V.
1983 — *The Civilisation of Prehistoric Cyprus*, New York (Alpine Fine Arts).

KENYON, K.
1970 — The Origins of the Neolithic, *The Advancement of Science*, 26, pp. 1-17.

LAMING-EMPERAIRE, A.
1962 — *La signification de l'art rupestre paléolithique*, Paris (Picard).

LEROI-GOURHAN, A.
1965 — *Préhistoire de l'art occidental*, Paris (Mazenod).
1984 — Le réalisme de comportement dans l'art paléolithique d'Europe de l'Ouest, in H.-G. Bandi *et al.* (ed.), *La contribution de la zoologie et de l'éthologie à l'interprétation de l'art des peuples chasseurs préhistorique*, pp. 75-90.

MALHOMME, J.
1959-61 — *Corpus des gravures rupestres du Grand Atlas*, Rabat (Service des Antiquités du Maroc), part 1, 1959; part 2, 1961.

MARSHACK, A.
1983 — European Upper Paleolithic-Mesolithic Symbolic Continuity, in E. Anati (ed.), *Prehistoric Art and Religion*, pp. 111-119.

MELLAART, J.
1967 — *Çatal Hüyük, a Neolithic Town in Anatolia*, London (Thames & Hudson).

MICHALOWSKI, K.
1968 — *L'art de l'ancienne Egypte*, Paris (Mazenod).

MORI, F.
1975 — Contributo allo studio del pensiero magico-religioso attraverso l'esame di alcune raffigurazioni rupestri preistoriche del Sahara, in E. Anati (ed.), *Les religions de la Préhistoire*, pp. 343-366.

PERICOT-GARCIA, L. *et al.*
1983 — *Prehistoric and Primitive Art*, London (Thames & Hudson).

RADMILLI, A.
1975 — Culti di fertilità della terra testimoniati in alcuni giacimenti neolitici italiani, in E. Anati (ed.), *Les religions de la préhistoire,* pp. 175-184.

ROME, L. & J.
1983 — *Primitive Eroticism,* Ware (Omega Books).

SREJOVIC, D.
1969 — *Lepenski Vir,* Beograd (Srpska Knijzevna Zadruga).

1975 — La religion de la culture de Lepenski Vir, in E. Anati (ed.), *Les religions de la préhistoire,* pp. 86-94.

TINE, S.
1975 — Culto neolitico della acque nella grotta Scaloria, in E. Anati (ed.), *Les religions de la préhistoire,* pp. 185-190.

UCKO, P.
1968 — *Anthropomorphic Figurines*, London (Szmidla).

VIALOU, P.
1975 — La figuration humaine au Paléolithique supérieur, in D Ferembach (ed.), *Les processus de l'hominisation,* p. 136.

OLD EUROPE: SACRED MATRIARCHY OR COMPLEMENTARY OPPOSITION?

Brian Hayden

In the past decade, it has become increasingly popular to view Neolithic cultures in general as being matriarchal or matrifocal. These cultures are portrayed as peaceful, harmonious, and artistic, in contrast to the warlike, destructive, and coarse patriarchal cultures that followed them. The matriarchal political and social organization is thought to be reflected in the Sacred sphere by cults of a Great Goddess which dominate religious life, a supernatural being from which all Life spontaneously and parthenogenetically stems. The claim is often made that *Homo sapiens* did, in fact, not know the facts of life in the Paleolithic or in the Neolithic. This interpretation of cultural evolution is essentially a restatement of the nineteenth century unilinear evolutionist views of Morgan, Marx, Engels and others. Most of twentieth century archaeology in Western Industrial countries has tended to argue that cultural evolution was considerably more complex than such unilinear schemes. However, in the contemporary climate of nuclear war threats and accelerating changes in women's status, it is easy to understand why such interpretations might become increasingly popular. To what extent is the matriarchal Neolithic scenario a verisimilitude? To what extent is it a hopeful and idealistic creation on the part of some contemporary writers in search of a social utopia? That is the topic of my paper.

Of all the Neolithic cultures that have been archaeologically investigated, perhaps none have been adduced to demonstrate the reality of the Neolithic matriarchy more strongly than the cultures of Old Europe and its neighbors, including Minoan, Mesopotamian, and Anatolian communities. Therefore, let us examine the Old European case in more detail.

One of the foremost archaeologists whose views have been used to support the matriarchal scenario for Old Europe is Marija Gimbutas. Gimbutas herself is somewhat ambivalent as to her exact position. In some passages, Gimbutas (1982:237) views both male and female deities manifesting side by side, the masculine force strengthening and affirming the creative feminine force. Neither masculine nor feminine Sacred force is subordinated to the other, but both work to complement the other yielding double power. In social terms, this is inferred to mean that women were not subject to males and that all human resources in Old European societies were used to their fullest.

On the other hand, Gimbutas presents other claims that stand in stark contrast to this balanced, complementary role of the sexes, in both the Sacred and profane domains.

1) She argues that the Old European pantheon reflects a society "dominated" by the mother (*ibid*);

2) She devotes the vast bulk (11/12's) of her book to the goddesses and their manifestations and deemphasizes representations of gods;

3) She argues that the principal deity — a Great Goddess — is androgynyous and a supreme creator that fashions all Life from herself (as opposed to the Indo-European Earth Mother that must be fecundated by a masculine deity in order to bring forth life — *ibid*: 196);

4) And finally Gimbutas raises the notion of Old Europe being a matriarchal society in the old nineteenth century sense (elsewhere as a matrilinear society), and from there goes on to contrast it with her idea of an extreme form of patriarchy represented by the Indo-Europeans. She claims that the Old European matriarchal societies were "savagely destroyed by the patriarchal element" and that patriarchy was thus imposed on Europe by invaders from elsewhere (*ibid*: 152, 238).

From these interpretations and arguments, it is quite easy to formulate an interpretation of beliefs and social roles very different from the balanced equality between the sexes that Gimbutas mentioned earlier. It could well be assumed that she endorses the traditional view of the matriarchal phase of cultural evolution. Although the format of this presentation precludes an in-depth discussion of each of her arguments, some general assessment of them can be attempted. They will be discussed in order.

THE DOMINANCE OF GODDESSES

In her treatment of goddess representations in Old European archaeological remains, it sometimes seems as though Gimbutas interprets everything that is not clearly phallic, and even somethings that are clearly phallic, as symbols of the Great Goddess or her variants. Thus, oblique parallel lines, horizontal parallel lines, vertical parallel lines, chevrons, lozenges, zigzags, wavy lines, meanders, circles, ovals, spirals, dots, crescents, U's, crosses, swirls, caterpillars, double axes, chrysalises, horns, butterflies, birds, eggs, fish, rain, cows, dogs, does, stags, toads, turtles, hedgehogs, bees, bulls, bears, goats, pigs, pillars, and sexless linear or masked figures all are viewed as symbols of this goddess. One wonders what is left.

Some of these interpretations are undoubtedly justified, such as the bear association since there are figurines that incorporate the features of women and bears. Other associations, such as those between toads or fish and a goddess form are not so certain because of the indeterminacy of the sex of the human forms or the animal forms. The toad figures are largely sexless, while the excavator of the Lepenski Vir fish-humans that Gimbutas uses as her main example, indicated that they represented a male divinity (*ibid*: 110).

Still other symbols that Gimbutas claims represent the Goddess seem entirely out of place, being more logically associated with masculine Sacred forces. These include the bulls, stags, rams, snakes, pillars, he-goats, and bucrania. Gimbutas claims alternatively that antlered animals really are the Goddess equipped with male defenses or that the Great Goddess dominates these horned animals so that when they are depicted, the viewer is really supposed to think of the Great Goddess. Sometimes, as in the case of Artemis, she even claims that the Goddess appears as a doe (elsewhere as a doe with stag's antlers), is represented by a stag, and goes around hunting stags. I would argue that there is something inherently inconsistent in the idea of a doe-stag going around hunting herself. I suggest that there is an alternative and more sensible way of interpreting this class of observations and associations. Namely that if Artemis hunts stags then the stags must represent something different from herself, a separate concept or form of Sacred force. Extended to the panoply of Neolithic sacred symbols, I would argue that many of the symbols that Gimbutas interprets as referring to goddesses, actually represent major forces in their own right — the missing masculine force that Gimbutas has chosen to minimize. This is a central concept in the rest of this paper.

Let us briefly see whether it makes sense to view the bull, the ram, the goat, the stag, the pillar, and the snake in terms of symbols of a Sacred masculine force, the complement of a Sacred feminine force. Here, even Gimbutas is forced to admit that in some circumstances the bull and the goat represent gods since there are numerous ceramic figurines of bulls and goats with horned human masculine heads. However, she relegates their origin to the Neolithic claiming that they did not exist prior to agriculture. Only the Great Goddess supposedly existed then (*ibid*: 216). Given what we know of Paleolithic religion, even this claim seems unfounded, as I shall argue in the next section. For the time being, it is adequate to note that bucrania, bulls, and rams were strongly associated with shrines and temples in Old Europe, the Minoan islands, Anatolia, and the Near East. From the earliest historic times, the bull and ram were intimately associated in Egypt with the pharaoh and the sun god, the masculine moon, and rebirth. Mellaart (1965: 94) and Singh (1974: 89) categorically state that masculine gods are represented by bull's horns or ram's heads while goddesses more generally take anthropomorphic forms in Anatolia.

As for the snake, Gimbutas again is equivocal about its symbolism. The aspects that she emphasizes are those she sees as representing the Great Goddess: water, rain, earth, cyclical change, eggs. However, she cannot avoid its strong association with Old European representations of male phalli, horns, and ithyphallic figures. She overtly refers to the snake as representing a "stimulating" force (*ibid*: 95). The meaning of snakes is thus at least ambiguous in Gimbutas' presentation. If we were to take a psychoanalytic approach, snakes would clearly be masculine forces. Taking a comparative religious approach, Eliade (1976:397-9) notes that snakes often are associated with the moon due to the cyclical shedding of their skins and disappearance into the earth. In these roles, the snake and moon are regarded as the "husband of all women", and Eliade gives a number of examples of societies that believe that the moon or snakes can impregnate women if they do not take precautions. Significantly, these beliefs occur among non-agricultural hunter/gatherers as well as among agriculturalists.

The pillar is yet another symbol that Gimbutas interprets as representing the Great Goddess, whereas all common sense and psychiatric wisdom would associate it instead with the phallus or masculine forces.

The fact that bulls, rams, pillars and snakes often appear with images of a goddess does not necessarily mean that they represent her, or even that she is in a dominant position over the forces they represent. It may simply mean that there is an important cosmic interaction in the scene, or it may represent an important sacred relationship between two important forces. The animal representations may even be considered the more important of the two elements in the portrayals. This is exemplified by Gimbutas herself when she notes that Dionysius is almost certainly a pre-Indo-European bull god of virility and rebirth close in meaning to the Great Goddess in her form as a vegetation deity (*ibid*: 227-28; 237). Significantly, Dionysius was crowned with snakes, and phallic cups were used to celebrate his rebirth in the spring. Even more interesting is the fact that his barebreasted female worshippers at Keos would wear horns or snakes as collars or belts to imitate him. At this point, there is no discernable difference between the Dionysian cult practices and what we know of the so-called Minoan or Old European "snake goddesses." A final note of interest is that the reborn Dionysius ultimately marries the Great Goddess and brings fertility to the land.

In addition to symbols that cannot clearly be related to either sex, and symbols that appear more logically to relate to masculine forces, there are also an entire series of abstract symbols that Gimbutas interprets as referring to the Great Goddess. While some of these symbols do legitimately appear to be symbols for goddesses and their fertility aspects, such as lozenges with dots in them, others are so abstract and so widespread that serious questions must be raised about interpreting them in any gender terms, or in any terms other than referrants to very broad concepts. King (1983:7) has recently criticized the over-interpretation of geometric designs, especially repetitive ones that can and do occur just about anywhere. When is a design a symbol, and when is it simply a decorative motif? When does a design have a specific meaning, and when is it only of the broadest significance? These questions are difficult to answer. Gimbutas ignores them completely in her headlong drive to establish the dominance and preponderant presence of the Great Goddess in Old Europe. Chevrons, parallel lines, crosses, crescents, zigzags, ovals, spirals, dots, continue in an unending avalanche of highly subjective interpretation. At least a few other art historians would argue that, contrary to Gimbutas' views, almost any linear representation should be interpreted in terms of masculine forces (e.g. Leroi-Gourhan 1965).

Another possibility is that many of the symbols that are interpreted as representing goddesses may simply symbolize general concepts. Symbols like chevrons that occur on goddesses and on rams may simply designate those elements as "Sacred." Meanders or spirals may serve a similar purpose, or as Campbell (1969) suggests, the spiral may represent a concept such as "Life" while the meander represents "Death." Marshak (1985) similarly suggests that meanders may represent "water," or "change" wherever they occur in the world. Surely, crosses and ovals might also represent similar concepts, and not be tied to specific deities of whatever gender.

Although Gimbutas is often inconsistent in the meanings she

attributes to symbols, resulting in pretzal-like accounts of epiphanies and the evolution of deity indicators, the overriding impression that she leaves is that of an inverted patriarchal pantheon for Old Europe, i.e. a matriarchal pantheon. Any attentive reader that examines the illustrations she provides to support her claims must be bothered at times by identifications and claims that seem to be verifiable only with the eye of faith. Nowhere is there even a mention of methodology, testing, statistics, chance variation, assumptions, or rigor.

ANDROGYNYOUS PARTHENOGENESIS OF THE GREAT GODDESS

Once again, Gimbutas sends out contradictory signals as to how the Great Goddess and her relation to the indisputable presence of some masculine deities is to be interpreted. On the one hand, she acknowledges that the god representations are "stimulators" without which nothing will grow. This is used to explain the phallic obsession of the Near East, Anatolia, and Old Europe since Natufian times (Gimbutas: 216). She even refers to the bull as an "invigorator" (*ibid*: 91).

On the other hand, Gimbutas argues that the Great Goddess was androgynyously all powerful, that she created everything out of her own powers, that phallicism was cathartic rather than erotic, and that Neolithic peoples did not understand the biology of conception (*ibid*: 196, 237).

It is easiest to deal with the last notion first. The idea that pre-Industrial humanity was ignorant of the facts of life is a popular one, primarily kept alive by sensationalistic writers. The idea that hunter/gatherers and early farmers could live intimately in an environment where they were surrounded by the facts of life for two million years and still be oblivious to how reproduction took place on the physical plane is similar to the notion that domestication of plants did not occur prior to 10,000 years ago because hunter/gatherers did not know how plants reproduced. Hunter/gatherers just about everywhere know what makes babies. One woman in the Australian outback even told the Berndts that she refused to live with her husband because she did not want any more children. There are copulation scenes in Paleolithic art (Begouen *et al.* 1982), and the realities of conception were undoubtedly known about throughout most of the Paleolithic. It is naive to believe that groups intelligent enough to invent language, fire, sewn clothes, complex technologies, and great art were so stupid that they could not make the association between sex and reproduction. The mere fact that *selective* genetic changes took place in domestic plants and animals in the Neolithic is proof that human beings knew the essentials of Mendelian genetics even then. Even today, peasant stock breeders in particular, are keenly aware of these facts of life. If it really was true that Neolithic communities were unaware of these facts, why should they insist on the Sacred Marriage and ritual copulation in order to insure crop fertility, as Gimbutas suggests they did in relation to the Dionysian cult? Accounts of groups in the world that did not recognize the realities of physical conception must be counted as exceptional and due to unusual conditions. Most reports of such groups must be categorized with the stories of storks that were told to children in Victorian Europe. Even today, many christians believe that God puts the souls in children and makes them live. The idea that Neolithic or Paleolithic communities were unaware of biological conception is simply untenable. And this means that much of the scenario written by the advocates of the Neolithic Sacred matriarchy is probably also flawed. If it takes both masculine and feminine principles to create life in this world, it is also logical to expect the same in the realm of the Sacred where the increase of plant, animal and human life is the highest priority. What does a review of the archaeological evidence reveal?

Gimbutas argues that the Great androgynyous Goddess is directly descended from the Paleolithic, citing in her support the well-known Venus figurines and a few sculptures that are visual tricks, depicting feminine or bird heads from one view and male genitals from another view. She dismisses the representations of horned men in the caves as being irrelevant because they are from different social and religious contexts than the bull and goat-men of the Neolithic, whereas presumably the ignorance of human reproduction was continuous. I would argue that this is an unduly biased interpretation of Paleolithic religion. While the goddess statues obviously did function in a very public, domestic context, there is no evidence that they were androgynyous or that they were the primary cult of importance. There are probably just as many phalli in the Paleolithic as there are Venuses. The few instances of visual double meanings can be accounted for in terms of artistic play and nothing more, just as such visual tricks appeal to psychology students, sculptors, and joke-shop clientele today. Many of the long necks that Gimbutas sees in phallic terms also occur on figures of male gods and can be found in the sculptures of other cultures such as Africa. It is worth considering that elongated necks may simply be a widespread indicator of beauty. Much more important in Paleolithic religion were the cults that absorbed great amounts of time and energy underground. On the basis of Leroi-Gourhan's work, most anthropologists now accept the view that some sort of basic duality underlay the construction of the cave sanctuaries. There is indisputably a sexual element in the cave art, and one of the most plausible dualities that may have been used for structuring the most fundamental religious concepts in these Paleolithic communities is the sexual duality, as Leroi-Gourhan himself has argued (1965). Many modern hunter/gatherers existing in conditions similar to the Paleolithic, such as the Eskimos and some Australian Aborigines, also explicitly incorporate such sexual dualities in their rites, myths, and basic religious concepts (Berndt 1951; McGhee 1977).

This same basic duality emerges even more clearly in the earliest sophisticated shrines in Eurasia, those at Çatal Hüyük. As Mellaart (1965:94) notes: "In the plaster reliefs only the goddess is shown in anthropomorphic form, the male god, however, appears only as a bull's or ram's head. The shrines were evidently the scene of a fertility cult, the main aim of the religion being the procreation of life, and the ensurance of its continuity and abundance both in this life and the next. Sexual symbolism is absent and attention is drawn to the navel, pregnancy or scenes in which the goddess gives birth to a bull's or ram's head." Like the Paleolithic cave sanctuaries, animals representing masculine forces are on different walls from those representing feminine forces, but they form a complementary whole.

Similar religious themes occur in the Neolithic farming communities of China in terms of the all-pervasive concepts of yin and yang, and in many other parts of the world. While Gimbutas would like to relegate the idea of a Sky-God/Earth Mother duality to Indo-European patriarchies, it actually appears to be relatively common throughout the world. Eliade (1976:205) observes its occurrence in Oceania, Asia, Africa, and both of the Americas, all of which were agricultural. In fact, on a comparative basis, Eliade and others have argued that some form of Sky God was universally present in all primitive cultures (Eliade 1978: James 1957; Narr 1964). All cultures also have a sacred center of their universe (Eliade 1976: 370). This is frequently seen as the meeting point of heaven and earth where creation began. It is the navel of the earth, a place where the sky and earth are unified in sacred marriage. Such sacred marriages are recorded in the earliest written records of the world, in which Ishtar lies with Tammuz on New Year's Day to insure terrestrial fertility. The complementary duality between sky and earth may also be reflected in the story of the cracking of the European cosmic egg into a bottom, earth half, and an upper, sky half. In fact, Von Franz (1972: 157) indicates that these two parts of the cosmic egg are frequently personified as mother and father. In Egypt, too, from the beginning of written accounts, a heavenly cow is connected with the bull of heaven (Kramer 1961: 31), and the king is associated with the strong, virile bull.

Thus, it is possible to follow a basic sexual duality in fundamental religious outlooks from the Paleolithic through the Neolithic and into historic times in the Old World and among a large number of agricultural and hunter/gatherer communities throughout the world. What about Old Europe? I have already referred to the way in which representations of goddesses in association with bulls, snakes, pillars, goats, and rams can be viewed as representing the unification of masculine and feminine forces. Even the depictions of ritual grain grinding may represent this duality if the grain was considered an epiphany of a male deity, as in the case of the well-known John Barleycorn. Given the widespread temporal and spatial distribution of sexual dualism, it presents at least a plausible alternate interpretation to that of Gimbutas. The fact that all forms of European witchcraft provide the goddess with a male consort known as the "Horned God" (Goldenburg 1979: 103) may well indicate that this duality has roots in European folk culture that go back to the Neolithic. The records from Dionysian cults provide another strong indicator.

OLD EUROPE: A MATRIARCHAL UTOPIA?

The final issue that I would like to address is the degree to which Old Europe may or may not have been a matriarchal utopia. While there can be no doubt that the Indo-Europeans that invaded the towns of Old Europe were savage and predatory, it is erroneous to assume that the cultures of Old Europe were social utopias for anyone but the elites. At one time it used to be thought that the European Neolithic was quite peaceful. However, it is beginning to appear more and more as though the initial peace of the era was more a product of isolation rather than a fundamental change in the social fabric. As soon as fertile lands began to fill up in central and northern Europe, significant and sometimes surprisingly ambitious evidence of warfare begins to appear (Milisauskas 1978; Dixson 1979; Mercer 1985). In the area of Old Europe many of the earliest Neolithic communities such as Nea Nikomedia appear to have had defensive walls and to have been planned in labyrinthine fashion so as to thwart easy penetration into the settlements. Mural scenes from the Minoan settlement of Akrotiri similarly show armed warriors, possibly carrying out engagements near North Africa at Minoan colonies. There was an indisputable Minoan expansion into the Aegean during the Late Bronze Age, also involving colonies. It is difficult to imagine such events as occuring without recourse to military means. In fact, it is difficult to imagine any complex society, especially those built on competitive trade, that could emerge or sustain itself without substantial armed conflict. The invading Indo-Europeans were simply better at such conflicts and took over the most lucrative trading routes as the Mycenaean expansion and Trojan war amply illustrate.

As for the role of women in Old European society, there are a number of indicators that women could and undoubtedly often did hold high status. The number and quality of female figurines from the Old European Neolithic seem to indicate this. There may have even been matrilineal inheritance. However, none of these observations warrant the extreme interpretation that the society was "dominated" by the mother. Matriarchal societies are unknown within the ethnographic present, and in all of the cross-cultural studies that have been carried out on women's status, there appear to be no societies where women's status exceeds that of men (Levinson and Malone 1980: 267; Rosaldo 1974; Sanday 1981: 165; Whyte 1978: 167-8; Schlegal 1972: 113, 138). Women sometimes have inferior status, and sometimes they have equal status to that of men. But on the whole it appears that men hold the critical reins of power in traditional societies, that is, physical and armed force. And males generally appear unwilling to relinquish these or to assume inferior status.

Harris (1979:96-7) has argued that matrilinear descent or inheritance occurs primarily in situations where men are absent from their communities for prolonged periods of time on raiding or trading expeditions. They do not feel they can trust family affairs to wives who come from other lineages, and therefore the men leave family affairs in their sister's hands. However, when lineage males are around, it is they that make the decisions. Even among the strongly matrilineal Haida, where women occupied high overall status, the society was still a male dominated one (Blackman 1982: 50). The same can be said of Sumerian society. In both cases, men were frequently on trading and warring missions. The mere fact that Old Europe was agricultural and may have emphasized female fertility goddesses associated with the earth does not by itself mean that women would have had high status. Many simple horticultural societies recognize Earth Mothers and associate the seeds with males, for example in Uganda, the Indies, Italy, Borneo, the Ewe of Africa, the Orinoco and Jivaro of South

America, Egypt, Finland. However, the status of women is often low in the simplest of these societies, such as those of the Amazon Basin and Highland New Guinea, where women are taken in raids and carry out the most laborious work of the household. Even in such societies, female deities may be the most prominent in the pantheon while in the profane world, women's status may be quite low. Werblowsky (1981) has explicitly cautioned against inferring relative social status of men or women from the nature of principal deities. Examples where female deities predominate but where women had markedly inferior status include hunter/gatherers such as the Eskimo as well as civilizations such as Classic Athens. The practice of animal and human sacrifice that has now been documented for Old Europe and Minoan Crete (Gimbutas 1982: 74, 87; Sakellarakis 1981) also somehow seems at odds with the utopian matriarchy that some people would like to believe existed in Old Europe.

In the last analysis, it seems highly dubious that Old Europe was either matriarchal, or matrifocal, or unusually utopian. At its climax, it was certainly rich, undoubtedly hierarchical, aggressive, and competitive. It may also have been matrilineal, and women probably had a relatively high status compared to that of Semitic, Mesoamerican or European medieval patriarchies. But it seems unlikely that they would have had as great an overall say in running society as males. In the murals, the sailors and the soldiers are all males representing a fairly traditional sexual division of labor. There is no evidence that society was dominated by the mother. There **is** evidence that the earth became increasingly important in religious ideology associated with agriculture and may have been most emphasized in the Old European pantheon. However, as Eliade (1976:391) notes, where this happens, masculine roles are generally also important, and, I would argue, reflect a fundamental view of the universe that has persisted since Paleolithic times in which masculine and feminine forces interact to enable Life to continue.

I would like to gratefully acknowledge the research assistance and critical thought that Lindsay Oliver contributed during the preparation of this article. Without her help it would have been a much cruder work than it is now.

Summary

Some recent authors have argued that early agricultural religions were dominated by the worship of a Great Goddess and later by a Mother Goddess. The strongest case for this interpretation has been made for the Neolithic and Chalcolithic of Southeast Europe. However, when these data and arguments are examined in detail, it can be seen that 1) they do not fit well with ethnological data; 2) that the interpretation of archaeological symbols lacks methodological rigor and is excessively subjective, and 3) that there are internal inconsistencies in the arguments. This article suggests that Paleolithic and early Neolithic religions more likely emphasised both a major male and female deity whose interaction insured the annual renewal of the world and most Life forms in it.

Résumé

Quelques auteurs ont recemment interpreté les religions dans le Nèolithique comme dominées par la vénération d'une Déesse Suprème ou plus tard par une Déesse Mère. Le cas le plus favorable à cette interpretation est le Néolithique et Chalcolithique du sudest d'Europe. Cependant, quand ce cas est examiné en detail, il est evident que 1) les arguments ne s'accordent pas avec les données ethnologiques; 2) les interpretations de symbols archaeologiques manquent de rigeur méthodologique et que ces interpretations sont excessivement subjectives; 3) les arguments ne s'accordent pas entre eux. Cet article suggère qu'il est plus probable que les réligions Paléolithiques et Néolithiques ont mis l'emphase sur l'existence d'un dieu mâle et d'une déesse qui étaient ensemble responsable de la renaissance annuelle du monde comprenant toutes les espèces vegetales et animales.

Bibliography

BEGOUEN, R., J. CLOTTES, J.P. GIRAUD and F. ROUSAUD
1982 — Plaquette gravée d'Enlene, Montesquieu-Avantes (Ariège), *Bullettin de la Société Préhistorique Française* 79: 103-109.

BERNDT, Ronald
1951 — *Kunapipi,* Melbourne (F.W. Cheshire).

DIXON P.W.
1979 – A Neolithic and Iron Age site on a hilltop in southern England, *Scientific American* 241 (5): 183-190.

GIMBUTAS, Marija
1982 — *The Goddesses and Gods of Old Europe,* Berkeley (University of California Press).

HARRIS, Marvin
1979 — *Cultural Materialism*, New York (Random House).

KING Mary,
1983 — On the origins and meanings of 'art', *Quarterly Review of Archaeology* 4 (4): 1, 6-8.

LEROI-GOURHAN, André
1965 — *Préhistoire de l'art Occidental,* Paris (Lucien Mazenod).

LEVINSON, David and Martin MALONE
1980 — *Toward Explaining Human Culture*, New Haven, Conn. (HRAF Press).

McGHEE, Robert
1977 — Ivory for the sea woman: the symbolic attributes of a prehistoric technology, *Canadian Journal of Archaeology* 1: 141-150.

MARSHACK, Alexander
1985 — On the dangers of serpents in the mind, *Current Anthropology* 26: 139-145.

MERCER, R.J.
1985 — A Neolithic fortress and funeral center, *Scientific American* 252 (3): 94:101.

MILISAUSKAS, Sarunas
1978 — *European Prehistory,* New York (Academic Press).

ROSALDO, Michelle Zimbalist
1974 — Woman, culture, and society: a theoretical overview, in M. Rosaldo and L. Lamphere (Eds.) *Women, Culture and Society*, Stanford (Stanford Univ. Press) 17-42.

SAKELLARAKIS, Yannis and Efi SAPOUNA-SAKELLERAKI
1981 — Drama of death in a Minoan temple, *National Geographic* 159 (2): 205-222.

SANDAY, Peggy
1981 — *Female power and male dominance: on the origins of sexual inequality,* Cambridge (Cambridge University Press).

SCHLEGAL, Alice
1972 — *Male dominance and female autonomy*, New Haven (HRAF Press).

WERBLOWSKY, R.J.Z.
1981 — Women...and other...beasts, or 'Why can't a woman be more like a man', *Numen* 29:123-131.

WHYTE, Martin
1978 — *The status of women in preindustrial societies,* Princeton, N.J. (Princeton University Press).

PHILOSOPHICAL PARADIGMS OF FERTILITY CULT INTERPRETATIONS: PHILOSOPHICAL PERSPECTIVES ON SEASONAL GODDESSES

Zak vàn Straaten

Why did fertility cults exist? What function did they have, if any? What are we to make of fertility cult figurines and artefacts? Can the differences of figurine design be explained? Is there a single unifying explanation of the fertility cult data? In this paper I propose answers to all of these questions and give a general explanation of the existence and function of fertility cults.

THE DATA

The data to be explained consists of the goddess figurines and other artefacts; together with associated retrodicted fertility cult behaviours, and associated semantics.

One may remain sceptical of the "mother-goddess" hypothesis such as is explicated in the works of Marija Gimbutas (1974) and in E. O. James's *The Cult of the Mother Goddess* (1959) but take James's careful record of the vast geographical dispersion of fertility cult figurines and artefacts as a good guide to part of what I am calling the data. The diffusion of the fertility cult artefacts took place on a vast geographical and historical scale. The data encompasses the sculptured venuses from the Gravettian culture of the Upper Palaeolithic era to the emblems and inscriptions of Western Asia, the Indus Valley, the Aegean and Crete between the 5th and 3rd millennia B.C. James thinks that with the rise of agriculture and domestication of animals the figure of the goddess was refined and sharpened: from unmarried mother — personifying divine principle in maternity — to association with the young god as son or consort. There was a dual aspect of seasonal drama in which both male and female played roles.

Palaeolithic cultures

The figurines are made of bone and ivory, — pendulous breasts, broad hips, round buttocks, and corpulency implying pregnancy. Examples have been found at Kostienki, Gagarino, and at Malta, near

Lake Baikal in Siberia. By contrast there is the Willendorf venus near Vienna, which is slim and grotesque. At Cogul, twelve miles from Lerida in Catalonia, the record consists of nine narrow-waisted women with long pendulous breasts, clad in caps and bell-shaped skirts which reach to the knees, with no facial features, who are shown in association with a small naked male figure. The male figure may have been added later.

Neolithic cultures

According to James, in the transition from food-gathering to food production, the female principle continued to dominate rituals which had grown up around the (mysterious) process of birth and generation. Worth noting are the arpachiyah figurines in Northern Iraq, within 16 kilometres of Tigris and the ancient city of Nineveh, at the Chalcolithic mound Tell Arpachiyah. These headless venus-type clay statuettes date from before 4000 B.C. They have pendulous breasts, prominent navels, slender waists and highly developed buttocks. Most are in a squatting posture suggestive of childbirth; some have the appearance of pregnancy. According to James these were precursors of later Eastern Mediterranean figures, associated with the double axe and the dove, bull's head and serpent, as in Crete and the Aegean. James claims there is a link between Palaeolithic and later Chalcolithic and Bronze Age evidence of the cult in Crete and the Aegean. Dr. Mallowan says that: "fertility worship connected with a "mother-goddess" cult must indeed be one of the oldest and longest surviving religions of the ancient world" (Mallowan 1935: 87). And James thinks that: "Once the maternal principle had been personified it was either as a single goddess, the Great Mother, with different functions and symbols, or as a number of independent and separate deities exercising several roles in the process of birth/generation/fertility" (James 1959: 24).

It is worth calling attention to the Iron Age Israelite occupation level at Tell Beit Mirsim in South Palestine, near the Canaanite city, Kirjathsepher. James speaks of an exaggerated protrusion of the vulva region in an attempt to suggest the descent of the head of an infant at the moment of birth.

There is no trace of relevant data from the north-east of early Iran and Turkestan. The fertility cult appears to have flourished in the south and south-west. Figures from the Elamite period (2800 BC) show one splayed hand on the stomach and one on the breasts, an example of which may be found in the Ashmolean Museum, Oxford.

Prior to the third millennium BC, in the mountain villages of Baluchistan, farming communities similar to early Iranian settlements were established. Numerous clay figurines have been found in the Zhob Valley and identical terracotta figurines have also been discovered at Dabar Kot, Periano Ghundai, Sur Jangal and Mogul Ghundai.

In the Indus Valley figurines dating from 2500 to 1500 BC at Harappa, Mohenjo-daro, and Chanhu-daro have been found. One female figure has a projection from the top of the head; this could represent horns or doves which are an important emblem in the goddess cult.

So much for the figurines and artefacts, and some of the historical *retrodicted* hypotheses to make sense of this part of the data. I shall refer to the "semantic" part of the data in section (c) below after I have introduced some of my explanatory structures.

THEORY

a) *Explanation of the Existence and Function of Fertility Cults*

To explain the existence and function of fertility cults I shall posit a gene replicational *hypothesis*. The ineluctable genetic imperative requires that replication must be the *primary concern* of the gene replicators at all times. Call this the main sentence. This is the reason for being. Fertility cult behaviours played a part in the optimization or maximization of the population relative to a set of survival conditions. They were part of the gene's strategy for survival, often under very unfavourable conditions. Two cases immediately present themselves.

(i) Replication is particularly to be stressed when survival is in question. An insufficient number of births at one time may result in an inadequate food store at another time. On the *underpopulation* view we must assume that the replicators think they require more hands as food gatherers, hunters, or defenders in pre-agricultural cultures, with the additional requirement of more farmers in agricultural communities. Since fertility rituals contributed (or were supposed to contribute), in the longer term, to more food gatherers, hunters, defenders or farmers, the ruling elites established and supported fertility cults. In hunter-gatherer communities a sufficient supply of food and an optimum number of offspring would be necessary conditions for survival. Since only one child can be carried easily by each mother, it is necessary to practice self-regulatory contraception; and to secure a trade off between procreation and procuring food. The initial conditions, data and universal generalisation are fairly explicit here.

(ii) Even at times of massive *overpopulation* fertility cults could continue to flourish as in (i) for a variety of reasons. The gene replication hypothesis may be true in a society when that society is *not* conscious of its truth.

There is evidence to show that the Trojan wars were caused by overpopulation and that from the 8th century BC many city states were over-populated. Do we therefore conclude that the functionalist explanation in (i) above must fail? Either (a) under-population was false for each tribe or whole city but true for each mating couple. For example, in India today the majority recognises over-population, yet each couple has just as many children as their parents had; — over-population can be true for all India but not for them; or (b) under-population is generally false. This latter conclusion could show the selfish gene theory to be true. Replication aided by fertility cults continues but no one knows why this should be so in a time of over-population. When communities become settled the advantages of cooperation in food production and defence show the need for enlarged social groupings. Under such conditions natural selection favours individuals who reproduce at maximum, as opposed to optimum, rates. The political leaders would see advantages in institutionalising fertility practices.

In either the under-population or over-population case the main sentence could be true for the reasons given above. The ruling elites may also make explicit ideological use of a set of *false beliefs* to further social ends. This can be a rational activity. For example those religions which make abortion taboo and are closely linked to state power can maximize birthings for reasons of their own even in times of gross over-population. (I shall not go into the class of cases dealing with self-deception or false consciousness here for lack of time. They are obviously linked to actions based on false beliefs.)

Maynard Smith first introduced the idea of an 'evolutionarily stable strategy' (ESS) which is put to such good use in Dawkin's *The Selfish Gene* (1978: 74). A "strategy" is a "preprogrammed behavioural policy". An example, given by Dawkins, is: "attack the opponent; if he flees pursue him; if he retaliates run away". The strategy need not be conscious (p. 74). An ESS is theoretically defined as a strategy which, if most members of a population adopt it, cannot be bettered by an alternative strategy.

The essential implication is that the best strategy for any individual will depend on what strategies are adopted by all the other individuals in the group. As the group consists of individuals each of whom is trying to maximize his own success, the only permanent strategy will be one which cannot be bested by any anarchic individual.

Using game theory one can compute whether a particular group of animals is in an ESS or not. Imagine a population of hawks and doves. Hawks by definition fight hard and unrestrainedly, and retreat only when badly injured. Doves merely threaten. What happens when a hawk meets a dove? If a hawk fights a dove, the dove flees. If a hawk fights a hawk, one dies or is seriously injured. If a dove fights a dove they only posture and there is no damage. Suppose you cannot tell in advance which is a hawk or a dove; and you allot 50 = win; 0 = lose; -100 = seriously injured; -10 = waste of time over a long contest. Is the hawk or the dove in an ESS?

> "Suppose we have a population consisting entirely of doves. Whenever they fight nobody gets hurt. The contests consist of prolonged ritual tournaments, staring matches perhaps, which end only when one rival backs down. The winner then scores 50 points for gaining the resource in dispute, but he pays a penalty of -10 for wasting time over a long staring match, so scores 40 in all. The loser also is penalized -10 points for wasting time. On average, any one individual dove can expect to win half his contests and lose half. Therefore his average pay-off per contest is the average of +40 and -10, which is +15. Therefore, every individual dove in a population of doves seems to be doing quite nicely.
>
> But now suppose a mutant hawk arises in the population. Since he is the only hawk around, every fight he has is against a dove. Hawks always beat doves, so he scores +50 every fight, and this is his average pay-off. He enjoys an enormous advantage over the doves, whose net pay-off is only +15. Hawk genes will rapidly spread through the population as a result. But now each hawk can no longer count on every rival he meets being a dove. To take an extreme example, if the hawk gene spread so successfully that the entire population came to consist of hawks, all fights would now be hawk fights. Things are now very different. When hawk meets hawk, one of them is seriously injured, scoring -100, while the winner scores +50. Each hawk in a population of hawks can expect to win half his fights and lose half his fights. His average expected pay-off per fight is therefore half-way between +50 and -100, which is -25. Now consider a single dove in a population of hawks. To be

sure, he loses all his fights, but on the other hand he never gets hurt. His average pay-off is 0 in a population of hawks, whereas the average pay-off for a hawk in a population of hawks is -25. Dove genes will therefore tend to spread through the population" (Dawkins 1978: 76).

If one does the arithmetic the stable ratio is 5/12 doves to 7/12 hawks. At this ratio the average pay-off for hawks is equal to the average dove pay-off. So the answer to the question asked above about the ESS is that in this hypothetical example at the hawk-dove ratio of 7:5 both doves and hawks are in an ESS.

Fertility cults contributed to the evolutionarily stable strategy of tribes within palaeolithic and neolithic cultures. It is advantageous for human replicators to establish and encourage fertility cult behaviours, since these behaviours will directly affect the optimization and maximization of a population relative to a set of survival conditions. The ruling elites could control and exploit fertility cult practices for political and social advantage.

The basic explanation of fertility cults as expressed above is that they contributed to the ESS of those communities which practised them. They were used as a seasonal reminder of the obligations the gene replicators had to their genes; and of the need to optimise birthings relative to survival conditions. In the periods considered in the data section there was no better survival strategy available. And as we have seen above the same strategy was applied at the level of the local group in times of both over-and under-population.

b) *Explaining the differences of figurine design*

Sculptured figurines of the fertility gods and goddesses seem to exhibit more *differences* in shape, size and design than similarities. I shall argue that the *differences* are not significant. Variation in design does not matter, since the function of the figurine is to call attention to the requirements of the genetic imperative in creating a stable replicational strategy. Then why do different designs proliferate? I find the study, made by P.F. Jenkins, of how mistakes are made in the learning of bird calls by the young of the saddleback family of birds in islands off New Zealand, very instructive. We can generalize from these cases to copying errors whenever messages or ideas are transmitted.

This is how Dawkins (1978: 203-204) describes the study.

"On the island where he worked there was a total repertoire of about nine distinct songs. Any given male sang only one or a few of these songs. The males could be classified into dialect groups. For example, one group of eight males with neigbouring territories sang a particular song called the CC song. Other dialect groups sang different songs. Sometimes the members of a dialect group shared more than one distinct song. By comparing the songs of fathers and sons, Jenkins showed that song patterns were not inherited genetically. Each young male was likely to adopt songs from his territorial neighbours by imitation, in an analogous way to human language. During most of the time Jenkins was there, there was a fixed number of songs on the island, a kind of 'song pool' from which each young male drew his own small repertoire. But occasionally Jenkins was privileged to witness the 'invention' of a new song, which *occurred by a mistake in the imitation of an old one.* He writes: 'New song forms have been shown to arise variously by change of pitch of a note, repetition of a note, the elision of notes and the combination of parts of other existing songs...The appearance of the new form was an abrupt event and the product was quite stable over a period of years. Further, in a number of cases the variant was transmitted accurately in its new form to younger recruits so that a recognizably coherent group of like singers developed'. Jenkins refers to the origins of new songs as 'cultural mutations'."

The different designs of fertility cult figurines can similarly be described as *cultural mutations due to copying errors*. There may be a local story to tell, relative to the time of the design, which would explain why the sculptor thought a particular feature should be emphasized but that story would not be significant in the context of the function of fertility cults as explained in (a) above.

c) *Explaining the associated symbolism, semantics and metaphysics*

The symbolism and semantics associated with fertility cult practices varies with changing geography or time. The literature and associated scholarship is relatively large. What is clear is that the literature tends to lack plausible explanations that are general and apply to many cases.

In his *The Meaning of Aphrodite*, Paul Friedrich (1978) argues that Aphrodite is quite properly a liminal figure. The application of the Friedrich/Turner concept of "liminality" to fertility cult gods/goddesses by Friedrich suggests that a set of opposite or contradictory properties inhere in the true description of Aphrodite. The very properties which distinguish "liminal" characters can apply to fertility goddesses. These are:

1. Transition "crossover" between social or metaphysical grids or frames; 2. Operating successfully between such cultural (universal?) oppositions as nature vs culture; 3. Asceticism or strong sexuality; 4. Verbal purity or excessive profanity and obscenity; 5. Silence or verbal efflorescence and brilliance; 6. Foolishness and silliness or great wisdom, seer-craft, prescience; 7. Social homogeneity or absence of relative status; 8. Nakedness or special costumes (Friedrich 1978: 133).

It was N.K. Humphrey who suggested that we view ideas as living structures. He proposed calling ideas "memes", and said:

> "Memes should be regarded as living structures, not just metaphorically but technically. When you plant a fertile meme in my mind you literally parasitize my brain turning it into a vehicle for the meme's propagation in just the way a virus may parasitize the genetic mechanism of a host cell — the meme "belief in life after death" is realized in the structure in the nervous system" (Dawkins 1978: 206ff).

For an idea or meme to survive it must have psychological or social appeal, and must be copied accurately. In the transmission of the semantic properties associated with seasonal gods/goddesses production of good copy is not important if the central idea, that of being a fertility cult figure identified with a social ritual, is copied. For it is this idea which results in behaviour which ensures an evolutionarily stable strategy. Friedrich lists many properties of seasonal goddesses. They have or are clearly associated with all or some of the following: 1. Location — islands and mountain peaks; 2. Fruits and flowers; 3. Birds — heron/cuckoo/quail; 4. Goldenness; 5. Sun/moon/stars; 6. Water — aquatic birth; 7. Origin from Zeus (descendent of the Proto-Indo-European sky god); 8. Kinship — parallel to nuclear and extended families of Homeric times; 9. Friendliness and intimacy — close to kinship; 10. Virginity (Athena — sexless, sororal friend of heroes); 11. Attendant nymphs and maidens; 12. Beauty (Aphrodite); 13. Intelligence; 14. Nature versus culture; 15. Abstract features, e.g. Mobility; 16. Fertility; 17. War; 18. Subjectivity (Friedrich 1978: 72ff).

It is important that each fertility cult goddess has enough semantic properties to identify her as a seasonal fertility goddess. But if my basic reductive explanation in (a) above is correct; and if my explanation of the function of fertility cult behaviours is correct; then the significance of any one semantic property can be discounted. It would be enough if some properties identified the goddess as a fertility goddess. The same can be said of "liminality". "Liminality" sets the tone or colour of the goddess by alluding to the collection of symbolic opposites she embodies, and emphasising her marginality and highlighting the tension between destructiveness and the mother principle.

According to the liminality thesis fertility cult goddesses are synthesizing symbols of powerful opposites. And liminality can be claimed to be true of a range of seasonal goddesses. But the thesis itself is not an explanation of the existence and structure of the semantics and symbolism associated with fertility cult figures. "Liminality" merely serves to give *colour* and *tone* to any explanation of the real function of the semantics and symbolism. Basic semantic features can be referred to local variation and can be explained as cultural mutations. These cultural mutations do not matter if we keep in mind our basic reductive gene-replicational explanation. For the reductive thesis has to be related to the data in a particular community or tribe by way of a functionalist explanation. At best liminality can give tone to the description of goddesses, who are themselves embedded in fertility cult behaviours, and contribute to an ESS for that community or tribe.

d) *Alternative views*

Attempts at explaining fertility cult behaviour as primarily religious in nature must fail if the basic explanation is that given in (a) above. It might be possible to show that the idea of the mother goddess was central to that development, as is argued by James (1935) and Gimbutas (1974). But this would not detract from the basic, reductive, gene-replicational thesis outlined above. If this religious thesis were true, it would like the liminality thesis, add tone and colour to the explication of the function of seasonal goddesses.

It could be argued that myth-making animals are preferred in the survival process. Natural selection could favour individuals with a propensity for myth making. Myths, held to be true by a community, help to stem neurosis, and to universalize the norms or whatever is held to be exemplary. Myths are models which serve to render the unknown comprehensible, and to create order out of seeming chaos. It is the perception of the idea that the earth produces all vegetation, and animals, that gives rise to the 'emergence-from-bowels-of-the-earth' myth, which sees earth as ultimately in control of vital, magical processes. While it is true that man, the ideology-creating creature, uses the unifying aspects of fertility rituals for social and political ends, this by itself cannot explain the existence and function of fertility cult behaviour at a sufficiently basic level. The explanation which holds that fertility cults contributed to the evolutionarily stable strategies of communities, and were a seasonal reminder of the obligations the gene-replicators had to their genes to optimise birthings relative to survival conditions, is sufficiently basic to count as a general, universalizable explanation.

I wish to thank Miss Jennifer Warren of the Institute for Advanced Studies in Philosophy for discussing the topic of this paper with me.

Summary

Is there a general explanation of the existence and function of fertility cult behaviour and artefacts? Is there an explanation of the symbols, semantics and metaphysics associated with fertility cults? This paper suggests affirmative answers. The data to be explained consists of the goddess figurines and other artefacts; together with associated retrodicted fertility cult behaviours, and associated semantics.

Man as a gene replicator is subject to the genetic imperative. His primary concern at all times must be replication. He can replicate both his genes and ideas or cultural messages. In gene replication he has a 50% (copying fidelity) investment in the resultant chromosome. But cultural messages and ideas are subject to copying errors. Fertility cult objects and behaviours can now be explained as follows. Man, the replicator, encourages (and the ruling elites exploit) fertility cults which exist to optimise or maximise population relative to survival conditions. The objective is to stress seasonal behaviour required for birth causation. Animals are subject to copying errors in the transmission of cultural messages. Any message can be miscopied. The divergent semantics and symbolism can be explained as copying errors. Friedrich using the concept of "liminality" cites lists of opposing semantic markers, such as: asceticism/strong sexuality; verbal purity/obscenity; foolishness/wisdom; nakedness/special costumes; as features of seasonal goddesses. These and other basic semantic features can be referred to local variation and explained as copying errors.

The design variation in figurines form Baluchistan, the Indus Valley, Nothern Iraq, to the Aegean and Malta can be explained as copying errors. The variation is irrelevant since the function of the figurine is to call attention to, and accentuate the demands of the genetic imperative in creating an evolutionarily stable strategy. Alternative hypothesis of fertility cult behaviour and semantics are found wanting. The religious explanation refers to primitive religion and man's need to the numinous dimension. This misses the point. A secular explanation claims that myth-making animals are preferred in the survival process. Man, the ideology-creating creature, uses unifying aspects of fertility rituals for social and political ends. This partly succeeds but misunderstands the workings of the gene replicational mechanism as explained in this paper.

Bibliography

CHADWICK, J.
1976 — *The Mycenaean World* (Cambridge University Press, New York).

DAWKINS, R.
1978 — *The Selfish Gene* (Granada, London).

ELIADE, M.
1960 — *Myths, Dreams and Mysteries: The Encounter between Contemporary Faiths and Archaic Realities,* (Harper and Row, New York).

FRIEDRICH, P.
1978 — *The Meaning of Aphrodite* (University of Chicago, Chicago).

GIMBUTAS, M.
1974 — *The Gods and Goddesses of Old Europe 7000-3500 BC,* (University of California Press, Los Angeles).

JAMES, E.O.
1959 — *The Cult of the Mother-Goddess* (Thames and Hudson, London).

KIRK, G.
1976 — *The Nature of Great Myths,* (Praeger, New York).

MALLOWAN, M.E.L.
1935 — *Iraq* Vol II, (Oxford University Press, Oxford).

TURNER, V.
1967a — 'Myth and Symbol' in *International Encyclopedia of the Social Sciences,* 576-82, (Macmillan and The Free Press, New York).

1967b — *The Forest of Symbols,* (Cornell University Press, Ithaca).

1969 — *The Ritual Process: Structure and Anti-Structure*, (Aldine Chicago).

ANCIENT RELIGIONS IN THE CONTEXT OF CULTURAL TYPES

Mimi Lobell

In this paper, I am very briefly presenting a typology of cultures, which spans from prehistory to the present. I have been developing this theory for over ten years and have completed a book manuscript on it. Here, I will necessarily be limited to outlining the theory and giving a synopsis of the six cultural types I have identified: the SENSITIVE CHAOS of the Palaeolithic hunter-gatherers, the GREAT ROUND of the Neolithic and Early Bronze Age farmers, the FOUR QUARTERS of the Bronze and Iron Age Chiefdoms, the PYRAMID of the nation state, the RADIANT AXES of the empire, and the GRID of the commercial-industrial network.

I will suggest only one or two direct applications to the subject of the conference, but many more are clearly implied. For those who wish to pursue this further, more details are available in my article, "Spatial Archetypes" in *REVISION* (1983).

I hope that this typology of cultures, which focuses on their religions, mythologies, and world views, can provide researchers with a useful context within which to evaluate archaeological evidence and other fragmentary information.

THE THEORY

This theory of cultural types originated in my observation that many cultures widely separated in space and time have produced very similar architectural forms. Because it is so familiar, the pyramid can demonstrate the pervasive nature of these forms. As we can see in these examples, it has appeared in nearly all parts of the world:

1. The Giza Pyramids, Egypt. 2500 B.C.
2. The Pyramid of the Sun, Teotihuacan, Mexico. 150 B.C. - 750 A.D.
3. The Ziggurat of Ur-Nammu in ancient Sumer. 2100 B.C.
4. Pusa Peak, China (a natural mountain enhanced by a Buddhist shrine with 108 steps).
5. A Classic Mayan pyramid, Tikal, Guatamala.

6. The Bakheng temple mountain, Angkor, Kampuchea. 9th c. A.D.
7. The Mount Li Tomb , Xian, China. About 210 B.C.
8. The Borobudur Stupa, Java. 9th c. A.D.
9. Pyramid of the Niches, Classic Period at El Tajin, Mexico.
10. A pre-European Royal Tomb at Apia, Samoa.

We can analyze the recurring form motifs in world architecture the way a comparative mythologist would analyze a mythic motif in world mythology — for instance, as Joseph Campbell did in *The Hero with a Thousand Faces* (1949), and Erich Neumann in *The Great Mother: Analysis of the Archetype* (1955). This enables us to differentiate their underlying structural similarities, which are universal, from their surface colorations, which vary from region to region and culture to culture.

The structural similarities in the recurring forms in world architecture point to their significance as archetypes. I find this a useful concept, not as an argument against cultural diffusion for I do not think it is an "either-or" issue, but rather as a model for the relationship between the *universal* and the *particular* in the various forms of cultural expression. There may be surface differences in the appearance or use of a type of structure from culture to culture at the same time that there are archetypal similarities of form and meaning. The pyramid can be planar or stepped, and it can serve as temple, tomb, or reliquary, but it is nearly always a model of the sky-aspirant World Mountain stretching between Heaven and Earth about the numinous *axis mundi.*

Without denying the importance of their differences, my study focuses on the similarities in the recurring forms in world architecture in order to penetrate their archetypal nature. Each spatial archetype thus revealed points to a different world view working powerfully within a culture to bind all its forms of expression into a coherent whole. Thus, its art, mythology and religion, architecture and town planning, social and economic system, prevailing family structure, moral code, etc., all coordinate to reinforce the culture's archetypal structure of meaning.

As we might expect, each archetypal form is consistently found in the same general social context. For example, whether in Egypt, Mesopotamia, Asia, Oceania, or the Americas, the pyramid consistently arises as an architectural form shortly after the social structure has coalesced into nation or city states governed by a dynastic succession of rulers, who are usually divine and mediate the axis between Heaven and Earth on behalf of their subjects. Once we recognize this pattern, we can see that the Gothic cathedrals and certain Greek temples are variants of the Pyramid archetype.

In Pyramid cultures, society is structured into a hierarchical pyramid of classes. Often this is mirrored in a concept of tiered Heavens and Hells to which one goes after death depending on one's station in life and the nobility of one's soul. Finally, the cosmos itself is mythically represented as the World Mountain modeled by the architectural pyramid. This Mountain may be the birthplace or abode of the gods and goddesses as in the "primeval hill" in Egypt and Mount Olympus in Greece, or it may be a complete conceptual model of the cosmos as in Mount Meru (Govinda 1976) in India and the Mayan *imago mundi* (Thompson 1970). In any case, the World Mountain models the cosmic pattern of the social order and of the purpose and meaning of life on earth.

What emerges from these efforts to let architecture, comparative mythology and religion, psychology, archaeology, and anthropology shed light on one another are models of *cultural types*, which usually succeed one another as stages of development in any given geographical area. There are indications in the research of Jean Piaget (1960, 1967), Erich Neumann (1954), and others that these cultural stages parallel stages of individual psychological development. I must omit most of these intriguing parallels in this brief paper, but they are more fully presented in my *ReVISION* article.

I feel strongly that each cultural type should *not* be seen as an inevitable stage in an inexorable evolution toward the type of culture we in the West enjoy today. Rather, it is a completely distinct way of life in its own right, and each type has a fundamentally different world view.

THE TYPES

I have identified six major spatial archetypes, which I have termed the Sensitive Chaos, the Great Round, the Four Quarters, the Pyramid, the Radiant Axes, and the Grid. Each is associated with a different cultural type. This does not mean that a spatial form can appear *only* in its associated culture, but rather that it is *dominant* and has its truest meaning in that type of culture.

1. The first type, the SENSITIVE CHAOS, (for the origin of the name of the archetype, see Schwenk 1965), is seen among *Palaeolithic hunter-gatherers* living in nomadic, egalitarian bands. Based on the meandering spiral that has no apparent geometric order or centralizing axes, it expresses the way of life of a people who do not build permanent architecture, and whose view of the world is of a fluctuating unified field of being in which one life form can transform into another through magical or shamanic states of mind.

This cultural type developed and prevailed in the first few million years of human evolution up to about 15,000 B.C. Among the precious few Sensitive Chaos cultures extant today are some Australian Aborigines, the Tasaday of the Philippines, and the Kung San and Pygmies of Africa.

2. The second type, the GREAT ROUND (name origin: Neumann 1955: 211-239), most concerns the subject of this conference and is associated with *Neolithic and early Bronze Age farmers*. Rooted in the land, they build permanent dwellings, shrines, granaries, and collective graves. Indeed, most megalithic structures can be credited to them. The Great Round as a circular form is often expressed in stone circles, passage mounds, sacred caves, and sanctuaries, although there are also non-circular structures. The spiritual focus is on the Great Goddess, and her sacred Womb-Cavern is a prevalent form motif that becomes the prototype for the *holy-of-holies* of nearly all later religions.

Worship of the Great Goddess in her various forms fosters the sensibilities and values of the feminine principle, much as the worship of male gods fosters the sensibilities and values of the masculine principle. Great Round cultures are female-centered, which does not mean that they simply reverse today's sex roles. It means that they have or had a fundamentally different world view, and consequently, fundamentally different social systems, institutions, religions, artifacts, settlement patterns, building types, technologies, etc.

In keeping with the female-centeredness of the Great Round, matrilineal families are common, and relatively egalitarian social structures persist, with little evidence of royal burial or status differentiated housing. The archetype is further amplified in the holistic psychological state which seems to prevail, judging both from the peacefulness prehistoric Great Round cultures sustained for thousands of years — which is nearly miraculous considering how commonly war is assumed to be inherent in human nature — and from their cyclical view of time based on continually recurring agricultural seasons.

Unlike the relatively static hunting-gathering cultures, the peoples of the Great Round exhibit a dynamic inventiveness, seen typically in the development of pottery, agriculture, animal domestication, metallurgy, astronomy, and permanent villages and towns.

Examples of Great Round cultures and sites include the Maltese temples and rock-cut tombs, the pre-Greek cultures of the Aegean, Khirokitea on Cyprus, most of the cultures discussed by Marija Gimbutas in *The Gods and Goddesses of Old Europe* (1974), the Boyne Valley culture in Ireland, Predynastic Egypt up to the Gerzean, Mesopotamia into the early Ubaid period, Çatal Hüyük in Anatolia, the Yang Shao culture in China, and the Jomon of Japan. Certain later Bronze Age cultures such as Minoan Crete and the Indus Valley Civilization also display a predominance of Great Round characteristics. Among contemporary Great Round cultures can be numbered the Hopi and Pueblo Indians of the American Southwest.

3. The third type is the FOUR QUARTERS (name origin: Perry 1966), seen in the warlike *hierarchical chiefdoms* of the Bronze and Iron Ages. The spatial archetype is represented by the cardinal axes bounded by a square, which is a major spatial motif in forts, temples, and walled cities. The cosmos is divided into quarters, and everything — including the seasons, colors, elements, castes, past ages, and human attributes — is aligned along the cardinal axes.

Spiritual life is centered on the archetypal "Lord of the Four Quarters", a heroic male god, usually of thunder and war like Zeus, Thor, and Indra, who rules from the central position in a hierarchical pantheon. He is mirrored by the chieftain as the central authority in a caste society, and by the father as the head of the new patriarchal family. The analog in individual development is the rise of the ego as the central reference point in the psyche. Other common mythical themes concern metallurgy and the blacksmith (Eliade 1978), the dragon-slayer (Neumann 1954: 131-133, 152-169), and the conquest and domestication (e.g. through marriage) of the goddesses of the older Great Round cultures (Graves 1960: 13-24).

Examples of the Four Quarters include Homeric Greece, the Etruscans, Bronze and Iron Age Indo-European language-speaking cultures in general, the Ubaid period in Mesopotamia, early Vedic India, the Shang and Chou dynasties of China, the Israelite tribes before David, and the Late Preclassic cultures of Mesoamerica; and I would also cite the "disk idols" of Malta's Tarxien cemetery culture as illustrations of the Four Quarters.

4. The fourth type is the PYRAMID, which, as we saw earlier, is associated with the *nation or city state*. As a "stage of cultural development", this is usually considered the Classical Period or "Golden Age" when a civilization reaches the height of its artistic and architectural florescence. Pyramid cultures are characterized by dynastic theocratic rule; reverence for the World Mountain; the building of architectural pyramids; and all the attributes of statecraft including standing armies, intensive agriculture, urban centers, and class-structured societies.

A growing dualism, expressing an increasing alienation between ego and Self (Edinger 1972), generates a spiritual emphasis on the *logos* principle. This can be seen in the proliferation of writing and mathematics; and in the idea that the universe is secretly ordered according to divine laws, mystical geometric relationships, sacred names, and numbers imbued with magical power, all of which are accessible only to the ruler and his elite priesthood. The operative maxim is "as above, so below", and the ruling dynasty is mandated to insure microcosmic harmony. Usually the dynastic tribal deity reigns at the apex of a syncretic state religion centering on the divine (or divinely inspired) ruler's ritualistic and symbolic mediation of the *axis mundi* — that spiritual axis between Heaven and Earth paralleled by the psychological axis between the ego and the Self (Edinger 1972: 5).

Examples of the Pyramid type include Old Kingdom Egypt, Sumer, the Kingdoms of David and Solomon in the Levant, Classical Greece, the Ch'in (Qin) through Sung Dynasties in China, the Buddhist and Hindu Dynasties in India, the Toltecs and the Maya, the Khmers at Angkor, the Sailendra Dynasty in Java, and the Gothic cathedral builders of medieval Europe.

5. The fifth type is the RADIANT AXES *empire*, which subsumes a number of nation states. The sun, with its seemingly infinite rays of power is a dominant image, mirrored for instance in networks of roads radiating from palaces like Versailles or from capitals such as Imperial Rome or Cuzco, the Peruvian capital of the Incan empire.

The gigantism and ego-inflated quality of this type are seen in colossal sculptures and structures such as those at Abu Simbel and Karnak (Giedion 1964: 25-26, 385), and in propagandistic murals or bas reliefs such as those at Persepolis, capital of the Persian Empire. A strong vertical axis is commonly embodied in the obelisk form, which can symbolize a ray of the sun.

In the Radiant Axes, a ceremonially pompous, spiritually empty state religion tends to prevail, focusing on the Sun God: Amon-Ra in New Kingdom Egypt, Apollo or Helios in Greece, Tonatiuh among the Aztecs, Inti in the Incan empire. The importance of the sun is illustrated also in Louis XIV's epithet "the Sun King" and in the acceptance of Copernicus's heliocentric theory of the universe just as Europe entered her Age of Imperialism.

6. Empires usually end abruptly through violent revolutions, which establish the last archetypal form: the GRID of the international, post-imperialistic *commercial-industrial networks.* These are characterized by secularism, bureaucracy, mercantilism, eclecticism, decadence, nihilism, and mass production industries (in part, Spengler 1939). The grid form appears in the layouts of worker's housing, bureaucratic land divisions, colonial cities, military camps, market and factory towns, assembly lines, office buildings, and industrialized farms. And, like the spatial archetype itself, the social system seeks to decentralize power, whether through republicanism or communism, socialism or democracy.

Rarely do Grid cultures create new forms; rather, they repeat, refine, standardize, and mass-produce old forms borrowed from previous eras and more creative cultures. They may, however, accomplish impressive feats of engineering, like those of the Roman, Incan, and modern Western civilizations.

Psychologically, the Grid parallels the deflated ego, bringing a sense of anonymity and despiritualization. Religion can become a free-for-all with eclectic experimentation, charismatic cults, and desperate zealotry. Whether in society, the psyche, or the spirit, the center cannot be found. Ultimately, however, the Grid can foster the perception that all the archetypal gods and goddesses, heroes and demons are within oneself, and religion then becomes the inner path.

Grid cultures include Ptolemaic Egypt, Hellenistic Greece, the late Roman Empire, China from the Manchu Dynasty to the present, and of course contemporary Western culture.

CONCLUSIONS

It is often possible to trace the whole sequence of archetypes in one civilization. For instance, in the Aegean, the Sensitive Chaos would have prevailed up to the time of the first agriculturalists about 6500 B.C. Then the Great Round began, with its relatively peaceful, goddess-centered way of life embracing the first farmers (such as those living at Nea Nikomedeia by about 5800 B.C.). Typified by the Early Cycladic culture, the Great Round continued in many ways even through the Minoan civilization, though signs of defensive fortifications and social hierarchy began appearing at sites such as Dhimini and Troy in the fourth millennium B.C. The Indo-European invasions from at least 2000 B.C. or earlier clearly initiated elements of the Four Quarters, but the true turning point was the shift of power around 1500 B.C. from peaceful Minoan Crete to warlike Mycenae. The Four Quarters — Archaic Greece's heroic, Homeric Bronze and Iron Ages — continued until the flowering of Classical Greece in the fifth century B.C. With its Olympian mythology, city states, Athenian Acropolis, and growing *logos* principle, Classical Greece was a true Pyramid culture, though it was not theocratic and did not build pyramids. By the time of his death in 323 B.C., Alexander the Great had established a Radiant Axes empire that had spread Greek civilization throughout the known world. The subsequent Hellenistic Period represented the Grid, with Greece being subsumed by Rome by 146 B.C.

A most important use of the theory, and the reason I wished to present it at this conference, is that it offers *contextual models* in which to interpret data and artifacts. For example, we can see that the Neolithic Maltese cultures responsible for the temples and rock-cut tombs strongly exhibit Great Round characteristics — including megalithic structures, peacefulness, goddess-worship, and collective burial. There is little or no physical evidence for the hypothesis advanced by Colin Renfrew (1979) that they were organized around chieftains (i.e., that it was a Four Quarters type of culture as were the Easter Island and Polynesian cultures he cites for comparison). This hypothesis seems to be based mainly on the assumption that no society could build such major structures without the central organizing authority of a chieftain. Renfrew writes, "The temples of Malta, for instance, are too big to have been the product of single small and independent farming villages" (1979: 156).

The same chieftain hypothesis is still sometimes advanced for other sites such as Silbury Hill, Newgrange, and the early stages of Stonehenge, which also clearly fall within the Great Round context. (In this regard, it would be useful to examine the Anasazi culture of the American southwest, which accomplished quite complex feats of building, astronomy, irrigation, and road-making within an egalitarian Great Round context, presumably acting on a consensus basis as do their descendents, the contemporary Hopi, Zuni, and Pueblo Indians).

By definition, prehistoric religion is lacking the written literature that would elucidate its nature and meaning. Thus it has been highly vulnerable to the assumptions and biases of researchers, most of whom have lived in Radiant Axes and Grid cultures. We can see this, for instance, in the use of the term "fertility cult" to describe the prehistoric religion of the Great Goddess. A "cult" is usually a small, possibly fanatic, fringe group in religion of the type often seen in Grid cultures. But there is profuse evidence that the religion of the Great Goddess was the *main religion* practiced nearly universally in prehistory for thousands of years.

The term "fertility" stresses only one aspect in a religion that also dealt with death, prophecy, calendrics, and astronomy, among other things. Indeed, the Great Goddess provided a complete world view different from our own. And, like women in our culture, the Goddess has suffered the trivialization of being seen merely as a fertility figure, or a doll or plaything, or a "pin-up" for sexual arousal, or simply a "fat lady".

The models outlined in this paper can lead to a new clarity by helping us to understand other cultures, including their artifacts and religions, in full recognition of their world views. And we can benefit greatly from the sources of meaning offered by comparative mythology and religion, psychology, and the studies of architectural symbolism that have contributed to this typology.

Summary

A cross-cultural study of spatial archetypes in architecture, town planning, art, mythology, cosmology, and social structures from prehistory to the present reveals six models of cultures, each with a distinct world view and religion:

1) The SENSITIVE CHAOS of Palaeolithic hunter-gatherers: "the world is one within the animal spirits"
2) The GREAT ROUND of Neolithic and Early Bronze Age farmers: "the world is one within the Great Goddess"
3) The FOUR QUARTERS of Bronze and Iron Age hierarchical chiefdoms: "the world is centered on the Lord of the Four Quarters"

4) The PYRAMID of Classic Period nation or city states and theocracies: "the world is the Sacred Mountain of the Father-God"
5) The RADIANT AXES of Postclassic empires: "the world is ruled by the Sun"
6) The GRID of post-imperialistic commercial-industrial networks: "the world has no center".

This typology of cultures and religions can enhance our understanding of the ancient world — especially of the ancient Mediterranean — giving us a useful context in which to evaluate archaeological evidence and fragmentary data.

Résumé

Une étude inter-culturelle des archétypes spatiaux en architecture, urbanisme, art, mythologie, cosmologie et sociologie des structures sociales de la préhistoire jusqu'à nos jours, révèle six modèles de cultures caractérisés chacun par une vision du monde et une religion distinctes:

1) Le CHAOS SENSIBLE des pratiquants de la chasse et de la cueillette de l'ère paléolithique: "le monde est un avec l'esprit des animaux"
2) Le GRAND CERCLE des agriculteurs de l'ère néolithique et du début de l'Age de Bronze: "le monde est un avec la Grande Déesse"
3) Les QUATRE QUARTIERS des clans hiérarchiques de l'Age de Bronze et de l'Age de Fer: "le monde a pour centre le Seigneur des Quatre Quartiers"
4) La PYRAMIDE des états-nations, des cités-états et des théocraties de la Période Classique: "le monde est la Montagne Sacrée de Dieu-le-Père"
5) Les AXES RAYONNANTS des empires post-classiques: "le souverain du monde est le Soleil"
6) La GRILLE des réseaux commerciaux et industriels post-impérialistes: "le monde n'a pas de centre".

Cette typologie des cultures et des religions peut accroître notre compréhension du monde antique — et surtout du monde antique méditerranéen — en nous fournissant un contexte utile au sein duquel évaluer les preuves archéologiques et les données fragmentaires.

Bibliography

BACON, Edmund
1974 — *The Design of Cities,* Revised Edition, New York (Viking Press).

CAMPBELL, Joseph
1949 — *The Hero with a Thousand Faces,* Bollingen Series XVII, Princeton (Princeton University Press).

CASSIRER, Ernst
1944 — *An essay on Man,* New Haven (Yale University Press).

EDINGER, Edward F.
1972 — *Ego and Archetype,* New York (G.P. Putnam's Sons).

ELIADE, Mircea
1964 — *Shamanism: Archaic Techniques of Ecstasy,* Bollingen Series LXXVI, Princeton (Princeton University Press).
1978 — *The Forge and the Crucible,* Chicago (University of Chicago Press).

FAGAN, Brian
1974 — *Men of the Earth,* Boston (Little, Brown & Company).

FRANKFORT, Henri
1978 — *Kingship and the Gods,* Chicago (University of Chicago Press).

GIEDION, Sigfried
1964 — *The Eternal Present: The Beginnings of Architecture,* Bollingen Series XXXV.6.II, New York (Pantheon).

GIMBUTAS, Marija
1974 — *The Gods and Goddesses of Old Europe: 7000 to 3500 B.C.: Myths, Legends and Cult Images,* Berkeley and Los Angeles (University of California Press).

GOVINDA, Lama Anagarika
1976 — *The Psycho-Cosmic Symbolism of the Buddhist Stupa,* Emeryville, California (Dharma Publishing).

GRAVES, Robert
1960 — *The Greek Myths: 1 & 2,* Middlesex (Penguin Books).

LOBELL, Mimi
1977 — Spatial Archetypes, *Quadrant,* Volume 10, Number 2, pp 5-44.
1983 — Spatial Archetypes, *ReVISION,* Volume 6, Number 2, pp 69-82.

MELLAART, James
1975 — *The Neolithic of the Near East,* New York (Charles Scribner's Sons).

NEUMANN, Erich
1954 — *The Origins and History of Consciousness,* Bollingen Series XLII, Princeton (Princeton University Press).

1955 — *The Great Mother: An Analysis of the Archetype,* Bollingen Series XLVII, Princeton (Princeton University Press).

PERRY, John Wier
1966 — *Lord of the Four Quarters: Myths of the Royal Father,* New York (Macmillan).

PIAGET, Jean
1960 — *The Child's Conception of the World,* Totowa, New Jersey (Littlefield, Adams & Company).

PIAGET, Jean and BÄRBEL, Inhelder
1967 — *The Child's Conception of Space,* New York, (Norton).

PRICHARD, James B.
1969 — *Ancient Near Eastern Texts,* 3rd Edition with Supplement, Princeton (Princeton University Press).

RENFREW, Colin
1979 — *Before Civilization: The Radiocarbon Revolution and Prehistoric Europe,* Cambridge (Cambridge University Press).

ROWLAND, Benjamin
1970 — *The Art and Architecture of India,* Middlesex (Penguin).

SPENGLER, Oswald
1939 — *The Decline of the West,* New York (Alfred A. Knopf).

SCHWENK, Theodor
1965 — *Sensitive Chaos,* London (Rudolf Steiner Press).

THOMPSON, J. Eric S.
1970 — *Maya History and Religion,* Norman (University of Oklahoma Press).

TRUMP, D.H.
1980 — *The Prehistory of the Mediterranean,* New Haven (Yale University Press).

VOLWAHSEN, Andreas
1969 — *Living Architecture: Indian,* New York (Grosset & Dunlap).

WENKE, R.J.
1980 — *Patterns in Prehistory: Mankind's First Three Million Years,* Oxford (Oxford University Press).

PROBLÈMES D'INTERPRÉTATION DES OBJETS MINIATURES DE DIKILI TASH (NÉOLITHIQUE RÉCENT)

Christina Marangou

Parmi les vestiges des occupations successives, datant du néolithique moyen et récent et du bronze ancien du site fouillé par Jean Deshayes à Dikili Tash en Macédoine Orientale, il existe des objets représentant la vie miniaturisée. L'ensemble de ces objets constitue un microcosme presque complet, qui comprend des habitations avec leurs équipement et leurs habitants: deux maisons, dix-huit meubles, dix fours, cinquante-et-un vases, quatre cuillères, soixante-deux figurines anthropomorphes et quatre-vingt-trois figurines zoomorphes — au total deux cent trente objets. Ils datent dans leur grande majorité du néolithique récent.

Il est certain que nous n'avons pas affaire à un cas exceptionnel: dans différents sites de civilisations appartenant aux mêmes périodes chronologiques et situés dans des régions du bassin méditerranéen et des Balcans les fouilles ont livré du matériel analogue à celui de Dikili Tash. La même problématique s'y pose, qui reste encore ouverte à toutes les tentatives d'interprétation.

Dans leur majorité, les objets miniatures de Dikili Tash sont fragmentaires, tandis que les renseignements concernant leur contexte précis au moment des fouilles font souvent défaut. Ceci dit, il existe cependant certains points fournissant des indices significatifs concernant les fonctions éventuelles de ce matériel. Ces points résultent premièrement des renseignements existant sur sa provenance, et deuxièmement de l'étude du matériel lui-même.

Les associations connues, arrivant au nombre de 80, montrent une tendance au regroupement des figurines humaines d'un côté (sept cas) et des figurines animales de l'autre (cinq cas), les groupes comprenant à chaque fois de 2 à 5 figurines, mais ils sont associés en même temps à d'autres objets. Par ailleurs, nous retrouvons parfois des corrélations entre les objets miniatures: dans deux cas une figurine humaine est associée à une figurine animale, dans deux cas aussi à des meubles miniatures, dans quatre cas à des vases miniatures, dans un seul cas une figurine animale est associée à un vase miniature, mais il n'y a pas d'association connue de figurine animale avec des meubles. En revanche, nous connaissons deux cas d'association de figurines animales avec des anneaux en argile, mais leur rapport ne peut, pour le moment, qu'être supposé.

En ce qui concerne le contexte des objets miniatures, mis à part la céramique et l'outillage lithique qui sont prépondérants, nous rencontrons de rares cas de vases zoomorphes et anthropomorphes, de cuillères et d'ossements. La fréquence de la parure en revanche paraît remarquable (20 cas), ainsi que celle des balles de fronde (9), des fusaïoles (8), rencontrées surtout en association avec des figurines humaines, et des pointes en os (11). Au moins deux de ces associations qui paraissent significatives coexistent dans les mêmes cas: figurine, balle de fronde, fusaïole, pointe en os, parure.

L'étude du matériel nous amène à nous poser un certain nombre de questions. Et d'abord celle de la fidélité de la représentation, ce qui revient à dire, la ressemblance à des objets ou à des êtres réels, l'existence ou non de prototypes, le degré du rôle de l'imagination et de la symbolique, de là la signification de certains motifs de décor.

Les vestiges de constructions réelles, et les restes d'ustensiles en vraie grandeur nous démontrent que les trois types de fours, les deux types de cuillères (à manche anthropomorphe et à section quadrangulaire ou en demi-lune) et la typologie variée des vases utilisés à Dikili Tash ont bien des imitations fidèles à des dimensions très réduites. Chose difficile à prouver en ce qui concerne le mobilier (tables, sièges, banquettes), dont l'original n'a pas laissé de traces; son polymorphisme suggère cependant une réalité aussi variée: des sièges avec dossier à deux ou à trois montants, ou à bord entourant deux ou trois côtés, à assise de forme circulaire ou quadrangulaire, des tabourets tripodes ou quadrupodes. La fidélité de la représentation est encore plus difficile à démontrer quand il s'agit de figurines. Les animaux figurés ne sont pas généralement identifiables, mais il semble que leurs caractéristiques les rapprochent des moutons, boeufs et, plus rarement, chèvres, dans un cas peut-être d'un chien, interprétations qui sont renforcées par les restes osseux du site. Quant aux figurines humaines, il s'agit surtout de femmes, avec l'exception de 2 figurines masculines et quelques cas assexués, ce qui ne veut certainement pas dire qu'à Dikili Tash nous aurions affaire à une société d'amazones.

Il est par ailleurs difficile de se prononcer sur l'ornementation riche de ces figurines; s'agit-il de tatouage, de vêtements, de décor fantaisiste, d'indices d'un culte, de traces de certains rites de magie ou d'initiation inconnus, ou de simple caprice du fabriquant ou de sa clientèle? Un type humain principal est représenté, une femme à longs cheveux, aux formes prononcées, aves les seins, les fesses et les cuisses fortement mis en évidence, alors que ses jambes aboutissent de façon abstraite à des pointes (Pl. 1). Elles sont richement parées, de ce qui parait être des colliers autour du cou, des bracelets autour des poignets et des avant-bras, d'une double ligne qui épouse les hanches comme une ceinture (Pl. 2) — ceci étant valable aussi pour une figurine masculine (Pl. 3) — de lignes incisées et de motifs pointés sur les cuisses et le torse. De nombreux points sont percés dans la "ceinture", d'autres sur les reins, symétriquement; ils ont pu servir à accrocher des dispositifs aujourd'hui perdus, ou des ornements, ou à stabiliser les figurines dans leur position "semi-allongée"; il semblerait pourtant que les maquettes de meubles auraient mieux fait l'affaire. Dans deux cas par ailleurs il y a association entre meubles et figurines.

Un point qui mérite l'attention est celui de la miniaturisation des objets miniatures eux-mêmes. Nous avons en effet des exemples de vases, de meubles, de figurines humaines et d'une figurine animale qui paraissent être des imitations, à une échelle encore plus grande — donc en dimensions encore plus petites — de vases ou meubles miniatures ou de figurines qui ont probablement servi comme prototypes intermédiaires à la fabrication de ces objets minuscules qui sont souvent — en particulier en ce qui concerne les vases et les meubles — faconnés avec maladresse. Il y a un contraste frappant entre ces derniers et leurs prototypes de petites dimensions également — d'objets miniatures aussi — dont le modelage et la décoration ont été effectués avec beaucoup de soin et d'attention. Cette différence serait-elle dûe à des intentions différentes ou à des capacités différentes des personnes qui les ont modelés? On pourrait même dire que les miniatures maladroites paraissent avoir été fabriquées par des enfants et les autres par des grandes personnes. Par ailleurs, les vases miniatures les plus grands ont une certaine contenance, et le fait qu'ils sont souvent associés à des objets de parure pourrait indiquer qu'il s'agirait plutôt d'équipement de cosmétique — ou autre.

Ici il faudrait ajouter un autre point intéressant: dans le contexte des objets de parure il y a souvent aussi des figurines humaines; un vase miniature très soigné a été même trouvé exactement en dessous d'une figurine; mais à qui appartiendraient les vases? plutôt aux adultes, d'autant plus qu'ils sont associés également à des fusaïoles et des pointes ou des aiguilles en os? ou plutôt aux enfants, et ils accompagneraient dans ce cas leurs poupées et autres jouets? Une explication plausible de ces situations serait selon nous l'hypothèse des utilisations variées des groupes d'objets miniatures. Et en effet, ils sont parfois differenciés.

D'une façon générale, les figurines humaines du type majoritaire, les maquettes de fours et quelques vases miniatures paraissent être particulièrement soignés et décorés de façon très détaillée; leur utilisation dans un but religieux ou rituel pourrait en être la raison. Par contre, les figurines animales donnent plutôt un aspect général de l'animal représenté, peut-être parcequ'il était déjà connu et reconnaissable, peut-être parceque la précision et le détail n'avaient guère d'importance pour les animaux — il y va pourtant tout autrement en ce qui concerne les vases zoomorphes, même miniaturisés — ; toujours est-il que la majorité des figurines zoomorphes, groupées en un type A, semblent figurer le même animal, ou l'idée de l'animal, si l'on veut (Pl. 4), tandis que les figurines du type minoritaire appelé B sont plus différenciées, mais aussi, chose curieuse, de dimensions plus réduites (Pl. 5), contrastant fort avec le type A qui a des dimensions importantes et un poids considérable; si les utilisateurs des figurines animales ont été des enfants, on pourrait plus facilement se l'imaginer pour les B, tandis que les A semblent trop lourdes pour avoir été déplacées, par exemple en jouant, par des petits enfants.

Nous arrivons à un autre point significatif de notre problématique lié à la question de l'utilisation: celle de la préhension.

Du point de vue de la préhension, nos objets peuvent être divisés en plusieurs catégories: ceux qui peuvent être posés, ceux qui semblent avoir été manipulés, ou du moins avoir besoin de prendre appui sur un dispositif pour rester en équilibre lorsqu'on les pose sur un support ou par terre; ceux qui auraient pu être suspendus par une perforation, mais qui peuvent en même temps être posés.

Dans la première catégorie nous avons les grandes figurines animales du type A, mais aussi les plus petites du type B, qui peuvent également être manipulées plus ou moins facilement; les modèles de fours, à face inférieure non décorée, la plupart des vases y appartiennent aussi; ces derniers présentent pourtant le même degré d'attention pour le rendu de toutes leurs faces; ils auraient pu être souvent déplacés d'un endroit à l'autre, ce qui paraît normal, s'agissant de récipients fonctionnels ou supposés comme tels. Le mobilier aussi est par définition destiné à être "posé", le déplacement n'étant cependant pas exclu.

La situation change en ce qui concerne les figurines humaines: elles ne peuvent pas rester debout sur leurs pieds inexistants (il s'agit du type majoritaire), mais sembleraient être confortablement assises, penchées vers l'arrière. Cependant cette position paraît peu naturelle, si l'on n'imagine pas un support quelquonque qui puisse les stabiliser — et pourquoi pas un siège en miniature? malheureusement, comme il a été déjà signalé, nous n'avons que deux cas de coexistence en association de meubles et de figurines humaines. Or, il est vrai que les figurines humaines offrent toutes leurs faces au regard, elles auraient donc pu être prises dans la main ou enfouies dans une ceinture.

Les objets qui auraient pu être suspendus comprennent: un petit animal, avec des pattes aplaties en dessous, et dont les yeux sont perforés horizontalement, et plusieurs vases perforés aux anses ou sous le bord, dont par ailleurs les originaux provenant de la céramique de Dikili Tash portent des perforations similaires. Il est possible qu'ils ont porté à l'origine des couvercles.

En fait nous allons de plus en plus, d'un côté vers une homogénéïté des miniatures — il s'agit de l'idée de l'imitation en modèle réduit d'objets réels plus ou moins fidèlement, ainsi que d'un contexte des différents objets miniatures qui présente fréquemment des analogies (parure, pointes, fusaïoles, balles de fronde) — et de l'autre côté, une différenciation à l'intérieur même de certains groupes d'objets miniatures, tels que les vases ou les figurines animales. Il est probable qu'une catégorie de vases, par exemple ceux qui sont manifestement plus précieux et paraissent effectivement utilitaires, aient un certain rapport avec les figurines, celles-ci avec les fusaïoles et les meubles; il est aussi possible qu'une autre catégorie de vases, les "imitations au second degré" soient en rapport avec de meubles (nous ne distinguons pas pour le moment de catégories différentes de meubles par manque de données).

Il y aurait donc eu des fonctions différenciées parmi les miniatures: ici il se pose déjà le problème de leur appartenance; prenons l'exemple des figurines humaines — auraient-elles appartenu à des adultes (père ou mère), ou à des enfants? s'agit-il de jouets utilisés par des enfants à côté de leur mère ou père occupés à leurs ouvrages (à cause des fusaïoles et des points en os ou les éclats de silex)? Les vases miniatures incisés auraient-ils appartenu aux parents? Est-ce que les objets miniatures servaient au culte ou à l'initiation des enfants, par exemple pour des rites de passage, ou, ayant servi dans le passé aux adultes en des occasions semblables ont été gardés par la suite? S'agit-il d'objets à fonctions multiples suivant la situation?

L'hypothèse d'une différenciation de l'utilisation et d'interprétations variées nous paraîtrait plus plausible. Cependant, pour le moment, on ne peut que discerner la complexité du problème, et espérer qu'un jour nous aurons la preuve si, et dans quels cas, il s'agit de maisons de poupées, de trésorerie rituelle, d'imagerie de la divinité et de ses paraphernales, ou, tout simplement, de plaisanterie imaginative et inoffensive.

Nous remercions vivement le Professeur Monsieur René Treuil d'avoir lu le manuscript, ainsi que l'Ecole Française d'Athènes d'avoir fourni des diapositives.

Summary

Miniature objects from Dikili Tash in East Macedonia (Greece) date mostly from the recent neolithic and comprise models of houses, furniture, ovens, vases, spoons, as well as anthropomorphic and zoomorphic figurines.

Interpretation problems of these objects still remain open. Nevertheless, there do exist some indications concerning their function; these are either given by evidence about their origin, associations or context, or result from the study of the material; in the latter case they concern style, method of prehension, fidelity of the representation and decoration.

The above mentioned points having been considered, it seems a unique way of interpretation should be avoided. We are, in fact, rather turning towards a solution consisting of multiple hypotheses showing different functions of various groups of miniature objects. There would be, therefore, no incompatibility with parallel uses for playing, for symbolic representation or, even, imagery of divinity, or for accomplishing magic or initiation rites. At the same time the manufacturers', owners', or, at least, users' identity would also vary.

Résumé

Les objets miniatures provenant de Dikili Tash en Macédoine orientale (Grèce) et datant dans leur majorité du néolithique récent comprennent des maquettes de maisons, de meubles, de fours, de vases, de cuillères, ainsi que des figurines anthropomorphes et zoomorphes.

Les problèmes d'interprétation de ces objets restent toujours ouverts. Cependant, certains indices relatifs à leur fonction sont fournis par les renseignements existant sur leur provenance.

associations ou contexte d'un côté, et résultent de l'autre côté de l'étude du materiel, concernant dans ce dernier cas le style, la méthode de préhension, la fidélité de la représentation et le décor.

Après considération des points sus-mentionnés il paraît que la voie unique d'interprétation est à éviter. En fait, nous nous orientons plutôt vers une multiplicité d'hypothèses, qui nous laissent entrevoir une différenciation de la fonction parmi des catégories des objets miniatures. Une utilisation parallèle à des fins de jeu, ou servant à une reprèsentation symbolique, voire d'imagerie de divinités, à l'accomplissement de rites de magie ou d'initiation ne parait pas incompatible. En même temps, l'identité des fabricants, des personnes à qui ces objets appartenaient ou, du moins, de leurs utilisateurs aurait été aussi variée.

Bibliographie

DAUX, Georges

1962 — Dikili Tash, *Bulletin de Correspondance Hellénique,* 86, pp. 912-933.

DESHAYES, Jean

1970a — Les fouilles de Dikili Tash et l'archéologie yougoslave, *Zbornik Narodnog Muzeja u Beogradu,* 6, pp. 21-41.

1970b — Dikili Tash, *Bulletin de Correspondance Hellénique,* 94 (1970-II), pp. 799-808.

1972 — Dikili Tash and the origins of the Troadic culture, *Archaeology,* 25, 3, pp. 198-205.

1973 — La séquence des cultures à Dikili Tash, *Actes du VIIIe Congrès International des Sciences Préhistoriques et Protohistoriques (Belgrade),* II, pp. 492-496.

1974 — Fours néolithiques de Dikili Tash, *Mélanges helléniques offerts à Georges Daux,* pp. 67-91.

DESHAYES, Jean, THEOCHARIS, Dimitrios et ROMIOPOULOU, Ekaterini

1961 — Anaskafai Dikili Tash, *Praktica tis Archeologikis Eterias* pp. 81-89.

SEFERIADES, Michel

1981 — Dikili Tash, un grand site protohistorique de Grèce, *Archéologia* 153, pp. 48-60.

1983 — Dikili Tash: Introduction à la Préhistoire de la Mácedoine Orientale, *Bulletin de Correspondance Hellénique,* 107, pp. 3 ss.

TREUIL, René

1983 — *Le Néolithique et le Bronze Ancien Egéens,* pp. 96-97.

SEATED CLAY FIGURINES FROM THE NEOLITHIC PERIOD, ISRAEL

Tamar Noy

Although early literary texts and documents as well as archaeological discoveries attest to the existence of fertility cults in antiquity, the identification of these cults in prehistoric periods still presents a problem (Ucko 1968; Cauvin 1972). The existence of such cults may, however, be seen in the abundant human and animal figurines in wall paintings, rock carvings, and significant groupings of particular objects. The carved bone sickle handles from the Natufian culture (10,300 - 8600 B.C.E.), for instance, could be interpreted as objects in fertility ceremonies by their combination of the sickle and the animal carved on the handle, which may represent the two kinds of food consumption — that of cereal crops and animal flesh.

During the Neolithic in the Levant (8200 - 4500 B.C.E.), fundamental and far-reaching changes took place, both in everyday life and in the social and religious aspects of society. It was in fact the achievements of the preceding Natufian culture which brought societies in this area to the threshold of the Neolithic revolution. Intensive research in Israel has brought to light rich material from the cultures which existed during the transition from the Epi-Paleolithic to the Neolithic, giving us even so but a fragmentary picture of the end of this period.

Among the principal changes characteristic of the Neolithic are the existence of large-scale settlements, the growth of population, and the dependence on early farming: all these were already present in the Pre-Pottery Neolithic A period (8200 - 7600 B.C.E.). Advance in farming life, changes in house shape, the development of crafts such as plaster-making, basketry, weaving, the use of flax fibres for textiles, and the increased trade in asphalt, obsidian, sea shells and semi-precious stones are well attested in the Pre-Pottery Neolithic B (7600 - 6200 B.C.E). Particularly striking is the presence of numerous artistic and cultic objects. These include both male and female human figurines of various shapes and sizes, masks and plastered skulls. This overwhelming amount of human representation suggests the possibility that men visualized their gods in their own image. Temples were built for the performance of cultic rituals, and mythological scenes were depicted on walls, as can be seen at Çatal Hüyük in Anatolia.

In spite of the fragmentary nature of the archaeological evidence from the sixth millennium, many pottery figurines are known from this period, appearing at the same time as the earliest pottery known.[1] Also at this time, the increasing scale of settlements and their locations indicate advances in agriculture.

During the fifth millennium, settlement spread into now arid parts of the country, taking advantage of an improvement in the climate. Local cultures of this period — some show a transition to the Chalcolithic — are known mostly from their pottery design and repertoire. Well-established settlements in fertile valleys indicate a heavy reliance on agriculture. The arid area has provided us with a unique example of an isolated temple, with an extraordinary representation of leopards outlined with small stones in front of the building as if guarding it.

The seated human figurines, found among other human representations, are known from as early as the early Neolithic. Their seated posture may represent the moment of giving birth — the mother goddess — or a combination of this and a goddess enthroned. The earliest known figurines are from Netiv Hagedud, the Sultanian phase of the PPNA (Bar-Yosef and Gopher, personal communication)[2] and Jericho (Kenyon and Holland 1982 a). These figurines are small, and their upper bodies are very stylized (Fig. 1)[3] No details of the limbs or features are shown, except for the eyes and small breasts. The lower part of the body is more detailed, two legs are shown, and a groove divides this part into two sections. The possibilities of iconographic comparison are very limited.

Although the PPNB in Israel has been so well documented, almost no seated clay figurines have been found. The few that were found in Jericho are a continuation of the previous culture's style (Kenyon and Holland 1982 b). However, the figurines found in other parts of the Levant from various phases of the PPNB demonstrate a new type: they are larger; most of the body elements, such as the breasts and belly, are well pronounced; and the lower part of the body is exaggerated. Although the head is still very stylized and the hands are not always represented, the image of this type of figurines is well established.[4]

Numerous well defined seated figurines are known from the Yarmukian culture of the sixth millennium B.C.E. The Kefar Giladi figurine may be the earliest of this period (Fig. 2) (Kaplan 1957-8). They are all made of the same clay as the vessels of the period. These figurines are more detailed, with certain elements receiving additional emphasis. Most of them are covered with red paint. The majority of these figurines were found in Sha'ar Hagolan (Stekelis 1972) (Fig. 3-4)[5] and H. Minha (Munhata) (Perrot 1967) (Fig. 5, Plate 6)[6], both sites in the Jordan Valley. In addition, a few have been found inland and on the coast. Such figurines are also known from Syria and Lebanon.

A special technique was employed to make these figurines: on a cylindrical core layers of clay were added for the main parts of the body. The entire figurine was then completed by a few more incisions, clay pellets and paint.

The naturalistic style together with the symbolism (including the use of red paint) are characteristic of the unique iconography of this type of figurine. The legs are divided into two parts, and the buttocks are steatopygous — this may have been the natural form, or may have been used to emphasize the seated position. The belly and breasts are clearly represented. One arm runs along the body, and the other is placed under the breasts. A "garment" covers the shoulders and the entire back, where it is divided into two parts. The head is triangular, wide at the bottom and usually pointed at the top. Hair dress is shown on the back of the head, which arches slightly backwards. The eyes, cheeks, ears and probably earrings were added at a later stage. It should be noted that only on two faces, both from Sha'ar Hagolan, was a mouth added. While we are still dealing with the details, the characteristic "coffee bean" or "lizard" eyes should be mentioned. They are elongated and narrow at both ends and grooved in the middle. Their oblique setting gives the face a particular form, perhaps recalling grains on a stalk (Noy 1984). The nose is prominent, and continues to be shown in this manner into the Chalcolithic.

Very few figurines had any additional features except for the "garment" — a ritual costume — hair and earrings. One example has animals depicted by means of incisions on the lower part of the head (Kaplan 1972) (Fig. 6). There is also a "seated figurine wearing a soutane and mask" (as it was described by Yeiven and Mosel 1977). However, no stools/thrones have been found in archaeological excavations. The importance of such stools or thrones can be seen at Çatal Hüyük, where the stool is emphasized by its size and by the depiction of two felines, one on either side of the goddess seated on it (Mellart 1967).

In the fifth millennium almost no pottery figurines are known until now, while the Chalcolithic period, in the fourth millennium B.C.E. is represented by an anthropomorphic vessel.

To summarize: we can observe that the seated figurines made of clay are known from the beginning of farming in the Early Neolithic period of the early eighth millennium B.C.E. Their posture and the cultural context of their appearance suggest their connection with fertility cults. In the course of time, the symbolic language they exemplify becomes more elaborate.

Notes

1 Clay is known as a raw material for the modelling of figurines as early as the beginning of agriculture. Clay figurines can be more expressive and skilfully modelled than those of stone, which are known even earlier.

2 The figurines, of which the complete one is 42 mm high, were found in the Excavations of Netiv Hagedud (Lower Jordan Valley), directed by O. Bar-Yosef and A. Gopher from the Institute of Archaeology, Hebrew University and sponsored by the National Geographic Society, Washington D.C.

3 Figures 1 - 3, 6 were drawn by F. Vainer.

4 Ain Ghazzal in Jordan (Rollefson 1985), Aswad III-II in Syria (Contenson 1985), Mureybet in Syria (Cauvin 1977).

5 Figure 4 from Sha'ar Hagolan is shown here for the first time. Fig. 3 is after Stekelis 1972: pl. 49, 1.

6 The drawing is after Cauvin 1972: fig. 29:1. Height: 10 mm.

Bibliography

CONTENSON, H. de
1985 — Early Agriculture in Western Asia, *Studies in Ancient Oriental Civilization* 36, pp. 57-59.

CAUVIN, J.
1972 — *Religions Néolithiques de Syro-Palestine,* Paris.

1977 — Les fouilles de Mureybet (1971 - 1974) et leur signification pour les origines de la sédentarisation au Proche Orient, *Annual American School of Oriental Research* 44, pp. 19-47.

KAPLAN, J.
1957-8 — The Excavation in Kefar Giladi in 1957, *Bulletin of Israel Exploration Society* XXII:1, pp. 92 ff.

1972 — The Archeology and History of Tel-Aviv Jaffa, *Biblical Archeologist* 31, pp. 68-69.

KENYON, K.M. and HOLLAND, T.A.
1982 a — *Excavations at Jericho* Vol IV, London, fig. 223/1.
1982 b — *Ibid.* fig. 223/3.

MELLART, J.
1967 — *Çatal Hüyük - A Neolithic Town in Anatolia*, London.

NOY, T.
1984 — Female figurine, *Highlights of Archeology, the Israel Museum,* Jerusalem, pp. 26-27.

PERROT, J.
1967 — La Palestine Préhistorique, Munhata Un Village Préhistorique, *Bible et Terre Sainte* 39, pp. 4-17.

ROLEFSON, G.O.
1985 — The 1983 Season at the Early Neolithic Site of Ain Ghazal, *National Geographic Research* Vol. 1, pp. 44-62.

STEKELIS, M.
1972 — *The Yarmukian Culture of the Neolithic Period*, Jerusalem.

UCKO, P.J.
1968 — *Anthropomorphic Figurines*, London.

YEIVIN, E. and MOZEL, I.
1977 — A "fossile directeur" figurine of the Pottery Neolithic A, *Tel Aviv* 4, pp. 194-200.

CULTIC FINDS FROM THE MIDDLE COPPER AGE OF WESTERN HUNGARY – CONNECTIONS WITH SOUTH EAST EUROPE

Eszter Bánffy

Until recently prehistoric objects considered to be cultic ones were mostly interpreted in two different ways: using the typological method on archaeological material, or on the basis of speculative anthropology, working from recent ethnographic parallels or from parallels to ancient religions.

In recent times the analysis of the pure archaeological context provides a third method of increasing popularity. It is in fact very important to study to what extent archaeology can help to solve problems of the history of art and religions, that is, to what extent archaeology can be a source of the history of religions (Bánffy, in print). To apply the method of contextual study to the Carpathian Basin and South East Europe, a collection of human figurines with well-observed contexts, as well as anthropomorphic vessels, house models and other finds having a cultic character is in progress (Bánffy 1986). Hopefully this work will provide useful data for a better knowledge concerning Neolithic and Chalcolithic cultural groups that lived in the study area (Fig. 7).

Nevertheless, even in this region there are periods where the above-mentioned three models could be used with difficulty, for no cultic finds have come to light yet. Such a period is the Early and Middle Copper Age of the Western Carpathian Basin, i.e. Transdanubia. The Late Neolithic of this area, that is the Lengyel Culture is fairly well researched. It is a close relative of the Moravian Painted Ware found in Lower Austria and Czechoslovakia; not only its ceramics, but its whole material culture and way of life fit the South East European Painted Pottery group very well.

In Eastern Hungary the Tisza culture, which is more or less contemporary with the Lengyel culture, goes on until the Early Copper Age (the Tiszapolgár Culture) without any severe break. In Transdanubia, however, it is still an open question whether, as in Eastern Hungary, the development of the final phase of the Lengyel culture led continuously to the Copper Age, or whether we can speak of new invasions — or perhaps a hiatus — after the Late Neolithic.

Between the Lengyel Culture and the Late Copper Age, i.e. the appearance of the enormously extended and also well-known Baden culture) there was a gap of several hundred years about which nothing was known. In 1966 in the course of a field survey, N. Kalicz was the first to find and publish sherds that he identified as belonging to the Middle Copper Age. He gave the name Balaton Group to the pottery. Later, perceiving its closer relations to the Croatian Lasinja culture, he changed it to Balaton-Lasinja Culture (Kalicz 1969: 86). Yet, up till now little was known about this period apart from a few pits with typically coarse ware thinned with sand (the so-called "Furchenstich - pottery) which is typical for the later phase. During further investigations a few isolated graves also came to light: from the older phase of the culture (Balaton I) skeletons with side-contracted position; from the later phases (Balaton II-III) cremation also came into use (Kalicz 1969: 86; Makkay 1970: fig. 26). Very little was known about the habitation and the way of life of this culture, and there was no information concerning its cultic life either.

In the summer of 1983 near the south-west coast of lake Balaton, in Balatonmagyaród - Homok, during a medieval rescue excavation a great number of sherds were found in the eroded soil that can be dated to the early Balaton-Lasinja culture.[1] A perfectly circular pit also came to light (Fig. 8). This pit was dated by a few pottery fragments from the filling. In the pit several burnt layers of clay and wattle-and-daub as well as layers of sterile white sand were observed. At the bottom of the pit a regularly circular mound of lime concretions stuck together was raised in the middle. Outside this mound, along the edge of the pit, the bottom was deepened forming a ring-like feature. This circular ditch was filled with much charcoal and wattle-and-daub, and here lay the skeleton of a five-year-old infant, probably a boy. The extended body lay on its back, and near it was found a large conglomerate slab (shaped like a grinding stone) together with the bottom of a fairly big pot.

This discovery raises the question of whether this pit had a ritual function. Following the logic of the previously mentioned methodological approach, I will present several alternative hypotheses to account for this find, trying to avoid the mistake of interpreting every phenomenon which is not fully understood as a cultic one.

The pit, being the first find of its kind, stands without any parallels within the cultural complex. We can probably exclude the assumption that this was an imitation without any meaning, borrowed from habits used in other regions, that is to say that the people who dug this pit and carefully buried the child in it had no idea what the reason for these efforts was. On the other hand, it would be just as ill-justified to assume that this phenomenon possibly had a large mythological background which can be compared with myths in the Ancient Near East.

A third possibility recommends itself as a possible explanation: that we have found the first archaeological traces of a Neolithic-Chalcolithic tradition; perhaps the most we can do is to find its type and image elsewhere, but it is not possible yet to delineate the tradition in the epic (verbal) way. Therefore, the phenomenon can only be judged on the basis of the typology of the individual features and contexts. So, features thought to be cultic that were observed in the pit have to be divided into individual details. Then we have to compare them separately with the immediately preceding and later cultic features belonging to cultures in the study area; and also with synchronous features in neighbouring regions. The features will be discussed as follows: 1. burial in the pit; 2. the skeleton of an infant; 3. the grinding stone; 4. the circular mound in the bottom; 5. levels in the filling.

1. Because the material found in the pit and nearby shows unambiguously typical forms of the early phase of the Balaton-Lasinja culture, it is reasonable to turn to the previous period, the end of the Neolithic, for parallels. Plenty of examples exist for burials in pits, indeed; this practice was wide-spread in the Lengyel-culture and occurred also in the Moravian Painted and Stichband groups. It also occurs southwards from the Balaton-Lasinja area, in the Sopot and Vinča cultures.

Among these finds the most important ones are as follows:[2] on the site Veszprém-Felszabadulás, belonging to the final phase of the Lengyel culture, an apsis-shaped house came to light with the skeleton of a child in its foundation ditch (Raczky 1974: 187-189). This find can hardly be much older than the Balatonmagyaród pit. One of the strange phenomena in the Lengyel culture, not very well understood today, is that while one can find fairly extended, regular cemeteries in the eastern area (Aszód, Zengövárkony, etc.), westwards in Austria and the Moravian Painted pottery there are only a few isolated skeletons of fragmented human bones in pits. Certainly, these cannot be thought to be customary burials, because those — for an up till now unknown reason — have not survived. Nevertheless, lack of research can also be to blame.

The Slovakian settlement and cemetery of Branč belongs to the eastern Lengyel area (Podborsky 1970). From the Nyitra-Brodzany and Ludanice phase, pit Nr. 271 contained the remains of a child who was thrown in head first. This habit is not unknown westwards in Bohemia, in the area of the Stichband-ceramics.

South of the Carpathian Basin I have found only one example of a pit burial on the site of Gomolava, belonging to the late Vinča culture (Brukner 1976: 12-14, fig. 2). Yet, the number of these pits can grow with further research.

As an unusual burial site, pit burial also occurs sporadically after the heyday of the Balaton-Lasinja culture. The cellar of the so-called "Herranhaus" in the Early Bronze Age fortified settlement at Vučedol was used by people of the previous Baden culture, and later on, in the Vučedol community, it served as a burial place for babies and small children. It is peculiar that the Vučedol habit of laying the women and men in a different way is identical with the ritual used in the Hungarian Baden and the earlier Bodrogkeresztúr cultures (Schmidt 1945: 41-45).

A greater part of the above mentioned graves came from pits probably belonging to settlements, some of them directly under houses or their foundation ditches. This is the reason why in most cases the excavators interpreted them as foundation sacrifices.

There is not much to know yet about the Chalcolithic Balaton-Lasinja culture apart from pottery and some pits. So it is unclear whether the foundation sacrifice was practiced. The analysis of the other objects and features found in the Balatonmagyaród pit could help resolve this problem.

2. Considering similar skeletons from pits, most of them belong to children, or at least to juveniles. Without entering into the details of this phenomenon, which is discussed very often and which occurred during the whole of prehistory, it is worth mentioning that apart from the Carpathian Basin in time and space dead babies and children are treated differently from adults. According to the lawbook of Manu, children who died under the age of two years could not be cremated as usual; they had to be buried in the earth. In West Africa, babies are buried along the road in jars instead of normal cemeteries, so that women passers-by can receive them into themselves earlier and thus bear them again (Dieterich 1913: 8).

These examples, together with many further ones not mentioned here, show that someone who was born a short while ago stands in close connection with earth and the world of forefathers and in such a body the chthonic ancestors of a family or of a larger community can move more easily. For this reason children often have separate burial places and their corpses are more effective for foundation offerings too. I certainly do not want to assert with this that we necessarily have to speak of human sacrifice or ritual murder. The several examples known are — perhaps with the exception of the pit in the Branč — of normal burials; this is an important common feature of theirs.

3. The piece of conglomerate found beside the skeleton of the small child has one side which is flat, slightly concave, while the other side is formed cylindrically. This shape makes it similar to a grinding stone; however, the pebbles are too rough and pitch-faced, so they could hardly serve the purpose. This allows two interpretations: either the maker realized that the conglomerate was unsuitable for use while preparing it, or he meant it for a grave good in advance. In both cases the conglomerate interpreted as a grinding stone has — practically in the first case or theoretically in the second — something to do with grain, and this always stands in connection with assuring fertility. And indeed, a rite which strove after the wealth of the community could be one main reason for foundation sacrifices.

4. It is also possible to interpret the specific shape of the bottom of the pit. The mound made of lime with the ring round it is a feature that occurs at several places in different types in the Neolithic and Copper Age of the Carpathian Basin. On the basis of their characteristics and contexts they can be connected with the well known "omphaloi" of the ancient world. We can find such navel-like formations made of clay on the floors of houses from the late neolithic tell Herpály (Kalicz-Raczky 1984: fig. 29). These houses can be dated to the Herpály and the so-called Prototiszapolgár culture, which means the beginning of the Copper Age in Eastern Hungary. A cultic place in Szarvas, belonging to the Bodrogkeresztúr culture, was shaped the same way (Makkay 1980/81: 45-57; 349-350), and the same "omphalos" can be seen on the floor of a painted shrine model, right in the middle. This latter comes from Öcsöd-Kováshalom[3], a tell settlement from the Szakálhát period. As it is known, the word "omphalos" means navel and the middle of something;in this way it must be the symbol of a central spot (Cirlot 1981). Knowing that the pit in Balatonmagyaród belonged to a settlement which had to be protected, these approximate denotations fit the assumption that the pit could have been a foundation sacrifice.

5. Because the surface was eroded, it is not clear whether the pit belonged to a house or was rather the foundation sacrifice of the whole community which was dug in the middle of a square-like space left

open among the houses — as suggested by a parallel in Herpály (Kalicz-Raczky 1984). This latter idea could perhaps be supported by the fact that the filling consists of closed strata. According to C. Colpe's traditional definition, unusual circumstances and repetition are the characteristics of a sacrificial pit (Colpe 1970: 34-39). The cultic place, pit, "bothros" was widely known in the Neolithic and Chalcolithic Middle and South East Europe, as well as in the Near East, as proven by many examples (Buren 1952: 76-92; Makkay 1975: 161-173, with further literature). The pit discussed here, however, differs from the "bothroi" in several aspects. Though it satisfies the unusual circumstances, the type of stratification, that is two burnt layers with charcoal and sterile white sand above each, is no proof for repeated use. There are no traces of plant or animal offerings, with or without blood. The explanation of the strata in the fill demands caution, anyway, as slow and natural filling can produce similar layers. Nevertheless, in our case the idea that the pit could be filled slowly and by chance is as improbable an assumption as that which opts for a "bothros" solely on the basis of the stratification. The fact that no foundation offering is known which served as a place for a repeated rite harmonizes with this negative result.

The gap between the life of the Lengyel-and the Boleráz-Baden cultures will only slowly disappear if it is filled with archaeological data. I have shown a few parallels from South East Europe for the first cultic find from a culture originally based on Middle European traditions. To throw a bridge between the two regions, another fill of the "missing link" could be the unusual burial from Čičarovce-Csicser (Vizdal 1978), where the rite recalls the western cultural groups in many respects; but the find complex belongs to the Tisza culture which shows plenty of strong south eastern connections.

It would be senseless to draw a too daring inference based on the Balatonmagyaród pit. Yet, it shows clearly that the beliefs and cultic life of the Balaton-Lasinja culture cannot be basically different from that of the Neolithic antecedents of the Carpathian Basin and South East Europe. This tradition could rather have played the role of the intermediary toward later Chalcolithic traditions.

Notes

1 The excavation was led by L. Horváth, Museum of Nagykanizsa.

2 Other sites with examples for pit burials: Brudek/Snehotice/; Cezavy/Blucina/; Unicov; Hluboké Masufky; Telnice; Hrabetice; Drbanice; Brno-Kralovo polje; Nagykosztolány/Vel'ké Kostolany/; Vicsápapáti/Výcypy Opatovce/ — Czechoslovakia; Poigen; Bisamberg-Parkring; Eggendorf-Zogeldorferstr.; Bernhardstal - Austria.

3 Unpublished; from an excavation conducted by the author and P. Raczky in 1984.

Summary

Considering finds with their archaeological contexts, a unique phenomenon from the West Hungarian Chalcolithic is discussed in this paper. The regularly formed pit from Balatonmagyaród-Homok can be dated to the Balaton-Lasinja culture. It contained alternating sterile and burnt layers in the fill. A heap of large-sized limestone concretions plastered together was observed on the floor of the pit surrounded by a trench. The extended skeleton of a small boy was found in this trench, accompanied by a grinding stone.

Being the first find of its kind in the Balaton-Lasinja culture, before suggesting a ritual function for the pit, features that were observed in it are dealt with individually: 1. burial in the pit; 2. the skeleton of an infant; 3. the grinding stone; 4. the circular mound in the bottom; 5. levels in the fill.

On the basis of the diachronous and synchronous parallels and also of their contexts it seems probable that the pit was a foundation sacrifice, which is a custom that fits well in ritual habits of the study area, both in the preceding Neolithic and the later Baden culture. This brief communication clearly shows that the cult life of the Balaton-Lasinja culture can probably be assigned a transition role towards later Chalcolithic cultures.

Résumé

Cette communication s'occupe d'un phénomène jusqu'ici unique dans l'âge de cuivre de la Hongrie Ouest, en considérant les trouvailles archéologiques avec leurs contextes. La fosse à la forme régulière, trouvée à Balatonmagyaród-Homok, peut être datée dans la culture de Balaton-Lasinja.

Le comblement de cette fosse était composé des niveaux stériles et brûlées. Au fond, il y avait un grand ramas de concrétion du calcaire entouré d'un fossé. Ici, dans ce fossé, on a trouvé le squelette d'un petit garçon avec un conglomérat de cailloux qui avait été transformé en moulin à main.

Étant donné que c'est la première trouvaille pareille dans la culture de Balaton-Lasinja, nous avons distingué les phénomenès décrits au-dessus avant d'y attribuer une fonction rituelle à cette fosse. 1. inhumation dans une fosse; 2. le squelette d'un enfant; 3. le moulin à main; 4. le ramas rond au fond de la fosse; 5. les niveaux dans le comblement.

D'après les analogies diacroniques et syncroniques et d'après leurs contextes, il semble être probable que la fosse mentionnée était un sacrifice de construction. Cette coutume convient bien aux habitudes rituelles dans la région examinée même dans le néolithique précédant comme dans la milieu de Baden qui suivait. Il nous semble, d'après cette courte explication que la vie cultuelle de la civilisation de Balaton-Lasinja aurait pu jouer un rôle intermédiaire envers les traditions des cultures tardives de l'âge de cuivre.

Bibliography

BÁNFFY, E.

in print — Bemerkungen zur Methodologie der Erforschung vorgeschichtlicher figuraler Plastic, *Prähistorische Zeitschrift.*

1986 – Unpublished dissertation at the Academy of Sciences, Budapest.

BRUKNER, B.

1976 – Gomolava, *Archeološki Pregled.*

BUREN, D.

1952 – *Places of Sacrifices, Iraq.*

CIRLOT, J.E.

1981 – *A Dictionary of Symbols,* London.

COLPE, C.

1970 – Theoretische Möglichkeiten zur Identifizierung von Heiligtümern und Interpretation von Opfern in Ur- und prähistorischen Epochen, in *Vergeschichtliche Heiligtümer und Opferplätze in Mittel- und Nordeuropa* (H. Jahnkuhn ed.) Göttingen.

DIETERICH, A.

1913 – *Mutter Erde,* Berlin/Leipzig.

KALICZ, N.

1969 — *A rézkori Balatoni-csoport Veszprém megyében/The Chalcolithic Balaton Group in County Veszprém,* Veszprém.

KALICZ, N. and RACZKY, P.

1984 — Preliminary report on the 1977-1982 excavations on the Neolithic and Bronze Age tell settlement od Berettyóujfalu-Herpály, *Acta Archaeologica Hung.,* Budapest.

MAKKAY, J.

1970 — A kökor és a rézkor Fejér megyében/The Neolithic and Copper Age in County Fejér, *Fejér megye története,* Székesfehérvar.

1975 — Über neolithische Opferformen, *Valcamonica Symp. 1972* (Actes du Symposium International sur les Religions de la Prehistoire), Capodiponte.

1980/81 — Eine Kultstätte der Bodrogkeresztur-Kultur in Szarvas und Fragen der sakralen Hügel, *Mitteilungen des Arch. Instituts der UAW.*

PODBORSKY, V.
1970 — Soucasný stav výskumu kultury s Moravskou Malovanou Keramikou, *Slovenska Arch.*

RACZKY, P.
1974 — A Lengyeli-kultúra legkésöbbi szakaszának leletei a Dunántúlon/ Finds from the latest phase of the Lengyel culture in Transdanubia, *Archeológiai Értesitö.*

1984 — see Kalicz-Raczky.

SCHMIDT, R.R.
1945 — *Die Burg Vučedol,* Zagreb.

VIZDAL, J.
1978 — Kultobject der Theiss-Kultur in der Ostslovakei, *Arch. Rhozledy.*

FÉCONDITÉ ET PRATIQUES FUNÉRAIRES EN ÉGÉE A L'ÂGE DU BRONZE

Robert Laffineur

L'aspiration à la fécondité est assurément une des composantes principales des religions de l'Egée au cours de la période du Bronze, spécialement de la religion crétoise. Son origine remonte, comme ailleurs en Méditerranée, au fond des âges préhistoriques. Elle y apparaît comme une préoccupation spontanée, en réponse à une impérieuse nécessité vitale, mais elle ne s'y exprime encore que d'une manière bien élémentaire. Le monde minoen en donne une image incomparablement plus diversifiée, qui correspond, à n'en pas douter, à une conception plus mûrie et plus élaborée. On s'est maintes fois intéressé à la manifestation la plus évidente de cette aspiration, la place prépondérante, quasi exclusive, qu'occupe dans le culte crétois la notion de fertilité.[1] Les documents archéologiques en avaient apporté, dès les premières fouilles, d'abondants témoignages. Mais l'intérêt s'est toujours concentré en priorité sur le domaine des vivants, alors qu'il y a des indices — moins nombreux, il est vrai, et plutôt continentaux que crétois — d'une relation entre les pratiques funéraires et la notion de fécondité. C'est à ces témoignages que je voudrais consacrer la présente communication.[2] Elle ne prétend pas vider le sujet, mais, plus modestement, livrer les premiers résultats d'une réflexion et d'une recherche en cours. Elle s'attachera à quelques uns des aspects du problème, en attendant d'autres occasions de compléter, voire de préciser, les observations et les suggestions d'aujourd'hui.

On admettra aisément que le concept de fécondité s'associe assez naturellement avec le monde des morts. L'accession des défunts à une vie nouvelle dans l'au-delà, qui, à en juger par le principe et le contenu des mobiliers funéraires, devait faire partie des croyances fondamentales,[3] suppose une sorte de seconde naissance et possède à ce titre des implications inévitables avec la fertilité et la fécondité.

On peut voir dans l'ensevelissement lui-même une garantie de régénération, à l'image de ce que montre le domaine végétal. Mais on peut être tenté de favoriser plus activement cette régénération par le choix de certaines offrandes funéraires.

J'ai cru ainsi pouvoir établir, dans des études antérieures, que les ornements figurés de la parure du défunt manifestent l'existence, au début de l'epoque mycénienne, d'une iconographie symbolique. On y trouve "des images apotropaïques qui font office d'auxiliaires précieux dans le monde hostile de l'au-delà, chouette, aigle, masque complet ou réduit aux seuls yeux, et des figurations d'animaux, papillon, cigale, abeille, grenouille, triton, poulpe et peut-être cervidé, dont la faculté de métamorphose — voire de génération spontanée —, la capacité de régénération ou les habitudes d'hibernation apparaissent comme autant de gages de survie après la mort ou d'accession à une vie nouvelle" (Laffineur 1985: 261).[4] On peut de même, et la relation est plus directe et plus évidente, intégrer au mobilier funéraire des images ou des objets qui sont des symboles de fécondité. C'est ce que l'on observe, à nouveau au début de l'époque mycénienne, avec les petites figures en feuille d'or de femme portant les mains à la poitrine (Karo 1930-33: no. 36) de divinité nue aux oiseaux au geste identique (*Ibid.* no. 27-28)[5], de divinité de type crétois au corsage ouvert et accompagnée de végétaux (*Ibid.*, no. 75) ou avec un collier de perles en forme de grenade (*Ibid.,* no. 77).[6] La destination de ce dernier n'est peut-être pas exclusivement funéraire, comme semble l'indiquer la facture relativement soignée des perles. Une éventuelle utilisation primaire comme amulettes de fécondité ne modifie toutefois en rien les intentions exprimées par le motif: l'affectation des perles à la parure du défunt va probablement de pair avec une adaptation de la signification symbolique primitive du motif au monde de l'au-delà. La même remarque vaut sans doute pour les chatons de bague ornés d'une scène de culte de fertilité,[7] conçus plus sûrement encore à l'origine comme ornements des vivants, mais choisis peut-être comme pièces de parure funéraire précisément en raison de la signification de leur décor.[8] Elle vaut peut-être également pour la divinité aux végétaux, qui sert d'ornementation à une épingle en argent,[9] et pour une des deux feuilles d'or à divinité aux oiseaux, que le système de fixation, constitué de clous à tête dorée (*Ibid.,* no. 27), identifie comme un élément d'applique décorant peut être primitivement une pièce de mobilier. Quant aux autres feuilles à figure repoussée citées plus haut, elles paraissent avoir été, au contraire, réalisées spécialement pour les besoins funéraires et les petites perforations qui en marquent le contour permettent de penser à des ornements cousus au vêtement mortuaire.[10]

D'autres éléments du mobilier funéraire, etaient probablement chargés d'une signification en rapport avec la fécondité. C'est spécialement le cas, semble-t-il, des figurines en terre cuite, bien attestées durant toutes les phases du Bronze et dans toutes les régions de l'Egée. Un inventaire rapide permet déjà — à défaut d'une étude systématique qui ne peut être envisagée ici — d'observer une prédilection évidente pour des types liés plus ou moins directement au concept qui nous retient. L'exemple des variétés mycéniennes est spécialement significatif, avec les figurines féminines en *phi* et en *kourotrophos*, ainsi qu'avec les figurines animales, qui sont quasi exclusivement — est-ce un hasard? —des figurines de bovidé.[11] Plus anciennement, les "idoles" cycladiques en marbre, qui ont été mises au jour principalement dans les sépultures, représentent une divinité qui n'est assurément pas étrangère au domaine de la fécondité (Pini 1968: 23).[12]

L'aspiration à la fécondité ne peut trouver cependant meilleure expression que dans l'incorporation d'oeufs d'autruche au mobilier funéraire. L'usage est attesté à l'époque mycénienne, avec les trouvailles du cercle A de Mycènes et de la tholos de Dendra. Les oeufs y sont toujours utilisés pour former un vase, en l'occurrence un rhyton, muni d'un col et d'un fond rapportés en faïence ou en or et éventuellement renforcé par un cerclage de bandes métalliques.[13] Les équilvalents de ces pièces ne font pas défaut, en Crète (Dawkins 1903-04: 202; Platon 1971: 159; Touchais 1978: 762), à Mélos (Renfrew 1981a: 31, 1981b: 73) et à Théra (Foster 1979: 151-152 et pl. 53-54; Doumas 1983: pl. 42), mais ils proviennent la plupart du temps de contextes domestiques ou cultuels.[14] Cela donne à penser que l'utilisation comme offrande funéraire doit être le résultat de ce que C. Renfrew appellerait volontiers une *interpretatio Mycenaea* (Renfrew 1981a: 32), [15] ou au moins d'une généralisation d'un usage apparemment secondaire en Crète. Les témoignages concernant l'utilisation de l'oeuf d'autruche en Méditerranée orientale ont été rassemblés tout récemment par A. Finet (1982: 69-77) et A. Caubet (1983: 193-198). La découverte de nombreux spécimens, entiers ou découpés en forme de vase, dans des sépultures, à Ur, Kish et Mari, au Luristan (Finet 1982: 72-74), en Syrie-Palestine et à Chypre (Caubet 1983: 194-195),[16] met bien en évidence la connotation funéraire. Son origine — comme celle de la tradition de nos oeufs de Pâques — tient sans aucun doute au fait que l'oeuf est considéré naturellement comme un "symbole de la vie qu'il contient en germe" et, dans l'au-delà, comme un gage "de la vie future et de la résurrection qu'il promet au défunt" (Deonna 1922: 160).[17] La taille inhabituelle de l'oeuf d'autruche est propre, de surcroît, à frapper l'imagination et à passer pour une garantie supplémentaire de régénération et de fertilité, davantage encore que le nombre éléve d'oeufs que pond l'oiseau.[18]

Cette signification paraît confirmée par la présence de petites figures de dauphin sur un des oeufs de Mycènes (Karo 1930-33: no. 828). L'interprétation que W. Deonna a donnée de cette association (Deonna 1922: 157-166) est peut-être excessive. "L'image de l'oeuf cosmogonique" et "l'allusion au mythe de la naissance de la déesse, sortie de l'oeuf aquatique et poussée eu rivage par les dauphins" (*Ibid.*, 166) répondent à des conceptions religieuses élaborées et organisées dont on hésite à admettre l'existence au milieu du deuxième millénaire. On préférera l'interprétation récente de P. Somville, qui se situe en cette occurrence précise au niveau des réalités observables et des croyances intuitives plus générales et plus fondamentales qui en dérivent: "la mer, porteuse de vie et nourricière,...la dauphin, animal maternel par excellence..." dans lequel "l'homme projette un destin de promesses: la vie, la mort et peut-être une nouvelle naissance, après" (Somville 1984: 4-7). Il n'y a là, après tout, que la juste affirmation d'une composante marine bien concevable en milieu égéen au niveau des croyances en une puissance fécondante universelle.

La valeur fécondante de l'élément liquide est également mise en évidence dans les libations funéraires. La pratique en est attestée en Grèce mycénienne. On a observé en particulier, au cours des fouilles, la présence fréquente, dans le dromos des tombes, parfois à proximité immédiate de l'entrée, de vases, principalement des kylix, qui avaient manifestement une fonction différente de celle de la vaisselle habituelle placée comme mobilier funéraire dans la tombe elle-même, et qui ont dû servir à des libations puis être jetés là après usage (Andronikos 1968: 93; Pini 1968: 70-71; Long 1974: 40).[19] Mais au total les témoignages sont ici moins nombreux et moins diversifiés qu'aux époques ultérieures, protogéometrique et géometrique. On n'a pas, ou très peu, d'exemples des pratiques apparentées, plus ou moins régulièrement représentées au début du premier millénaire (Andronikos 1968: 93-97): vases placés sur la couverture de la sépulture, témoins d'un rite accompli au moment de la fermeture de la tombe;[20] éléments tubulaires en terre cuite disposés verticalement et vases à fond perforé (Kübler 1954: 33-34), destinés à faciliter — en partie symboliquement sans doute — la pénétration du liquide dans le sol de la tombe. Les éléments tubulaires n'ont d'équivalents que dans les "tubes à serpents" minoens, mais il s'agit à nouveau de documents qui appartiennent au mobilier du culte, en l'occurrence du culte domestique, à Gournia et Koumasa par exemple, et leur fond n'est pas toujours percé.[21] A moins qu'il ne faille faire le rapprochement — mais la distance chronologique est importante — avec les curieux "vases-pantalons", à une extrémité dédoublée, trouvés dans les tombes de la Mesara (Xanthoudides 1924:

39, 94 pl. XXVIII et L), dont l'usage est incertain, mais dont la structure est de nature à suggérer une fonction comme instruments à libation.[22] Quant aux vases à fond perforé, s'ils sont connus en assez grand nombre en Egée, ils proviennent eux aussi essentiellement de sites d'habitat ou de sanctuaires.[23]

On pourrait considérer cette apparente pauvreté en témoins de l'usage des libations funéraires à l'epoque mycénienne comme le résultat d'un concours de circonstances: les indices cités sont localisés généralement en dehors des tombes et on ne les a peut-être pas observés au cours de la fouille des sépultures.[24] Et il est vrai que le type toujours bien défini des tombes de l'Egée, en particulier des tombes mycéniennes, n'invite pas effectivement à étendre les recherches aux abords de la fosse ou du dromos ou sur le pourtour de la chambre, dans des zones qui sont pourtant, les fouilles systématiques récentes l'on montré,[25] susceptibles de livrer des vestiges importants. Mais en réalité, cette impression de pauvreté disparaît quand on veut bien chercher les témoignages ailleurs, c'est-àdire à l'intérieur même des tombes. On observe alors la présence dans le mobilier d'un autre type de rhytons, le vase en forme de tête animale, pour lequel on note, plus clairement encore que précédemment, car la documentation est ici plus abondante, la même opposition entre une utilisation cultuelle en Crète et une utilisation funéraire sur le continent mycénien.

On sait que le rhyton — l'étmymologie en témoigne — est, en raison de la présence d'un orifice de remplissage et d'un trou de vidange, le vase à libations par excellence dans le monde créto-mycénien (Tuchelt 1962: 36-45; Koehl 1981: 179-188). Si l'origine des différentes variétés est incontestablement minoenne, ainsi que l'indique l'évolution générale des formes, aujourd'hui bien assurée (Koehl 1981; Petit 1984: 71-80), et si les exemplaires continentaux les plus anciens sont même probablement des objets crétois d'importation (Hood 1978: 163), il n'en reste pas moins que les contextes de trouvaille sont fondamentalement différents d'un domaine à l'autre et que la signification du rhyton devait être en conséquence différente à Mycènes de ce qu'elle était en Crète. Il n'y a pas là contradiction: l'adoption d'une forme ou d'un motif étrangers — voire des deux simultanément quand il s'agit, comme ici, essentiellement de vases plastiques — n'implique pas nécessairement l'adoption de la signification et de l'utilisation particulières qui sont celles du modèle (Laffineur 1985: 264-265). C'est ce qu'a bien noté récemment R.B. Koehl, au terme d'un recensement de la documentation: "The evidence and interpretations presented here indicate that rhyta were used by the

Minoans from Middle Minoan IIB to Late Minoan III in both domestic and cult activities. Rhyta first appear on the Greek Mainland in the Late Helladic I period. Most come from graves, although domestic contexts are also known. The presence on Crete of large groups of rhyta in repositories of cult implements is striking in contrast to the infrequency of rhyta in Mycenaean shrines. The presence of rhyta in Mycenaean graves and their absence in Minoan before Late Minoan III is another significant difference" (Koehl 1981: 187).[26] En se reportant à l'usage général des rhytons, on verrait volontiers dans cette différence des contextes de trouvaille une préfiguration de la dichotomie classique des σπονδαί, libations destinées aux dieux, et des χοαί, libations destinées aux défunts.[27]

C'est à une même distinction, sans pour autant la nommer, qu'aboutit, Ch. R. Long au terme de sa récente analyse des scènes du sarcophage peint d'Aghia Triada, encore qu'en l'occurrence les deux variétés soient intégrées au rituel funéraire. Le type de la scène de libation d'un des longs côtés du monument résulterait de l'association de deux rites distincts: une pratique de tradition minoenne, qui s'adresse à la divinité,[28] et l'usage mycénien du "toast d'adieu" au défunt, qui implique sans doute un nombre plus élévé de participants que le premier rite et exige donc une quantité de liquide aussi importante que celle que l'on verse dans le cratère de l'extrémité gauche de la scène (Long 1974: 40, 73).[29]

Il semble que la destination des rhytons en tête animale déposés dans les tombes ne puisse correspondre à aucune de ces deux pratiques. La forme spécifique du récipient, bien différente de celle des cruches ou des coupes à boire, et surtout son caractère figuré inviteraient plutôt à y voir un ustensile utilisé pour une libation versée sur le sol même de la tombe, au moment de l'inhumation, et dont le défunt est la bénéficiaire naturel. L'écoulement d'un liquide semble de nature à évoquer et à susciter l'action d'une force régénératrice et l'efficacité du processus se trouve assurément renforcée quand le récipient prend la forme d'un animal, le plus fréquemment réduit à la seule tête,[30] et peut-être davantage encore quand il s'agit de l'image du taureau, dont la puissance fécondante peut aisément passer pour une garantie supplémentaire de survie ou de nouvelle naissance. Les documents archéologiques incitent même à envisager la possibilité d'une libation de sang, le liquide de vie par excellence, qui conférerait à la terre et au défunt qui y est déposé sa propre substance vitale.

Le sarcophage d'Aghia Triada apporte ici à nouveau un témoignage de première importance. On y voit une représentation unique d'un sacrifice de taureau, dans lequel le sang de la victime est recueilli dans un récipient tronconique, équivalent de l'ἀμνίον classique. L'anse unique de celui-ci montre, on l'a bien noté, qu'il s'agit d'une forme différente de celle des seaux de la scène de libation du long côté opposé (Long 1974: 36, 62-63).[31] L'observation a amené Ch. Long à y renonnaître non pas un vase complet posé sur le sol mais la partie supérieure d'un rhyton-cornet à demi enfoncé dans le sol (*Ibid.*, 63),[32] à travers lequel le sang peut pénétrer dans la terre et y accomplir son action vivifiante.[33] Le principe des cavités à libations est bien attesté en Egée et Ch. Long en a rassemblé les exemples (*Ibid.*, 63, n. 37). On y associera, d'un point de vue plus général, le témoignage des bassins des salles à pilier minoennes (Gesell 1985) et celui des nombreuses "salles lustrales", sans doute en partie au moins à destination cultuelle, dont le sol était enfoncé par rapport à celui des quartiers voisins.[34] Quant à la représentation de l'enfoncement d'un élément dans le sol, on en a un autre exemple sur le sarcophage même avec la figure du défunt (Long 1974: 46) et un équivalent exact sur un vase-anneau de Mycènes (*Ibid.*, 63, fig. 92). Le document appartient à une série bien connue, dont il sera question encore dans la suite. On observera seulement pour l'instant, à la suite de Ch. Long, que l'anneau supporte un vase à demi enfoncé qui est incontestablement un rhyton-cornet, muni d'un petit bucrane en ronde bosse, allusion probable au sacrifice animal. On ajoutera que l'anneau dans lequel le rhyton s'enfonce représente sans doute le sol, puisqu'il est parsemé de fleurettes et sillonné par un serpent plastique. La libation est donc présentée ici aussi comme devant pénétrer profondément en terre. On notera encore que cette identification précise de l'ἀμνίον du sarcophage implique un rejet de l'hypothèse défendue par R. Paribeni (1908: 36, 57) et récemment par J. Sakellarakis (1970: 185, 193), selon laquelle le cratère de la face opposée était destiné à recevoir le sang du sacrifice. Si le sang de la bête immolée s'écoule au fur et à mesure dans le sol à travers un rhyton, on ne peut guère imaginer qu'il soit possible de le recueillir pour le vider dans un second récipient, même si celui-ci ne paraît pas d'une capacité excessive pour contenir le sang d'une seule victime (Long 1974: 69 n. 25).

Une seconde catégorie de témoignages concerne l'éventuelle pratique de sacrifices d'animaux dans le cadre des rites d'inhumation. Les ossements d'animaux ont été trouvés en grand nombre dans les tombes crétoises et mycéniennes, mais en l'absence de données précises sur les circonstances et les contextes de trouvaille on peut y voir indifféremment des restes de provisions de nourriture destinées au défunt, des reliefs du repas funèbre ou des vestiges de sacrifice (Pini

1968: 27-28, 68-69; Sakellarakis 1970: 158-161;. Long 1974: 68). L'hésitation s'applique en particulier aux ossements de bovidés, pour lesquels le matériel disponible amène à constater une nouvelle fois l'opposition relevée précédemment: ils ont été trouvés en Crète essentiellement dans des contextes domestiques et cultuels et leur apparition dans les tombes de l'île, assez rare de surcroît, se situe à une époque récente et résulte sans doute d'une influence continentale.[35] L'hypothèse du sacrifice vaut en tout cas sûrement pour la trouvaille de la tholos A d'Arkanes, de date MR IIIA, à laquelle J. Sakellarakis a consacré une étude extrêmement documentée. Il en ressort que le crâne de taureau déposé au milieu de l'entrée donnant accès à la chambre latérale est certainement — la fouille minutieuse ne laisse ici aucun doute — une partie isolée d'un animal sacrifié offerte au défunt à l'issue d'une immolation intervenue pendant le rituel d'inhumation (Sakellarakis 1970: 187-192).[36] Le choix de la tête, partie essentielle s'il en est, n'est certes pas un hasard. Quant à l'usage de l'offrande de la tête *pars pro toto*, il est attesté ailleurs par les trouvailles archéologiques (*Ibid.*, 188 n. 388),[37] mais également par les têtes animales que l'on rencontre dans la glyptique et qui sont davantage, à coup sûr, que de simples motifs décoratifs de remplissage (*Ibid.,* 173-174).

Dans ce contexte, l'usage des rhytons en forme de tête animale — ou plutôt l'adaptation au rituel funéraire qu'en ont fait les Mycéniens — apparaît ainsi comme le résultat d'une association des deux principes qui viennent d'être examinés, celui de la libation de sang destinée au défunt, l'αἱμακουρία, et celui de l'offrande *pars pro toto*. Mais il procède encore d'un troisième concept. La tête en terre cuite ou en métal précieux doit en effet être interprétée sans doute comme un substitut de la tête animale réelle et, à ce titre, comme un substitut du sacrifice réel.[38] Cette interprétation semble confirmée par le détail des cornes dorées dont sont pourvus les rhytons en tête de taureau en pierre ou en métal. G. St. Korres a montré récemment que l'application d'une couche de dorure sur les cornes des taureaux conduits au sacrifice est un usage bien attesté en Egée depuis le période créto-mycénienne jusqu'à l'époque contemporaine (Korres 1973: 879-913 et 1977: 205-221). La substitution pourrait tenir à des raisons d'économie, puisqu'aussi bien les exemples des tombes d'Arkanes et d'Aghia Triada se révèlent finalement assez isolés et concernent très probablement, ainsi que J. Sakellarakis l'a bien montré, des personnes de rang élevé (Sakellarakis 1970: 187-188). Mais la véritable raison est peut-être qu'une tête fabriquée dans un matériau non périssable est susceptible de remplir plus longtemps la fonction qu'on lui prête. L'ustensile avait, à n'en pas douter, un rôle effectif et ponctuel à jouer dans le rituel funéraire au moment de l'inhumation.[39] Mais son incorporation au mobilier de la tombe assurait une présence que la résistance du matériau rend en quelque sorte indéfinie et permettait ainsi de prolonger éternellement, de manière virtuelle, le rituel de libation régénératrice dont bénéficie le défunt. On a là la manifestation d'une croyance quasi universelle, selon laquelle l'accomplissement des rites se continue grâce à la seule présence de l'ustensile adéquat, de la même manière qu'il se poursuit virtuellement par l'intermédiaire de la représentation figurée du rite lui-même (Cassimatis 1973: 122). On a là également une manifestation de la tendance à l'expression symbolique qui paraît bien caractériser l'art mycénien et conférer aux objets et aux images une valeur active. C'est précisément dans le contexte funéraire que cette conception trouve les applications les plus nombreuses.[40] On connaît déjà les éléments de parure funéraire mentionnés plus haut, dont l'iconographie est fréquemment en rapport avec la protection ou la régénération du défunt et qui apportent ainsi symboliquement une sorte de garantie pour l'au-delà.[41] On citera également l'usage des masques funéraires et autres plaques de revêtement corporel, dont la fonction était de dissimuler les effets de la décomposition du corps, ou au moins de sa partie considérée comme essentielle, et de conserver au défunt les apparences de l'existence (Laffineur 1985: 252). La plupart de ces documents sont réalisés en or, matériau inaltérable, aisément compris comme un gage de la pérennité des vertus magiques que l'on prête aux ornements funéraires. L'efficacité de ces derniers est encore accrue par le caractère volontiers emblématique de l'imagerie et par la répétition fréquente des motifs (Vermeule 1975: 16-18, 23, 25, 40-47).

La même signification d'ustensile de libation symbolique était probablement attachée aux rhytons-cornets trouvés dans des contextes funéraires (Pini 1968: 67)[42] et on doit admettre ici aussi une adaptation d'une forme d'usage sans doute à l'origine essentiellement cultuelle (Koehl 1981: 184-186).

L'interprétation s'applique aussi aux vases-anneaux de type élaboré, mais ces récipients sont surtout typiques du domaine chypriote et leur utilisation se prolonge abondamment au début du premier millénaire, dans les sanctuaires et surtout dans les tombes.[43] Ils méritent de faire à eux seuls l'objet d'un examen détaillé qui dépasse largement le cadre de la présente contribution. En se limitant à des observations générales, on remarque toutefois que les éléments fixés sur l'anneau sont le plus souvent des petits vases qui communiquent avec le corps principal du récipient et permettaient donc d'assurer l'écoulement d'un liquide dans la partie annulaire. Mais on note aussi la présence d'autres éléments constitutifs en ronde bosse, qui sont manifestement en relation avec les rites examinés plus haut et, plus généralement, avec l'idée de fécondité: tête de taureau, munie habituellement de l'orifice de vidange de l'ensemble du vase,[44] figure de grenouille,[45] grenade,[46] coquillage.[47]

On rangera enfin dans cette même catégorie des instruments de libation funéraire les coquilles de triton et leurs imitations en pierre, en terre cuite ou en faïence, dont les exemplaires ont été rassemblés récemment par P. Darcque dans le cadre de la publication du triton en pierre MRIA de Malia (Baurain-Darcque 1983: 59-73).[48] On a montré à cette occasion qu'une identification de ces documents comme des rhytons[49] devait être préférée à l'interprétation habituelle qui veut y voir, sans arguments déterminants, des trompettes à usage rituel (*Ibid.*, 52-58).[50] Si le contexte de trouvaille de ces objets est souvent domestique ou cultuel, il y a cependant aussi de nombreux exemples de leur association au mobilier des tombes, au MR principalement.[51] La valeur d'instrument de libation funéraire, réelle puis symbolique, doit sans doute être admise ici aussi. Cela est d'autant plus vraisemblable que l'on prêtait dans l'antiquité au triton une faculté de génération spontanée et que son mode de vie se caractérise par une période d'hibernation (Laffineur 1985: 257-259). Ces deux particularités n'ont certes pas le même degré de réalité, mais elles sont de nature à passer pour des garanties de l'accession à une vie nouvelle dans l'au-delà. C'est le sens qu'il faut donner aux petites figures de triton en or de la tholos 3 de Peristeria (Marinatos 1967: 12, fig. 16). C'est probablement aussi la signification qu'il convient d'accorder aux tritons naturels et à leurs imitations. De même que pour les vases en forme d'animal ou de tête, l'écoulement du liquide de libation, qu'il soit effectif ou virtuel, était sans doute conçu ici comme le moyen symbolique de transférer la substance et les vertus régénératrices du mollusque à l'intérieur de la tombe. Un principe analogue a présidé à la conception des rhytons en forme de buste féminin aux seins perforés trouvés dans les nécropoles de Mochlos[52] et de Malia.[53] Le lien est là plus direct encore avec la fécondité, mais le fonctionnement symbolique du récipient n'est pas différent.

Au terme de la présente étude, on perçoit mieux la relation qui s'est établie en milieu égéen entre les pratiques funéraires et la notion de fécondité. On a pu constater à plusieurs reprises le rôle décisif que paraissent avoir joué les Mycéniens dans l'enrichissement de cet aspect des conceptions funéraires, en particulier par l'adaptation qu'ils ont faite d'usages traditionnels empruntés au domaine cultuel. Mais il convient d'être prudent dans les conclusions que l'on peut tirer de cette observation. Le hasard des trouvailles est peut-être responsable, dans une mesure non négligeable, de la différence fondamentale que l'on a pu noter plus d'une fois entre les pratiques minoennes et mycéniennes. Les tombes crétoises du MM et du début MR ne sont connues qu'en nombre relativement restreint et une lacune correspondante concerne par ailleurs les sites d'habitat du début de l'époque mycénienne (Koehl 1981: 187 no. 40). Il n'est pas douteux non plus que les rites dont les traces nous sont parvenues sont les plus élaborés et sans doute ceux qui étaient accomplis en l'honneur de défunts de haut rang. Le bilan, dès lors, serait à coup sûr différent si l'on pouvait faire intervenir les données concernant la masse des inhumations des classes moyenne et inférieure (Sakellarakis 1970: 188; Long 1974: 50). Il faut enfin, au moment de conclure, se garder également d'oublier que les vestiges matériels des rites funéraires sont d'importance éminemment inégale et que l'essentiel de leurs manifestations nous échappe ainsi probablement en grande partie, d'autant qu'il s'agit de phénomènes de nature essentiellement spirituelle. Mais quoi qu'il en soit, une chose paraît certaine. Par leurs implications avec le concept de fécondité, les croyances et les rites qui accompagnent la mort sont étonnamment proches dans le monde égéen de ceux qui s'attachent à la naissance. Les deux moments primordiaux de la vie se trouvent ainsi réunis, comme les deux composantes de la dichotomie fondamentale de l'existence, ou, pour reprendre l'heureuse formule de P. Somville, comme une incarnation de "la même constante anthropologique de la dualité attrayante-fascinante de qui donne la vie et la reprend, incarne et désincarne, fait croître et se corrompre, alternativement" (Somville 1984: 4-5).

Notes

1 Voir notamment à ce propos Ch. Picard, *Les religions préhelléniques (Crète et Mycènes)*, Paris 1948 et M.P. Nilsson, *The Minoan-Mycenaean Religion and its Survival in Greek Religion*, 2e éd., Lund 1950, *passim*. La bibliographie à ce sujet a été rassemblée dans I.M. Ruud, *Minoan Religion. A Bibliography*, Oslo 1980 (voir l'index, p. 57, *s.v.* Mother Goddess).

2 Il sera question ici des pratiques liées à l'inhumation propremnet dite, non des manifestations possibles d'un culte du défunt accompli après la mise en terre, de manière répétée, éventuellement à intervalles réguliers. La différance a bien été précisée par G.E. Mylonas, qui a justement mis en garde contre toute confusion dans ce domaine: The Cult of the Dead in Helladic Times, *Studies Presented to David Moore Robinson*, I Saint Louis 1951, p. 64-65.

3 Sur l'au-delà, voir Picard, *op. cit.*, p. 161-175 et Nilsson, *op. cit.*, p. 619-633. La pratique fréquente du "nettoyage" des sépultures pour faire place à des nouvelles inhumations implique peut-être seulement la croyance et une survie brève. Voir à ce propos Mylonas, *op. cit.*, p. 92 et 98-99; *id.*, Homeric and Mycenaean Burial Customs, *AJA*, 52, 1948, p. 70-71; Cassimatis 1973: 121 ("...il n'est pas impossible qu'il existat [*sic*] la croyance en une survie très courte: le temps que prend le corps à se décomposer, ou le temps pour la vie "spirituelle" de passer dans un autre monde. Le mobilier servirait à faciliter ce passage, en assistant le défunt dans son attente et ses transactions avec les forces souterraines, après quoi, corps et offrandes perdant leur importance pouvaient être impunément violés) et 165 ("Mais la tombe n'est pas la demeure de la vie future. Elle sert à faciliter le passage d'un état à un autre et les offrandes ouvrent la voie tout en aidant le mort dans cette transformation et en sauvegardant sa personnalité. Sinon, chaque caveau resterait inviolé"). Voir aussi Long 1974: 18, 32, 46 (le sarcophage d'Aghia Triada utilisé au moins deux fois successivement). *Contra*, Pini 1968: 73.

4 Pour le symbolisme de protection, voir R. Laffineur, Le symbolisme funéraire de la chouette, *AC* 50, 1981, p. 432-444. On observe les indices de croyances analogues en rapport avec le monde végétal: certaines plantes sont naturellement considérées, de même que leur simple figuration, comme gages de fertilité, en particulier de la régénération annuelle de la vie végétale. Le fait a bien été mis en évidence récemment par P. Warren à propos de la scille de mer, mais les témoignages recueillis concernent exclusivement le domaine cultuel (Of Squills, *Aux origines de l'hellénisme. La Crète et la Grèce. Hommage à Henri van Effenterre*, Paris 1984, p.17-24). On peut s'étonner que les vertus de cette plante n'aient apparemment pas été mises à profit dans le contexte funéraire, étant donné la connotation d'immortalité qui s'y attache aujourd'hui encore (*op. cit.*, p. 17).

5 Pour l'interprétation de l'oiseau, voir Nilsson, *op. cit.*,p. 330-340.

6 Pour le symbolisme de la grenade, voir *RE, s.v. Malum Punicum*, col. 939-940.

7 Voir les nombreux exemples recensés dans *CMS, passim* et E.T. Vermeule, *Götterkult, Archaeologia Homerica,* V, Göttingen 1974, p. 14-16.

8 L'iconographie mycénienne exprime également d'autres formes de symbolisme. Voir à ce propos R. Laffineur, Iconographie mycénienne et symbolisme guerrier, *Art & Fact. Revue des historiens d'art, archéologues et musicologues de l'Université de Liège*, 2, 1983, p. 38-49.

9 Les détails de la description de Karo 1930-33: 54, no. 75 montrent que l'association des deux éléments n'est pas douteuse.

10 Sur l'usage du vêtement mortuaire, voir Andronikos 1968: 7, 9, 97.

11 Sur les terres cuites mycéniennes, voir l'étude fondamentale d'E. French, The Development of Mycenaean Terracotta Figurines, *BSA*, 66, 1971, p. 101-187 (spécialement p. 107-108 pour l'interprétation) et la mise au point récente de la même spécialiste, Mycenaean Figures and Figurines, their Typology and Function, *Sanctuaries and Cults in the Aegean Bronze Age, Proceedings of the First International Symposium at the Swedish Institute in Athens (1980),* Stockholm 1981, p.173-178. Voir aussi pour l'interprétation G.E. Mylonas, *Mycenae and the Mycenaean Age,* Princeton 1966, p. 114-116; Andronikos 1968: 98 et Long 1974: 47.

12 Une interprétation apparentée mais plus ébalorée a été proposée par J. Thimme: les "idoles" seraient les images d'une divinité astrale et constitueraient pour le défunt une garantie magique de renaissance (voir en dernier lieu dans *Kunst und Kultur der Kykladeninseln im 3. Jahrtausend v. Chr.,* Karlsruhe 1976, p. 453-456).

13 Mycènes, tombe IV: Karo 1930-33: no. 552 (oeuf), 567 et 573 (embouchure et fond en faïence), avec traces d'un revêtement en feuille de bronze: Mycènes, tombe V: Karo 1930-33: no. 828 (oeuf avec dauphins en faïence appliqués) et 651 (fond en or), no. 832 (fragment d'oeuf) et 774 (embouchure en faïence); tholos de Dendra: A.W. Persson, *The Royal Tombs at Dendra near Midea,* Lund 1931, p. 37 et 54 et pl. III (bandes de bronze doré). Pour la reconstitution des exemplaires de Mycènes, voir Foster 1979: 130-134, fig. 87-88 et pl. 41-42. Un autre spécimen est mentionné dans A.W. Persson, *New Tombs at Dendra*, Lund 1942, p. 146. Les bandes en bronze de l'oeuf de Dendra correspondent sans doute à la dénomination *ko-no-ni-pi / kononiphi,* "avec des barres, des bandes", qui accompagne l'idéogramme *217 VAS sur la tablette linéaire B KN K 434 (Fr. Vandenabeele et J.P. Olivier, *Les idéogrammes archéologiques du linéaire B,* Paris 1979, p. 241-245).

14 Seul, l'exemplaire de Palaikastro (Dawkins 1903-04: 202) provient d'un contexte funéraire.

15 La priorité chronologique des spécimens de Mycènes, que l'on pourrait envisager, inviterait à retenir le processus inverse d'une signification primitivement funéraire — et originaire de l'Orient, ainsi qu'on va le voir — adaptée ensuite en Crète et dans les îles au domaine cultuel. Mais si cette priorité semble confirmée par les trouvailles de Théra (Foster 1979: 151-152) et peut-être par celles de Phylacopi et de Zakro, les contextes respectivement MA et MMIII des rhytons trouvés à Palaikastro et à Kommos (Touchais 1978: 762) obligent à écarter cette hypothèse. On le fera d'autant plus facilement que les imitations en terre cuite de vases en oeuf d'autruche remontent en Crète jusqu'au MMII (Sir A. Evans, *The Palace of Minos*, I, Londres 1921, fig. 436, entre les p. 594-595 et II, Londres 1928, fig. 129; voir aussi G. Walberg, *Kamares. A Study of the Character of Palatial Middle Minoan Pottery,* Uppsala 1976, p. 42) et que les oeufs de Mycènes ne sont sans doute, avec leurs accessoires en faïence, que des produits crétois d'importation, ou du moins des productions inspirées de modèles crétois (Vermeule 1975: 19-20 et Foster 1979: 134, 136-137).

16 Les oeufs d'autruche sont également attestés dans les tombes puniques. Voir en dernier lieu M. Ponsich, *Recherches archéologiques à Tanger et dans sa région,* Paris 1970, p. 130-140 et P. Cintas, *Manuel d'archéologie punique,* II, Paris, 1976, p. 282-284.

17 Sur la signification funéraire de l'oeuf, voir aussi J. Wiesner, *Grab und Jenseits,* Berlin 1938, p. 218, et M.P. Nilsson, *Das Ei im Totenkult der Alten, Opuscula selecta,* I, Lund 1951, p. 3-20.

18 Aristote, *H. Anim.*, IX, 15, 616b5; Aristote, *Gen. Anim.*, III, 1, 749b17; Pline, *H.N.*, X, 143. Voir à ce propos *RE, s.v. Strauss,* col. 341-342. Les autres raisons que l'on peut invoquer paraissent moins déterminantes: l'oeuf d'autruche déposé comme nourriture pour le défunt (Finet 1982: 72, n. 26) ou considéré comme symbole de résurrection parce qu'il éclôt de lui-même quand il est enfoui dans le sable (Deonna 1922: 160, n. 9).

19 Les nombreux vases trouvés dans les pièces annexes des tombes circulaires de la Mesara — lesquelles ne contenaient pas d'inhumations — témoignent sans doute des mêmes pratiques (Pini 1968: 29-30; K. Branigan, *The Tombs of Mesara,* Londres 1970, p. 98-103). Pour la Crète du Bronze récent, voir aussi Long 1974: 66.

20 Le mobilier de la tombe à fosse 36 de Zafer Papoura à Cnossos (la "chieftain's grave") est disposé pareillement sur la dalle de couverture (Pini 1968: 62 et fig. 81), mais il ne s'agit pas de vases spécialement destinés aux libations.

21 A propos de ces objets, voir G. Cadogan, Clay Tubes in Minoan Religion, Πεπραγμένα τοῦ Γ' διεθνοῦς Κρητολογικοῦ συνεδρίου A, Athènes, 1973, p. 34-38; G.C. Gesell, The Minoan Snake Tube, *AJA,* 77, 1973, p. 213-214 et The Minoan Snake Tube: A Survey and Catalogue, *AJA*, 80, 1976, p. 247-259.

22 Le rapprochement avec des cônes de Malia (Pini 1968: 26) n'éclaire pas la question, car ces objets n'ont qu'une extrémité perforée (l'extrémité étroite).

23 A. Maiuri, Jalisos, *ASAtene,* 6-7, 1923-1924, no. 7, p. 131 et fig. 51 (Ialysos, tombe 19); J.-Cl. Poursat, Un sanctuaire du Minoen Moyen II à Mallia, *BCH*, 90, 1966, no. 11, p. 537 et fig. 28-29, p. 538; Koehl 1981: 181, fig. 2a-d; P. Warren, Minoan Crete and Ecstatic Religion, *Sanctuaries and Cults...*, p. 156 et Of Squills, *Aux origines de l'hellénisme...*, p. 20 et pl. VIII, 1-2 ("cup-rhyton"); W.W. Cummer et E. Schofield, *Keos,* III, *Ayia Irini: House A,* Mayence 1984, no. 999, pl. 30; B. Wells, *Asine II,* 4, *The Protogeometric Period,* 1, *The Tombs,* Stockholm 1976, fig. 32, p. 25 (date incertaine, peut-être HR).

24 Voir cependant l' "autel" situé au-dessus de la tombe IV du cercle de l'acropole de Mycènes (en dernier lieu L. Pelon, *Tholoi, tumuli et cercles funéraires,* Paris 1976, p. 146-147) et, en Crète, les quelques exemples de fosses à mobilier séparées des sépultures proprement dites (Pini 1968: 31).

25 Voir par exemple le mur de péribole circulaire autour de la grande tholos de Peristeria et le tumulus mésohelladique autour de la tombe de Voïdokilia (G. St. Korres, Πρακτικά 1976, p. 481-485 et 1977, p. 242-295).

26 Les rhytons en tête animale sont rassemblés dans Sakellarakis 1970: 191, n. 429. Les seuls exemplaires crétois trouvés dans une tombe sont les fragments de la "tombe des doubles haches" de Cnossos (Sir A. Evans, *The Tomb of the Double Axes and Associated Group and Pillar Rooms and Ritual Vessels of the 'Little Palace' at Knossos,* Londres 1914 [Archaeologia LXV], p. 72, fig. 50), un spécimen de Ligortyno (E. Pottier, Documents céramiques du Musée du Louvre, *BCH*, 31, 1907, p. 117, no. 1 et pl. XXIII, en haut) et, peut-être, un rhyton inédit de

Platanos mentionné par J.A. Sakellarakis. Le deuxième document est cependant daté du MRIIIA, c'est-à-dire de l'époque de l'occupation mycénienne en Crète.

27 Sur ces deux formes de libations, voir notamment J. Rudhardt, *Notions fondamentales de la pensée religieuse et actes constitutifs du culte dans la Grèce classique,* Genève 1958, p. 240-248.

28 Sans doute une divinité (ou des divinités) protectrice du défunt comme sur le modèle en terre cuite de la tombe de Kamilari (Long 1974: 45-46; pour le monument, voir D. Levi, La tomba a tholos di Kamilari presso a Festos, *ASAtene*, 39-40, 1961-1962, p. 123-139.

29 Cette pratique du "toast d'adieu" peut se restituer d'après les nombreuses trouvailles de fragments de coupes à boire découvertes dans le dromos des tombes (*supra*,p.82).

30 Outre les exemples de têtes dont il a été question plus haut (*supra*, n. 26), on mentionnera les rhytons en forme d'animal entier, en particulier ceux des tombes de la Mesara (Branigan, *op. cit.*, p. 81).

31 J.A. Sakellarakis note également cette différence, mais il estime qu'il s'agit pourtant d'un vase à deux anses et avoue l'impossibilité d'en trouver des équivalents (Sakellarakis 1970: 180).

32 On préférera cette hypothèse à celle d'un seau sans fond proposée par E.O. James (*The Cult of the Mother-Goddess,* Londres 1959, p. 131). On observera toutefois que la cavité où s'enfonçait le vase devait être assez profonde, faute de quoi le trou de vidange de l'extrémité inférieure du vase aurait été en contact avec le fond de la fosse, qui l'aurait obturé, rendant ainsi impossible l'écoulement du liquide.

33 L'idée est bien exprimée par E.O. James (*op. cit.*, p. 131): "...the life-giving blood of the victim being conveyed to them [the deceased] by means of ritual jars which carry the offering to Mother-earth, regarded as the ultimate source of rebirth". Voir aussi Wiesner, *op. cit.*, p. 187-188.

34 Voir en dernier lieu à leur propos J.W. Graham, Bathrooms and Lustral Chambers, *Greece and the Eastern Mediterranean in Ancient History and Prehistory. Studies Presented to Fritz Schachermeyr,* Berlin et New York, 1977, p. 110-125.

35 Voir la liste des trouvailles dans Sakellarakis 1970: 215-217. La présence d'ossements de bovidés n'est attestée qu'une seule fois dans un sanctuaire à l'époque mycénienne (Sakellarakis 1970: 164).

36 L'auteur admet que le sacrifice se faisait hors de la tombe, à l'air libre. Il note un seul cas de sacrifice accompli à l'intérieur de la sépulture, mais l'indice utilisé, la prétendue table de sacrifice en pierre du "cénotaphe" de Dendra (A. W. Persson, *The Royal Tombs at Dendra near Midea,* Lund 1931, pl. XXIX, à gauche), doit être aujourd'hui rejeté. Le document a été réinterprété récemment de manière convaincante par Å. Åkerström comme le support d'un sarcophage en bois (Mycenaean Problems, *Op. Ath.*, 12, 1978, p. 69-73). Sur la valeur sacrificielle du taureau et de son sang, voir aussi M.C. Loulloupis, The Position of the Bull in the Prehistoric Religions of Crete and Cyprus, *Acts of the International Archaeological Symposium "The Relations between Cyprus and Crete ca. 2000-500 B.C.",* Nicosie 1979, p. 216-217.

37 Sur le principe de l'offrande partielle, voir aussi Pini 1968: 68.

38 Les figurines animales des sanctuaires et des tombes sont interprétées pareillement comme des substituts du sacrifice, de même que la représentation du rituel, sur le sarcophage d'Aghia Triada par exemple (Pini 1968: 28, 70).

39 Le liquide versé à cette occasion n'était probablement pas du sang, qui aurait nécessité un sacrifice, mais un liquide également de substitution, peut-être du vin (Long 1974: 68) ou simplement de l'eau.

40 Les indices de l'existence d'un symbolisme guerrier sont toutefois également observables (voir *supra,* n. 8).

41 *Supra,* p.80.

42 Les spécimens mycéniens sont rassemblés dans A. Furumark, *The Mycenaean Pottery. Analysis and Classification,* Stockholm 1942, p. 618 (type 199).

43 Voir le catalogue de A. Pieridou, Κυπριακὰ τελετουργικὰ ἀγγεῖα *RDAC* 1971, p. 18-26. Le type est attesté également à Mycènes (Furumark, *op. cit.*, p. 618, type 197).

44 Pieridou, *op. cit.*, pl. IX-XI; H.-G. Buchholz et V. Karageorghis, *Altägäis und Altkypros,* Tübingen 1971, no. 1271; E.T. Vermeule, *Götterkult, Archaeologia Homerica,* V, Göttingen 1974, pl. VIIb. Ce dernier document est un spécimen exceptionnel de l'Héraion de Samos, daté des environs de 600 et de fabrication probablement rhodienne (voir H. Walter et Kl. Vierneisel,

Heraion von Samos. Die Funde der Kampagnen 1958 und 1959, *AM*, 74, 1959, p. 29-30 et Beil. 67 et Kl. Vierneisel, Neue Tonfiguren aus dem Heraion von Samos, *AM*, 76, 1961, p. 28-34 et 52-59 et Beil. 24-32). La même signification symbolique était peut-être attachée à un trépied en stéatite à tête de taureau de la collection Stathatos (D. Levi, Mobilier funéraire de Kharvati, *Collection Hélène Stathatos*, III, Strasbourg 1963, no. 8, p. 24-25 et 28).

45 Sur le vase-anneau de l'Héraion de Samos cité à la note précédente. Sur la signification symbolique de la grenouille, voir Laffineur 1985: 257.

46 Sur le même vase de Samos et dans Pieridou, *op. cit.*, pl. X, 1 et XI, 1-2.

47 Sur le vase de Samos. Pour le signification du coquillage, voir ci-dessous.

48 Pour les trouvailles de coquillages en faïence, voir aussi Foster, *op. cit.*, p. 83-85 et 137-140.

49 L'absence de perforation à l'extrémité pointue de certains spécimens (P. Warren, *Minoan Stone Vases,* Cambridge 1969, p. 91) n'est pas suffisante pour écarter l'interprétation comme vases à libations. Comme le font observer Cl. Baurain et P. Darcque, les rhytons ne sont pas les seuls vases à libation et il faut, dans le cas des tritons sans orifice de vidange "supposer que le liquide offert était introduit, puis reversé par la même ouverture" (Baurain-Darcque 1983: 57).

50 Pour une signification possible — mais peu vraisemblable — de cet usage dans le contexte funéraire, voir Long 1974: 13-14.

51 Aux spécimens repris dans le catalogue de P. Darcque (Baurain-Darcque 1983: no. 2, 7 et 20, p. 62, 65 et 71-73), il convient d'ajouter les nombreux tritons naturels, qui n'ont pas été recensés et qui proviennent tous de sépultures. On en trouvera mention dans Pini 1968: 67, n. 790 et on renverra également à Dawkins 1903-04: 197, 202. On notera que la tombe du sarcophage d'Aghia Triada a livré aussi des fragments de triton naturel (Long 1974: 13).

52 Sp. Marinatos et H. Hirmer, *Kreta, Thera und des mykenische Hellas,* Munich 1973, pl. 10, en haut (l'auteur interprète curieusement le personnage comme une figure masculine: p. 111).

53 Buchholz et Karageorghis, *op. cit.,* no. 1193. Sur l'interprétation de ces rhytons, voir F. Muthmann, *Mutter und Quelle. Studien zur Quellenverehrung im Altertum und im Mittelalter,* Bâle 1975, p. 198 et 270.

Summary

Burial customs manifest during the Aegean Bronze Age close relations with the idea of fertility. This is especially true for the Mycenaean world and it is a further indication of the predilection of the Mycenaeans for the various forms of symbolism. The relation may be expressed by the image of different living beings, more or less directly connected with fertility, or by placing more significant elements such as ostrich eggs within the tomb. The best examples of those elements, however, are the animal head rhyta. Their funeral use is limited to continental late Bronze Age Greece. Their meaning seems to be that of a substitute of a sacrifice *pars pro toto* which is supposed to supply the deceased with the guarantee of a symbolic and eternal regenerating blood libation in the after-life.

Résumé

Les coutumes funéraires du domaine égéen présentent au cours de l'âge du Bronze (IIIe et IIe millénaires) des implications nombreuses avec le concept de fécondité. C'est spécialement le cas du monde mycénien, qui donne ici un indice supplémentaire de sa prédilection pour les diverses formes du symbolisme funéraire. La relation peut aller de la simple figuration d'éléments qui sont en rapport plus ou moins direct avec la notion de fécondité, jusqu'à l'intégration aux mobiliers funéraires d'objets plus directement évocateurs, comme les oeufs d'autruche. Mais la manifestation la plus révélatrice est donnée par les rhytons en tête animale, dont la destination funéraire est propre à la Grèce continentale du Bronze récent et dont la signification semble être celle d'un sacrifice *pars pro toto* de substitution qui apporte symboliquement au défunt la garantie d'une libation de sang régénératrice.

Bibliographie

ANDRONIKOS, M.
1968 — *Archaeologia Homerica* W, *Totenkult*, Göttingen.

BAURAIN - DARCQUE
1983 — Un triton en pierre à Malia, *BCH*, 107, pp. 3-73.

CASSIMATIS, H.
1973 — Les rites funéraires à Chypre, *RDAC*, pp. 116-166.

CAUBET, A.
1983 — Les oeufs d'autruche au Proche Orient ancien, *RDAC*, pp. 193-198.

DAWKINS, R.M.
1903-04 — Excavations at Palaikastro. III, *BSA*, 10, pp. 195-235.

DEONNA, W
1922 — L'oeuf, les dauphins et la naissance d'Aphrodite, *Revue de l'histoire des religions*, 85, pp. 157-166.

DOUMAS, Chr.
1983 — *Thera, Pompeii of the ancient Aegean*, Londres.

FINET, A.
1982 — L'oeuf d'autruche, *Studia Paulo Naster oblata*, II, *Orientalia antiqua*, Louvain, pp. 68-77.

FOSTER, K.P.
1979 — *Aegean Faience of the Bronze Age*, New Haven et Londres.

GESELL, G.C.
1985 — *Town, Palace and House Cult in Minoan Crete*, Göteborg.

HOOD, S.
1978 — *The Arts in Prehistoric Greece*, Harmondsworth.

KARO, G.
1930-33 — *Die Schachtgräber von Mykenai*, Munich.

KOEHL, R.B.
1981 — The Function of Aegean Bronze Age Rhyta, *Sanctuaries and Cults in the Aegean Bronze Age, Proceedings of the First International Symposium at the Swedish Institute in Athens (1980)*, Stockholm, pp. 179-188.

KORRES, G. St.
1973 — Ἐπιβιώσεις ἐκ τῶν θυσιῶν ταύρων, Ἀθηνᾶ, 73-74, pp. 879-913.

KORRES, G. St.
1977 — Ἐπιβιώσεις ἐκ θυσιῶν ταύρων - Β', Ἀθηνᾶ, 76, pp. 205-221.

KÜBLER, K.
1954 — *Kerameikos VI. Die Nekropole des 10. bis 8. Jahrhunderts*, Berlin.

LAFFINEUR, R.
1985 — Iconographie minoenne et iconographie mycénienne à l'époque des tombes à fosse, *L'iconographie minoenne. Actes de la Table Ronde d'Athènes (1983), BCH,* suppl. VI, pp. 245-266.

LONG, Ch.R.
1974 — *The Ayia Triadha Sarcophagus. A Study of Late Minoan and Mycenaean Funerary Practices and Beliefs,* Göteborg.

MARINATOS, Sp.
1967 — Problemi archeologici e filologici di Pilo, *SMEA,* 3, pp. 6-25.

PARIBENI, R.
1908 — Il sarcofago dipinto di Haghia Triada, *Mon. Ant.,* 19, pp. 20-74.

PETIT, Fr.
1984 — Les rhytons égéens en forme de tête animale, *Art & Fact. Revue des historiens d'art, des archéologues et des orientalistes de l'Université de Liège,* 3, pp. 71-80.

PINI, I.
1968 — *Beiträge zur minoischen Gräberkunde,* Weisbaden.

PLATON, N.
1971 — *Zakros. The Discovery of a Lost Place of Ancient Crete,* New York.

RENFREW, C.
1981a — Questions of Minoan and Mycenaean Cult, *Sanctuaries and Cults in the Aegean Bronze Age, Proceedings of the First International Symposium at the Swedish Institute in Athens (1980),* Stockholm, pp. 27-33.
1981b — The Sanctuary at Phylakopi, *Sanctuaries and Cults...,* pp. 67-80.

SAKELLARAKIS, J.A.
1970 — Das Kuppelgrab A von Archanes und das kretisch-mykenische Tieropferritual, *PZ,* 45, pp. 135-219.

SOMVILLE, P.
1984 — Le dauphin dans la religion grecque, *Revue de l'histoire des religions,* 201, pp. 3-24.

TOUCHAIS, G.
1978 — Chronique des fouilles et découvertes archéologiques en Grèce en 1977, *BCH,* 102, pp. 641-770.

TUCHELT, Kl.
1962 — *Tiergefässe in Kopf - und Protomengestalt,* Berlin.

VERMEULE, E.
1975 — *The Art of the Shaft Graves of Mycenae,* Cincinnati.

XANTHOUDIDES, St.
1924 — *The Vaulted Tombs of Mesara,* Londres.

OF EARRINGS, SWALLOWS AND THERAN LADIES

Iris Tzachili

It seems that religious concepts in the Late Bronze Age settlement at Thera are essentially Minoan. Almost every phenomenon of Minoan religious life is present at Thera; moreover religious iconography is thought to be in a high degree dependent, or at least strongly influenced by Minoan themes (Sapouna-Sakellaraki 1976: 487-509; Cameron 1978: 580-592). The subject has in the last years been linked with an attempt to investigate the political schemes in the Aegean; that is whether Thera was, or was not, a Minoan colony and which was the role of religion in this political dependence (Marinatos 1984a: 176).

Yet one becomes easily conscious of some diverging details, either in the form of absences of well known Minoan themes, or of some particular features occurring almost exclusively at Thera. Usually these peculiarities are assigned to the older Cycladic tradition, (Barber 1978: 378-9; Thorpe-Scholes 1978: 444; Höckmann 1978: 615); or to Mycenaean influences (Doumas 1983: 132). The aim of this paper is to deal with two of them, not so arbitrarily chosen as it may seem at first sight; the earrings and the swallows.

The great majority of the Theran ladies depicted in the wall paintings are adorned with earrings. The priestess from the West House wears big, wheel-like ones (Pl. 7), and the two female figures from the House of the Ladies wear earrings of the common crescent form (Pls. 8-9) as do the women who are depicted in the Crocus-gatherers fresco in the house known as Xesté 3. The earrings of one of the crocus gatherers (Pl. 10) are of exactly the same form as the golden ones found in Mycenae in Shaft Grave III (Sapouna-Sakellaraki 1976: 509), and thought to be Cretan work of Late Minoan Ia. Earrings are also worn by young boys, namely, one of the young boxers (*Thera IV* pl. E) and one of the recently found male figures in the Xesté 3.

This fact is hardly remarkable by itself; what is more natural for the glamorous Theran ladies than to be adorned with earrings along with necklaces, bracelets, diadems and so on? Earrings, furthermore are found in graves in Crete and the mainland, though not so numerous as the necklaces (Hood 1978: 194-207). It assumes significance only by comparison; in the whole Aegean iconography (Knossos, Mycenae, Pylos, Tiryns, Thebes) none of the female personnages wear earrings. They wear rich gowns, rich jewellery but no earrings (Tzachili 1985: 395).

Even after this observation the Theran earrings would not appear to be more than an additional refinement. But this does not seem so. There are indications that suggest that earrings are invested with a derived, secondary meaning, that they might be functioning as signs. This is denoted by the other puzzling representations of earrings in Theran iconography. We see them decorating vases around the handles in the form of rings as if handles were ears (Pl. 11). Not in any kind of vases. Only in nippled-ewers and sometimes flower-pots. The nippled-ewer, considered as a typical cycladic vessel, is characterized by two, non utilitarian features: the imitation of female breasts and the bird-like spout. The combination of these and the large "fertile" belly lead to ideas or images related to birds, women and fertility. Consequently this vase is often considered as a ritual one even though there are no archaeological data to confirm this assumption (Marinatos 1984a 177). Besides, the most important point is perhaps that the nippled-ewer is so far in Thera the only type of vase represented on another vase. Ewers, besides, are represented on a skyphos from Phaistos: one of the rare representations of a vase on another vase outside Akrotiri (Stümer 1985: 127, fig. 12). When a nippled-ewer is represented on a vase, two of its elements are emphasized, the nipples and the earrings, which are excessively big as if the artist wanted to make sure that people's attention would instantly be drawn on them. In one case the representation of a nippled-ewer on a large pithoid amphora is characterized by huge wheel-like earrings, the same as those worn by the priestess in the West-House.

This type of vase is frequently decorated with swallows, the other subject we are proposing to examine in this paper. Swallows are depicted frequently on Theran frescoes and vases, more frequently than in any other part of the Aegean (Marinatos 1969: 68), a curious phenomenon in the light of the fact that swallows do not stay to make nests in Thera, they just migrate through (Doumas 1983: 81). They are the main theme in the spring fresco (Marinatos IV, pl. A, B, C) a wall painting whose religious character has been doubted by none (Doumas 1983: 76) (Pl. 12). Swallows are also depicted in two fresco fragments; one from the Xesté 3 which represents a swallow near a crocus cluster and another belonging to the Monkeys fresco (Marinatos, III pl. B a). We find them on a kymbe, on strainers and often on ewers. A nippled ewer with a swallow which was found in Mycenae comes probably from Thera (Marinatos 1969: 68). In 1984 beneath the ground floor of the West House several nippled-ewers were found all of them decorated with swallows. They were deposited in shallow pits whose function appears quite enigmatic.

Swallows are always rendered in the same conventional manner, black-and-white and with the bifurcated tail. Very often they are associated with crocuses and lilies, flowers well known for their symbolic dimension (Chirassi 1968: 126-134) and, being bulb plants, often brought in connexion with the cycle of regeneration (*Ibid*: 128-129).

Finally there is one document of crucial importance since it permits a glimpse in the subtle play of the successive subtitutions. A bird, possibly a swallow, is depicted wearing earrings identical to those of the West House priestess (Pl. 13). Is the swallow standing for a girl? Is a definite female character visually symbolized by the swallow and emphasized by the earrings? As we shall see later, swallows as well as earrings point to a common path, youth and its ambiguities.

What kind of approach or interpretation may enable us to comprehend this sequence of related subjects? We may, of course, easily enough classify them in the current conceptual frames of the Minoan religion such as the cycle of life and death or the epiphany of a goddess in the form of a bird. These concepts were elaborated mostly by Evans, Persson and Nilsson. In their syntheses they tried to build a general and coherent system often on the base of similitudes with classical Greek religion. Therefore, we are equipped with interpretative concepts created for the needs of a descriptive synthesis. If we use these as a frame into which every single detail must find a way to fall, even those which tend to differentiate the religious elements in time, space and meaning, this mental procedure which seeks to explain the diverging details with interpretative concepts, seems to me a useless and meaningless tautology which can't help us to define the differences or catch the nuances. As a possible method to enlarge the scope of potential analysis, apart from sorting out the material and establishing the associations or visual connotations, I tried to follow in the Homeric poems the semantic field of the Greek word whose referent is depicted.

Let's have a look again at the Crocus-gatherers fresco. One trait that gets confirmation as restauration and research advances is the fact that the female persons form groups according to their age, presumable role in the ritual or social position. This is suggested by various details in the appearance, which are symbolical. Pausanias describing a fresco in Delphi mentions the same detail on a fifth century wall-painting: "Andromache and Medesicaste wear hoods; but Polyxena has her hair braided after the manner of the maidens" (Pausanias, 10, 25, 10). The same custom seems to prevail here; all girls who take part in these scenes, often considered as an initiation ritual (Marinatos 1984b: 73-84), have their hair uncovered, or seen through a transparent veil, whereas the others, who seem older, have their hair well covered by what in Greek is called the *kredemnon*. These last figures form another group but they still belong to the same pictorial programme. The interesting fact is that all the younger girls who have their hair uncovered wear earrings whereas the elder ones do not. Earrings together with other external features seem to assign them to a social group, determined by age. This kind of female communities must have been an important factor of social integration. In the *Iliad* (III, 175) when Helen evokes the beloved people she left behind, she mentions her daughter and her ὁμηλικίην ἐρατεινήν, the lovely companions of her own age.

In the Homeric poems earrings are mentioned twice with the same formula "ἕρματα τρίγληνα μορόεντα". The first time is in the *Iliad* (XIV, 182). Hera prepares herself for the love-meeting with Zeus: "In her pierced ears she put earrings with three clustering drops; and abundant grace shone therefrom". She wants to convince him to stop helping the Troyans and to achieve this temporary neutrality she asks the assistance of Aphrodite and Hypnos. In doing so she will bring the wrath of Zeus upon herself and disaster on the Greeks. Her intervention by way of seduction threatens the natural and social order of the world expressed by the will of Zeus. The second time is in the *Odyssey* (XVIII, 297). One by one, Penelope's pretenders present to her their gifts. Eurydamas gives her a pair of earrings, the third in importance after a gown and a necklace. Here again we have an attempt of seduction which threatens directly Penelope's marriage. In both cases it is an attempt against the social order and in both cases it gets seriously repressed. In the Homeric context earrings seem to belong to the string of malefic jewels presented to young women by ill-intentioned persons in order to persuade them to forget their duty. They often possess magic powers. This dangerous ambiguity can hardly find a visual expression. We can only see the emphasis put on this detail; as it seems to be the case in the Theran wall-paintings.

Swallows are comparatively rare outside the Cyclades. At Akrotiri we have seen them on wall-paintings associated with lilies and crocuses as well as on vases. Here the interpretation seems plausible. Swallows throughout the whole Greek tradition (Classical, Byzantine and modern Greek) bring the message of spring, the renewal of hope, the resurrection of the earth and the whole nature (Marinatos 1968, 65-66). We find them in Classical vase-paintings, in Byzantine verses and in modern Greek folk-songs. Yet the contrary tradition exists as well. In the *Odyssey,* the swallow brings again a message, but it is one of disaster. Athena takes the aspect of a swallow during the killing of the suitors (XXII, 240) and the sound of Odysseus' bow is compared with the sound of a swallow (XXI, 411). The swallow is connected in mythology with Philomela, the unfortunate heroin who has been deprived of speech. The name of the swallow was used to express the incomprehensible speech, that is, the language of the barbarians. More significant for our scope is the use of the word swallow as a metaphor for the female sexual part (Aristophanes, *Lysistrata,* 770) and this in a context of a reversed order, where the revolt of the Athenian woman threatens their social role. Expression of youth and consequently immaturity, the swallow appears as the visual and mental metaphorical realization of youth, beneficent but socially uncontrollable and therefore potentially malefic.

At the end of this detour, in our attempt to understand the multiple levels of meaning, let us return to our iconographic details. They point to a female personality, young, versatile, ambiguous, dangerously attractive. It is impossible to say by which goddess or goddesses these elements are epitomised. Nevertheless she seems to be the counterpart of the fertility figures, desired, needed and controlled by agricultural societies. Here we are in the cultural sphere of a society whose wealth was acquired by trade, which can afford enough surplus time to permit its female members to elaborate on their appearances and send thus back to it the image of grace and wealth it obviously desires.

Summary

The paper deals with some minor details occurring almost exclusively in the iconography of the prehistoric settlement of Akrotiri on Thera. These details, i.e. the persistent representation of ladies wearing earrings, the decoration of vases with painted earrings — and especially those called nippled-ewers which are frequently associated with fertility and ritual — and the persistent association between swallows, nippled-ewers, earrings and some flowers well known for their symbolic values (lilies, crocuses), tend to differentiate the religious concepts or, at least, denote the multiple levels and meanings of a religion thought to be Minoan.

Résumé

L'étude de quelques détails iconographiques des représentations à Akrotiri (Théra) peut conduire à des conclusions intéressantes quant à leurs particularités et surtout quant aux traits spécifiques de l'iconographie de Théra. Concernant leur interprétation, une possibilité autre que l'application des schémas bien connus de la déesse mère et de son conjoint, serait de s'appuyer aux textes homériques qui peuvent fournir des renseignements instructifs sur les multiples niveaux de signification et les ambiguités de sens de ces mêmes détails.

Bibliography

BARBER, R.L.N.
1978 — Cyclades in the Middle Bronze Age, in Doumas (ed.), *Thera and the Aegean World,* 367-379, London.

CAMERON, M.A.S.
1978 — Theoretical Interrelations among Theran, Cretan and Mainland Frescoes, in Doumas (ed.), *Thera and the Aegean World,* 579-592, London.

CHIRASSI, I.
1968 — *Elementi di culture precereali nei miti e riti greci,* Roma.

DOUMAS, C.
1983 — *Thera, Pompei of the ancient Aegean,* London.

HÖCKMANN, O.
1978 — Theran floral Style in relation to that of Crete, in Doumas (ed.), *Thera and the Aegean World,* 605-616, London.

HOOD, S.
1978 — *The Arts in Prehistoric Greece,* (Penguin Books).

MARINATOS, N.
1984a — Minoan Threskeiocracy on Thera, in Hägg, R. and Marinatos, N., (eds) *The Minoan Thalassocracy, Myth and Reality,* 167-178, Stockholm.

1984b — *Art and Religion in Thera,* Athens.

MARINATOS, S.
1968 — Chelidonisma, *Archaiologika Analekta Athinon,* 65-69.

1968-1976 — *Thera I-VII.*

SAFFLUND, G.
1981 — Cretan and Theran Questions, in Hägg, R. and Marinatos, N. (eds), *Sanctuaries and Cults in the Aegean Bronze Age,* 189-208, Stockholm.

SAPOUNA-SAKELLARAKI, E.
1981 — Oi toichographies tes Theras se schesi me ten minoiken Kreten (Theran frescoes in relation with Minoan Crete), in *Pepragmena tou* Δ*Diethnous Cretologikou Synedriou.* (*Acts of the IV International Congress for Crete*),479-509 Heraklion.

STÜRMER, V.
1985 — Schnabelkannen: eine Studie zur darstellenden Kunst in der minoisch-mykenischen Kultur, in *L'Iconographie Minoenne, Bullettin de Correspondance Hellénique,* Supplement XI, 119-134.

THORPE-SCHOLES, K.
1978 — Akrotiri, Genesis, Life and Death, in Doumas, C. (ed), *Thera and the Aegean World,* 437-447, London.

TZACHILI, I.
1985 — Ta skoularikia tes theas tes Kyprou kai oi mastoprochoi tes Theras (The Earrings of the Goddess of Cyprus and the Nippled-ewers of Thera), in *Praktika tou B' Diethnous Kypriologikou Synedriou* (*Acts of the 2nd International Congress for Cyprus*), Vol. I, 391-401, Nicosia.

UNE INFLUENCE DES RELIGIONS MÉDITERRANÉENNES? ANTHROPOMORPHES, ZOOMORPHES ET PICTOGRAMMES DANS LA MOITIÉ SUD DE LA FRANCE AU 8eme S. AV. J.C.

Jean-Pierre Pautreau

LES DECORS SUR CÉRAMIQUE:

Dans le midi de la France, la Mailhacien montre une utilisation soudaine au Bronze final III b des représentations humaines et animales associées souvent à des signes géométriques symboliques. La quasi totalité des schématisations est effectuée avec la technique du double trait (quelques stylisations au trait simple existent à Mailhac, Sextentio et Mireval-Lauragais) en gestation dans le Bronze final IIIa local. Les incisions devaient être remplies de pâte blanche.

L'interprétation de ces figures reste souvent difficile. Les zoomorphes demeurent le plus souvent assimilés à des chevaux (Millas, Montredon, Mailhac, Las Fados, Mireval-Lauragais...) et l'on trouve parfois des attelages (Lansargues) et des groupes de cavaliers. Certains ont cru voir des bovidés ou des oiseaux (animaux à deux pattes: Las Fados, Mailhac...). Les plus belles gravures animales se rencontrent à Sextantio de Castelnau, Languissel de Nimes, Camp Redon de Lansargues, Montpeyroux de Causses-et-Veyran, Vendres, Grèze de Lodève, Las Fados, En-Bonnes, Montredon et Millas. A Mailhac, sur le Cayla comme à la nécropole du Moulin, on aboutit à une schématisation extrème qui passe sur certains récipients, sans transition nette, à la représentation géométrique pure.

En ce qui concerne les anthropomorphes le problème d'interprétation reste le même et il n'existe pas de frontière entre certaines figurations humaines abstraites, certains animaux stylisés et de simples motifs géométriques. Si l'on considère certaines gravures de Vendres comme étant celles de personnages ithyphalliques, il faut admettre comme humaines d'autres de Montredon, Millas, Vidauque et peut-être certaines zoomorphes de Las Fados. Il n'y a pas de séparation nette entre les rondes manifestes mais stylisées de Las Fados, Mailhac, Vendres, Canet et certains décors en arête de poisson souvent, il est vrai, plus tardifs.

Cet ensemble figuratif s'étend dans toute la zone mailhacienne, de la Provence occidentale à l'Empurdan (Punta del Pi, Agullana, La Verna) (Fig. 9). Il semble que les schématisations les plus poussées correspondent aux horizons les plus tardifs. Les représentations périphériques en direction de l'Aquitaine (Lot, Basses-Pyrénées) sont dans ce cas.

La signification de ces motifs schématiques restera longtemps sujet de débats; toutefois, comme l'a souligné O. Taffanel, il paraît indubitable que nous soyons en présence de la figuration simplifiée de processions, danses ou défilés. Parmi les constantes nous remarquons les personnages se donnant la main, l'association quadrupède-attelage qui évoque des chars, la disposition en files et aussi la mise en valeur du sexe de certains personnages masculins (les assexués sont-ils en fait des représentations féminines?). Quelques figurations montrent des individus dans la position de l'orant (Le Cayla, Sextantio) et d'autres avec les bras levés en "V".

L'ensemble du phénomène présente un caractère religieux fort probable. Les comparaisons restent malgré tout rares; elles se limitent aux deux autres groupes francais puis aux ensembles de la péninsule italienne. La région de Cumes, comme l'aire proto-villanovienne permettent quelques comparaisons. (Aris-Jully 1968: 82; Combier 1972: 41; Louis-Taffanel 1955; 1960; Pautreau 1972: 218; Mohen 1980: pl. 118-182; Pons I Brun 1982: 181).

Dans le Sud-Est de la France, le groupe du Bas-Dauphiné et de la moyenne vallée du Rhône constitue, comme le mailhacien, un groupe original par son utilisation soudaine au même moment (transition Bronze-Fer) de représentations animales et humaines sur sa céramique (Fig. 10). Le traitement des figurations au trait unique par incision plus ou moins profonde, parfois après cuisson, diffère nettement du double trait mailhacien. Cette technique existe pourtant, nous l'avons signalé, dans l'aire mailhacienne (Mireval-Lauragais...). La disposition des motifs n'est pas exactement la même dans les deux groupes.

Les découvertes exceptionnelles de Moras-en-Valloire forment la pièce maîtresse de cet ensemble avec des anthropomorphes isolés et se donnant la main, des oiseaux, chevaux, cervidés et probables bovidés attelés. Les oiseaux (ou du moins zoomorphes bipèdes) existent également à Vidauque de Cheval Blanc (Vaucluse) et Ranc-Pointu de St. Martin en Ardèche. Des chevaux stylisés et attelés ont été mis au jour à Virignin dans l'Ain.

Il faut probablement associer à ce groupe le vase, isolé, des palafittes du lac du Bourget où les petits personnages se donnant la main sont obtenus par application d'étain sur une incision. Les mêmes rives lacustres ont produit un fragment de chenet incisé. Il est probable que les personnages tête-bêche sur bronze de la Ferté-Hauterive en Allier se rattachent au même mouvement. Dans la périphérie de cette même zone, les découvertes de Polignac en Haute-Loire, comme celles de Möringen au Lac de Bienne (Suisse) présentent des techniques légèrement différentes.

Si l'on met à part les rares découvertes lacustres et le tesson de Polignac, l'ensemble apparaît bien homogène. Plus que les motifs, assez proches en fait de ceux du Mailhacien, excepté leur traitement au trait simple, c'est leur disposition et leur organisation qui est ici intéressante. La figuration de scènes de processions ou de défilés du Mailhacien semble ici faire place dans certains cas à Moras-en-Valloire à un message écrit étant donné la disposition cohérente des signes.

La datation de ce groupe semble relativement aisée. Les associations avec des jattes carénées, des vases globuleux à col éversé et fond ombiliqué (Ranc Pointu en Ardèche) et la présence de panneaux de cercles concentriques estampés (Virignin dans l'Ain, St. Uzé dans la Drôme) placent bien cet ensemble à l'extrème fin du Bronze final. On a vu dans ces expressions figuratives le résultat de contacts avec l'Italie du Nord, soit au travers des Alpes (gravures rupestres), soit par le couloir rhodanien et une relation éventuelle avec le Mailhacien (Bocquet 1969: 343; Bocquet-Lebascle 1983: 98; Bocquet-Raymond 1976: 33; Combier 1973: 106; Delporte 1972: 477; Egloff 1980; Nicolas 1978: 56).

Dans le Centre-Ouest de la France, les décors anthropomorphes et zoomorphes qui ornent plusieurs céramiques relèvent du même esprit et permettent de définir un troisième ensemble culturel, parallèle à ceux du Mailhacien et du groupe Bas-Dauphiné-Rhône (Fig. 11).

La belle urne polychrome à décor de lamelles d'étain de Sublaines (Indre-et-Loire) figurant un char attelé à des quadrupèdes rappelle techniquement la découverte de Grésine au lac du Bourget et reste isolée. Une petite écuelle à bord rentrant et fond ombiliqué de la grotte du Quéroy en Charente est ornée d'une remarquable frise où l'on trouve trois petits personnages assexués et deux zoomorphes (chevaux ou oiseaux?) superposés. La grotte de Rancogne a livré une petite urne globulaire à panneaux avec des bonshommes se donnant la main; leur tête est un estampage de cercles concentriques. La couche 3 du Camp

Allaric à Aslonnes (Vienne) a produit les restes de petites urnes ornées par panneaux en damier avec des anthropomorphes se donnant la main et d'autres longilignes séparés par des lignes verticales. Il s'agit dans tout les cas de profondes incisions. Plus à l'Est, les vases de Villement à Ste Aoustrille dans l'Indre sont dans une nécropole contenant des épées hallstatiennes mais pas en association avec celles-ci. Une figuration masculine obtenue par de fines incisions parallèles évoquant la Mailhacien vient de l'Ilot-les-Vases à Nalliers (Vendée). Tout ces éléments, sauf le dernier cité, hors contexte, sont indubitablement associés au Bronze final IIIb et aux premiers instruments en fer régionaux.

La disposition de ces figurations appelle quelques remarques. Nous trouvons encore des rondes, processions (Villement), une apparente notation pictogrammique (Le Quéroy) et surtout la fréquente association de personnages par groupe de trois, identiques et se donnant la main. Cette "triade" se retrouve à Rancogne, au Quéroy, au Camp Allaric, comme elle existe sur plusieurs sites des Alpes et du Mailhacien; il ne s'agit certainement pas d'un phénomène fortuit. (Cordier 1976: 451; Gomez 1974: 72; 1978: 412; Guillien 1968: 321; Meloizes 1889: 15; Pautreau 1980; Pautreau-Gendron-Gomez: 1972).

Les trois groupes: Mailhacien, Dauphiné-Rhône et Centre-Ouest présentent des caractères originaux mais leur ferments semblent identiques. La France du Nord paraît à l'écart de ce phénomène (les figurations du Fort Harrouard à Sorrel-Moussel dans l'Eure restent bien isolées pour l'instant). Il est curieux que les groupes du Massif-Central et du Périgord, pourtant très proches culturellement de ceux du Centre-Ouest, ne connaissent pas dans l'état actuel de la recherche de figurations similaires.

LE DEBUT DU MESSAGE ECRIT:

Les débuts de l'écriture pictogrammique s'inscrivent dans la même période de transition et semblent intimement liés au renouveau des schémas de pensée qui entraine subitement l'éclosion de décors figuratifs. Les régions ayant produit des signes ou ensembles de signes montrant un notation sinon une écriture primitive se limitent aux zones où l'art figuratif et les chars cultuels sont connus: Palafittes, vallée du Rhône, Languedoc, Roussillon et Centre-Ouest (Fig. 12). De rares éléments se trouvent à l'extérieur de ces contrées (Fort-Harrouard et Clayeures).

Les plats mis au jour à Moras-en-Valloire (Drome) et le vase du

Quéroy à Chazelles (Charente) montrant des signes similaires disposés de facon cohérente constituent les éléments majeurs de ces débuts de l'écriture. D'autres récipients (Camp Allaric, Le Quéroy) rassemblant des curieux signes impressionnés strictement géométriques et bien abstraits, appartenant aux mêmes niveaux, peuvent correspondre à un autre système de notation.

Il est fort probable, au regard des signes le plus souvent utilisés (soleil, croix de St. André, svastikas, anthropomorphes se donnant la main, attelages, chevaux, oiseaux...) que la préoccupation de ces messages soit d'ordre religieux. Là encore, le phénomène n'atteint principalement que les régions méridionales de la France et nous invite à chercher des comparaisons ou des origines vers les cultures méditerranéennes. C'est au 8ème siècle que les écritures grecques et étrusques se mettent en place (Gomez 1974: 143; Gomez 1978: 394; Nicolas 1978; 56; Nicolas-Martin 1972: 35).

LES MODELAGES EN ARGILE, LES BRONZES:

A la même époque, mais sur une aire legérement différente de celles des céramiques à décor figuré — et il ne s'agit vraisemblablement pas du même phénomène — se rencontre toute une série de représentations humaines et animales modelées en argile ainsi que quelques bronzes. Ces modelages schématiques ne se trouvent pas dans les régions bordières de la Méditerranée (à l'exclusion de la statuette d'oiseau de Mourèze dans l'Hérault) où on les rencontre plus tardivement; mais ils sont connus dans le Centre-Ouest, la région palafittique et un peu plus au Nord. Bien qu'un genre similaire de statuettes soit connu au Néolithique, celles-ci appartiennent bien au Bronze final III b.

Dans le Centre-Ouest, des petites figurines théromorphes, modelées en argile ont été mises au jour sur le gisement de l'Ermitage dans le littoral du pays de Retz et au sein du niveau 3 du Camp Allaric. L'habitat de Chalucet à St. Jean-Ligoure (Haute-Vienne) a livré trois figurines anthropomorphes en argile cuite. Il faut associer à ces modelages une tête d'oiseau, extrémité brisée d'une chenet en terre cuite du Coteau de Montigné à Coulon (Deux-Sèvres) et un possible tronc de statuette à la grotte du Quéroy.

A ces figurations d'argile modelée, il convient d'ajouter quelques représentations en bronze comme la petite tête de cervidé ornant la brôche à rôtir de Challans en Vendée, le quadrupède de l'instrument similaire de Notre-Dame-d'Or (Vienne) et peut-être le canard sans contexte de Chédigny (Indre-et-Loire). Bien datées dans les dépôts de l'extrême fin du Bronze, les broches à rôtir ornées se trouvent dans une bonne partie de l'Europe (forêt de Compiègne, Portugal, Sardaigne) montrant l'européanisation des croyances (les clefs des régions palafittiques portent des décors zoomorphes similaires).

Dans l'Est, à Euvry (Marne) on rencontre trois petites statuettes anthropomorphes associées à un matériel du début du Ier âge du Fer; à Cercy de Gumery (Aube) une figurine schématique féminine est dans un contexte Bronze final. Sur les rives du Lac de Bourget, plusieurs modelages anthropomorphes et zoomorphes ont été mis au jour; il est possible de les rapprocher de ceux rencontrés en Suisse à Corcelette (oiseau et porc). Dans le Massif Central, à Brézet, une statuette quadrupède ayant servi de support entre dans la même catégorie.

Il faut probablement inscrire dans cette ambiance culturelle les vases zoomorphes et les figurines d'Alsace (Haguenau, Hoxlandsberg et Marlenhiem). Les régions du Centre-Est et du Sud-Est connaissent également des objets figuratifs en bronze; si la pendeloque de Charroux (Allier) avec disque solaire et tête de cygne date du passage Bronze-Fer, d'autre figurations appartiennent pleinement à l'âge du Fer, qu'il s'agisse des trépieds de Ste Colombe et d'Auxerre ou de quelques bronzes du Vaucluse, des Hautes-Alpes et du Jura.

L'usage rituel de ces objets bien divers ne fait pas de doute: les figurines du Camp Allaric étaient disposées près du foyer; on a parlé de "sanctuaire" pour les statuettes d'Euvry; le caractère d'instrument de culte du chenet est bien connu; le décor d'oiseaux et de cervidés, l'aspect luxueux des broches à rôtir les destinent certainement au repas rituel. L'oiseau mythique (canard ou cygne), les cervidés se retrouvent dans une grande partie de l'Europe sur les vases et chars votifs.

Nous avons là une émanation incontestable des religions liées à la "culture" des champs d'Urnes, apparue avec les premiers courants Rhin-Suisse (vase ornithomorphe de Tigy, Loiret, Bronze final II). Le phénomène n'est probablement pas sans rapport aucun avec les décors de vases évoqués plus haut, mais il s'agit d'une manifestation d'essence bien différente qui va se prolonger dans l'âge du Fer sur une immense partie du territoire européen alors que le décor "céramique" disparaît rapidement dans les cultures françaises et ne perdure pas du tout au Ier âge du Fer.

LES CHARS, LEUR FIGURATION ET LE CULTE SOLAIRE:

La présence de figurations d'attelages et probablement de chars a été soulignée sur les décorations des céramiques en association avec les anthropomorphes, zoomorphes et autres signes. Il est indéniable que la roue et le char, symboles du disque solaire, connaissent un développement sans précédent lors de la période qui nous intéresse. La plupart des chars processionnels à roue massive en bronze trouvés en France peuvent être attribués aux 8ème et 7ème s., qu'ils soient munis de 5 ou 6 rayons: Coulon, Triou (Deux-Sèvres), La Côte-St. André (Isère), Nîmes (Gard), Langres (Haute-Marne), Fâ (Aude). Les chars à roue de bois renforcée de garniture en bronze, parfois considérés comme utilitaires à la différence des précédents, nous aménent dans les mêmes horizons chronologiques (Choussy, Ouroux-sur-Saône, Vénat) (Fig. 13).

Si l'on examine la carte de répartition des restes de char, des roues miniatures et des figurations de char sur céramique ou pierre, on constate qu'elle recouvre exactement celle des représentations anthropomorphes et zoomorphes, mettant en valeur les trois foyers culturels de la moitié Sud de la France: Mailhacien, Bas-Dauphiné - Vallée du Rhône et Centre-Ouest où les changements sont profonds et où le fer apparaît précocement.

REMARQUES GENERALES:

A la suite de ce court exposé, quelques remarques s'imposent:

— L'existence de figurations anthropomorphes, zoomorphes, d'attelages associés à plusieurs signe géométriques est attestée sur des céramiques de trois régions du Sud de la France et ceci dans un contexte culturel et chronologique bien défini: le Bronze final IIIb ou si l'on veut la période charnière entre les âges du Bronze et du Fer (8ème s. av. J.C.).

L'absence de ces décors figuratifs incisés dans les autres régions méridionales et au Nord de la France au même moment ne semble pas la conséquence d'une indigence de la recherche (mais il faut demeurer prudent: les fouilles d'habitat restent rares).

— Les reproductions de chars, les fragments de chars eux-mêmes, correspondant à la même époque, se cantonnent quasi strictement aux régions déjà définies.

— Les ensembles culturels dans lesquels apparaissent ces

représentations résultent de l'évolution locale d'un substrat d'origine Rhin-Suisse qui s'est mis en place au plus tard au Bronze final II b, même dans les régions les plus périphériques (Côte Atlantique avec l'Ile de Ré; Catalogne avec Can Missert) avec les nouvelles coutumes funéraires. On y trouve les caractères propres au Bronze final IIIb. Les figurations sur céramique n'existent pas dans les groupes septentrionaux à la culture matérielle assez similaire et restent exceptionnelles dans les régions palafittiques.

— Le caractère religieux de ces schématisations (orants, processions, ithyphalliques) est quasi certain.

La majorité des auteurs ont toujours expliqué ces manifestations comme le résultat d'une influence méditerranéenne. Toutefois, si l'on examine les expressions graphiques des religions de la Méditerrnée au même moment, on s'apercoit que les éléments absolument similaires s'avèrent rares. Certes on peut rapprocher quelques figurations mailhaciennes de celles de Cumes en Campanie avec tête en chapeau chinois, bras et jambes en V renversé. Les anthropomorphes se donnant la main se rencontrent bien dans l'Helladique moyen puis en Crète; mais il n'existe pas de véritable solution de continuité. On ne trouve de ressemblances que dans le Proto-villanovien puis plus tard au ler âge du Fer dans la culture de Golasecca.

Ces décors, étant donnée leur répartition différente de celle des statuettes et figurations en bronze de cervidés ou oiseaux "des Champs d'Urnes", leur absence dans les groupes septentrionaux de tradition Rhin-Suisse, n'appartiennent vraisemblablement pas à l'ambiance culturelle des Champs d'Urnes et n'en constituent pas du moins une phase évolutive normale.

L'éclosion semble sumultanée dans le Proto-villanovien et dans les trois groupes francais. On pourrait envisager une origine commune dans les montagnes alpines (où les figurations rupestres sont bien connues) avec diffusion vers la plaine du Pô d'une part puis vers la vallée du Rhône et le Languedoc d'autre part. Cette hypothèse ne tient pas compte du groupe Centre-Ouest et il serait étrange que les cultures lacustres, toutes proches des Alpes, soient restées en dehors du phénomène.

Les pictogrammes à caractère religieux apparaissent dans la France méridionale comme dans la péninsule italienne au moment où vont se mettre en place les écritures étrusques et grecques. Les processions, cortèges et chars traités schématiquement sur les céramiques du Centre-Ouest, du Bas Dauphiné ou du Languedoc-Roussillon peuvent être des expressions d'une mythologie comparable à celle que l'on retrouve sur les céramiques grecques d'alors. Les figurations très stylisées, periphériques, ne sont peut-être que des copies par des potiers étrangers, de symboles religieux ayant perdu leur signification première. La culture de Golasecca qui prolonge ces expressions en plein ler âge du Fer semble n'être qu'un épiphénomène ou tout simplement l'expression des croyances de tradition Champs d'urnes comme le sont les bronzes et statuettes déjà évoqués.

Les contacts de la France du Sud avec le monde méditerranéen sont une permanence. A l'époque qui nous intéresse ici, les fibules de type sicilien se retrouvent dans les dépôts atlantiques, les pointes de flèche à barbelure et pédoncule allongé et renflé, marquant des rapports avec les cultures égéennes se rencontrent dans le Mailhacien mais aussi dans l'embouchure de la Loire et même le bassin de la Seine (mais leur usage a pu s'étaler du 8ème au 5ème siécle).

Bien que l'état de la recherche ne permette pas encore des interprétations précises, nous pensons que anthropomorphes, zoomorphes et pictogrammes de la moitié Sud de la France au 8ème siècle ac. J.C. sont vraisemblablement la manifestation graphique du changement de mentalité qui affecte, plus sensiblement que les autres, les régions en contact avec le monde méditerranéen. C'est de là que semblent issus la plupart des éléments novateurs: écriture, aristocratie de guerriers prètres et surtout changement du mode de vie avec tendance à l'urbannisation. Le nouvel équlibre socio-économique, mélé aux apports orientaux, se diffuse assez vite à l'ensemble du territoire.

Résumé

Au 8ème s. av. J.C., les céramiques de trois régions de la France du Sud portent brusquement des décors figuratifs schématiques. Ces expressions picturales d'essence religieuse semblent devoir se rattacher aux influences des cultures méditerranéennes que se font jour alors.

Bibliographie

ARIS R., JULLY J.

1968 — A propos d'un fragment de céramique inédit, à décor incisé, provenant de Cessero (Saint-Thibéry, Hérault), *Cahiers Ligures de Préhistoire et d'Archéologie,* 17, pp. 82-101.

ARNAL J., PRADES H.

1976 — L'art de la civilisation des Champs-d'Urnes et les chars processionnels en France. IXème congrès U.I.S.P.P., colloque 27, *Les gravures protohistoriques dans les Alpes,* Nice (prétirage) pp. 39-51.

BOCQUET A.

1969 — L'Isère préhistorique et protohistorique, *Gallia-Préhistoire,* XII, 1-2, pp. 121-400.

BOCQUET A. - BALLET F.

1979 — *Il y a 3000 ans...les artisans du Lac du Bourget.* Centre de documentation de la Préhistoire Alpine, Grenoble.

BOCQUET A., LEBASCLE M.C.

1983 — *Metallurgia e relazioni culturali nell'Età del Bronzo finale delle Alpi del Nord Francesi,* La memoria della terra 1.

BOCQUET A., REYMOND J.

1976 — Deux vases protohistoriques d'un abri-sous-roche de Virignin (Ain), *Etudes Préhistoriques.* 13. pp. 33-35.

CHEVILLOT C.

1976 — Trois statuettes anthropomorphes en argile cuite provenant de l'habitat protohistorique de Chalucet, commune de Saint-Jean-Ligoure (Haute-Vienne), *Bulletin de la Société d'Etudes et de recherches préhistoriques des Eyzies,* 25, pp. 61-69.

CHEVILLOT C. - GOMEZ J.

1979 — Roues de char et statuettes en terre cuite de Chalucet (Saint-Jean-Liguore, Haute-Vienne). Leur signification culturelle, *Bull. Soc. Préhist. Fr.,* 76, 10-12, pp. 434-444.

COMBIER J.

1972 — Figures zoomorphes et anthropomorphes, *Etudes Préhistoriques,* pp. 41-44.

CORDIER G.

1975 — Les tumulus hallstattiens de Sublaines (Indre-et-Loire). I Etude archéologique, *L'Anthropologie,* 79, 3-4, pp. 451-579.

DEDET B.

1978 — L'habitat de hauteur du Grand-Ranc à Boucoiran (Gard) et le Bronze final III B dans les Garrigues du Languedoc oriental, *Gallia-Préhistoire,* 21, pp. 189-206.

DELPORTE H.
1972 — Informations archéologiques, circonscription d'Auvergne et Limousin, *Gallia-Préhistoire,* 15, 2, pp. 457-485.

DUVAL A., - ELUERE C., - MOHEN J.P.
1974 — Fibules antérieures au VIème siècle avant notre ère trouvées en France, *Gallia,* XXXII, pp. 1-61.

FORRER R.
1932 — Les chars cultuels préhistoriques et leurs survivances aux époques historiques, *Préhistoire,* I, pp. 19-123.

GARMY P.
1973 — *L'oppidum protohistorique de Roque-de-Viou (Gard).* A.R. A.L.O. 1.

GOMEZ J.
1974 — Décors et signes gravés sur les céramiques de la grotte du Quéroy à Chazelles (Charente), *Revue Hist. et Arch. du Libournais,* pp. 72-77, 152-154, 145.

1978 — La stratigraphie chalcolithique et protohistorique de la grotte du Quéroy à Chazelles, Charente, *Bull. Soc. Préhist. Fr.,* 75, pp. 394-421.

GUILAINE J.
1972 — *L'Age du Bronze en Languedoc occidental, Roussillon, Ariège,* Mém. Soc. Préhist. Fr., Paris.

GUILLIEN Y.
1968 — Informations archéologiques, circonscription de Poitou-Charentes, *Gallia-Préhistoire,* XI, pp. 281-335.

LOUIS M., - TAFFANEL O., - TAFFANEL J.
1955 - 1960 — *Le premier âge du Fer languedocien. I - Les habitats; II - Les nécropoles à incinération; III - Les tumulus. Conclusions.,* Bordighera, Montpellier.

MELOIZES A. des
1890 — Un cimitière gaulois à épées de bronze découvert à Villement, commune de Sainte-Aoustrille et Thizay (Indre). Note sur deux épées de bronze trouvees à Bourges et à Déols, *Mémoires de la Société des Antiquaires du Centre,* pp. 15-36.

MOHEN J.P.
1977 — Broches à rôtir articulées de l'âge du Bronze, *Antiquités Nationales,* 9, pp. 34-39.

1980 — *L'Age du Fer en Aquitaine,* Mém. Soc. Préhist. Fr. 14, Paris.

MORDANT C.
1981 — La figurine en terre cuite des "Hauts de Fourches" à Cercy, commune de Gumery (Aube), *Bull. Soc. Préhist. Fr.,* 78, 1, pp.14-15.

NICOLAS A.
1978 — Inventaire des Picto-idéogrammes de la fin de l'âge du Bronze et de début de l'âge du Fer. *Bull. Soc. Préhist. Fr.*, 75, pp. 56-64.
NICOLAS A., - MARTIN B.
1972 — La céramique incisée de Moras-en-Valloire (Drôme), *Etudes Préhistoriques*, pp. 35-38.
PASSELAC M.
1983 — L'habitat du Bronze final IIIb de l'Estrade à Mireval Lauragais (Aude), *Documents d'Archéologie méridionale,* 6, pp. 7-12.
PAUTREAU J.P.
1972 — Un vase hallstattien à décors anthropomorphes, au Camp Allaric, commune d'Aslonnes (Vienne), *Bull. Soc. Préhist. Fr.,* 69, pp. 218-224.
1984 — Les figurations humaines et animales du ler âge du Fer dans le Centre-Ouest de la France, *Eléments de Pré et Protohistoire européenne,* Hommages à J.P. Millotte, pp. 449-457.
PAUTREAU J.P., - GENDRON C., - BOURHIS J.R.
1984 — *L'Age du Bronze en Deux-Sèvres. La cachette de Triou,* Niort.
PAUTREAU J.P., - GENDRON C., - GOMEZ J.
1972 — Une figuratio.. anthropomorphe hallstattienne à l'Ilôt-les-Vases, commune de Nalliers, Vendée, *Revue du Bas-Poitou et des Provinces de l'Ouest,* pp. 247-250.
PERRIN A.
1870 — *Etude préhistorique sur la Savoie, spécialement à l'époque lacustre (Age du Bronze),* Paris, Reinwald, Chambéry.
PERRIN J.
1936 — Une figurine en terre cuite de l'Age du Bronze découverte à Cercy (Aube) par M. Lapôtre, *Bull. de la Société de Sens,* 39, pp. 333-388.
PESCHECK C.
1976 — *Das Kultwagengrab von Acholshauser.* Wagweiser zu vor und frühgeschichtlichen Stätten Mainfrankens, Haft 3, Hürsburg.
POINS I BRUN E.
1982 — La poblaciò mailhaciana establerta a l'Empordà. Noves aportacions, *Estat Actual de la recerca arqueològica a l'Istme pirinenc,* 4ème Colloqui internacional d'arqueologia de Puigcerda, 1980, pp. 181-194.
ROUDIL J.L.
1972 — Chars protohistoriques, *Etudes Préhistoriques,* 2, pp. 38-40.
TAFFANEL O.J.
1948 — La nécropole hallstattienne de Las Fados (Pépieux) (Aude), *Gallia*, pp. 1-29.
TESSIER M.
1965 — Sites côtiers de l'Age du Bronze du Pays de Retz (Loire-Atlantique), *Annales de Bretagne*, LXXII, pp. 75-85.

SECTION II: PREHISTORY, MALTA

THE PREHISTORIC MALTESE ACHIEVEMENT AND ITS INTERPRETATION

Colin Renfrew

It is a privilege and honour to be speaking here at the University of Malta, and for us to be celebrating together one of the most important achievements of World Prehistory. It is, at the same time, I think, one of the least understood achievements of World Prehistory. The great temples of Malta and the art of prehistoric Malta are not yet perhaps as well known universally as they ought to be. They are famous among archaeologists but I think they deserve still greater celebrity! Certainly when I was looking again at those great temples at Mnajdra and Ħaġar Qim yesterday, and then going down the Hypogeum at Ħal Saflieni, I felt that if one were to draw up a list of the seven great monuments, the seven wonders of the prehistoric world, there is no doubt that one of these (perhaps one would choose Ħal Salfieni, perhaps it would be the Ġgantija), would be on the list. What I would like to do first is to set the scene, as it were, and to stress the point that we now know that the full development of these monuments, in the Ġgantija phase, took place somewhere around 3500 B.C. in calendar years. In the early phase in their development we are speaking therefore of a phenomenon which is comfortably earlier than the pyramids of Egypt. The apogee of development in the Tarxien period can be placed somewhere between 3000 and 2500 B.C. These remarkable and complex monuments, with their extremely sophisticated art, including wonderful spirals, are thus to be placed in the third millennium B.C. Among those extraordinary works of art, the most remarkable certainly must have been the monumental figure of a woman, probably a deity set in the temple at Tarxien. As you know only the legs remain, but she must rank as one of the earliest monumental sculptures in the world, the only competitors perhaps being the sculptures of Egypt in the Old Kingdom.

We can indeed celebrate these achievements, but how well can we interpret them? It is when we come to the religious interpretation, which is part of the focus of our Conference that matters become very much more obscure. I think they are obscured partly because we have inherited a series of myths, as it were, only some of which we have yet learnt to put aside. In this paper what I want to do, as well as speaking some cautionary words and I hope indicating where some hope of progress may lie, is to focus on some of those myths which we have already learnt to discard, which formerly obscured the way to further progress, and to indicate one or two myths which I think we could with benefit also set on one side.

In the face of these great monuments, it is appropriate for us to remember one or two of those people who have contributed so much to our understanding of them. The first was Sir Themistocles Zammit with his early and pioneering excavations at these sites. We have all certainly learnt a very great deal from Professor John Evans whose standard work *The Prehistoric Antiquities of the Maltese Islands* (1971) will remain, probably for ever, one of the fundamental statements on these sites. Then we have profited much from Dr. David Trump and from his wife Bridget through their excavations at Skorba (Trump 1966) and subsequently. I would also like to acknowledge those Maltese colleagues who over the years have been very generous with their time and help — Mr. Francis Mallia, formerly Curator of Antiquities, and Mr. Tancred Gouder, who is at present, of course, Curator of Antiquities here in Malta. I would like to thank Dr. Anthony Bonanno also for bringing about this Conference.

Now for the myths! We can recognise very easily one or two which today we can see impeded earlier progress. The first was the myth of the Minoan connection. For certainly, it so happened that some of the early discoveries in Malta were being made at the very time that the important excavations of Sir Arthur Evans and his associates in Crete were bringing to light the Minoan civilisation. Perhaps for that reason, and because of the relative proximity of the two islands, it was natural that early Maltese scholars and early interpreters of the temples thought in terms of Minoan influence. Of course that remains an active hypothesis to this day. But it was assumed rather than demonstrated, and I think it became one of the impediments to further study of the monuments.

Secondly, there is the simple notion, which is no doubt quite reasonable in a sense, that the Maltese momuments are 'megalithic'; they are built of large stones. Nobody could dispute that simple truth. But this has led many to relate them directly to the megalithic monuments of western and north-western Europe, particularly coastal Europe, Atlantic Europe: a questionable point. Moreover to relate the deity or deities of the Maltese megalithic temples to whatever deities may have been associated with the various megalithic phenomena in western Europe makes a very dangerous assumption.

There are other myths to doubt, and Dr. Bonanno has already referred to one, which has been very effectively questioned some time ago by Dr. Peter Ucko and also by Mr. Andrew Fleming. That is the myth of a universal Great Earth Mother. The curious thing about many of these myths is that they came into our minds, into the scholarly world that is, in the very early days of scholarship, long before there was much evidence which might or might not justify them. So as archaeologists we started off with the assumption of a universal Earth Mother; you can read it in the writings of Schliemann and others even before the Minoan civilisation was discovered, although it was only after the discovery of the relevant material that this myth gained its greatest force. But the circumstance that the explanation was available before the evidence for it came to light underlines, I think, the very hypothetical and indeed dubious nature of that explanation. Now I do not doubt that we can with great profit discuss the possibility of a universal or at any rate a Mediterranean fertility cult in the early period. That would be an interesting hypothesis. I have rarely seen it presented as a hypothesis, but often offered instead as an accepted truth, (although not accepted by me, and I hope it is not accepted as an *a priori* truth by yourselves).

So my moral is that one must be ready to reject these old myths and to start anew with the Maltese antiquities. Of course, one must indeed be willing to study other religious manifestations and particularly religious manifestations whose iconography has some resemblances with that of early Malta. Let us indeed look at any cults which give us products in the religious iconography similar to those wonderful human figures of the Maltese temples. Let us then look at different structures in different classes of religion. No doubt there may be much to learn from discussion of Demeter and Persephone, from Phoenician deities and from the Near-Eastern precursors of those Phoenician deities. But what I would like to stress is that in the study of early religion we still lack, in my view, a coherent methodology for accurate comparison. For that reason it is all too easy to observe some figure in some other part of the world, whether nearby or distant, to recognise it as a 'fat lady', and since we have fat ladies in the Maltese temples, to conclude there must be some relationship. Well of course there is a resemblance! We live in a world which is partly inhabited by fat ladies after all, and so we must not be surprised sometimes to see them represented in the iconography. The same remark, can be made about spirals. We live in a world where, if one doodles with pen and paper, or with a stick on sand, it will be a miracle if one does not get some spirals very quickly. One of the great truths, (perhaps the only truth) of semiotics is that symbols have meanings which are often arbitrarily ascribed. That is to say that when one sees an object which has some symbolic function, one may well be able to recognise that is a symbol but one cannot *a priori* know *of what* it is a symbol, because the meaning is likely to be arbitrarily ascribed. So that when we look at spirals we can think of the sky, or we can think of the sea, or we can think of eyes or breasts or even of genital organs. Our imagination can run riot. Perhaps it will run riot during the course of this Conference! But it is important for us to remember the underlying point that we do not know *a priori* the meaning of symbols. When in another part of the world we see two spirals we should not be quick to recognise the *oculus* motif, the eyes of the Great Mother looking at us. Nor should we identify two spirals as representing procreation in the form of the reproductive organs of the Great Mother. Nor again should we immediately see breasts or twin suns or whatever. These symbols have to be analysed within their own context.

The right way to proceed is to look at the religious iconography of a given region first of all, in its own terms. And while we may make these far-ranging comparisons to give ourselves ideas, we must be sober in trying to assess them within their own context. I would like to give you two examples where I think this has been accomplished so successfully — one is the work of Martin Nilsson, that great scholar, who wrote so effectively about the Minoan and Mycenaean religions and their iconograpgy (Nilsson 1950). The other, happily here with us at this Conference, is Professor Marija Gimbutas, who has made such an intensive study of the iconography of the figurines of the neolithic period of south-east Europe (Gimbutas 1974).

FOUR KINDS OF CONTEXT

It is necessary to establish three or four contexts in any study of early religion. First of all we have to define very closely the temporal context: to define with great clarity what are the dates we are speaking of. Secondly we have to establish the spatial context. That is very much more difficult, for while of course we know where we are, where the finds have been made, the question is where we shall draw the borders of our study. In my own view we should in the first instance be willing to draw the borders quite narrowly. Then of course, we can look beyond them. If we are studying the Maltese prehistoric religion, the relevant borders are first of all those around the Maltese Islands. Then of course we can look beyond and examine other areas which may have had interaction with Malta. But we have to demonstrate what can be said about Maltese prehistoric religion first of all in that context.

The third context is the social context. It is imperative if we are going to speak about early religion that we have at least some general notion of the structure of society. It is a truism, yet perhaps one that has some validity, that when there are very hierarchical societies, for instance state societies, there are often very hierarchical pantheons as well. So that when one looks at the very hierarchical societies of the Near East or of Geometric and Archaic Greece, it is not surprising to find hierarchical pantheons too. Often there is a reflection of the social organisation in the religious organisations. Without wishing to exaggerate the significance of that notion, it is useful to look at the context in that way.

The point has already been made that until only 15 or 20 years ago the spirals of the Mycenaean shaft graves, dating from around 1600 B.C. (found by Schliemann at Mycenae, a century ago), and their comparison with the spirals from the temples at Tarxien, offered the principal dating evidence for the Maltese temples. Even John Evans put some emphasis on the similarities here which led him to give a date of around 2000 B.C. for the developed phase of the Tarxien temples. And he put great emphasis also on the spirals on the ceiling at the Ħal Saflieni hypogeum.

Today largely through the work of Evans in establishing a reliable stratigraphic sequence, and then that of Dr. Trump in refining that sequence, and providing radiocarbon samples to be dated, there is a sound radiocarbon chronology. With the calibration of radiocarbon dating it was possible to see that chronology in a new light (Renfrew 1972). It is clear that this was one of the myths, and that one would be wrong today to relate these spirals directly with those of Crete.

The next myth, as we saw, was the relationship between the Maltese temples and the megaliths of north western Europe. In the 1930s and 1940s this notion of a movement of people and ideas from Crete was widespread. So the megalithic tombs of Italy and Sicily, and the Maltese temples were considered as part of the same movement, which continued to Spain and to the megaliths of Europe in general. That idea again has now been discarded so that when we look at one of the great monuments, for instance in the Orkney Islands, in North Scotland, we can recognise something whose architecture we can admire and study but which has no relationship to the Maltese architecture other than in being very sophisticated, and very old and pre-urban. We are still in a sense suffering from that sense of surprise which to start with we all feel when we perceive that these great achievements in Malta, or in this case Scotland, were indeed achieved by a pre-urban society. One cannot strictly speak here of a 'civilisation' since in the English language we relate civilisation and *civitas* whereas in French 'civilisation' is used in a wider cultural sense.

More recent work has suggested that there was independent development in different parts of Europe for the megalithic tombs and undoubtedly also independent development in Malta for the Maltese temples. The calibrated dates for the Maltese sequence, which it was possible to establish a decade or more ago, indicated the important periods here; the Mġarr period of the early temples, the Ġgantija period about 3000 B.C., which is the period of the major development of the great temples, and then the Tarxien period which is the climax when most of the art was produced. It must have ended around 2500 B.C. That gives us a chronological context.

As concerns the spatial context, it is clear that mistakes were made in relating Malta to the Aegean. I am not suggesting that we should not be free to make these comparisons, but I think recent experience makes us cautious of accepting them too readily. I am also cautious about possible comparisons with Sardinia. Recent developments in Sardinian archaeology have shown us the great wealth to be seen there and we know also that these are roughly contemporary with developments in Malta. We do have some ways of monitoring the extent of contact between Malta and other areas — for instance the obsidian trade, which shows that obsidian from Pantelleria and Lipari was reaching Malta already in the earliest Għar Dalam period. There are indications of contact and movement, but no suggestion that the contact becomes more intense at the period of the temples; indeed it may have become less so.

In considering social context and comparing the achievements, for instance the great buildings, in pre-state societies, sometimes it is useful to use the concept of the chiefdom. That is a very general concept and may have weaknesses in that respect, but it allows us to think at the same time of Polynesia — or of some of the great monuments of the British Isles like the henge monuments, and it allows us to consider what the society was like. Without a very highly stratified society, without a very hierarchical society in Malta, what was the society like which produced these great temples? The answer surely has to be that there must have been some centralised organisation to bring about these great achievements, albeit without the strict hierarchy of a state society, for we find no evidence in the artifacts for individuals of great personal wealth. It is perhaps legitimate to use as a first approximation this concept of the chiefdom.

The spatial distribution of the monuments perhaps supports that. Some years ago I produced a map (Renfrew 1973: 154), (later improved by Dr. Trump 1983: 72), to suggest that it may be possible to think of the Maltese Islands as a number of territories, each territory with a small group of temples, typically two temples, sometimes more, which will have served as a focal point of the territory. In the early phase of Maltese temples, in the Ġgantija phase, it is perhaps appropriate to think of some territorial distribution in this way. Here one can also use the idea of competition. It is quite useful to compare the Maltese parishes, where the churches vie with one another (and that firework display last Saturday night was a fine example of conspicuous consumption of wealth!) Above all one is impressed by the construction of the churches, these enormous churches — I think it is quite legitimate to use our insights into these achievements of modern construction, and indeed of modern faith. We could of course misinterpret them, I have no doubt, but I suggest that in the competitive territoriality of some of the more pious and energetic of the Maltese parishes today we may see something of the same phenomenon which we note in these remarkable and gargantuan constructions of prehistoric Malta. That sets the scene, as it were, in terms of the social context insofar as we are able to do.

THE STUDY OF EARLY RELIGIONS

I now want to make one or two remarks about the study of early religions, because as I said at the beginning we have very little in the way of a framework. I want to say something first of all about analogy, because in this Conference we are deliberately looking at other religions, and therefore are making analogical comparisons. When we see a similarity between one fat lady and another, if we are talking about a fertility cult we should be able to realise there are at least four possible underlying causes for such an analogy.

One is common ancestry. When we see a fat lady sculpture in Malta and a fat lady in prehistoric Greece, then it may well be that they are similar because they have a similar ancestry. In other words there could be a common cultural background.

Secondly and quite separately is the question of what one might call structural homology. That may be a rather pompous term, but it simply means resemblance of form coming about without a direct common cause. In this case, one might expect to find a fat lady in the iconography of Greece and a fat lady in Malta because in real life you may equally find a fat lady in each place. One has nothing to do with the other; there is no relationship between the two.

Thirdly, it may be a question of analagous process. In other words there may be sequences of development in the religion in each area, quite independent developments, which lead to an emphasis on certain properties of similarity.

And fourthly it may be a question of convergent evolution, to borrow a term from the biologists, where the similarities become progressively more evident.

So I think we have to try and bear in mind these possibilities and each time we are offered an analogy we have to consider the relative merits. I would like to stress that there is absolutely no presumption in favour of the first, in favour of common ancestry. One has to *demonstrate* the common ancestry if we are going to use that as a conclusion. There is therefore no presumption in favour of an Early Neolithic Great Mother. The Early Neolithic of the West Mediterranean is in any case not particularly abundant in those female figurines which we do see at Çatal Hüyük, and indeed in south east Europe. The absence of such a widespread abundance of such figurines predisposes me not to accept too readily the notion of a universal Great Earth Mother. So I am not in the least chastened by the discoveries at Çatal Hüyük, to which Dr. Bonanno referred in his opening remarks.

TRANSFORMATIONS

Religious like social organisation undergoes transformations and these transformations have their own internal dynamic. That may not seem a very remarkable statement. But there is the tendency among archaeologists, when changes take place, to try to derive from outside the reasons, the underlying causes for these transformations. Usually we should look instead inside within the developing trajectory of the society for the underlying dynamic of the transformation. If we use the notion of internally produced transformations then we can perhaps begin to see how in the very early beginnings in the Żebbuġ phase we come to developments which grow in the Mġarr phase. We don't always have to be drawing from outside for our inspiration.

This may be illustrated with reference to the religions of the Aegean. My reason for making this comparison is not to liken the Aegean finds with those of Malta, but on the contrary to emphasise how in the Aegean we have an autonomous series of transformations, which again have sometimes been explained through external agencies, but I think needlessly so. We may begin with the Greek fat ladies — for instance from the isle of Crete, in the neolithic period. In the early bronze age there were indeed these remarkable marble figures which have sometimes been called fertility figures, but they are very rarely fat. On the contrary they are extremely thin, and if you prefer thin ladies it is to the Cyclades that you should turn! When we come to Early Minoan Crete we do indeed see some splendid representations of women in the form of pottery vessels. Some of them may relate to fertility, and some of them also relate to liquids — milk, water, wine perhaps. Then in the Middle Minoan period, the early period of Cretan palaces, we do indeed have development of some sort of pantheon. There may be a whole range of deities. The most remarkable figure comes from the Temple Repositories at Knossos in the Middle Minoan III period. But interestingly the Minoan palaces themselves do not seem to have been temples, and the main religious centres seem to have been outside in the hills, the peak sanctuaries. And then we come to the Late Bronze I period around 1500 B.C. in Crete, and the apogee of the palace civilisation. The wonderful stone vase from one of the Cretan palaces at Zakro may actually give a representation of a peak sanctuary. It represents a mountainside with mountain goats at the top. Contemporary with it are the gold double axes from the sacred caves at Arkalochori. When you look across to Mycenae on mainland Greece, you find influences from Minoan Crete well represented in the great gold finger rings found there, but Mycenae developed its own different traditions so that by the Late Helladic IIIA and IIIB periods around 1400 B.C. and a little later, one finds the remarkable terracotta figures from the temple at Mycenae. This represents a further development and the gesture with the upraised arms is significant. This is picked up in Crete after the collapse of the Cretan palaces when the great religion of the Cretan palaces must have suffered a setback. It must have lost its priests, and have become a popular religion. One then finds a whole series of little shrines, with the Minoan Goddess with upraised arms. Now I indicate this sequence of forms simply to illustrate how the iconography changed with the centuries. Things of one period are not the same as those in another. This is a series of transformations. And late in the Minoan period in Crete there appear Mycenaean figurines during the Late Helladic IIIC period around 1100 B.C. Now it is worth noting that until recently most of the deities known in the Mycenaean world in the form of figures or figurines were female. It is not until the Geometric period in Greece that we see male deities clearly represented. But my own recent excavations in Melos have shown us that the transformations there began earlier. On the island of Melos, at the site of Phylakopi, we found a Sanctuary which began its life sometime in the 14th century B.C. and continued right on into the 11th century. It takes us right through the late Mycenaean period. I haven't time to describe the buildings in detail to you. The main shrine is quite a small and modest room, but the Sanctuary had a large number of items of iconography (Renfrew 1985), including a small gold head, perhaps from some cult figure and a whole series of splendid bovid figures, which are amongst the finest from the Mycenaean world. We had the great good fortune to find one beautiful figure about 40 cm high, the 'lady of Phylakopi' (*ibid.*pl 31). She is a remarkable work of art. But she too illustrates the difficulty of making gender distinctions. If you looked at the head alone you might think it was bearded. But some other convention is being followed there: I don't believe it is bearded and most scholars agree that this is a female deity. In addition we have a series of male figures which are really without close comparison in the Mycenaean world. This is why I am taking your time to indicate these things: it is to illustrate this idea which I want to emphasise of internal transformation within a religion. The conventional view of the Greek religion has sometimes been that there was a Mycenaean religion and then a collapse, and a Dark Age and then a new religion, namely the Greek religion. Sometimes this change is associated, quite erroneously I think, with ideas about the Indo-European languages. Now we see that the development of the Greek religion should be seen instead as a whole series of transformations and that one of the major transformations was occurring already during Mycenaean times. We should expect, when we are looking at the development of Maltese religion to see in the same way a series of transformations, and we shouldn't necessarily be looking for external causes for these transformations. Interestingly, we had at Phylakopi two male figurines in bronze of this period which are imports from the Near East, so I am not trying to argue the case for complete isolation. Certainly there were contacts and sometimes significant interactions between different areas. But I think these should be seen in perspective.

THE MALTESE CASE

Now let us turn to Malta again and use the background of the notion of spatial context, temporal context and the social and the cognitive contexts, and the idea of transformation, to look again briefly at the Malta temples and their associated cults.

It is very important to start with Dr. Trump's find at Skorba of female iconography. These female figurines are amongst the earliest representation from Malta of the human form. The Skorba phase is a millennium or so before the great temples, and we do perhaps have some indication of the early religious observances. It is difficult of course to correlate the small figurines found in any area with any coherent religious observance because we don't have a very good context for them. But it is a fair assumption perhaps to make that they have such a significance.

And then in the Żebbuġ phase, the time when the rock-cut tombs make their appearance, there is the important find of the menhir from Żebbuġ. John Evans was amongst those who suggested that the rock-cut tombs could be a starting point for the development of the Maltese temples and it is significant that we have this early iconography. It may well be female iconography, but that is not easy to establish from the head alone. It may be relevant to the later development of the temples. Then you will remember that from among the earlier temples, namely the temple at Mġarr, there came the delightful little temple model (Evans 1971: pl. 33, 11-12), which also helps us to realise how the temples may have been roofed. From the Tarxien period comes an exciting fragment of a temple, a model which has been reconstructed by Professor Stuart Piggott (*ibid.* pl 47, 7-9; Trump 1983: 68, fig. 5). It is a wonderful thing that we have these graphic representations from the Neolithic period of what these temples looked like. I think it is essential to remember one of the reasons for the technical accomplishment of the Maltese temples; that the rock was such as to allow easy construction. This no doubt is true for some of the great modern achievements of Maltese architecture also. So it was in Orkney in Scotland, which I referred to earlier. If you have a wonderful stone which is easy to work, then it is not surprising that you may find remarkable architectural achievements. This of course must be one of the contributory reasons for the accomplishments of Maltese civilisation. But when we come to the spirals, I have no easy explanations to offer for their great sophistication. For me these are really the high point of Maltese art, in the great sophistication of these abstract motifs which I enthused about earlier and in the very great variety in their forms.

One factor then, if we are looking at the internal development in the architecture and the art, is the ease of carving the stone. Another is the very feature of insularity. When we analyse the position of Malta, it is ready-made for strong interaction. But of course that has been one of the principal themes of Maltese history. If we look at the Knights of Malta or the great days of Malta as a naval centre, Malta's very existence was as a focal point, as a centre of interaction. But in periods when transport is less easy, islands are also obviously a locus for insularity, and insularity is in some ways almost the opposite of such interaction. It is a remarkable feature in prehistory that in many different cases we find insularity allowing a sort of exaggeration, a sort of hothouse effect as if the reverberations of the culture can't get out and don't spread themselves more widely, but are reinforced by the insular status. That is of course what we find so clearly in Polynesia. So that when we look at Easter Island, we see great monuments which arose partly because of the remarkable insularity of Easter Island, partly through local social developments towards a chiefdom society. Clearly there were very competitive tribes and chiefdoms. I am not presuming here to give an explanation of the achievements of Easter Island or of Malta but I am emphasising relevant features. In Malta we have remarkable developments in art: in Easter Island you have the development of the rongorongo writing and indeed the remarkable local artistic developments.

My last point is to stress that I think we can recognise deities in Malta. If I had more time I would give a more coherent background to this observation, but I think there is certainly one, perhaps more than one, female deity in the Maltese temples. There are two arguments that would lead me to this conclusion. One is the great scale of the major statue at Tarxien. It is rare to make monumental, larger than life-size statues unless you are referring either to a great ruler (and I don't think in a non-state society that is appropriate), or to a deity figure. The other argument is one of relationship in scale. There are two very important sculptures in the Museum of Valletta. The first piece is unfortunately much damaged and shows the feet of a seated fat lady and on the back or the side there are remarkable little figures of standing ladies who are subordinate to the great figure (Evans 1971: pl. 48, 1-3). I think that when there are artistic representations of *subordination* then the depiction either represents a great human leader with little human people, (which one often finds in a state-society), or it represents a divine figure with little human people. The same observation occurs in another place in the Museum in Valetta, again incomplete (*ibid*. pl. 48, 4-5). Here one sees the legs and skirt of one of these great ladies and with her there is a little seated figure of an acolyte. If we are looking for concrete arguments for the divine status of this figure, then I find this conjunction, really quite a significant one.

In conclusion I would like to mention that if one is analysing the early Maltese religion one should certainly note the presence of the various phallic representation, although curiously in the developed phase, the Tarxien phase, one sees groups of two if not three phalli represented rather than a single one. One should not, however, get carried away, if I might say so, by these phallic representations. There is clearly something of religious significance here, but religion can have many sides, many aspects, and it is not appropriate to try and unite everything into one central simplifying idea of "fertility".

One should offer a further cautionary word about the famous sculpture sometimes identified as a priest (*ibid.* pl. 49, 11-13). First of all it could easily be female because the torso, is restored. Secondly there is absolutely nothing that teaches us that this it not a divine figure rather than an acolyte.

My final thought is that far from understanding the Maltese religion well, we do not in fact know a great deal about the contexual background, as I have tried to show. It may well be that we are on the threshold of making the necessary significant observations, and in order to make them properly I think we have to cast aside the older interpretations of a universal Great Mother, and the automatic belief in the existence of a fertility cult. It is not clear to me precisely what the notion of a fertility cult entails and I shall be interested to see if anybody else at this Conference really knows what they mean by the concept of "fertility cult". That is something that I hope we shall learn in the days to follow!

Bibliography

EVANS, J.D.

1971 — *Prehistoric Antiquities of the Maltese Islands*, London (Athlone Press).

GIMBUTAS, M.

1974 — *The Gods and Goddesses of Old Europe*, London (Thames and Hudson).

NILSSON, M.P.

1950 — *The Minoan-Mycenaean Religion and its Survival in Greek Religion*, 2nd ed., Lund.

RENFREW, C.

1972 — Malta and the calibrated radiocarbon chronology, *Antiquity*, 46, 141-4.

1973 — *Before Civilisation*, London (Jonathan Cape).

1985 — *The Archaeology of Cult: The Sanctuary at Phylakopi*, London (Thames and Hudson).

TRUMP, D.H.

1966 — *Skorba* (Reports of the Research Committee of the Society of Antiquaries of London XXII), Oxford.

1983 — Megalithic architecture in Malta, in C. Renfrew (ed.), *The Megalithic Monuments of Western Europe*, London (Thames and Hudson).

THE SIGNIFICANCE OF THE NUDITY, OBESITY AND SEXUALITY OF THE MALTESE GODDESS FIGURES

Cristina Biaggi

The Maltese Goddess figures from the late Neolithic (3200 - 2500 B.C.) stand out as unique expressions of their creators' conceptions of the numinous. They represent the continuation of a philosophical idea given visual form by a long line of female deity figures originating in the Paleolithic. Because of their particular characteristic — some figures are nude, other clothed, some do not show primary sexual traits, and all are obese — there have been considerable and diverging speculations about their significance. Although there has been abundant research and writing on the Maltese archaeological material since the beginning of this century resulting in a variety of different interpretations, so new comprehensive examination as to the specific morphology and meaning of the figures has been made for the past two or more decades.

It is the purpose of this paper to focus on the morphology, archaeological context and derivations of these images, to discuss various interpretations concerning the significance of their nudity, obesity and sexuality, and to offer additional explanations concerning their form and meaning.

About thirty of these figures ranging in size from 20 cm to about 3 meters have been found in the late Maltese temples and in the Hypogeum. Most of them were carved from Globigerina limestone and then painted with red ochre. They seem to be a product of local development, for there is nothing else quite like them in the Mediterranean. The prototypes for these figures reside in the Paleolithic — e.g., the Venus of Willendorf, the Venus of Lespugne and the Savignano Venus — via the Mediterranean early Neolithic — e.g., the Anatolian figures at Hacilar and Çatal Hüyük, the early Neolithic figures of Greece and the Balkans, the Seated Fat Lady of Saliagos, the Predynastic figures of Egypt, and many others.

There are basically two varieties of figures: nude and clothed. The nude figures share certain characteristics. They are all represented as being enormously fat, with huge buttocks, bulbous thighs, legs, arms, and forearms, a corpulent chest and tiny hands and feet. A further feature is that they lack all sexual characteristics, either male or female. They appear in various positions and stylized poses. There are standing figures, and squatting or seated figures with legs folded to the left or right (Pls. 14-16).

The seated figures average 22 cm in height. Hands are placed gracefully either at the sides or on the folded legs. Some figures lack heads but have a hollow socket between the shoulders for a separate head. Small holes around the neck area indicated that a head was attached by means of a dowel or string that could be used to make the head move (Evans 1959: 142). The separate carved heads are small in proportion to the bodies (Evans 1959: pls. 55 - 56). The face is oval, the hair close to the head, the eyes small and set horizontally, the nose wide with a definite ridge, the mouth small with full lips, and the chin barely indicated. Prototypes for the poses of the seated figures were found among Predynastic Egyptian figures (Weinberg 1951: 1) and in the Balkans (Renfrew 1969: 28 - 29); figures with small separate heads were discovered at Hacilar (Mellaart 1970: 168-178).

The standing figures are less numerous, but much larger — 49 cm in height. Usually three rolls of fat appear at the abdomen, and the legs are so stylized that sometimes the figures seem to be wearing shorts. Some figures stand on pedestals that have carved motifs on the sides.

Clothed figures are represented sitting on stools or couches (Pls. 17-18). These figures are dressed in bell-shaped skirts that reach halfway down the legs. About seven of these clothed figures, either complete or fragmented, have been found in various sacred inner areas of the Maltese temples and in the lower chambers of the Hypogeum. They vary in size from 23 cm high to an estimated 2.75 m. Some display a necklace or dècolletè which is reminiscent of earlier deity figures along the Mediterranean. One fragment from Tarxien shows part of the calf and fringed skirt of a draped figure seated on a stool (Evans 1971: pl. 48, 4-5). Four small figurines of the nude fat variety are represented below the figure's skirt. The largest seated goddess figure which, when complete, was about 2.75 m high, belongs to this variety. She wears a full pleated skirt and is supported by small feet. She stands on a pedestal that is decorated by a relief reminiscent of the "egg and dart" pattern of Classical Greece. (Pl. 19).

It is significant that the Maltese Goddess is depicted both nude and clothed. Clothing and adornment are and always have been symbolic of rank and status; nudity has been used symbolically in art to elicit emotions and to express ideas. That some of the figures are nude and others clothed might signify that they were meant to have different functions in Maltese religion. Perhaps their special sanctity and magical power was increased by their nudity. Perhaps they represented different aspects of the same deity to be invoked on different occasions and for different reasons, or perhaps they even represented different deities.

That the clothed and nude figures represented a similar divine being is suggested by their similarities: both are fat, are approximately the same size, show traces of red ochre, are made of stone, had moveable heads, stand on pedestals, come from the same period and neither shows sexual characteristics. The moveable heads could have been made to move in ritual to assent or dissent a particular request made by a worshipper. Their differences show that they represented different numinous aspects of the Goddess: the clothed figures are often seated on a stool decorated with sacred symbols, wear a bell shaped skirt, and are shown with much smaller figures crowding below; while the nude figures stand or squat and are always alone. These trappings of rank, the sacred stool, the bell shaped skirt, and the necklace, suggest a special numinous quality and are found in other recognized deity figures around the Mediterranean — e.g., the Enthroned Goddess of Çatal Hüyük or the Snake Goddess of Crete. The clothed Goddess or her priestess had to be approached and addressed in a certain manner, after certain preliminary rituals had been completed, much like the Pithia of Archaic Greece.

The clothed and nude figures could represent two aspects of the Goddess, perhaps invoked at different times and for different reasons. The seated figure could be the Great Mother of all, while the nude figures could be the quintessential fecund vegetation Goddess. The clothed figures could be the Goddess, shown sometimes with her votaries or acolytes depicted much smaller than herself and seated under her skirt. She could represent the Goddess as queen, sitting properly gowned and adorned on her earthly throne. The queen may have been considered to be the human manifestation of the Goddess, her divine representative on earth, just as the Egyptian Pharaoh was regarded as the human manifestation of Horus, while the nude figures could simply depict the Goddess in her extreme opulence. Perhaps the nude figures, representing the opulent sensual Goddess, were ritually clothed during certain sacred periods of the year. Finally the nude and clothed figures could have represented two aspects of one deity worshipped by different groups in Maltese society.

The claim that the purpose of the nudity of the figures was to "excite the senses of males" (Battaglia 1927: 141) is unwarranted given the fact that the figures were found in the sacred areas of the temples and that they were covered with red ochre, the sacred annointment of death and rebirth. The nude figures could have evoked erotic-mystical emotions in both sexes in the early Maltese society which was unencumbered by later patriarchal sexual codes that objectify and therefore preclude the mystical in the female body.

The significance of the figures' obesity is based on a long tradition dating from the Paleolithic period. "...The 'Monstrous Venus' of prehistory was one manifestation of a long-enduring tradition of cosmogonic myth as old...as human culture. Its evolution may be seen in later form, even in historic times. The 'Monstrous Venus' is a religious representation — the reification of the Life Genetrix" (Gimbutas 1981: 18). The obesity of the Maltese figures may have been a measure of their sanctity. Zammit believes that obesity was associated with power, wealth and fertility; that it was related to sanctity and was considered a desirable and beautiful condition (Zammit 1924: 77). Ugolini thinks that it symbolized prosperity (Ugolini 1934: 124).

Although these scholars believe that the obesity of the Maltese sculptures was symbolic, Battaglia seems to think that it was inspired by obese living models who were considered special in their society (Battaglia 1927: 159). According to Battaglia there are two problems to solve: 1) the nature of this obesity, and 2) the reasons for reproducing obese female figures.

Battaglia divides the figures into three groups according to geographical and chronological distribution: Mediterranean-Balkan (Malta, Crete, Aegean, the Balkans), Egyptian-Ethiopian (Egypt, Ethiopia), and Berber (West Sahara, Gran Canaries). In each group the figures are dealt with in slightly different ways. In some cases (Gran Canaries), neither the breasts nor the pubic region are shown. In others (Balkans), the breasts are not emphasized, but the pubic triangle is slightly visible. Still others (Bulgaria), which are very stylized, stress the pubic triangle, but not the breasts. Breasts are not a necessary component in the representation of females. Obesity in Neolithic representations can take several forms: in some cases specific parts of the body are enlarged (the legs and hips, as in the Canary Islands); in others, the entire body is obese (Malta, Rumania).

To support his contention about living models, Battaglia draws evidence from a number of writers, both ancient (Xenophon) and modern (Jãos dos Barros, John Speke, Mehmed Emin Paşa), who had witnessed actual examples of extreme, artificially produced obesity around the Mediterranean and in Africa (*Ibid.* 159). Artificially induced obesity was still practiced in Tunisia, Algeria and Morocco at the time of Battaglia's writing (*Ibid.* 151).

Obesity in women could have had a magical function, to favor fecundity (*Ibid.* 159). According to Neolithic and even Paleolithic peoples, a woman is endowed with magical powers which, among other things, have influence on the growth of vegetation. "Therefore, according to the law of mimetic magic, to increase the volume of her body by fattening is to increase the intensity of the magic powers which emanate from her" (*Ibid.* 159). Although natural obesity in women may have been thought to favor fecundity in ancient times, I think that artificially produced obesity is a product of a patriarchal culture because it presupposes the loss of woman's control over her own body, which is not a characteristic of early Goddess worshipping cultures.

It is my contention that the stylized obesity of the Goddess figures was established to create an aesthetic-symbolic connection with the temples. Rachel Levy believes the shape of the Maltese temples was inspired by the seated deity figures (Levy 1946: 111-113). Even though Levy's theory is valuable because it establishes a link between Maltese sculptures and architecture, I believe that the sculptor was inspired by the architect, and not the other way around. There is a strong and undeniable affinity between the shape of seated goddess figures and the shape of the temples. This becomes apparent when one compares the temple shape with the little clay temple model and then compares it with the goddess figure, especially as seen from the back (Pls. 20-22). Because Maltese sculptors could see the contour of the models at one glance, they may have realized that the shape of temples resembled seated figures. This may have inspired them to stylize their sculptures so that they echoed the temples, rendering them more effective as sacred images.

There are diverging opinions concerning the sexuality of the Goddess figures, for they lack primary sexual characteristics. The nude figures do not have apparent breasts nor evident vulvas. However, a roll of fat appears on the chest. The fact that there is no central division within this mass of fat to separate the breasts in a naturalistic fashion has caused scholars to claim that the figures represent males. However, if one examines the seated or standing figures from the back, one will notice that the furrow of the buttocks is not delineated — in fact the buttocks appear as a continuous surface. This stylized departure from realism was obviously adopted in the depiction of the breasts (Battaglia 1927: 143). Furthermore, the vulvas of the figures are not visible in the seated or standing figures because they are obfuscated by the fat.

Zammit claims that the sexless figures are male, even though there is never any indication of a phallus or a beard (Zammit 1924: 74). The lack of sexual attributes can be discerned in other Neolithic representations thought to be female, such as the goddess images of Çatal Hüyük. In these the reproductive organs are not shown (Mellaart 1967: 202). Evans states that the sexless quality of these figures, probably the result of a gradual evolution, had become incidental and did not detract from their power as deities (Evans 1959: 142).

Christopher Kininmonth thinks that the figures might have represented eunuchs (Kininmonth 1979: 54). After lengthy examination of the figures, I concluded that, despite the lack of clearly defined sexual characteristics, the statues appeared more female than male. Their lack of sexual characteristics might be due to extreme stylization and to a change in ideology. In early art, male figures usually exhibit male characteristics (a beard, a phallus), or their physical shape and their stance designates them as males (the Sumerian priest figure and the Cycladic cupbearers). In the so-called Maltese priest figure the reconstruction of the chest area which eliminates breasts seems totally arbitrary (Evans 1959: pl. 60). It's more likely that the figure was a priestess. Therefore, I do not think that the nude deity figures represent males. It is difficult to believe that more than twenty statues, laboriously carved in stone with stone tools, were meant to represent eunuchs, beings who have been shorn of their fertility, which was considered so crucial in early societies.

The lack of sexual characteristics is prevalent in the Paleolithic and early Neolithic female figures, which far outnumber male figures. The femaleness of a figure is gleaned from other characteristics such as morphology, context, or its similarity and derivation from other female figures. At Hacilar "The absence of marked breasts...a possible indication of youth, frequently contrasts with marked opulence" (Mellaart 1967: 178). The wide hips and narrow shoulders of the Maltese figures certainly are more female than male; no male figures in early art look like the Maltese figures. Red ochre with which the figures were painted, which may have been menstrual blood in its earliest manifestation, is the color of fertility, death and rebirth — the color of the Goddess.

The lack of sexual characteristics might represent the result of a process of evolution from figures whose power as sacred images lay in well defined sexual characteristics, to figures whose power lay in their opulence. The sex of the figures may have been deliberately left out to concentrate on the most important thing — the fatness and therefore the opulence and sanctity of the figures. The lack of sexual delineation in the late figures might also be interpreted as a recognition of the similarities between the sexes, as in the Medieval angels, whose sexuality was not apparent. But, because they are the product of Maltese religion, which was female oriented, these nude figures were more female than male. The Medieval angel, on the other hand, is assumed to be male, because he is the product of the patriarchal Christian religion. The Maltese figures seem to embody cosmic power and overflowing fullness on a superhuman scale which is beyond dualism, beyond sex.

These very fat sexless goddess figures contrast with the earlier Skorba figures (Trump 1966: pl. 26) and with other contemporary figures, such as the Sleeping Priestess (Evans 1971: pl. 36, 6-9) and the Venus of Malta (Evans 1959: pl. 65) all of which (the Skorba figures) have strongly emphasized pubic regions. All of these figures are made of clay and are much smaller than the earlier figures. The attributes of the earlier figures could be the result of the newly established religion brought to Malta by the first colonists and influenced by the prevailing artistic depiction of the numinous which, at that point, emphasized sexual characteristics. Depictions of the numinous tend to increase in size and elaboration or stylization when a religion becomes entrenched in a society. The Sleeping Priestess figure is not the Goddess, she is a priestess engaged in dream incubation, adept in giving oracles, interpreting dreams, or suggesting cures for illness. The Venus of Malta is very different from the larger stone goddess figures because of her size and her naturalistic proportions and stance. Her slightly voluminous yet natural form recalls Paleolithic figurines, e.g., the Savignano figure (Antonielli 1925: pls. 1-2). The faint traces of red ochre on her body suggest that she must have been important, either as another aspect of the Great Goddess that had its roots in the Paleolithic, as a priestess, or a fetish figure. The position of her arms might be significant in identifying her as a fetish figure, created to insure the fertility of a particular woman.

The worship of the Great Goddess was universal from the upper Paleolithic to the late Neolithic in Europe and the Near East. The Maltese goddess figures represented the very stylized visual manifestation of that worship in Malta. The nude and clothed figures represented two aspects of the Goddess; their obesity was important because it implied power, sanctity and fecundity, because it strengthened their symbolic connection with the temples which they resembled in shape; and their sexlessness signified their universal quality — female in identification, but beyond the dualism of male and female.

The Maltese scenario may have gone like this. The Maltese had a female centered culture and worshipped a Great Goddess. Priestesses guided in temporal as well as religious matters. But, contacts from abroad put the Maltese — especially a dissatisfied contingent dominated by men — in touch with new ideas. Men became more and more active in the religious practices; their temporal power also increased, as perhaps in trade. In the meantime, the economy of Malta was failing. Over-population and soil exhaustion caused disease and famine (Trump 1966: 51). A political crisis ensued and a large part of the population migrated to the mainland. The balance of power was thus upset, the priestesses lost their credibility and the remaining Maltese were weakened, thus making it easy for the bronze wielding people to come in and take over without much struggle.

Summary

This is an examination of the Maltese Goddess figures from the late Neolithic (3000 - 2500 B.C.) that represent the continuation of a philosophical idea given visual form from a long line of female figures originating in the Paleolithic. Thirty of these figures, both nude and clothed, have been found in the late Maltese temples and in the Hypogeum. The product of local development, they share two important characteristics: obesity and lack of sexual traits. After evaluating the figures themselves and what has been said about them, I concluded that the nude and clothed figures represented two main aspects of the Goddess. Their obesity was important because it implied power, sanctity and fecundity, because it strengthened their symbolic connection with the temples which they resembled in shape. And their sexlessness signified their universal quality — female in identification, but beyond the dualism of male and female.

Résumé

Il s'agit d'une étude des sculptures maltaises de la Grande Déesse parvenant du Néolithique tardif (3000 - 2500 B.C.); elles représentent la suite d'une idée philosophique qui a pris forme à partir d'une longue ligne de sculptures féminines qui eurent leur origine à l'époque paléolithique. Trente de ces sculptures nues et vetues, ont été trouvées dans les derniers temples de Malte et dans l'Hypogée. Produit du développement local, elles ont deux caractéristiques en commun; l'obesité et l'absence de traits sexuels. Ayant évalué les sculptures elles mêmes et ce qui a été écrit à propos j'ai conclu que les sculptures nues et vetues représentent deux aspects de la Déesse; leur obesité était importante parce qu'elle impliquait le pouvoir, le sacré et la fecondité, car elle renforçait leur relation symbolique avec les temples dont elles ressemblaient la forme; l'absence des traits sexuels signifiait leur qualité universelle — d'une identification féminine, mais celle-ci outre le dualisme du mâle et du féminin.

Bibliography

ANTONIELLI Ugo

1925 — Una Statuetta femminile di Savignano sul Panarò ed il problema delle figure dette "Steatopigi", *Bollettino di Paletnologia Italiana,* XIV, 1-3.

BATTAGLIA Raffaelo

1925 — Le statue neolitiche di Malta e l'ingrassamento muliebre presso i Mediterranei, *IPEK,* Vol. II.

EVANS J.D.

1959 — *Malta,* London (Thames and Hudson).

1971 — *The Prehistoric Antiquities of the Maltese Islands,* London (Athlone Press).

GIMBUTAS Marija

1981 — The "Monstrous Venus" of Prehistory or Goddess Creatrix, *The Comparative Civilization Review No. 7,* 10, 3.

KININMONTH Christopher

1979 — *Malta and Gozo*, Revised Edition, London (Jonathan Cape).

LEVY Gertrude Rachel

1946 — *The Gate of Horn*, London (Faber & Faber Ltd.).

MELLAART James

1967 — *Çatal Hüyük,* London (Thames and Hudson).

1970 — *Excavations at Hacilar,* Edinburgh (The University Press).

RENFREW Colin

1969 — The Development and Chronology of Early Cycladic Figurines, *American Journal of Archaeology,* 73, 1.

TRUMP David H.

1966 — *Skorba* (Reports of the Research Committee of the Society of Antiquaries of London XXII) Oxford.

UGOLINI Luigi M.

1934 — *Malta Origine della Civiltà Mediterranea,* Rome (La Libreria dello Stato).

WEINBERG Saul S.

1951 — Neolithic Figurines and Aegean Interrelations, *American Journal of Archaeology,* 55, 2.

ZAMMIT Themistocles

1924 — Neolithic Representations of the Human Form from the Islands of Malta and Gozo, *Journal of the Royal Anthropological Institute of Great Britain and Ireland,* LIV.

THE MEGALITHIC TEMPLES OF MALTA
An Anthropological Perspective

Giulia Battiti Sorlini

Malta is the biggest island of an archipelago that lies about sixty miles from the south-east corner of Sicily and about two hundred miles from the coasts of Africa. It covers an area of ninety three square miles. The other islands are Gozo, Comino, Cominotto and Filfla, but only Gozo is here of importance not only for the archaeological memories of the Ġgantija temple, but because of a legend still lingering in the memory of the people regarding a female ruler of Ġgantija. According to this legend, "the temple was built not by a man, but by a woman with a baby at her breast. Strengthened by a meal of magic beans, she is said to have taken the huge blocks of stone (some of which are forty to fifty tons) to the site in a single day, and then to have built the walls by night" (Cles-Reden 1962: 78). The legend is very simple but its originality lies in the protagonist, a woman with a child at her breast for once not represented as a helpless creature looking for shelter and protection, but as the heroine of an epic poem, the maker of the temple and maybe of the Universe.

Malta is scattered with the ruins of thirty odd megalithic structures in which evidence has been found that witnesses to the existence in prehistoric times of a religion in which the image of a woman godhead was paramount. This religion, dispatched by many scholars as fertility cult because apparently lacking the manifestations of a full fledged organized state religion of historic times, might have been the really first universal monotheistic cult. The archaeological evidence for the possibility of the existence of this religion is provided by thousands of statuettes of the so-called Venus figurines type found in different contexts and sites, which at Malta, most scholars agree, were the representation of the Maltese Goddess.

Until the coming of radiocarbon dating and, later, the more precise technique of radiocarbon dating calibrated through dendrochronology, the chronology of the Old World prehistory was based on the theory of diffusion. This theory, postulated by Childe and other scholars, assumed the spread of culture to be a continuous process from the Eastern Mediterranean toward Europe. But even Childe found it difficult to explain the temples and other artifacts of Malta as a mere development of ideas coming from the East. In 1925 he wrote: "No significant parallels are at the present known to the temples, the carvings, the statuettes, or the pottery. Motives adorning the 'neolithic' buildings and ossuaries have been derived by Sir Arthur Evans from the Middle Minoan II repertoire; Professor Schuchardt has found in the same ornaments the prototypes of the Cretan. It is still quite impossible to say whether Malta played the role of master or disciple among her neighbours, and fruitless speculations on this topic had best be omitted" (Childe 1925: 133).

Later on J.D. Evans, another scholar who studied Malta's temples in great detail, wrote: "It is, I hope, abundantly clear...that the Maltese temples and tombs were something indigenous, rooted in the beliefs and customs of the people whose religion they express, and they evolved step by step with these. There seems to be no question of their having been introduced as a result of influence from other cultures" (Evans 1959: 133). And in 1981, D.H. Trump again points out Malta as one independent center of megalithic architecture: "That island offers perhaps the clearest argument for the ability of the prehistoric Mediterranean peoples to make startling progress without having to await stimulus from more advanced centres elsewhere" (Trump 1981: 102).

In the light of the previously mentioned recent dating techniques, the temples of Malta become the oldest known stone buildings of such magnitude in the Ancient World and the preceding theory of diffusion, "ex Oriente lux", is challenged.

The Maltese sequence can be broadly divided in two periods: the period of the so called Temple People and the successive period of the Tarxien Cemetery. This paper will deal with the former period only.

Malta has an area of about ninety square miles and it is scattered with remains of megalithic structures varying in size between buildings that cover only a few square yards and buildings that cover several thousands square yards. These buildings were once believed to be tombs, but no burials have been found in them and most scholars seem to arrive to the same conclusion that these buildings were temples.

Who were the people who built them, why they built them and why they shaped them as they did are some of the questions that we can only try to answer.

The shape of the Maltese temples is unique and the main characteristic of this architecture is the absence of straight lines (as visible in any picture representing the planimetry of a temple). This is true for the architecture proper of the temple and for the decorations which are based primarily on the spiral motif. The emphasis is on curving lines: "...the circular snake, the uroboros, which as The Great Round, or sphere, is a still undifferentiated whole, the great vault and vessel of the world, which contains in itself the entire existence of early man and so becomes the Archetypal Feminine..." (Neuman 1961: 42). This characteristic shape seems to have no counterpart anywhere else in the world.

It is rather difficult to describe the shape of the temples because they cannot be satisfactorily enclosed into any known geometrical figure, nor do they resemble any existing architectural structure. Commenting on the possibility of simpler shapes for buildings in stone, Evans calls the plan: "...odd and arbitrary, yet is obviously deliberately chosen and followed. One gets the irresistible impression that an attempt is being made to reproduce something from another medium, so clumsy and ill-adapted does it seem" (Evans 1959: 88). Could the other medium that was attempted have been, instead, another dimension? That is, could it be that the makers of the temples were trying to reproduce in two dimensional form the three-dimensional curves of the body of the Goddess?

The origin of the shape of the temples, always according to Evans, might be the reproduction above ground of rock-cut tombs already existing in Malta. Since the temples, apparently, were never used for burial, why then should their shape imitate that of a tomb?

To this Evans answers as follows: "...the rites to be celebrated there have to do with the dead. That this was the case is confirmed by everything that we can learn about the religion of the ancient Maltese and it can be further supported by calling in evidence from abroad. The collective rock-cut and megalithic tombs of Western Europe, whose close analogies with the Maltese monuments have already been referred to, are all in some degree shrines whose rites for the propitiation of the ancestor-spirits were carried out, often in the area enclosed by a monumental concave facade, like those of the Maltese temples. In these collective tombs we frequently meet with representations of a female figure, a sort of personification of fertility (often thought of in primitive religion as being under the control of ancestor-spirits), comparable to the obese deity who plays such a large part in the later development of the Maltese cult" (Evans 1959: 91).

But all this still does not explain the very peculiar and unique shape of these buildings. To me, a better explanation is that given by

Guenther Zuntz, which, by the way, coincides with the one I personally had after seeing many statuettes representing the Maltese Goddess and the layout of the temples. "These buildings reproduce, in a fixed symbolic form, the body of the Great Mother; as medieval churches reproduce the cross of Christ" (Zuntz 1971: 8).

This possibility becomes even more appealing when we take into consideration the results of ethnographic studies by J. W. Fernandez in "Fang Architectonics". By architectonics Fernandez means "...the particular relatedeness in the quality of experience in various kinds of space — mythical, cosmological, domestic, social and personal" (Fernandez 1977: 38). The condensation of the complex symbolism of the Fang is represented by the structure of the cult house and its assimilation to the womb. We will never be able to know exactly what kind of rites were taking place in the Maltese temples, but the vivid description given by Fernandez and the interpretation of the ritual dances taking place inside the chapel are worth being considered as hypothetical ethnographic parallels.

After the gathering of all members outside the chapel: "The men and women then divide into two dance groups. ... The women enter first. The three senior female members of the cult, Yombo, are clothed in white and precede the rest of the membership which is clothed in regular red and white ritual garments. These women, candles in hand, dance into the chapel bringing a small stone found in a clear sacred pool in the forest. This stone, sent to man by Nyingwan Mebege, the female principle of the universe, is the principle of creation — the stone of birth — ..." (Fernandez 1977: 34). Immediately after the entrance of the women, the men's dances take place: "The men arriving at the birth entrance of the chapel halt there. The leaders place their hands on the thatch or the lintel piece above them, then the entire group in close packed formation backs up and comes forward again, this time proceeding a short distance into the chapel. This process continues until the male group arrives entirely within the chapel to begin their circles therein.... These ritual actions at the birth entrance are variously explained as 1) the difficult birth of men out of this life into the spiritual world of the ancestors, and 2) the entrance of the male organ into the female body. The first explanation confirms the assimilation of the chapel space to the spiritual world and the second explanation confirms the assimilation of the chapel to the female body. ...In the multilevel explanation for the men's ritual entrance we have an association between the primary processes of sexual orgasm, birth and death — for the entrance dance represents the sexual entrance, the dying out of this world and the birth into the next" (Fernandez 1977: 35).

The spiritual reality that exists within the cult house of the Fang might have existed in the temples of Malta, and the plan of the temples might indeed represent the shape of the body of the Goddess.

Neumann too describes the temple "...as a symbol of the Great Goddess..." and the temple gate as "...the entrance into the Goddess..." (Neumann 1961: 158). He who entered the temple was entering the body of the Goddess, that same body that had received the dead, whose bodies had been sprinkled with red ochre.

Traces of red colour have been found on plaster covering the walls of the temples, on statuettes of the Goddess and on dead bodies as well.

Since paleolithic times, the sprinkling of red ochre on the bodies of dead people has been interpreted by most scholars as having some kind of magical power related to death, usually associated with a non-belief in an after life. I am of a completely different opinion and I think that the red ochre represented the colour of life, the colour of blood, the colour which surrounds the body of the baby coming out of her mother's womb and, by consequence, the same colour that should surround the dead going back into the Great Goddess' womb. Actually, if we consider the presence of the women figurines as possible evidence of a Fertility cult, I think we should consider a fertility cult as another possible explanation for the lack of a cult of the dead and, moreover, for the absence of secular and funerary monuments expressing some kind of social stratification and/or differentiation. To this purpose I would like to submit a theory quite different from the general view on the subject, even though I do not have any ethnographic support for it, yet.

Assuming that a fertility cult stems from the belief in a Mother Goddess, seen not as an omnipotent figure above Nature and Man, but as a figure very much in tune with Nature, its rhythmical changes, the cyclical processes and the symbolic passages between Life and Death, then it is possible to see death as a simple natural process. In the value system of this type of culture, death is not something that has to be conquered or from which we might expect a better treatment depending on the wealth of our burial or the offerings and gifts that accompany us. The Underworld, in a society that believes in a Mother Goddess, is a place without a class system, where wealth and status have no significance. The wealth of burials is not only to prove the importance of people when they were alive, but also to influence the Underworld where another place with a class system is supposed to wait for the dead, it is a reiteration of that system of values that was present in the living world. For people who believe in a Mother Goddess, the act of dying is as natural as the act of being born, and death can be seen as another state of being, an obligatory passage preannouncing the return to the maternal womb of the Goddess. Both the acts of birth and death are magical in the sense that they go from a state of non-being to a state of being to a state of non-being, and they are both sudden: we are not before we are born and we are not after we are dead. If we understand this, we do not need to believe in an after-life, because the after-life and the supernatural are all parts of the Mother Goddess, who is before and after, Life and Death. For the people of the Goddess there was no dichotomy between opposites and maybe this is a symbolic significance of the spiral motif so prominent in the ornamentation of the temples. Besides the spiral decorations, actual figurines of the steatopygous kind have been found in the temples. Some of these have definite female sexual characteristics, while some seem to: "...lack all sexual characteristics..." (Evans 1959: 142). Zuntz explains this a-sexuality "...as a widening and not a reduction of that basic character; these figures are not really 'a-sexual', but 'supra-sexual' " (Zuntz 1971: 50). In comparison with the magnificence of the temples, very little is known of the ancient Maltese, their everyday life and their social, political, economic and judicial organization. Very little is known of their settlements: some huts have been found as possible habitations, but they were poorly preserved because they had been built with clay and not with lasting stone.

If we assume, by the evidence that has been found, that people were at least partly agriculturalists, then there can be another explanation for the megalithic temples and their function.

It is extensively believed by many anthropologists and archaeologists that woman had, possibly, a greater role in the discovery of the art of agriculture than previously thought. By the study of existing societies of hunters and gatherers, anthropological models have been drawn that give factual information on the division of labour in the procurement of food. The results obtained seem to determine that, in most cases, men are doing the hunting and women the gathering. As a consequence, women could have been more in touch with the flora of a certain environment than with the fauna and might have noticed certain peculiarities and recurrences about certain grasses that could not only be gathered, but also stored and pounded to provide for staple food on a yearly basis. This discovery might have brought about the so called agricultural revolution and one of the most radical changes in the way of life of our forebears. The possibility of having a continuous supply of certain kinds of grasses without having to move around, probably brought with it the realization that it could be convenient to adopt a far less nomadic way of life and people started to settle down and to put down roots. Seeds have been found in Malta and the palynological analysis of the fossilized record points to the possibility of indigenous species of wild cereals. If the information is reliable, then Malta and its archipelago might have been an insular model of an agricultural society with well established rituals connected with the decay and revival of vegetation. Probably, as men had their rituals of sympathetic magic to assure and enhace the result of the hunt, women also had sympathetic rituals to assure and enhance the success of their work in the fields. In primitive communities a program of periodical ceremonies had its function in that it provided the means to ensure a renewal of the vitality and the continuation of the community. The performance of public ceremonies was the means by which the revolving of the seasons and the coming and going of the years were sanctioned. One of these rituals seems to have been connected with the cyclic spiralling coming and going of vegetation and, in the presence of cereals, with the annual growth of corn. The fact that a female Goddess, rather than a male God, was later chosen for the personification of the corn could add some weight to the suggestion that women had a preponderant part in the development of primitive agriculture. Or, simply, it might mean that equating the fertility of the Earth to that of a woman, the earlier aniconic image of the creative power was transformed in the anthropomorphic image of the Goddess. Her main attributes were an abundance of round forms and the presence of those sexual characteristics that are typical of a pregnant woman. This Goddess, I believe, did not need a specific and/or uniform representation of facial features that could make her recognizable and distinguished from other goddesses. Her facial features and expressions were not iconographically essential to her symbolic significance of femaleness, fecundity and universality. This fertility Goddess should remain purposely without a name and not to be associated, as it always happens when talking about corn, with Demeter-Persephone; these two Goddesses being the much later impersonifications in anthropomorphic form of the old and the new corn in Greek mythology.

L.R. Farnell, in his book "Cults of the Greek States", argues that the worship of Demeter's whole character cannot be simply reduced to a transformation from aniconic corn fetish into anthropomorphic corn-Goddess. "...There is the shadowy personality of an Earth-Goddess in the background, of larger dimensions than a corn sheaf, which lends magnitude and grandeur to the Demeter religion" (Farnell 1977: 37). Could this magnitude and grandeur be the magnitude and grandeur that are reflected and expressed in the architecture of the Maltese temples? The temples that, with their curved lines, represent the continuous state of pregnancy and consequently of fertility of the Goddess? If we assume that the Maltese megalithic structures were temples and that the image worshipped there was one of the Goddess, then we could speculate that Her religion was embracing a very large number of people and places and, maybe, Malta and its archipelago were a site of pilgrimage for the Ancient World. The spiral motif found so often in the temples could lend some evidence to the fact that the Goddess' image was much more complex than a simple vegetation impersonification, but also had eschatological values. Malta could have been a Lourdes *ante litteram* where the ancient religion of the Goddess could have had its focal point.

The megalithic structures, besides being places of worship, could have been at an earlier time, or at the same time, storing places where the Goddess was presiding over the redistribution of wealth, in this case represented by the produce of staple foods accumulated there previously. This double function of the temples could have been later diversified and transformed into the earliest form of the Demeter cult and the Maltese archipelago have been its place of origin.

According to Mylonas (Mylonas 1961), the cult of Demeter was introduced to Eleusis about the fifteenth century B.C., but its place of origin is still uncertain. Mylonas favours a Northern Greek origin from Thessaly or Thrace, while other scholars have proposed Egypt or Crete, to which I would like to add Malta.

One of the reasons why we do not have written records of the Eleusinian Mysteries is the fact that they were transmitted by oral tradition and were restricted to initiates who were sworn to secrecy.

The religion of Demeter, with its chthonic undertones of Life and Death, of Hope and Resurrection, might have been just the revival of a much more ancient religion, the religion of the Goddess and its mysteries as they were carried out in the Maltese megalithic temples, before those rituals were tinged and suppressed by the people of the later Maltese sequence. The Maltese mysteries might have had rites that re-enacted the decay and birth of the vegetation and, at a deeper level, the spiralling cycle of Life and Death over which the Goddess presided and of which the Goddess knew the secrets.

The temples themselves might indeed have represented the cavity of the womb of the Goddess, where people could enter and experience an almost tangible state of communion with Her.

Maybe they were experiencing the same happiness that, much later, Sophocles attributes to the people participating in the Eleusinian mysteries:

"Thrice happy are they of mortals who have looked upon these rites
they go to Hades' home; for over there these alone have life:
the rest have not but ill."

Summary

At Gozo, one of the smaller islands of the Maltese Archipelago, there is still lingering in the memory of the people a legend about a woman Giant that is told to the visitors of the Ġgantija Temple (Temple of the Giants). Is it possible that the woman of the legend and the Great Goddess worshipped in prehistoric Malta were one and the same?

The shape of the Maltese temples could be assimilated to the shape of the body of the Goddess. I looked for ethnographic parallels and I found one in the Fang people of Africa; accordingly, in the very condensed and complex symbolism of the Fang, the structure of the cult house is assimilated to the womb.

In a preliminary study, I propose Malta and its Archipelago as a model for an agricultural society where the much later religion of Demeter-Persephone had its origin and its mysteries.

Résumé

A Gozo, une des plus petites îles de l'Archipel Maltais, il y a encore dans la mémoire des habitants une légende à propos d'une femme Géante que l'on raconte aux visiteurs du Temple de Ġgantija (Temple des Géantes). Est-il possible que cette femme légendaire et la Grande Déesse préhistorique Maltaise soit la même?

Nous pouvons voir une similitude entre la forme des temples Maltais et le corps de la Déesse. Après une recherche d'un parallèle ethnographique je l'ai trouvé chez les Fang d'Afrique; suivant le symbolisme complexe des Fang il y a une analogie entre la structure de la maison de cult et l'uterus.

D'une façon preliminaire, nous pourrions voir dans Malte et son Archipel un modèle d'une société agricole ou le mythe de Déméter-Perséphone et ses mystères ont pris naissance.

Bibliography

CHILDE, V.G.
1925 — *The Dawn of European Civilization,* London (Routledge, 1st Edn).

CLES-REDEN, S. von
1962 — *The Realm of the Great Goddess,* New York.

EVANS, J.D.
1959 — *Malta,* London (Thames and Hudson).

FARNELL, L.R.
1977 — *The Cults of the Greek States,* New Rochelle, N.Y. (Caratzas Brothers Publishers).

FERNANDEZ, J.W.
1977 — *Fang Architectonics,* Philadelphia (Institute for the Study of Human Issues).

FRAZER, Sir J.G.
1963 — *The Golden Bough,* New York, N.Y. (Macmillan Publishing Co., Inc. abridged edition).

MYLONAS, G.E.
1961 — *Eleusis and the Eleusinian Mysteries,* Princeton N.J. (Princeton University Press).

NEUMANN, E.
1961 — *The Great Mother,* Princeton, N.J. (Princeton University Press).

TRUMP, D.H.
1981 — *The Prehistory of the Mediterranean,* Harmondsworth, Middlesex, (Penguin Books Ltd.).

ZUNTZ, G.
1971 — *Persephone,* Oxford (Clarendon Press).

NEW VIEWS ON THE HYPOGEUM AND TARXIEN

Ian F.G. Ferguson

One of the tasks set us by archaeologists and scientists is to conceptualise spans of time ever increasing with the refinements of science, such as radiocarbon dating and its calibration. Our current task in this field is to conceptualise the millennia back to 10,000 B.C., the end of the last Ice Age, and beyond. The calibrated radiocarbon dates, as established by Professor Renfrew and others, place the first wave of immigrants to Malta around 5000 B.C., and the second wave around 4000.

With such immense periods, the dangers of unconscious anachronisms are considerable. These dangers include treating such concepts as "goddesses and gods" as being personified and named deities, the concept of "worship" in relation to cult activities, and the idea of human conception, that is, of the male role as well as of the self-evident birth-giving act of the female. Major problems also exist in interpreting cultic, religious and philosophical ideas from material remains. "The beliefs of past societies are an integral aspect which the archaeologist cannot afford to ignore, however difficult their reconstruction may seem." (Champion et al. 1984: 142). Different types of material remains are discovered; a quern has an easily recognisable function, but an icon does not. The correct technique must be the detailed examination of the object per se, comparison with similar objects, and then reference back to its archaeological context.

"THE FAT LADY"

The Tarxien temples form the largest temple complex in Malta, and this figure, the so-called "Fat Lady" (Pl. 19) is found inside the Western Temple, one of the last of the Maltese temples, dated to around 3000 B.C. This figure, which must originally have been over 2 metres high, is perhaps the earliest piece of monumental sculpture in the world's history. Sadly she has been quarried away till only her impressive lower parts remain. Professor Evans comments, "The figure was undoubtedly portrayed as seated. Some of the statuettes at Tarxien give a good idea of what she must have looked like when complete. The base of the statue is set into the slab, which is cut out to receive it (Pl. 24). This slab is 1.30 m long and 16.5 cms high and the front of it is sculptured with a kind of primitive egg and dart motif."

(Evans 1971: 129). A related view is given by Mr Ridley: "The motif carved on the panel is both unique and interesting. It consists of a row of horizontal ovoids with pointed ends, 'eggs', separated by 'double axes' or concave and convex lines" (Ridley 1976: 78). At this conference we have already heard Mr. Cutajar's interesting interpretation that they represent bobbins and loom-weights, an idea I do not wish to discount as the art here, in its religious context, is clearly symbolic and symbols are normally polyvalent. However Mr Cutajar himself admits that the perforation of the bobbins is missing.

It is easy to think of eggs here, but unfortunately the domestic fowl is an anachronism, as it was not introduced into Europe from India until the first millennium. And how about the other elements, the 'darts' or 'double axes'? There is no evidence that the neolithic Maltese had either, and in fact there is a good alternative explanation. In the Museum at Tarxien are three upright querns about two feet high, two of which have just this outline (Pl. 23); another is in the National Museum in Valletta. The typology of the Maltese neolithic querns has not received enough attention: many types exist, including the long low quern of coralline limestone built into the temple at Kordin and having seven compartments, various simple querns, some of lava from Sicily, suitable for individual households, and these raised querns which appear suitable for ritual use while standing in front of a cult figure. So, the motif now appears, not as 'eggs and axes', but as exactly seven ritual querns which separate six enlarged representations of wheat or barley grains. This interpretation is completely compatible with the neolithic Maltese farming community.

If correct, this helps dramatically in identifying the "Fat Lady". By Roman times the slab was buried under over a metre of silt, but any Roman looking at the motif and the cult figure would have thought of her as Ceres, while the Greeks would have related her to Demeter—Demeter was actually a pre-Greek goddess only tardily accepted into the Greek Olympus, and she was especially characterised as the goddess of corn responsible for the fertility of the tilled soil. I am not claiming that the "Fat Lady" was called by some such name as Ceres or Demeter: this would be an anachronism, as the personifying anthropomorphisms of the deities in this area was a feature of the late second and the first millennia. Now the older and more correct title of Athene was "*potni' Athenai*", using the genitive, "Our Lady of Athens." This corresponds to the earlier Cretan goddess whose style, according to our translation of the Linear B tablets was "Our Lady of the Labyrinth." So our neolithic Maltese, whatever their language, probably referred to their local form of the Goddess by a title equivalent to "Our Lady of Tarxien."

II. THE HYPOGEUM: BURIALS

The Hypogeum at Hal Saflieni is unique, though there may well be others awaiting future archaeologists in the Maltese limestone. It was discovered in 1902, but since its systematic excavation from 1904 -11 by the father of the Maltese archaeology, Sir Temi Zammit, little further progress has been made, apart from the Survey in 1953 by Professor Evans and Mr Wright. I quote now from Dr Trump: "This must be the most remarkable monument in the Mediterranean, in Europe, perhaps in the world, but we are almost totally ignorant of what went on in it, or the other temples" (Trump 1980, 143). This is a challenge I wish to take up.

The Hypogeum is comparable to a mediaeval cathedral in that it was a sacred place gradually developed and extended over the course of many centuries (probably more than a millennium), coming to contain a variety of uses in its three levels. Its use ended with the abandonment of the temples and the end of the neolithic Maltese civilisation around 2500 B.C. and extends back from this point in time to the early part of the fourth millennium. We have evidence of various activities being performed there, of which the most evident is that of burial. When Dr Zammit excavated the Hypogeum, he estimated the large number of human bones as belonging to around 7000 individuals. These came from the upper and middle levels and were generally covered with earth. He also discovered an intact crouched human skeleton which probably represents the last individual to be buried there. So we are probably justified in distinguishing between an initial primary burial following the individual's death, followed at a discrete interval by dispersal or secondary burial, still within the Hypogeum. This interval quite likely corresponds to the period of mourning which would have followed the funeral rites and lasted until the secondary burial when the spirits of the departed "joined those of the ancestors." A smaller chamber or cave, when full, would have been cleared of its bones and soil to make way for new occupants, the earlier burials being disposed of collectively in a larger ossuary area.

Professor Renfrew has estimated the Neolithic population of Malta as approximately 11,000, averaging about 2000 for each of the six major centres. The figure could perhaps be around 2500 here, as Tarxien boasted the largest temple complex, and the Hypogeum could have been used by the inhabitants of Kordin as well. Now the average lifespan in contemporary Neolithic Orkney was around 20 years, and if the average lifespan in Mediterranean Malta was as high as 30 years, even at a population of 2500, the Hypogeum could have reached its total of 7000 in less than a century. However, in the absence of substantial radiocarbon readings, all the available evidence (pottery, etc) points to its use over many centuries. Hence, burial in the Hypogeum was probably strictly selective, possibly being inherited by certain families. Yet this was essentially collective burial without noticeable grave goods.

Linked with its primary function as a place of burial was presumably a cult of the dead ancestors, probably linked with animal sacrifice at the funeral itself. The Main Hall here is the most remarkable room left us by the ancient Maltese. Like the rest of the Hypogeum it has been carved out of the living globigerina limestone, yet unlike all the other rooms it does not have the feeling of a cave. This is because a concave temple facade of noble and harmonious proportions has been carved out of the rock, and this combines with three long lintels which introduce the features of a corbelled vault. This is architecture: the combination of an external temple facade with internal 'corbelling' is most admirable and ingenious, and with the high polish of the stone endows this 'chapel' with an air of great serenity and solemnity. However, the scale precludes congregational worship (itself an anachronistic Christian idea), so we have probably to envisage the funeral ceremonies being attended mainly by the members of the extended family group.

Evidence of cult usages elsewhere in the Hypogeum are the stone figurines of 'Our Lady', the painted designs in red ochre, and possibly the various entry trilithons which are also found in the temple entrances. Another indication of cult use, that of incubation, is provided by the famous terracotta Sleeping Lady and her companion piece which we will be considering shortly, associated with two cubicles opening into the Main Hall. There was possibly an oracular use too; this is more problematic and is linked to the so-called oracle-hole: this does indeed provide remarkable echoes, but echo does not constitute real proof of its use. The oracle-hole could equally well have been used to contain a stone icon; its interior is painted with three red discs which do seem to indicate some cultic function.

III. THE SLEEPING LADY

We now come to the famous Sleeping Lady of the Hypogeum, a terracotta figurine which is a small masterpiece of the craftman's art. The lady, whoever she is, dressed in a full-length skirt, ample-hipped and topless *à la maltaise ancienne*, is lying full length on a low couch or bed, head on a block in lieu of a pillow, clearly asleep, almost visibly dreaming. But who was she? What was she doing sleeping in this most spooky of all possible places, and why was the piece made? Was she indeed a priestess?

This fascinating piece is generally taken as representing the rite of incubation. In the classical world, which is almost all we have to go by, incubation was closely associated with cults of healing, and none of these was more famous than that of Asklepios at Epidauros. Medical treatment was beginning to gain some scientific status in the Greek world, but incorporated many weird and many superstitious elements. Sufferers from bodily and mental ailments were common then as now, treatment inevitably was often unsuccessful, and the centre at Epiduaros, with its temple to the divinised hero Asklepios, had gained a wide reputation for successful cures by the fifth century B.C.

The treatment at Epidauros consisted of an initial purification of the patient by washing and fasting, followed by a night spent in the temple of Asklepios. The next morning the patient's dreams were recounted to the attendant priest who used this information to develop a prescription which paid attention to general régime and diet. So this cult at Epidauros was a kind of medical divination using dreams. Votive offerings from cured and grateful patients were a common feature at the sites of healing cults in the ancient world. The offerings were typically terracotta models of the body or bodily parts cured — legs, arms, breasts, even wombs. The Romans inherited such cults from the Etruscans, the Greeks from the Minoans who had such a cult centre at Petsofa. Even today many Mediterranean churches have chapels with similar votive offerings, often now in plastic. Lourdes itself is a sacred centre associated with a cult of healing. And the ancient Maltese apparently had such a centre of their own at the temple of Mnajdra, where the 'oracle' was associated with a cult of healing. Several terracotta models of diseased or deformed bodies have been found there, and among these Dr Zammit diagnosed one, a woman with an abnormally swollen abdomen, as suffering from an abdominal tumour. The Hypogeum has been linked with an oracle, and if so, the piece called the Sleeping Lady could be a votive offering from one who successfully passed through the rite of incubation in the Hypogeum. But if so, what was she suffering from? I shall attempt to answer this question shortly.

IV. THE HYPOGEUM: CONTEXT FOR INCUBATION

We have already seen the link that existed in ancient times between incubation, oracles and cults of healing, but we have yet to consider one of the most important medical complaints. Perhaps the clay models of wombs are our clue, pointing to the problems of the women who were barren. Certainly to a neolithic community of farmers, a woman who was barren would seem like one accursed, one suffering from that curse they must have feared falling on their land, their animals and themselves. Even today, with all the benefits of modern science, hormonal treatment, artificial insemination, etc., there are plenty of women who experience great difficulty in becoming pregnant. The Old Testament bears witness to the plight of the barren wife in a patriarchal society.

Symbolically the Hypogeum at Ħal Saflieni represents a labyrinthine womb, and it is most unlikely that the early Maltese were not conscious of this symbolism. Our Lady must have been their symbol of fertility and new life. Just as these early farming folk depended on the good earth producing rich, not meagre, harvests of cereals, pulses and other crops, so they depended on the reproductive fertility of their cows, sheep, goats and pigs and — equally important and fundamental — on their own fertility to maintain the numbers of the Maltese community. Here in Malta the temple-builders had established a successful relationship with the forces of nature that regulated their destiny. We cannot test their ideas about destiny, but it is likely that, like similar groups elsewhere, they held beliefs about the perpetuation and periodic renewal of the vital forces of life.

However, up to the present there has been a general but tacit assumption on the part of prehistorians and archaeologists that prehistoric communities normally shared the view of historic societies about the causal relationship between sex and reproduction. This well could be a serious anachronism, and it is not a view shared unreflectingly by all. Anthropologists, sociologists and cultural historians have recognised this problem. Sir James Frazer was one of these; in his *Golden Bough* (Part IV, Book I) he quotes specific cases of some two dozen twentieth century communities where there was common denial of any male role in reproduction. His examples assemble the Hurons, various European groups including Slavs, several African tribes, a Syrian community (this is an Islamic society!), various tribes across India, others in Australia.

A classic in anthropology is Bronislaw Malinowski's description of his field work during World War I among the Trobriand Islanders in the Pacific, who, he found, did not share our ideas; they viewed sexual intercourse as a natural event to be enjoyed from puberty onwards, but they had established no causal nexus between human sexual activity and pregnancy. On the contrary, they believed in a form of reincarnation in which spirit children who wished to be reborn would cross to the Trobriand Islands where they would choose their future mothers and enter their wombs. They rejected the usual view when it was explained to them, and it is both remarkable and significant that they ascribed no role to the male in the reproductive process. None of this, of course, amounts to proof for the neolithic Maltese, but the range of examples in time as well as in space undoubtedly establishes it as a serious possibility. Here I wish to quote Professor Gimbutas: "There is no evidence that in Neolithic times mankind understood biological conception" (Gimbutas 1983: 237). With her I submit that the onus of proof in this matter lies just as heavily on those who assume, without proof, that neolithical peoples shared our own ideas: I think this is a serious anachronism.

This problem of conceptualising the different roles of male and female in reproduction could well be the cause of another related contrast phenomenon, that between the matrilinear and the patrilinear way of tracing descent. In fact there is just a little evidence to hint that our ancient Maltese may, in the course of the millennia, have made the discovery of the male role for themselves. I refer to the erection of cylindrical phallic stones, baetyls or *lingams* (to use the Indian term) within or beside the temples. They are especially associated with Ġgantija, Ħaġar Qim and Tarxien, and in the first two cases were deliberately associated with a downpointing triangular or 'female' stone. These baetyls are not integral parts of the temples, they were later additions. To this evidence we must add the late carving of bulls on the walls at Tarxien, and also the carved stone phalli from the same site; these must surely have had ritual use — one is actually double! Would it be surprising if these Maltese farmers, as their control and knowledge of stock-breeding increased, had made this discovery for themselves, and had developed new ritual, incorporating these symbolic stone structures in their temples?

V. REINCARNATION

I return now to the Sleeping Lady and the other sleeper, two terracotta figurines which are posing us some searching questions. Why should mature women from the neolithic farming community have visited the Hypogeum, their sacred burial ground, perhaps by night, for some kind of dream? The commonest explanation is that they went there to induce dreams, possibly prophetic or oracular dreams, which they could subsequently interpret with the aid of the priesthood. Though extrapolated back in time by two millennia, this is a possible explanation: we all know the tale of Joseph intrepreting Pharaoh's dream. Yet this practice was never common; even the Etruscans, those master-diviners of the ancient world, are not known to have practised divination by dream. Another point: unlike the goddess figurines, our neolithic Maltese sleepers are buxom, emphatically female; so there is another possibility to consider.

The fact is that, from the evidence, this was no general form of dreaming, but a specific act deliberately planned to take place inside the Hypogeum, so perhaps the Hypogeum, the context of the rite, itself contains the key to the riddle. We see that the walls and ceilings of two rooms carry paintings which depict meandering vines bearing round, disc-like fruit which could easily be pomegranates. Clearly the paintings are symbolic rather than naturalistic, they apparently depict some Tree of Life, here given features of the vine but also — since its fruits are not grapes — perhapes pomegranates. Equally significant is the use of red ochre: out of all available pigments this red oxide of iron was chosen, clearly for its traditional and close resemblance to blood, which the ancient Maltese, like so many others, surely thought of as the life-force, and which in all probability they collected from the dying animal during sacrificial ritual and poured as a libation to the Earth. There is sufficient evidence that this rite was performed in the Hypogeum itself, as well as in the Maltese temples and over much of the ancient world. And this act of libation was no idle act, but one performed with the deliberate, pious and conscious intent of revitalising the Earth from which all life ultimately springs. At Ħal Saflieni the blood-coloured ochre is painted directly onto the walls and ceilings of the Hypogeum, itself symbolically a womb. The symbolism could hardly be clearer, especially as the Trees of Life painted there bear fruits which are perhaps pomegranates, the fruit associated in the Persephone myth with death and the rebirth of life. The one intact burial was crouched in the foetal position, as if awaiting rebirth.

Here finally I have deliberately passed into the realm of philosophy. There is nothing impossible or improbable about a Maltese belief in reincarnation, which could come quite naturally to a people 'worshipping' a corn goddess associated with vegetative death and rebirth. Such ideas were indeed common in the ancient world. Among the classical Greeks, two of the most brilliant minds, Plato and Pythagoras, deliberately used myths of reincarnation, and both were consciously archaising. India provides an example where this ancient belief, not destroyed by subsequent religious reforms, survives to the present day. Indeed, knowledge of an afterlife is not possible, though reflecting and imagining about it is part of the common human heritage. The neolithic Maltese were pre-literate, but in their temples and the Hypogeum they developed an art form that is symbolic. It is either anachronistic or simplistic to write off this sacred art as 'decorative': the spiral carvings at Tarxien and Ġgantija could very well symbolically represent a belief in reincarnation, associated with a matrilinear genealogy. I have consciously wandered far from verifiable facts in order to derive the beliefs of the ancient Maltese from their material remains, so far as this is possible. Although my attempt is only a hypothesis, it has the virtue of being a reasonable explanation, of being self-consistent, and also of being consistent within the archaeological context left by the neolithic Maltese farming community. They would have been exceptional had they had no beliefs.

At last we are in a position to explain why certain of these farming women may have gone to the Hypogeum for 'incubatory dreams'. They went there, as they thought, to conceive, to become pregnant, or, more exactly, to improve their chances of doing so. Throughout the Early Neolithic period, like many, presumably most, very early societies, the ancient Maltese had neither worked out nor articulated the causal relationship between sexual intercourse and pregnancy. Instead we deduce that their ideas included some kind of reincarnation, that is, of pregnancy occuring due to a spirit-child choosing and entering a woman's womb and developing there. In Malta it seems that some of the women of the Tarxien clan or kinship group went to the Hypogeum, that sacred resting place of their ancestors, to have an 'incubatory dream' in one of the chambers there, in order to be chosen by a spirit-child and come out pregnant. This ritual act would in no way have interfered with their leading a normal and healthy sex life with their consorts! They simply did not connect the sexual act with pregnancy. And so perhaps the terracotta model of the Sleeping Lady was sculpted as a result of a pregnancy which coincided with an act of ritual incubation, and was in fact presented as a votive thank-offering to the ancestral cult site, the Hypogeum.

Summary

As prehistory reaches further back into forgotten millennia, we run the risk of serious anachronisms. Different categories of material objects are unearthed, some quite enigmatic; study techniques should incorporate description, comparison, and reference to archaeological and social contexts. At Tarxien the 'Fat Lady' stands on a plinth sculpted with shapes best interpreted as querns and grains, pointing to a corn-goddess of the Demeter type. The Hypogeum's main function was burial, probably of a minority group and associated with reverence for ancestors. Evidently there was also a cult of incubation, classically associated with healing. Red ochre paintings in the Hypogeum show vines (Trees of Life) with perhaps pomegranates, associated with death and rebirth as in the cult of Persephone, who apparently had a temple in Malta. A general knowledge of the male role in procreation is unproved for the Early Neolithic. As the Hypogeum was the context for the cult, incubation there appears linked with death and rebirth, possibly some 'reincarnation'. The Sleeping Lady could be an ex-voto terracotta given for a pregnancy posterior to an act of incubation.

Resumé

Notre connaissance des millénnaires préhistoriques augmente toujours, mais porte le danger d'anachronismes sérieux. Certains objets trouvés restent énigmatiques: nous devons les étudier avec référence à leur contexte archéologique et sociologique. A Tarxien, la grande figure d'une déesse reste sur une plinthe gravée en images mieux interpretées comme meules et grains, indiquant une déesse des céréales du type de Déméter. La fonction principale de l'Hypogée serait la sépulture d'une minorité, lieu donc de révérence aux ancêtres, et aussi d'un probable culte d'incubation, associé par les Grecs avec la guérison. Dans cet Hypogée la pienture en ocre rouge démontre des vignes (Arbres de la Vie) et peut-être des grenades, associées avec la mort et la renaissance, surtout dans le culte de Persephone, qui apparemment avait un temple à l'île de Malte. Une connaissance générale du rôle masculin dans la procréation reste sans preuve pour le Néolithique inférieur. Comme l'Hypogée était le contexte pour le culte, l'incubation était évidemment liée à la mort et à la renaissance — ou une réincarnation. Peut-être la figurine *The Sleeping Lady* est un ex-voto en terre-cuite presenté pour une grossesse postérieur à une acte d'incubation rituelle dans l'Hypogée.

Bibliography

CHAMPION, GAMBLE, SHENNAN & WHITTLE
1984 — *Prehistoric Europe*, London.

EVANS, J.D.
1971 — *Prehistoric Antiquities of the Maltese Islands*, London (Athlone Press).

RIDLEY, M.
1976 — *The Megalithic Art of the Maltese Islands*, Poole (Dolphin Press).

TRUMP, D.H.
1980 — *The Prehistory of the Mediterranean*, London (Alien Lane).

HARRISON, J.E.
1980 — *Prolegomena to the Study of Greek Religion,* London (Merlin).

EVANS, J.D.
1979 — *Blue Guide, Malta,* London (Ernest Benn Ltd.).

GIMBUTAS, M.
1983 — *The Goddesses and Gods of Old Europe,*London (Thames & Hudson).

TWO RELIEF-CARVINGS OF CHALCOLITHIC MALTA

Dominic Cutajar

This communication is intended to draw attention to two relief-carvings from the late Copper Age temples of Tarxien, in particular because the first of these — a panel with a decorative motif — may chronologically stand at the head of a line of development that evolved through the ages and has come to be designated as the Egg-and-Dart motif. References will also be made to the later stages in the evolution of the motif's history that apparently occurred in the Aegean area. One may here add that in the writer's own belief, there was little actual contact between Chalcolithic Malta and the Aegean. The evolution of the Tarxien motif does neither rest upon nor postulate such a linear development; the nature of the relationship is more likely to have been a collateral one.

At the same time one cannot help feeling some uneasiness about hypotheses of cultural development in complete isolation, the more so inside the Mediterranean. Neolithic Malta appears to have been an extension of Stentinello Sicily (Evans 1971:208-209; Bonanno 1986: 17-46) although during the Conference, in the course of a visit to the National Museum of Archaeology in Valletta, Prof. E. Anati drew attention to a closer relationship between the material culture of the Għar Dalam phase and that of Neolithic Hazorea in Israel.

To-date the cultural antecedents of Chalcolithic Malta have remained obscure. As is well known, its external contacts were few and far between, although there is some evidence that some tenuous contacts may have been maintained even with the Aegean area, as one can presume from the occurrence of the so-called *Thermi cups* during the Tarxien period (Trump 1966: 46).

The Mediterranean has often been a sea which kept its people divided, but not infrequently it did bring them together. The level of sophistication reached by the Chalcolithic culture of Malta could neither realistically have been attained in isolation, nor in a complete cultural vacuum. In the final analysis cultural developments can be better understood as an extension of a much broader texture — even if at times they degenerate into cultural dead-ends.

More difficult to assess is the degree of indigenuous contribution to any transmitted culture; there can be no doubt that the contribution of the inhabitants of Chalcolithic Malta to the consistency of their culture was substantial, especially in architecture. But let us remember, it did not happen in a vacuum, nor could it even evolve in rigid isolation.

* * *

Of the Copper Age temples in Malta, the west or third temple at Tarxien has the richest repertoire of relief-carvings, many in fact consisting of oblong bands of decorative motifs of vaguely abstract character. That early man had not arrived at a truly "abstract" expression is sufficiently well-known, although eventually and with time a number of abstractions were evolved. Frequently these came to be utilised in part for their decorative qualities, but largely — one suspects — for their symbolic connotations. However, most have reached us in their fully evolved and *abstracted* form, and thus present a veritable challenge to the decipherment of their original inspiration.

The object here is to suggest that one of the relief-motifs in the west temple at Tarxien seems to have preserved the proto-type — rather, the iconic form — that in subsequent ages became one of the commonest decorative motifs in the repertoire of Western art, thanks largely to its vast diffusion through the classical relief-sculpture of the Graeco-Roman world. I am referring to the motif carved in bold relief on the base of the monumental limestone statue of the so-called Mother-Goddess in the east apse of the third Tarxien temple (Pl. 24; Evans 1971: pl. 19/5; Ridley 1971: 23, no. 31).

The limestone relief in question measures 14cm × 146cm and appears to represent, in alternating order, spindle-whorls (or bobbins) and ovoid-shaped loom-weights. Actual specimens of precisely these spinning implements were recovered in dated archaeological contexts at Ħaġar Qim, Saflieni, Mnajdra and Tarxien — apart from other places — thus leaving no doubt as to their being well-known and very likely common during the Maltese Chalcolithic (Evans 1971: 66, 93, 94, 104, 165, pls. 65, 1-6 and 66, 1-3).

In the relief-carving, the whorls or bobbins are shown without their central perforation, probably due to these being pierced at their narrowest section. Luckily there also exists a single specimen from Mnajdra which is actually unperforated as in the relief-carving. Some of the loom-weights recovered at Ħaġar Qim were fashioned from globigerina limestone, although most samples recovered were moulded in clay. The writer has himself picked up half one of these clay spherical loom-weights from a field adjacent to the temple at Borġ in-Nadur.

The above would seem to indicate that the representation of a band of alternating whorls and loom-weights beneath a statue — commonly presumed to be a representation of the Mother-Goddess — is in itself both suggestive and significant, being tantamount to designating *that* particular female figure as *the Spinner*. The monumentality of the sculpture — in fact, the largest of the kind in the Maltese Chalcolithic context — serves to underscore dramatically the uniqueness of the figure, even when viewed against the background of Malta's entire corpus of Copper Age limestone sculptures — the individual specimens of which are themselves large, bulky and very heavy works. The Tarxien sculpture is thus conceived on such an impressive and monumental scale that it sharply contrasts with the negative criteria examined by Prof. P.J. Ucko (Ucko 1968: 427-434), justifying its designation as a representation of the Mother-Goddess.

This interpretation derives substantial support from the fact that an identical motif — more formally integrated — reappears in the stela mounted atop the Lions Gate at Mycenae. There the motif is carved beneath the pillar-altar, itself flanked by the "heraldic" lions — usually interpreted as a representation of the tutelary deity of the Mycenaean citadel. The close formal parallelism in the latter utilization of the motif at Mycenae, with that of the Tarxien monumental sculpture should not be underrated.

The motif recurs again in the Palace of Knossos, this time as a decorative mural frieze painted along the lateral sides and on top of the entrance to the Women quarters — where, incidentally, evidence of spinning activity was discovered. The Knossos painted frieze — probably Late Minoan III — seems to be later than the Mycenaean stela; yet, it too has a significance of its own, demarcating as it does the gateway to *the female domain*. The implication — if our reading of the signs is right — is that spinning being intrinsically a feminine occupation, its implements came to symbolize the female sex itself. Both the Tarxien relief and the Mycenaean stela appear to document an earlier stage when the feminine deity *par excellance* was thus designated.

The foregoing can hardly fail to suggest somehow the *Moirai* or the "Fates" — ancient Hellenic deities consisting of a triad of old spinning women, individually identified as Clotho, Lachesis and Atropos — originally venerated as birth-spirits, the Allotters to every new-born child of his portion of life.

Whatever the case may be, the "egg-and-dart" motif at Tarxien seems to constitute yet another small link between Chalcolithic Malta and the civilizations of the Aegean area. Whichever way this traffic flowed during the Chalcolithic is a question that has in the past bedevilled the chronology of prehistoric Malta — that is, before the advent of radiocarbon dating. It could well be that the two areas of separate development — Malta and the Aegean world — might have been *both* dependent in certain ways on cultural stimuli from the earlier Balkan civilizations. It is a hypothesis well worth examining.

* * *

With reference to the same temple at Tarxien, it might prove of some interest to discuss briefly the representation in relief of the two bulls and another animal, most times presumed to represent "*a sow suckling her litter of piglets*" (Ridley 1971: 28, nos 68-69). These animals were carved in shallow relief on the walls of a small enclosed area tucked between the third and middle temples (Pl. 25).

Michael Ridley has already cast serious doubts as to the correctness of the sow's identification. The animal is shown hornless — or it might well be its horns were lost through weathering. Yet on closer examination, its legs are proportionately far too long to suggest a sow. On balance we seem to have a depiction of a bull and its female counterpart — presumably a heifer.

The main objection to such an interpretation is of course the presence of its large litter, that on surface would seem to rule out a young female bovine. Yet the very size of the litter — thirteen young, carved side by side beneath the female animal — might well be a hint suggesting a solution. It appears that the carved animals were intended to be read symbolically. The bull — representing the male principle — would stand for the Sun, while his consort would naturally be the Moon, generally represented in the form of a cow. If such is the case at Tarxien, the latter's litter of 13 young would be nothing less than the thirteen lunar months of most primitive calendars.

Of course the point cannot be taken to be conclusively settled. It is yet not without significance that the two Tarxien relief-carvings here discussed seem to highlight in an overwhelming manner feminine interests, activities and functions, which the Chalcolithic temples of Malta strongly hint at on a score of other considerations.

Summary

The west temple of the Tarxien complex is certainly the most elaborately decorated of the Chalcolithic temples of Malta. The repertoire of stone-carved motifs is fairly extensive, among which one — carved beneath a monumental limestone statue of the 'Goddess' — seems to represent the prototype of the egg-and-dart motif before it was abstracted to become, presumably through the agency of the Aegean civilizations, one of the most popular architectural decorative motifs of western art.

A second carving — in an adjacent room to the west temple — represents a bull and a female animal with its young, usually taken for a 'sow with litter'. The writer suggests an interpretation connected with the calendar.

Bibliography

ANATI, E. *et al.*
1973 — *Hazorea I,* Capo di Ponte (Centro Camuno di Studi Preistorici).

BONANNO, A.
1986 — A socio-economic approach to Maltese prehistory. The Temple Builders, in *Malta - Studies of its Heritage and History,* Malta (Mid-Med Publication).

EVANS, J.D.
1971 — *The Prehistoric Antiquities of the Maltese Islands,* London (Athlone Press).

RIDLEY, M.
1971 — *The Megalithic Art of Malta,* Christchurch (Dolphin Press).

TRUMP, D.
1966 — *Skorba,* London (Society of Antiquaries).

UCKO, P.J.
1968 — *Anthropomorphic Figurines of Predynastic Egypt and Neolithic Crete...,* London.

SECTION III: PHOENICIAN AND NEAR EASTERN RELIGIONS

UNI-ASHTARTE AND TANIT-IUNO CAELESTIS

TWO PHOENICIAN GODDESSES OF FERTILITY RECONSIDERED FROM RECENT ARCHAEOLOGICAL DISCOVERIES

F.O. Hvidberg-Hansen

As you are not doubt aware, Phoenician and Punic studies have undergone an enormous and rapid increase during the last two decades, based on the intensive archaeological activity all over the Mediterranean: Phoenicia proper, Cyprus, North Africa, Spain, Sardinia, Sicily and Malta; numerous congress-volumes published during the last decade provide the proof: from *Proceedings of the 2nd International Congress of Studies on Cultures of the Western Mediterranean, Malta 23-28 June 1976* (1976/78, Vols. I-II, Alger), to *Atti del I° Congresso internazionale di studi fenici e punici, Roma 5-10 novembre 1979* (1983, Vols. I-III, Roma) and the colloquies in Belgium, the latest in December 1984 in Namur entitled: "La religion phénicienne" (published in *Studia Phoenicia IV,* Namur 1986).

Of the greatest importance for our acquaintance with the Canaanite or Phoenician cult and religion is the comprehensive text material from Ugarit, appearing since the beginning of the nineteen-thirties. A solid and first-hand knowledge basis for our understanding of Semitic religion in the middle of the 2nd Millennium has here come to hand — the religion of the population, which nowadays with a common designation may be called "Canaanites" or "Phoenicians". On this occasion I shall not lose myself in the semantic problem of whether "Canaanite", derived from *kinaḫḫu* (Nuzi) (*Kinaḫnu* in a Mari-text from the 18th century (Dossin 1973; 277-82)), perhaps *ka-na-na-um* in Ebla, and "Phoenician" or *Phoinix,* derived from *po-ni-ke, po-ni-ki-jo/a,* in the Linear-B texts, in reality have the common meaning: "purple" or "dyer" or "merchant", but refer to the paper of G. Garbini: "Chi erano i fenici?" (1983, I; 27-33) and to two recent articles of C. Tzavellas-Bonnet (1983a: 113-122; 1983b: 3-11).

The Canaanite-Phoenician religion undergoes from the middle of the second Millennium and till the Hellenistic Period considerable changes — I shall at once mention two important alterations: 1) the relation between the goddesses Ashtarte and Anat, and 2) the almost total disappearance of the goddess Athirat (Asherah) as a distinct character. Still, at least one constant element may be noted in the

Canaanite-Phoenician-Punic religion during the long space of time from about 1400 BC until the Late Punic Period, 2nd cent. AD: the god El as a Creator: *El qone arṣ*, from Ilu or El in Ugarit and Elkurniša in Boghazköy and in the Old Testament (*Genesis* ch. 14), passing by Karatepe in the 8th cent. (KAI, 26, III, 18) to Palmyra (Cantineau 1938: 78-79) and Leptis Magna (KAI, 129), 1st-2nd cent. AD (Röllig 1959: 403-16). On the other hand this does not mean that the nature of El should be considered as being static during the fifteen hundred years which the texts just mentioned include; this can be illustrated from the well-known Punic stele from Hadrumetum, 5th cent. BC, representing Ba'al Ḥammon, having on the stele mainly the same traits as El has on the famous Ugaritic stele (the Hadrumetum-stele: Picard, *Catalogue*, no. Cb 1075; the Ugaritic stele: Le Glay 1966: pl. VI). The rather identical character of the Canaanite El and the Punic Ba'al Ḥammon illustrates — as pointed out by M. Le Glay (1966: 432 sq.) — that the Canaanite fertility-god Ba'al Ḥammon has absorbed the outward appearance of El as well as some of his functions, El being the universal Creator-god. In this so to speak mixed shape we have to suppose that Ba'al Ḥammon was brought to the Occident by the Phoenician colonizers, having their point of departure in particular in Tyre, from where originates a recently published amulet, dedicated to Ba'al Ḥammon *and* to Ba'al Saphon (Bordreuil 1986: 77 sqq.).

The cultic and mythological texts from Ugarit thus being our most important source of knowledge of the Canaanite-Phoenician goddesses of fertility, Ashtarte, Anat and Athirat, I shall briefly recapitulate the nature of these goddesses as the essential background of the following. In order not to be considered an exponent of the so-called "Pan-Ugaritism" (Craigie 1981: 99 sq.), I shall furnish the recapitulation with a few elements from the most recent discoveries from outside Ugarit.

When the first and "euphoric" phase of the studies of the Ugaritic texts had come to an end and a comprehensive view of the contents and character of the texts had been gained, one could note that the goddess Ashtarte, who was dominant in the Phoenician inscriptions and in the Old Testament, plays a rather secondary role in the drama of the Ugaritic texts: here Ashtarte is the helper of Ba'al against the Sea-god Yamm, and together with Ḥoron she acts as a violent and warlike goddess, but bearing the title "Ashtarte-Name-of-Ba'al" (*'ṯtrtšmb'l*), a title indicating her special relation to Ba'al, cf. the Eshmunazar-inscription from Sidon, 5th cent. BC (KAI, 14).

As granting fertility, Ashtarte appears only sporadically in Ugarit, mainly in administrative texts: so "the wine-press of Ashtarte" (*gt 'ṯtrt*) is mentioned (PRU II, 46) as well as deliveries of wine to the temple of Ashtarte (PRU II, 88); it is obvious that she is the giver of wine as well as taking care of the cattle — as reflected in the Old Testament (Deuteronomy 7, 13; 28, 4. 18. 51) by: *'ashterot ṣonaeka,* together with: *shegar 'alapaeka*, i.e. "the ashtartes of your small cattle" parallel to: "the growing force of your oxen", these terms now having a parallel in the Ugaritic text RS 24. 643, *rev.* 9 (Virolleaud 1968: 584), mentioning a sheep as a sacrifice to Ashtarte, to Shagar and to *Iṯm* respectively (*Iṯm* according to J.C. de Moor 1969: 178) the Arabic *waṯim:* firm-fleshed (cattle)). As the name of a god or a goddess we now see Shagar in an Aramaic text from Deir 'Alla, Transjordania (7th cent. BC) where Shagar and Ashtar (male) are listed together (Hoftijzer/van der Kooj 1976: 174; 273 sq.). It is tempting, with M. Delcor (1974a: 7 sq.) to translate Ashtarte simply by "fertility" (*fécondité*). More doubtful (and *contra* Delcor) is "Ashtarte of the field" (*'ṯtrt šd* (PRU II, 106; PRU V, 4; RS 24. 643, *recto*, 18 (Virolleaud 1968: 582))) as being an indication of the goddess of fertility, *šd* = "field" more likely alluding to the Netherworld, parallel to Ishtar *ṣeri, - ṣeru* being the name of the Netherworld in the Babylonian texts describing the descent of Ishtar in the Tammuz-liturgies (Tallqvist 1934: 17 sq.). But I agree with Delcor (*loc.cit.*) that the Ugaritic name Ashtarte *ḫurri* in an alphabetic text (CTA, 33, 1) as well as in a syllabic one (PRU IV, 18, 01) means "the Hurrian Ashtarte" and not: "Ashtarte of the cave"; the translation last mentioned is possible, however, in the Phoenician dedication on the Ashtarte-statuette from Cerro del Carambolo, Spain, as demonstrated by Delcor (1969: 321 sqq.), although I now prefer the translation proposed by E. Lipinski (1984: 102 sqq.): "Ashtarte-in-the-Window" — to whom I shall return later.

As a belligerent goddess, connected with Ba'al by her title "Name-of-Ba'al" Ashtarte acts in the Ugaritic texts, but — and this is important — often together with Anat (PRU V, 8, 7; RS 24. 258, 9. 22 and RS 24. 244, *recto*, 20 (Virolleaud 1968: 545-47; 565)); so in the Legend of Keret (CTA, 14 IV, 145 sq.) Princess Ḥuray is described as she, "whose beauty is as the beauty of Anat and whose loveliness is as the loveliness of Ashtarte". The same juxtaposition: Ashtarte and Anat often occurs in texts from the Ramesside-Period of Egypt (Hvidberg-Hansen 1979: I, 84; 100).

A surprise to the students of the Ugaritic texts was the dominating role of Anat, in the dramatic texts as well as in the sacrificial tariffs, being closely connected with Ba'al Saphon, and sometimes called Anat Saphon herself (CTA, 36, 17 sq. and RS 24. 253, *recto*, 13. 17

(Virolleaud 1968: 592)) — surprisingly because before Ugarit appeared, Anat was known rather sporadically: in a few Phoenician inscriptions from Cyprus, from Egyptian texts in the Ramesside-Period and from personal names in the Elephantine texts. The very detailed and varied picture we get of Anat makes it necessary to sum up (without citations) the nature of Anat in four points (the material as it was known until 1977 may be found in: Hvidberg-Hansen 1979: I, 79-105; II, 100-146; notes):

1. Anat is a violent and bloodthirsty goddess; her strength and her agility is legendary, e.g. she is called "Anat of the Dance" (*'nt ḥl,* cf. Hvidberg-Hansen 1979: II, 106, n. 31); compare "Anat, strength of life" identified with Athena Soteira Niké in a bilingual text from Larnax Lapithou, Cyprus (KAI, 42).

2. Being devoted to hunting and thus desiring the bow of the hero Aqhat, she acts in a cruel manner – having this and other traits in common with Artemis, as demonstrated already in 1939 by Th. H. Gaster (1939: 109 sqq.) and confirmed by texts discovered later; in a recension H. Cazelles remarks that Anat is more an Artemis than an Aphrodite (1982: 306).

3. Anat is a sky-goddess, called *ba'alat shamem rumem,* i.e. "Mistress of the lofty heavens", and she is a flying, i.e. a winged goddess — iconographically surely depicted on an Ugaritic cylinder seal (Caquot/Sznycer 1980: pl. XXIII, a) and on an Ugaritic stele, here carrying a lance (ANEP, 492).

4. She is the goddess of love, celebrating with Ba'al the sacred marriage "in the land of the plague, in the field of the strand of Death" and acting here in the shape of a cow or a heifer, as does Ba'al (CTA, 5 V, 16 sq.) — Ba'al, the young bull is recently confirmed by bronze figurines from the so-called "Bull-Site", from Iron Age I (about 1200 BC) not far from Dothan, Central Palestine (Mazar 1982: 27 sq.). Anat is a mother, too, so indicated by a personal name in a syllabic text from Ugarit: *A-na-ti-um-me* (Virolleaud 1951: 174 sq.). She is — together with Athirat — nursing (*Nutrix*) (CTA, 15, II, 25), and under the name of *Raḥmay* she is, together with Athirat, a bearing goddess (bearing Shahar and Shalim, the Ugaritic Dioscures). Her title is *betulat*, meaning "a young marriageable woman", even though often translated "Virgin", but then not signifying "Virgin *intacta*"; in relation to Anat "virgin" indicates eternal youth — as it is reflected in an Egyptian text from the Ramesside Period mentioning Anat and Ashtarte as "the two goddesses who conceive but do not bear" (*Papyr. mag. Harris*; Lange

1927; 30 sq.). I wonder if this could be a sublime hint at the sacred prostitution, well-known in the Near East and in the Mediterranean, from Abydos to Mt. Eryx (Fauth 1966: 359 sqq.)?

The third goddess in Ugarit, already mentioned as nursing together with Anat, is Athirat, the mother-goddess *par excellence*, "the Creatress of the gods" and "Mother of the gods", mother of seventy sons. She is *rabbat*, i.e. "the great Lady", a title almost reserved for her and borne only a few times by the Sun-goddess Shapshu. Since Athirat is associated with El, whose abode is "at the sources of the two Rivers, in the midst of the streams of the two Deeps", i.e. the cosmic or primordial waters, one understands why she bears the title "Athirat of the Sea" (*a̠trt ym*) i.e. "She who treads on the Sea" (Albright 1942: 77 sq.) and having a servant, "Fisherman of Athirat" (*dgy a̠trt*). Another title is "The Holy one" or Qudshu (*qdš*), a name which cannot be disregarded by an identification of the goddess on the well-known "Qudshu-steles" from the nineteenth dynasty in Egypt. As an argument for this goddess being identical with Athirat is the text published by D.B. Redford (1973: 36 sqq.) running so: "An offering...to Ptah, ... to Ashtarte, lady of heaven, to Anat, the daughter of Ptah, ... to Resheph, lord of heaven, to Qudsh, lady of the stars of heaven" (about 1400 BC) — combined with the Qudshu-stele from the Winchester Collection, dedicated to Qudshu-Anat-Ashtarte (Edwards 1955: 49 sq.) — Athirat then being Qudshu. From Ugarit then, we know Athirat as the supreme mother-goddess — one could call her "matronly" (Gese 1970: 149 sqq.); but as the young and active goddess of fertility — as such depicted on the Qudshu-steles: nude, young and with strongly marked sexuality — she is anything but matronly! As a Qudshu she had her cult in the temple of Jerusalem, until the end of the 7th cent. BC, with sacred prostitution (2 Kings 23). The Old Testament mentions her being symbolized by the sacred tree or the sacred grove (Lipinski 1972: 101 sqq.) — this recently confirmed by the discoveries from Kuntillat 'Ajrud (50 kms south of Qadesh Barnea); the inscriptions on two pithoi from the 9th-8th cent. mention "Yahweh and his Asherah"[1], and one pithos (pithos A) depicts the goddess sitting on a throne; further symbols are a stylized tree, the "sacred tree", and beneath it a striding lion (Dever 1984: 21 sqq., figs. 1, 7). The lion is commonly the symbol of Ashtarte and especially of Anat — compare the two inscriptions on an arrowhead from El-Khadr, not far from Bethlehem: "Servant of the lioness" (*'bdlb't*) and "Son of Anat" (*bn 'nt*) (Cross 1980: 1 sqq.) — but the lion-symbol connected with Athirat motivates W.G. Dever (1984: 28) to remark that there is "an extraordinary, almost bewildering fluidity in the Northwest Semitic deities" and that "we might conclude either that all is a meaningless chaos, or that the ancients were somewhat less rigidly 'logical' than we", concerning the variant use of the symbols of the deities. The symbolism about Athirat on pithos A can be enriched by two ithyphallic figures of Bes wearing feather crowns, the Bes-figures being taken by Dever as symbols of fertility and perhaps having an apotropaic function, too.

Connected with Yahweh, the goddess Asherah also appears in the inscription from Khirbet el-Qom, near Lachish (Dever 1969/70: 139-204), dating from the 8th cent. too. The inscriptions from Kuntillat 'Ajrud and from Khirbet el-Qom show Athirat or Asherah having in the 9th-8th cent. a distinct role in Palestine — apparently in contradiction to the case in the Canaanite or Phoenician cities Byblos, Sidon, Tyre — the two last mentioned having a cult of Athirat in the last half of the 2nd Millennium, according to the Keret-texts from Ugarit, which mention "Athirat of the Tyrians" parallel to "the Goddess of the Sidonians" (CTA, 14 IV 201-202: *aṯrt ṣrm wilt ṣdnym*). In the cities just mentioned Athirat has apparently been merged with Ashtarte and Anat (both of them listed in the Asarhaddon-treaty in the 7th cent. (Borger 1956: 107 sq.)) In this connection it should be mentioned that the claim of J.W. Betlyon that the so-called Ashtarte-chapel by the temple of Eshmun at Bostan esh-Sheikh (Sidon) belongs to Athirat is insufficiently proved — lacking the epigraphical proof (1985: 53 sq.).

That the maritime aspect of "Athirat of the Sea" during the 1st Millennium BC has merged with what H. Gese has called "the Ashtarte-conception" (1970: *passim*) in the Phoenician cities — in a period proved by the Phoenician inscriptions to be dominated by the cult of Ashtarte — can be deduced from the coinage and from other monuments. The coins of the Phoenician cities bearing from the Persian and Alexandrine period the motif: "Ashtarte, standing in galley or on prow" (Hill 1911/1965: *passim*) indicates Ashtarte's taking over the maritime aspect of Athirat in Tyre, Sidon etc. as well as in the more southern cities such as Ascalon. A few coins from the Imperial epoch (Gordianus) with the Phoenician inscription: '*lt ṣr* = "the Goddess of Tyre" may be a late reminiscence of the "Athirat of the Tyrians" (Hamburger 1954: 201 sq.), as suggested by F.M. Cross, jr. (1973: 31).

Various monuments of Atargatis (the contamination of Ashtarte and Anat) showing maritime symbols, especially the dolphin, are well-known among the Nabateans (Khirbet Tannur), these marine symbols being taken over from among others Ascalon, as N. Glueck rightly supposes (1965: 382 and *passim*) , Ascalon being the city which according to Diodorus Sic. had a temple of Atargatis-Derceto, with a fish-shaped cult-image (Diod.Sic. II, 4). The Nabatean goddess Allat (from *al-ilat*, cf. the Ugaritic *ilt*), called "Mother of the gods" in a Nabatean inscription (CIS II, 185), whom Herodutus calls *Alilat*, is the goddess of Ascalon, whom he too calls Aphrodite Ourania — whose temple Herodotus considers the eldest and the one from which the cult of Aphrodite Ourania has been spread westwards, to Cyprus and Cythera (Herod. I, 105. 131; III, 8). But this goddess is stated as being armed (Pausanias III, 23; Hesychius, *s.v. enkheios*); this aspect, however, corresponds to the cult at Ascalon, where the coinage of Roman imperial time shows the armed goddess called *Phanebalos*, occasionally with the so-called Sign of Tanit. These coins are thus supposed to have the aspect of Anat, the cult of whom is indicated from the very name Derceto, having now been documentated as an Ugaritic epithet of Anat (*drkt* = "rule, dominion"), and from the mention of "Anat at Gaza" (near Ascalon) in an Egyptian text from the 12th cent. (Grdseloff 1942: 35 sq.; Hvidberg-Hansen 1979: I, 85, 95 with note 210). The Oriental (Ascalonite) Aphrodite Ourania, *alias* Anat plus Ashtarte added to the maritime functions of Athirat, is an important contribution to the cult and religion of the Occident (cf. M.P. Nilsson considering the Aphrodite *Euploia* as an Oriental characteristic, 1967: 521).[2]

Summing up the elements from Ashtarte plus Anat and from Athirat, we have the Great Oriental Goddess (as a common denominator):

1. Mother and *Nutrix*; fertility together with the maritime aspect.
2. A sky-goddess.
3. Young and attractive (Virgin, but not *intacta*).
4. Warlike and sometimes even cruel — comparable to Artemis.

* * *

From about the beginning of the 1st Millennium BC, then, we notice — especially from the Phoenician inscriptions — the changes of the Canaanite-Phoenician religion known from the Ugaritic texts. These innovations are surveyed by H. Gese (1970: 182 sqq.) and G. Garbini (1981: 29 sqq.).

One of the most important Phoenician or Punic inscriptions discovered in the last two decennia is the one from Pyrgi, together with the longer Etruscan one constituting a *quasi*-bilingual text. The identification of Ashtarte with the Etruscan Uni or Iuno confirms — as is well known — the statement of St. Augustine: *lingua punica Iuno Astarte vocatur* (Hept. VII, 16).

Among the numerous problems in the Semitic text, I shall — referring to the translation of G. Garbini (1980a: 207 sqq.) — mention the *crux* of the text, being the verb *'rš* (line 6), which should be taken (with Gårbini) cognate to the Hebrew verb *'arash*, "ask for, wish", here being an intensive form: "give in possession, give in hand", i.e. "to allow"; lines 5-9 then: "and he (king Thefarie) built a mark (*tw* = "temple" or the like) because Ashtarte had given him in hand to reign for three years, in the month of *Krr*, on the day of the burial of the deity". The buried deity is most likely Melqart, to whom lines 9-10 may allude: "May the years (granted) to the statue of the deity in its temple be (as many) as these stars!" — as demonstrated by S. Ribichini (1975: 41 sqq.; cf. also Lipinski 1970: 35 sqq.). Further evidence for a cult of Ashtarte and Melqart is adduced by M. Verzár, who in her well-documented study on Aphrodite at Pyrgi (1980: 35-84) demonstrates that the iconography of the antefixes from Temple B at Pyrgi together with "the burial of the deity", related to the ritual burning of Melqart, "in the month of *Krr*", i.e. the month of the sacred dance, indicate that the cult of the sanctuary at Pyrgi was a cult of Ashtarte-Melqart. According to M. Verzár this cult was so to speak within the sphere of Aphrodite-Heracles, and Aphrodite was identical with the Oriental Aphrodite *Parakyptousa* or Venus *Prospiciens alias* "Ashtarte-in-the-Window". This goddess must then have come via Cyprus to Rome, and was there assimilated to the Italic *Mater matuta*. The last mentioned — as for her being a matronly goddess and an Aurora — was for her part identified with Leucothea and Eileithyeia; according to R. Bloch this identification mediates that of Iuno with Leucothea and Eileithyeia, just as is the case at Pyrgi, where *Theisan* (Aurora) is proved epigraphically (Bloch 1976: 1 sqq.; 1981: 124 sqq.). Concerning the name of the month *Krr* as "the month of the dance" one can refer — semantically— to the Arabic name of the month *ḏu-l-hiğğa* and the Hebrew name of the feast of Passover, *pesaḥ* (Wellhausen 1897: 109; Delcor 1974b: 68 sq.).

We have a rather late confirmation of Heracles being connected with Leucothea in a Greek dedication from the Severan period in Tyre (Chebab 1962: 17sq). More important, however, is the above-mentioned Phoenician inscription from Cerro del Carambolo, if the interpretation of E. Lipinski is correct, the Ashtarte *ḥr* being "Ashtarte-in the-Window" ("Ashtarte à la fenêtre") (1984: 100-117), especially if the provenance of the inscription is Phoenician proper. The inscription then confirms the motif of Ashtarte (Aphrodite) *Parakyptousa* as this is well known from Syria, Phoenicia, Cyprus, etc. (Fauth 1966: *passim*). A hint of this aspect of the fertility-goddess we may have — as E. Lipinski states — in an Ugaritic passage: "when Ashtarte-of-the-Window enters the *lupanar* of the temple of the king" (CTA, 33, 1; Lipinski *loc. cit.*).

Leucothea of the Greeks is noted to be the goddess of navigation and of seafarers — so characterized by I. Krauskopf as "die freundliche und hilfreiche Meeresgottheit" (1981: 137-148). But if in the cult of Ashtarte-Uni-Leucothea at Pyrgi — as has been demonstrated by M. Verzár — there actually are elements which can be traced back, via the Greeks or via the Phoenicians themselves, to the Aphrodite from Cyprus — then it raises the question of whether in the character of the goddess at Pyrgi there may be some elements which have their background in the Aphrodite Ourania, *alias* the goddess from Ascalon, the nature of whom is a contamination of the violent Anat/Ashtarte (Anat being in Ugarit the "Anat of the Dance") with "Athirat of the Sea". I. Krauskopf touches on this by referring to Aphrodite *Euploia,* who we have seen may be traced back to the Near East (as stated by M.P. Nilsson) (Krauskopf 1981: 147). The mother-aspect of Anat and not least of Athirat may here have been a stimulating element, cf. the hypothesis of R. Bloch concerning *Mater matuta* mediating the identification of Uni-Iuno with Leucothea.[3]

It is no wonder that Uni at Pyrgi is called Ashtarte, and not Anat; this fits well with the fact that neither in the rest of the Occident does Anat act under her own name, but is partly assimilated to Ashtarte, and partly — as I still believe — has her Occidental existence in the Punic Tanit.

It has been discussed whether the inscription from Pyrgi was Phoenician or Punic, or — in other words — whether its provenance is due to Phoenicians who, via Cyprus, have reached the Italian coast, or to Carthaginian relations with the Etruscans — these relations being relevant in the period about the battle of Alalia (535) or the treaty between Carthage and Rome (509). If the text is Punic one has also wondered why Iuno is identified with Ashtarte, and not with Tanit (a survey of this discussion: Garbini 1980a: 205 sqq.; Hvidberg-Hansen 1979: II, 65). This question being important in itself is not, however, decisive for the relation of Ashtarte to Iuno when we take into consideration that the cult of Ashtarte was well established in Carthage from the earliest times (cf. the Ashtarte-Pygmalion inscription from the 8th cent. BC (KAI, 72, cf. Krahmalkov 1981: 117 sqq.)), as G. Garbini rightly states (*op.cit.*, 208); the tradition about the role of Cyprus in the foundation of Carthage should not be forgotten here.

More difficult is the problem of why Ashtarte or Ashtarte-Anat in the Occident is at one moment identified with Iuno-Hera, at another with Aphrodite-Venus. A general answer cannot, I think, be given. (The argument of F. Della Corte: that the Semitic goddess was worshipped at Paphos in a non-human form (a conic baetyl), so that one non-Semite would consider the baetyl a Iuno, and another an Aphrodite, is insufficient (1983: 651 sqq.)). The problem has to be solved, if possible, by searching behind general terms and names, e.g. the common use — by St. Augustine among others — of the name of Ashtarte, cf. the well formulated remarks of W. Röllig (1981: 71), and one has to draw the tracks back to the Near East, taking one's basis in the Canaanite texts as just mentioned. One has also to take account of local cultic conditions as well as political events, as for example at Selinunt (Sicily) where the Magna-Grecian culture from about 400 BC came under the political dominance of Carthage (White 1967: 335 sqq.).

The setting up of the Phoenician-Punic and Etruscan inscriptions at Pyrgi has been compared with that of a Greek and Punic one by Hannibal to Hera *Hoplosmia*, the armed Hera, in the temple of the Lacinium Promontory near Croton in 205 (Bloch, 1972, 388), Hera having there her sacred grove and cattle. We learn from Cicero (*de divin.* I, 24) that during the 2nd Punic War Hannibal intended to pillage the golden column of Hera, but warned by Hera herself he returned the column and set upon its top a Golden calf (*buculam*). This symbolized Hera together with her cattle, but no doubt — cf. Hannibal's two inscriptions — the Carthaginian goddess Tanit, too, just as E. Vassel (1912: 36), V. Basanoff (1945: 64 sq.) and G. Dumézil (1966: 450) suppose. This tradition being late, it must be admitted, may yet indicate that the Golden calf is a symbol of Tanit; F. Lenormant maintained as early as 1881 that "la vache était aussi un des principaux symboles de Tanit ou Junon coelestis" — but unfortunately without any concrete reference (1881: II, 226 sq.)! Yet, on a Punic mosaic from the 4th-3rd cent. BC at Selinunt we may have such a reference: next to the so-called Sign of Tanit is the head of a cow (or bull) (Tusa 1971: 61 sq.; fig. 20). If we take into account that Anat — sometimes acting in the shape of a cow — has been merged with "Athirat of the Sea", the mother-goddess represented herself by the sacred grove, and has been merged in some respect with Ashtarte, protectress of the cattle (as we learn from the Old Testament), and if we take into account that the natures of these goddesses constitute, to a large extent, the nature of Tanit, then the somewhat hazardous statement of F. Lenormant now gains a more solid basis. And Tanit as an armed goddess — we remember the *Phanebalos*-coins from Ascalon, some of them with the Sign of Tanit — may have been a centre of attraction to an armed Hera *Hoplosmia*, as is Athena Soteira Nike to Anat in the bilingual inscription from Larnax Lapithou (KAI, 42), about 4th cent. BC.

Which of the two goddesses, Ashtartę or Tanit, was locally identified with a Pre-Phoenician goddess of a given sanctuary, may be determined from the prevailing aspect of the local deity; for instance at Mt. Eryx sacred prostitution was characteristic in the Phoenician-Punic period, but if this element was Pre-Phoenician it may have been just that element which attracted Ashtarte, she herself being influenced by the Paphian cult. In fact literary traditions as well as archaeological discoveries affirm a relation between Cyprus and Mt. Eryx (as for the literary traditions, cf. Galinsky 1969: 75 sq.; for the archaeological material, cf. Grotanelli 1981: 121 sq.; Bisi 1966: 239 sq.; 1981: 134 sqq.). The Carthaginian Ashtarte, on the other hand, does not — like Tanit — seem to have been a sky-goddess, and this aspect in connection with the function of the Carthaginian Tanit as a tutelary goddess seems to have been decisive in the identification of the Roman Iuno with Tanit, evocated to Rome as she was by a ritual *evocatio* under the name of Iuno Caelestis (Basanoff 1945: 3 sq.; 63 sqq.).

* * *

Talking on Tas-Silġ at a Conference in Malta may seem to "carry coals to Newcastle", but the results of the discoveries here: the *fanum Iunonis* definitively localized as the sanctuary of Ashtarte and Tanit, are very important. Today everybody knows, that the cult at Tas-Silġ has — just as at Mt. Eryx — a pre-historic substrate, which the so-called "fat lady" demonstrates (*Missione* 1964: 75; pl. 30). As stated by M. Guzzo Amadasi and G. Garbini, the dedications to Ashtarte are numerous, contrary to the few to Tanit, and those of Ashtarte are dated to the 5th-4th cent. and on, whereas those of Tanit date from the 3rd-2nd or from 2nd-1st cent. BC (Guzzo Amadasi 1967: 27-52; Garbini, *Missione* 1965: 55 sqq.). The scanty appearance of Tanit is explained by M. Sznycer by the condition of Malta, having to a large extent conserved its original Phoenician character, and thus being less "Punified" so to speak — which is underlined by the two famous bilingual dedications to Melqart-Heracles (CIS I, 122-122 *bis*), which, though dating from the 2nd cent. BC are written in Phoenician characters, not in Punic ones (Sznycer 1973-74: 131 sq.; *id.*, 1974-75, 199). This is not contradicted by the two dedications to Ba'al Ḥammon, dating from the 6th cent. BC (CIS I, 123-123*bis*), given the Phoenician origin of this deity and of the name of Ba'al Ḥammon — as formerly stated.

Ashtart and Tanit, then? As is well known, they are mentioned side by side in a Carthaginian dedication: "to the great Ladies, to Ashtarte and to Tanit in *Lbnn*" (KAI, 81). The discovery of the ivory-inscription from Sarepta, Phoenicia, according to the already common opinion dedicated to Tanit-Ashtarte, means — with the dating of the inscription by J.B. Pritchard to the 7th-6th cent. BC (1982: 83 sqq.; Garbini (1980b: 1035 sq.) says 6th cent.) — that Tanit can now be found under her very name Tanit in the Phoenician homeland even before Tanit appears in the 5th cent. BC on the Carthaginian steles. The conclusion then, is, that we now either have Tanit in her supposed homeland from the beginning, or as a re-introduction to Phoenicia from the Punic Occident. The last mentioned possibility, however, is difficult to accept, taking into account the just mentioned date of the oldest Tanit-inscriptions from Carthage.

I admit, however, being a little in doubt as to whether Tanit really is to be found in the Sarepta-inscription, the two last words of which are: L/TNT' ŠTRT. Some years ago F.M. Cross, jr., put forward the hypothesis that the name Tanit is a feminine form of the Hebrew name of the Sea Dragon, Tannin: **tannintu* > *tannittu* (1967: 12; 1973: 32-33) (a hypothesis, however, put forward already in 1912 by E. Vassel (1912: 55 sq.)). Cross supported this by referring to the Proto-Sinaitic inscriptions where the word TNT occurs, this (according to Cross) being the name of the "Lady of the Serpent" (ḎT B ṮN) or Ba'alat. Albright, however, has demostrated that the Proto-Sinaitic TNT means "gift", deriving it from the root *ytn* or *ntn* (1948: 13 sq.; 1969: 17; he is followed by A. van den Branden (1962: 208) and by E. Puech (1983: 577)).

From the Proto-Sinaitic inscriptions of the 15th cent. BC to the Sarepta-inscription there is a long space of time — longer, however, is that between the inscriptions from Sinai and the Punic inscriptions at Tas-Silġ, where we have the two characters LT, which G. Garbini supposes to be an abbreviated form of the root *ytn,* "to give", LT then meaning "to a gift" or the like (*Missione* 1964: 83; *ibid.* 1965: 61). The words L/TNT'ŠTRT in the Sarepta-inscription, then, I should like to propose, may perhaps somewhat provocatively be translated: "to a gift of (i.e. to) Ashtarte" — TNT then being, as in the Proto-Sinaitic inscriptions, a *t*-affixed infinitive or noun from the root *ytn*; the initial Y has been elided (cf. the infinitive of *natan* in Hebrew) and the final N has been retained, cf. the Punic MTNT = "gift" and the Canaanite or Phoenician personal name Mitinti (*Mi-ti-in-ti*) in Assyrian texts (Tallqvist 1914: 138; Benz, 1972, 356 and Friedrich-Röllig 1970: 22, 97). TNT is here further taken as an objective genitive to the following word 'ŠTRT.

The Sarepta-inscription hereafter runs (the vocalisation of the personal names tentative): "The statue which Shillem, son of Maph'al, son of Uzza, made to a gift for (to) Ashtarte". — Being aware of the difficulty that one will prefer the formula TNT L'ŠTRT, I wish, however, to offer this translation for futher discussion — but, as it may be known and as stated by me above, I, too, am of the opinion that Tanit should be found (as a goddess distinct from Ashtarte) in the very Canaanite or Phoenician area).

How difficult the materials are in this respect may be seen from the problems of the so-called Sign of Tanit; the sign has been interpreted differently: from the most concrete (a conic baetyl like that at Paphos) via the Egyptian Sign of Life (*ankh*), to a speculative meaning with parallels in Jewish cabbalistic symbolism (so Barreca 1977: 165 sqq.; a survey of the interpretations is given in Picard, *Catalogue*: 22 sq.) The Sign of Tanit has recently been taken by G. Garbini as a combination of the *ankh* with the triangle — the triangle known as a symbol of fertility from the *tophet* at Sulcis (Sardinia) and from Ras il-Wardija (Gozo) (Garbini 1980b: 1035 sqq.) and — as I am more inclined to believe — as a schematized form of the nude, feminine figures with uplifted arms, which can be found on golden lamine and stone cassettes from Cyprus, dating from the Cypro-Geometric I to the Cypro-Archaic I period (i.e. from about 1000 to 600 BC), as proposed by A.M. Bisi (1980: 213 sqq.). How complicated the materials are, however, is demonstrated by the discovery of a Sign of Tanit at Ashdod, Palestine, in an archaeological stratum from the 9th cent. BC, as referred by Bisi (1979: 18, with reference to Dothan-Freedman 1966: 132, 148-149). But the form of the sign in question is closely related to that of the steles from Carthage in the 3rd cent. BC, and in addition the sign from Ashdod seems to be of a male form! One is not far from wishing that the discovery coming from the 9th-century stratum at Ashdod is due to a mere chance (as A.M. Bisi hints; *loc. cit.*).

Having just mentioned the male aspect of the fertility cult, I will end my paper by mentioning Melqart, whom — in Malta — it would be rather impolite to disregard! The two aforementioned bilingual inscriptions dedicated to Melqart-Heracles, called "the Lord of Tyre", of which the provenance in Malta is unfortunately unknown, as recently demonstrated by Dr. A. Bonanno (1982: 190 sqq.), must, however, have belonged to the temple of Heracles, referred to by Ptolemy (*Geogr.* III, 3), although the actual site of this sanctuary is still unknown, as far as I know. Given the identity of Melqart and Milkashtart, at least in the later Phoenician and Punic period (cf. Dussaud 1948: 229; Gese 1970: 198; Lipinski 1984: 93-100), one will be tempted to ask whether the dedication to Milkashtart at Tas-Silġ, published by M. Guzzo Amadasi (*Missione* 1970: 92 sq.) and dated by her to the 4th cent. BC, indicates the sanctuary at Tas-Silġ as belonging not only to Iuno *alias* Ashtarte-Tanit, but also to Melqart *alias* Milkashtart. I put forward this question, well aware that the placings by Ptolemy of the temples of Hera-Iuno and of Heracles-Melqart are somewhat different (concerning the geographical indications of Ptolemy, cf. V. Borg, *Missione* 1963: 12).

Thanks to the studies of S. Ribichini and P. Xella concerning Milkashtart. we can now consider this god to be an old Canaanite deity, whose nature was chtonic and who was connected with the Ugaritic Rephaim (*rpum*), the meaning of which is "to heal", and who later on is connected with Melqart (Ribichini - Xella 1979: 145 sqq.). Making at last an attempt to clarify the ancient problem concerning the name of ṢDMB'L (Ṣadamba'al) in the Punic inscription from Gozo (CIS I, 132 = KAI, 62), I take for granted the following identifications, mentioning them only very briefly:

In the Punic period the god Shadrapha', whose name implies a healer-god (cf. the Ugaritic *rpu, rpum*), stands side by side with Milkashtart, so at Leptis Magna in the beginning of the 1st cent. BC (KAI, 119); at Leptis Magna we also see Shadrapha' identified with *Liber Pater* in a bilingual inscription from the 1st cent. AD (KAI, 127), and *Liber Pater* (*alias* Shadrapha') standing side by side with Heracles (cf. Levi della Vida 1942: 29 sqq.; 1959: 299 sqq.). From Antas, Sardinia, we know that Shadrapha' is identified with Ṣid *alias Sardus Pater* in the 4th-3rd cent. BC (Sznycer 1969: 69 sqq.; Ferron 1976: 425 sqq.), and in Carthage Ṣid stands side by side with Melqart (CIS I, 256). In other words: Shadrapha' and Ṣid, being identical, are standing *vis à vis*, or side by side with Milkashtart and Melqart, respectively.

These facts may help us explain the name of ṢDMB'L from the Gozo inscription mentioning a temple of Ashtarte and of the deity ṢDMB'L (Ṣadamba'al), whose name has provoked such different explanations: as being an error in writing for ṢLMB'L, occurring in

Greek as *Salambò* or *Salambas*, which in their turn may be either a name of a goddess mourning for Adonis (according to Hesychius and to *Etymol.magnum, s.v.*), and perhaps to be related to the feminine personal name Salambò (*Slmbw*) from Gaza, according to South-Arabic (Minean) texts (so Robin 1975-76: 184 sqq.), or of a god of the Adonis-type (Cumont 1927: 330 sqq.; Gressmann, *s.v.* Salambo, RE). Or ṢDMB'L has been equated with Ba'al ṢMD from Kilamuwa (KAI, 24, 13, cfr. vol. 2, 78). The last mentioned explanati‹ .s seem to be rather improbable, however, the name of Ba'al ṢMD at Kilamuwa being geographically far from Gozo, and in addition involving an error in writing (ṢMD instead of ṢDM). The explanation first mentioned suffers from the difficulty of how to explain the spelling of the name of the deity with *daleth* instead of *lamed*. The reference to the very name of Gozo, which can be found in Greek as Gaulos or as Gaudos (Schröder 1869: 105), does not seem to hold good in the inscription in question, where the name of Gozo occurs as GWL, i.e. with *lamed* (line 1); this letter, then, should be expected to be found in the name of the deity, too. The statement of F.C. Movers, cited by P. Schröder (*loc. cit.*), that "in the Phoenician language we do not have any example of changing *daleth* - *lamed* nor do we have any sure example of a confusion of the two letters" is still valuable.[4]

Returning to the name of the deity ṢDMB'L, we have stated that the cult of Milkashtart and of Melqart being present in Malta, then — bearing in mind the juxtaposition of these gods with Shadrapha' and Ṣid, respectively, and the identity of the two gods last mentioned — it will be tempting to read ṢDMB'L so: "their Ṣid, Ba'al" taking ṢDM as the divine name of Ṣid connected with the pronominal or possessive suffix *-m,* either being 3rd plural masculine, or 3rd singular masculine (both of which are possible in Punic, cf. Friedrich-Röllig 1970: 47 sq.); the suffix then referring to "the people of Gaulus" in the foregoing line of the inscription. The beginning of the fragmentary text then runs:

"The people of Gaulus made and restored the three (?) ...(lacuna) / the sanctuary of the temple of their (or: its) Ṣid, the Lord". Or ṢDM may be taken, too, as a plural *majestatis*, then: "the temple of Ṣid, the Lord". Against the objection that the reading of ṢDM as "their (or: its) can be argued that this phenomenon is not unknown in the Semitic languages, e.g. Arabic and Ugaritic (Driver 1954: 125 sqq.) or probably in Aramaic (so the divine proper name Gad occurs in a determined form (article or suffix) GD', cfr. DISO: 47 (e.g. RES 53, 1)) and in Hebrew (Kuntillat 'Ajrud and Khirbet el-Qom: "Yahweh and his Asherah" (*lyhwh...wl'šrth*), cf. the discussion by Dever 1984: 22, note 5; 30 sq.; Zevit 1984: 44 sqq.).

The interpretation just proposed for SDM has the merit of avoiding textual emendations as well as far-fetched names of gods, and if the interpretation turns out to be correct, it further means that the Phoenician-Punic cult in Gozo (*via* the name of Sid), together with the cult of Milkashtart at Tas-Silġ and with that of Ṣid *alias* Shadrapha'at Antas and at Leptis Magna, enters the sphere of the chtonic, healing and fertility-giving gods — as they are stated as early as in Ugarit (the *rpum*) — and is a cult connected with "Melqart, the Lord of Tyre" (CIS I, 122-122*bis*).

To sum up:

The theme of the Conference: "Archaeology and Fertility Cult in the Ancient Mediterranean" is a vast and complicated affair, especially, perhaps, in respect of the Phoenician-Punic period. The lack of a Phoenician or a Punic mythology, handed over *directly* from the Phoenicians themselves during the 1st Millennium BC, forces us to combine the archaeological results (among those the often ambiguous inscriptions), with the — rather late — traditions found in the Classical Greek and Latin literature. No wonder, then, that our conclusions are so uncertain and have to be currently revised.

Notes

1 To "Yahweh and his Asherah" see below.

2 Among the various etymologies of the name of Aphrodite, that proposed by P. Kretschmer about ninety years ago (Kretschmer 1895: 267) should be mentioned; according to Kretschmer, Aphrodite means "She who walks on the sea-foam"; even if this etymology may be incorrect, it touches — as is evident from what has just been mentioned concerning "Athirat of the Sea" (*aṯrt ym*) = "She who treads on the Sea" — the very Oriental background of the goddess Aphrodite.

3 For a similar establishment of a Phoenician cult on Italian soil, cf. the studies of D. Van Berchem (1960), A. Piganiol (1962) and R. Rebuffat (1966) on Melqart-Heracles and Iuno *Maxima* in *Forum Boarium*, Rome, the Phoenician Melqart being introduced there as early as in the 7th-6th cent. BC. (The epithet *Maxima*, according to Rebuffat (1966: 22 sq.) being unique, I suggest that it is a translation of the Phoenician *rbt* ("the Great Lady"), cf. *rbt 'štrt* at Pyrgi).

4 A Greek etymology of the name (in Greek characters) *Ṣalambô* or *Salambas* remains uncertain (Frisk 1960/70: 11, 673); the best explanation still being that proposed by O. Blau and others: *Salambo* is the Phoenician Salamba'al, i.e. "likeness (or: image) of Ba'al" (Blau 1860: 649 sqq.; cf Hvidberg-Hansen 1979: I, 17 sq., note 70). Gozo (Gaudos) has recently been interpreted as a Latin-Castilian translation of the Semitic GWL (from the root GYL = "rejoice") by Diez Merino (1983: 276 sqq.).

Summary

From the middle of the 2nd till the beginning of the 1st millen. BC our acquaintance with the Canaanite-Phoenician religion is based on the text material from Ugarit. The most important deities are El and his consort Athirat, and Ba'al with the two goddesses Anat and Ashtarte attached to him — the role of the last mentioned, however, being rather modest. During the 1st millen. the position of El and Ba'al is in essentials unchanged, though the nature of Ba'al absorbs elements formerly being those of El, as is the case with Ba'al Ḥammon. In the 1st millen. BC the maritime aspect of Athirat is further assimilated to Anat and Ashtarte, and in the Hellenistic period the nature of the two last mentioned tends towards a contamination, in Phoenicia proper resulting in Atargatis. In the Punic religion the essential elements from Anat supplied with the maritime aspect of Athirat can be found in the goddess Tanit. In the Cypro-Greek culture we find the nature of the Semitic goddesses in Aphrodite Ourania.

In the Occident a syncretism between the Semitic goddesses and the local ones goes on: so at the Etruscan Pyrgi *Uni*-Ashtarte, at the South Italic Croton Hera-Tanit. On Mt. Eryx (Sicily) and at Tas-Silġ (Malta) the Pre-Phoenician goddesses are succeeded by Ashtarte and Tanit; in the Hellenistic period the Eryx goddess is called Venus whereas the Semetic one at Tas-Silġ is called Hera-Iuno. In Carthage Tanit exists as Iuno Caelestis in the Roman period.

The Canaanite-Phoenician origin of Tanit is likely, even if the ivory inscription from Sarepta as a proof of this can be questioned. Open to discussion is further the origin of the so-called Sign of Tanit. Finally it is stated that a dedication to Milkashtarte (mainly identical with Melqart) from Malta may help us to explain the rather enigmatic name in the Punic inscription from Gozo: ṢDMB'L, which can be understood as the Phoenician-Punic Ṣid who in the Occident stands side by side with Melqart-Heracles, both of whom are well-known from the two bilingual inscriptions from Malta (CIS I, 122-122*bis*).

Résumé

Pour la période qui va du milieu du deuxième millénaire au début du premier av. J.-C., nos connaissances de la religion cananéo-phénicienne se basent sur les textes ougaritiques. Les dieux les plus importants sont El, son épouse Athirat et Ba'al, auquel s'associent les deux déesses Anat et, avec un rôle plus modeste, Astarté. Au cours du premier millénaire, les positions d'El et de Ba'al restent sans changements essentiels, bien que la nature de Ba'al s'approprie des éléments qui avaient appartenu à El, comme c'est le cas pour Ba'al Ḥammon. Au cours du même millénaire, l'aspect maritime d'Athirat est attribué également à Anat et à Astarté, et dans la période hellénistique, celles-ci tendent à se confondre, en s'unissant, dans la Phénicie proprement dite, en Atargatis. Dans la religion punique, les éléments essentiels d'Anat, joints à l'aspect maritime d'Athirat, se retrouvent dans la déesse Tanit. Dans la culture chypro-grecque, nous retrouvons la nature des déesses sémitique dans Aphrodite Ourania.

En Occident, le syncrétisme des déesses sémitiques avec les déesses locales se perpétue, ainsi *Uni*-Astarté à Pyrgi en Etrurie, Héra-Tanit à Crotone en Italie du Sud. Au mont Eryx (Sicile) et à Tas-Silġ (Malte), les déesses préphéniciennes sont supplantées par Astarte et Tanit; pendant la période hellénistique, la déesse du mont Eryx est appelée Vénus, alors que la déesse sémitique de Tas-Silġ est appelée Héra-Junon. A Carthage, Tanit existe pendant la période romaine sous le nom de Junon Caelestis.

L'origine cananéo-phénicienne de Tanit est probable, même si l'on peut douter de la valeur probante de l'inscription sur ivoire de Sarepta. L'origine du soi-disant Signe de Tanit reste également ouverte à la discussion. Enfin, on a suggéré qu'une dédicace à Milkashtart (en grande partie identique à Melqart) de Malte, pourrait nous aider à expliquer le nom assez énigmatique qu'on lit dans l'inscription punique de Gozo: ṢDMB'L: on peut l'interpréter comme le Ṣid phénicéo-punique qui, en Occident, est mis à côté de Melqart-Héraclès, tout deux bien connus par les deux inscriptions bilingues de Malte (CIS I, 122-122*bis*).

Abbreviations

Besides the system of abbreviations according to the *American Journal of Archaeology* (AJA) the following abbreviations have been used:

Actes	*Actes de la XVIIe Rencontre assyriologique internationale. Université Libre de Bruxelles, 30 juin - 4. juillet 1969. Étud. rec. par A. Finet,* 1970.
Akten 1981	*Akten des Kolloquiums zum Thema Die Göttin von Pyrgi. Archäologische, linguistische und religionsgeschichtliche Aspekte (Tübingen, 16-17 Januar 1979*), Firenze 1981.
ANEP	*Ancient Near East in Pictures, relating to The Old Testament.* 2nd ed., by J.B. Pritchard, New Jersey 1969.
Atti 1983	*Atti del I. Congresso Internazionale di Studi fenici e punici, Roma 5-10 novembre 1979,* I-III, Roma 1983.
CIS I	*Corpus Inscriptionum Semiticarum. Pars prima, Inscriptiones Phoenicias continens,* Paris 1881 sqq.
CIS II	*Corpus Inscriptionum Semiticarum. Pars secunda, Inscriptiones aramaicas continens,* Paris 1889 sqq.
CTA	*Corpus des Tablettes en cunéiformes alphabétiques,* I-II, éd. A. Herdner, Paris 1963.
DISO	*Dictionnaire des inscriptions sémitiques de l'Ouest,* éd. Ch. -F. Jean et J. Hoftijzer, Leiden 1960.
Eugenio Manni 1980	*Miscellanea di studi classici in onore di Eugenio Manni,* I-VI, Roma 1980.
Festschrift J. Friedrich	*Festschrift Johannes Friedrich zum 65. Geburtstag am 27. Aug. 1958 gewidmet,* Heidelberg 1959.
KAI	H. Donner - W. Röllig: *Kanaanäische und aramäische Inschriften,* I-III, Wiesbaden 1966-1968/69.
Missione 1963 sqq.	*Missione archeologica italiana a Malta. Rapporto preliminare della Campagna 1963 sqq.,* di V. Bonello *et al.*, Roma 1964 sqq.
MRS	*Mission de Ras Shamra,* dirigée par Cl. F. - A. Schaeffer, Paris.
Picard, *Catalogue*	*Catalogue du Musée Alaoui, Nouv. série (Collections puniques I)* par C. Gilbert Picard, Tunis *s.d.*

PRU II	*Le Palais Royal d'Ugarit II,* publ. sous la direction de Cl. F. - A. Schaeffer, Paris 1957.
PRU V	*Le Palais Royal d'Ugarit V.,* publ. sous la direction de Cl. F. - A. Schaeffer, Paris 1965.
RE	*Paulys Realencyclopädie der klassischen Altertumswissenschaft,* hrsg. G. Wissowa, Stuttgart 1894 sqq.
Religione 1981	*La Religione fenicia. Matrici orientali e sviluppi occidentali. Atti del Colloquio in Roma, 6 marzio 1979,* Roma 1981.
Saggi Fenici 1975	*Saggi Fenici* - I, di G. Benigni *et al.*, Centro di Studio per la Civiltà fenicia e punica. Roma 1975.

Bibliography

ALBRIGHT, W.F.

1942 — *Archaeology and the Religion of Israel,* Baltimore.

1948 — The Early Alphabetic Inscriptions from Sinai and their Decipherment, *BASOR* 110, pp. 6-22.

1969 — *The proto-Sinaitic Inscriptions and their Decipherment* (Harvard Theol. Stud. XXII), Cambridge (Harvard Univ. Press).

BARRECA, F.

1977 — A proposito di una scultura aniconica rinvenuta nel Sinis di Cabras (Oristano) *RivStFen* V, pp. 165-179.

BASANOFF, V.

1945 — *Evocatio,* Paris.

BENZ, F.L.

1972 — *Personal Names in the Phoenician and Punic Inscriptions* (Studia Pohl 8), Rome.

BETLYON, J.W.

1985 — The Cult of ʻAsherah/ʻElat at Sidon, *JNES* XLIV, pp. 53-56.

BISI, A.M.

1966 — Studi punici - III. Testimonianze fenicio-puniche ad Erice, *Oriens antiquus* V, pp. 238-48.

1979 — Les sources syro-paléstiniennes et chypriotes de l'art punique, *AntAfr* XIV, pp. 17-35.

1980 — Ancora sull'origine del segno di Tanit, *Eugenio Manni* 1980, pp. 213-229.

1981 — Intervento di A.M. Bisi, in *Religione* 1981, pp. 134-135.

BLAU, O.
1860 — Phönikische Analekten, *ZDMG* XIV, pp. 649-662.

BLOCH, R.
1972 — Héra, Uni, Junon en Italie centrale, *CRAIBL,* 1972 (1973), pp. 384-395.
1976 — *Recherches sur les religions de l'Italie antique,* Genève (Droz).
1981 — Le culte étrusco-punique de Pyrgi vers 500 avant J.C., *Akten* 1981, pp. 123-129.

BONANNO, A.
1982 — Quintinus and the Location of the Temple of Hercules at Marsaxlokk, *Melita historica* VIII, no. 3, pp. 190-204.

BORDREUIL, P.
1986 — Attestations inédites de Melqart, Baal Ḥamon et Baal Ṣaphon à Tyr, *Religio Phoenicia: Studia Phoenicia IV,* pp. 76-86. Namur

BORG, V.
1963 (1964) — Tradizioni e documenti storici, *Missione* 1963 (1964), pp. 41-51.

BORGER, R.
1957 — Der Vertrag mit Baal von Tyrus, *ArchfOrient, Beiheft* 9, pp. 107-109.

CANTINEAU, J.
1938 — Tadmorea, *Syria* XIX pp. 72-82.

CAQUOT, A. et SZNYCER, M.
1980 — *Ugaritic Religion* (Iconography of Religions XV, 8), Leiden (E.J. Brill).

CAZELLES, H.
1982 — Review of: S. Ribichini, Adonis, *RivStFen* X, pp. 305-307.

CHEBAB, M.
1962 — Tyr à l'époque romaine *MélUnivSJoseph,* XXXVIII, pp. 12-40.

CRAIGIE, P.C.
1981 — Ugarit and the Bible, *Ugarit in Retrospect. Fifty Years of Ugarit and Ugaritic,* ed. G. Douglas Young (Winona Lake, Indiana), pp. 99-111.

CROSS, F.M.
1967 — The Origin and Early Evolution of the Alphabet, *Eretz-Israel,* 8, pp. 8-24.
1973 — *Canaanite Myth and Hebrew Epic*, Cambridge, Massachusetts.
1980 — Newly Found Inscriptions in Old Canaanite and Early Phoenician Scripts, *BASOR* 238, pp. 1-20.

CUMONT, F.
1927 — Les Syriens en Éspagne et les Adonies à Séville, *Syria* VIII, pp. 330-341.

DELCOR, M.
1969 — L'inscription phénicienne de la statuette d'Astarté conservée à Séville, *MélUnivSJoseph* XLV, pp. 321-341.

1974a — Astarté et la fécondité des troupeaux en Deut. 7, 13 et parallèles, *UF* VI, pp. 7-14.

1974b — Le hiéros gamos d'Astarté, *RivStFen* II, pp. 63-76.

DELLA CORTE, F.
1983 — La Iuno-Astarte virgiliana, *Atti* 1983, pp. 651-660.

DE MOOR, J.C.
1969 — Studies in the new Alphabetic Texts from Ras Shamra, *UF* I, pp. 167-188.

DEVER, W.G.
1969/70 — Iron Age Epigraphc Material from the Area of Khirbet el-Kôm, *HUCA* XL-XLI, pp. 129-204.

1984 — Asherah, Consort of Yahweh? New Evidence from Kuntillat 'Ajrud, *BASOR* 225, pp. 21-37.

DIEZ MERINO, L.
1983 — GWL-GOZO: un topónimo fenicio-castellano, *Aula Orientalis* I, 2, pp. 276-280.

DOSSIN, G.
1973 — Une mention de Canaanéens dans une lettre de Mari, *Syria* L, pp. 277-82.

DOTHAN, M. and FREEDMAN, D.N.
1966 — *Ashdod I. The First Season of Excavations 1962. 'Atiqot* VII, Jerusalem.

DRIVER, G.R.
1954 — Reflections on Recent Articles, *Journal of Biblical Literature* LXXIII, pp. 125-136.

DUMÉZIL, G.
1966 — *La religion romaine archaïque avec un appendice sur la religion des Étrusques,* Paris.

DUSSAUD, R.
1948 — Melqart, *Syria* XXV, pp. 205-230.

EDWARDS, I.E.S.
1955 — A Relief of Qadshu-Astarte-Anath in the Winchester College Collection, *JNES* XIV, pp. 49-51.

FAUTH, W.
1966 — Aphrodite Parakyptousa, *Akademie der Wissenschaften u. der Literatur, Abhandl. Geistes- und Sozialwissenschaftliche Klasse,* Jahrg. 1966, Nr. 6 (Akad. d. Wissensch. und Lit. in Mainz), pp. 327-437.

FERRON, J.
1976 — Ṣid: État actuel des connaissances, *Le Muséon* LXXXVI, pp.425-440.

FRIEDRICH, J. - RÖLLIG, W.
1970 — *Phönizisch-punische Grammatik (*Analecta orient. 46), Roma.

FRISK, H.
1960/70 — *Griechisches Etymologisches Wörterbuch* I-II, Heidelberg.

GALINSKY, G.K.
1969 — *Aeneas, Sicily and Rome,* Princeton, New Jersey.

GARBINI, G.
1964 (1965) — Le iscrizioni puniche, *Missione* 1964 (1965), pp. 79-87.
1965 (1966) — Le iscrizioni puniche, *Missione* 1965 (1966), pp. 53-67.
1980a — *I Fenici. Storia e Religione,* Napoli.
1980b — Reflessioni "sul segno di Tanit", *Eugenio Manni* 1980, pp. 1035-1040.
1981 — Continuità e Innovazioni nella religione fenicia, *Religione* 1981, pp. 29-42.
1983 — Chi erano i fenici? *Atti* 1983, pp. 27-33.

GASTER, TH.H.
1939 — "Baal is risen..." An Ancient Hebrew Passion-Play from Ras Shamra-Ugarit, *Iraq* VI, pp. 109-143.

GESE, H., HÖFNER, M. und RUDOLPH, K.
1970 — *Die Religionen Altsyriens, Altarabiens und der Mandäer,* Stuttgart-Berlin-Köln-Mainz (W. Kohlhammer).

GLUECK, N.
1965 — *Deities and Dolphins,* New York.

GRDSELOFF, B.
1942 — *Les débuts du culte de Rechef en Égypte,* Le Caire.

GROTANELLI, C.
1981 — Santuari e divinità delle colonie d'Occidente, *Religione* 1981, pp.109-133.

GUZZO AMADASI, M.G.
1967 — *Le iscrizioni fenicie e puniche delle colonie in Occidente* (SS 28), Roma.

HAMBURGER, H.
1954 — A Hoard of Syrian Tetradrachms and Tyrian Bronze Coins from Gush Halav, *IEJ* IV, pp. 201-226.

HILL, G.F.
1911/1965 — *Catalogue of the Greek Coins of Phoenicia,* London (reprint Bologna).

HOFTIJZER, J. and VAN DER KOOIJ, G.
1976 — *Aramaic Texts from Deir 'Alla,* Leiden (E.J. Brill).

HVIDBERG-HANSEN, F.O.
1979 — *La Déesse TNT. Une étude sur la religion canaanéo-punique* I-II, Copenhague (G.E.C. Gad).

KRAHMALKOV, CH.R.
1981 — The Foundation of Carthage 814 B.C. The Douîmes Pendant Inscription, *JSS* XXVI, pp. 177-191.

KRAUSKOPF, I.
1981 — Leukothea nach den antiken Quellen, *Akten* 1981, pp. 137-148.

KRETSCHMER, P.
1895 — Zum pamphylischen Dialekt, *Zeitschrift f. vergleichende Sprachforschung,* XXXIII (NF XIII), pp. 258-274.

LANGE, H.O.
1927 — *Der magische Papyrus Harris.* Det kgl. Danske Videnskabernes Selskab, Hist.-Filol.Meddelelser, XVI, 2, København.

LE GLAY, M.
1966 — *Saturne africain. Histoire,* Paris (E. de Boccard).

LENORMANT, F.
1881 — *La Grande-Grèce, paysage et histoire,* II, Paris.

LEVI DELLA VIDA, G.
1942 — The Phoenician God Satrapes, *BASOR* 87, pp. 29-32.
1959 — Tracce di credenze e culti fenici nelle iscrizioni neopuniche della Tripolitania, *Festschrift J. Friedrich,* pp. 299-314.

LIPIŃSKI, E.
1970 — La fête de l'ensevelissement et de la résurrection de Melqart, *Actes* 1970, pp. 30-58.
1972 — The Goddess Aṯirat in Ancient Arabia, in Babylon, and in Ugarit, *OLP* III, pp. 101-119.
1984 — Vestiges phéniciens d'Andalousie, *OLP* XV, pp. 81-132.

MAZAR, A.
1982 — The "Bull Site" — An Iron Age I Open Cult Place, *BASOR* 247, pp. 27-42.

NILSSON, M.P.
1967 — *Geschichte der griechischen Religion*[3], vol. I, (Handbuch d.Altertumswissenschaft), München.

PIGANIOL, A.
1962 — Les origines d'Hercule, *Hommages à A. Grenier*, éd. M. Renard, pp. 1261-64.

PRITCHARD, J.B.
1982 — The Tanit Inscription from Sarepta, *Phönizier im Westen* (Beiträge Internation. Symposiums, Köln 1979. Madrider Beiträge Bd. 8), pp. 83-92.

PUECH, É.
1983 — Quelques remarques sur l'alphabet au deuxième millénaire, *Atti* 1983, pp. 563-581.

REBUFFAT, R.
1966 — Les Phéniciens à Rome, *MEFR* LXXVIII, pp. 7-48.

REDFORD, D.B.
1973 — New Light on the Asiatic Compaigning of Ḥoremheb, *BASOR* 211, pp. 36-49.

RIBICHINI, S.
1975 — Melqart nell'iscrizione di Pyrgi? *Saggi Fenici* 1975, pp. 41-47.

RIBICHINI, S. - XELLA, P.
1979 — Milk'astart, MLK (M) e la tradizione siropalestinese sui Refaim, *RivStFen* VII, pp. 145-158.

ROBIN, C.
1975/76 — *apud* M. Sznycer, *Antiquités et épigraphie nord-sémitiques, École pratique des Hautes Études, IVe section, Sciences hist.et philol., annuaire,* 1975/76 (Paris 1976), pp. 184-189.

RÖLLIG, W.
1959 — El als Gottesbezeichnung im Phönizischen, *Festschrift J. Friedrich*, pp. 403-416.
1981 — in: *Akten 1981*, pp. 70-72.

SCHRÖDER, P.
1869 — *Die phönizische Sprache,* Halle.

SZNYCER, M.
1969 — Note sur le dieu Ṣid et le dieu Ḥoron d'après les nouvelles inscriptions puniques d'Antas (Sardaigne), *Karthago* XV, pp. 67-74.
1973/74 — Antiquités et épigraphie nord-sémitiques, *École pratique des Hautes Études, IVe section, Sciences hist. et philol., annuaire* 1973/74 (Paris 1974), pp. 131-153.
1974/75 — Antiquités et épigraphie nord-sémitiques, *École pratique des Hautes Études, IVe section, Sciences hist. et philol., annuaire* 1974/75 (Paris 1975), pp. 191-208.

TALLQVIST, K.
1914 — *Assyrian Personal Names* (Acta Societatis Scientiarum Fennicae XLIII, 1), Helsinki.
1934 — *Sumerisch-Akkadische Namen der Totenwelt* (Studia Orient. ed. Societas Orientalis Fennica V, 4), Helsingforsiae.

TUSA, V.
1971 — Selinunte punica, *RivIstArch,* XVIII, pp. 47-68.

TZAVELLAS-BONNET, C.
1983a — La légende de Phoinix à Tyr, *Studia Phoenicia* I (OLA 15), ed. E. Gubel - E. Lipinski - B. Servais-Soyez, pp. 113-23.

1983b — Phoinix, *Les Études classiques* LI, pp. 3-11.

VAN BERCHEM, D.
1960 — Hercule Melqart à l'Ara Maxima, *RendPontAcc* (ser. III), XXXII (anno accad. 1959/60), pp. 61-68.

VAN DEN BRANDEN, A.
1962 — Les inscriptions protosinaïtiques, *Oriens antiquus* I, pp. 192-214.

VASSEL, E.
1912 — *Le panthéon d'Hannibal* (Extrait de La revue Tunisienne), Tunis.

VERZÁR, M.
1980 — Pyrgi e l'Afrodite di Cipro, *MEFRA* XCII, pp. 35-84.

VIROLLEAUD, CH.
1951 — Six textes de Ras Shamra provenant de la XIVe campagne, *Syria* XXVIII pp. 163-179.

1968 — Les nouveaux textes mythologiques et liturgiques de Ras Shamra, *Ugaritica* V (*MRS* XVI), pp. 545-606.

WELLHAUSEN, J.
1897 — *Reste arabischen Heidentums*[2], Berlin.

WHITE, D.
1967 — The Post-Classical Cult of Malophoros at Selinus, *AJA* LXXII, pp. 335-352.

ZEVIT, Z.
1984 — The Khirbet el-Qôm Inscriptions mentioning a Goddess, *BASOR* 225, pp. 39-47.

EGYPTIAN FERTILITY MAGIC WITHIN PHOENICIAN AND PUNIC CULTURE

Günther Hölbl

A striking cultural element within the Greek and Phoenician world of the earlier first millennium B.C. are the Egyptian and Egyptianizing objects. They spread along with the Greek and Phoenician expansion, and can be found — generally speaking — wherever these seafaring peoples established themselves and wherever they had closer relations. Thus the Aegyptiaca arrived as far as the Northern coast of the Black Sea; they were distributed all over Italy (Hölbl 1979) as well as over the whole Phoenician and Punic West. The first important phase of diffusion of Egyptian cultural values, however, took place already in the second mill. B.C. and resulted from the Egyptian imperialism in Asia as well as from the close connections with the Minoan and Mycenaean world. The Sea People's invasion stopped all at once this expansion of Egyptian culture. Whereas we are confronted in the Greek area according to the actual state of our knowledge, with an absolute hiatus in the 11th and in the 1st half of the 10th cent.[1], the Egyptian Bronze Age cultural substratum in the Middle East survived in certain regions in spite of the general cultural regression. Here we think first of the Philistines with their anthropoid clay coffins and the Egyptianizing pottery (Dothan 1982). But I would like to point towards another aspect of the Egyptian element, that is the popular Egyptian magic, which is recognizable from innumerable small Aegyptiaca, scarabs and amulets of many different shapes, which penetrated into Syria and Palestine during the Late Bronze Age (Hölbl 1986, I: 11-53). This part of Egyptian popular religion can be traced in some places, especially at Megiddo (Hölbl 1986, I: 30-31) or at Tell Abu Hawam (*ibid.*: 33), also during Iron Age I. This old Egyptian substratum in Syria and Palestine receives a considerable impetus from renewed influences and imports from the 10th cent. onwards. The essential factor is now the activity of the Phoenicians. We can follow the formation of the Egyptian component in Phoenician art in several waves, above all in two periods: during the 8th and 7th centuries in the ivories and metal work, and thereafter, during the Persian period, in the Phoenician and Punic glyptics of hard stone. The unification of Egypt and Phoenicia in the Achaemenid empire obviously caused a cultural wave from Egypt to Phoenicia, at least in the sense of intensification of influence (Hölbl 1986, I: 16, 41, 43, 53).

Which areas of the complex Phoenician and Punic culture were affected by the Egyptian element? If one looks at the Egyptian component as a whole (at the noble arts — e.g. the jewellery of Carthage and Tharros — as well as at the mass-production of simple scarabs and amulets etc.), one will probably arrive at the conclusion that nearly all artistic manifestations of the Phoenico-Punic culture in the broadest sense (perhaps with the only exception of pottery) were more or less influenced by Egypt. In my opinion Garbini (1983: 32) rightly stressed the Egyptian component as the most important and unifying criterion of the Phoenician culture. But if one tries to look upon the Egyptian element in a more differentiated way, one will recognize that in Sidon, for instance, anthropoid sarcophagi (Kukahn 1955; Buhl 1983) and embalment (Torrey 1919-20: 21) are characteristic of the upper classes. And when we look for the scarabs and other little amulets (figurines of divinities, udjat-eyes etc.), we find them, admittedly, also with the rich people of Sidon (Torrey 1919-20: 27); but we arrive in this case at more specific results. At first we meet them in temple deposits, e.g. in a Libyan Period deposit of the temple of Baalat Gebal at Byblos (Dunand 1937: pl. LXXIII; 1939: 174-180), as votive offerings of rather poor women in the shrine of Tanit-Ashtart (or Tanit *and* Ashtart) at Sarepta (Pritchard 1975: 13-40, fig. 43, 44, 58; 1978: 140-148), or in the *bothroi* of the temple of Ashtart at Kition (Clerc *et al.* 1976). Regarding Cyprus it has been shown that scarab decoration, which is carried round the neck by female statuettes, became a sacred emblem of the local fertility goddess as well as of her priestesses (Clerc *et al.* 1976: 171); these scarabs had, therefore, a significance of cult and their magic value must have referred to fertility. Even the so-called Cypriot Temple Boys can carry scarab necklaces (De Salvia 1983a: 93-94, pl. X, 1). From these facts we conclude that the Egyptian popular beliefs concerning the protective power of the scarab for fertility and for the health of the little child was adopted unadulterated within the Phoenician and Cypriot area. (De Salvia 1978; 1983b: 210, n. 29).

Of great interest is a group of amulets in the shape of rectangular plaquettes which carry on one side the picture of a cow and which are distributed in Egypt, East-Phoenicia, Cyprus, Carthage, Mozia, Sardinia and Spain (Hölbl 1986, I: 103-105, 147-153). (Pl. 26). On the other side of the plaquette we find mostly the apotropaeic udjat-eye or the head of Bes (Hölbl 1986, II: pl. III, 6) who, like the cow, belongs in particular to the sphere of fertility; furthermore on such plaquettes there is often a scenic representation with the divine child protected by winged goddesses (Pl. 27). This infant god, with his implications of birth and resurrection, is known to the Egyptians for the most part as Horus-Harpocrates, being likewise a personification of the sun child, and in the Middle East as Mot, Tammuz, Adonis, etc. He embodies and secures the regeneration of nature, fertility in every sense, and rebirth in the other world. On the cow plaquettes the boy can be represented also above the lotus flower (Pl. 28). It is the motif of the god upon the lotus that the Phoenicians elaborated creatively and in various ways beyond the Egyptian iconography and in accordance with their own religious ideas[2]. But who is the cow? From the iconography and the Egyptian point of view it is the Hathor cow. That holds good for the finds from outside Egypt too. Thus, for example, a plaquette from Carthage shows the Egyptian gold hieroglyph, the designation of Hathor, above the cow (Pl. 29). At Kition a cow plaquette has been found among the votive offerings of Ashtart (Clerc *et al.* 1976: 144, Kit. 554, pl. XVIII). Like many other examples these plaquettes demonstrate, therefore, that Egyptian iconographic models were adopted and applied to Phoenician concepts, but still in accordance with their Egyptian significance. I do not know any examples of usage of an Egyptian motif contrary to its original sense. That means that together with the iconography the Egyptian content, too, was accepted[3]. The Hathor cow, for example, did not loose anything of her cultic quality[4], in the sense that the Egyptian picture as well as the substantial Egyptian content, which referred to fertility, survived in the Phoenician and Punic culture.

Very important is the fact that the Egyptian amulets of Sarepta originate from the social background of poor women, a circumstance which underlines the significance within the **popular** religion. And from that point of view, I would like to claim that even the Aegyptiaca from the rich tombs of Sidon or from the anthropoid sarcophagus of a woman found in 1980 at Cádiz in Spain (Freijeiro, Sánchez 1981: 242, pl. 21e) should be considered in relation to their efficacy for female fertility.

We can perceive the importance of the magical Aegyptiaca within the Phoenician and Punic world not only from votive deposits but perhaps even more from grave finds. Aegyptiaca are met nearly exclusively in graves of women and children, so far as it is evident from the excavation reports. In the east the cemeteries of 'Atlit (Johns 1933) and Kamid el-Loz (Poppa 1978) are especially significant; they belong to the Persian period. Most expressive, regarding amuletic forces in the sphere of fertility, is the position of the amulets in grave L 23 at 'Atlit, in which 31 Egyptian type amulets were found between the legs of a woman (skeleton c-VI) in a chain stretching from the waist to the ankles (Johns 1933: 48, 86, fig. 61; 87-88). That Aegyptiaca belong to the world of woman and child is confirmed in the west by numerous tombs in Sardinia, or by the Egyptian type amulets in the *Tophets* of Sulcis, Tharros (Hölbl 1986, I: 54, 61, 63, 70-71), and Carthage (Stager 1982: pl. 18d). Of course, the amulets in tombs do provide protection for the dead woman and the dead child. But the comparatively small number of certain specific Aegyptiaca for use in the other world[5] shows that the Egyptian-type amulets, which we discuss in this paper, had their place first in daily life and became effective only secondarily after death. Their function in this world is evident from their presence in votive deposits.[6]

In the study of the Aegyptiaca from Sardinia one could distinguish 65 different kinds of amulets, divinities and powerful symbols (Hölbl 1986, I: 79-107). Checking through these amulets type by type we see that in Egypt they either possess general and comprehensive protective forces (against dangerous beasts etc.) or else they promote, among other things, especially fertility and the upbringing of the little child (Hölbl 1986, I: esp. 114, 116, 119, 128, 135). It is not only female fertility that the amulets proclaim, but even special virile forces connected with the ram and bull figurines have their place within the female world (Hölbl 1986, I: 140) (Pl. 30). What the amulets express from the Egyptian point of view on one side and the archaeological circumstances in the Phoenico-Punic area on the other side fit together perfectly, while special Eygptian beliefs connected with particular divinities like Sekhmet and Nefertem, which we find everywhere, were mostly not known in all probability outside Egypt. But we see from the contexts outside the Nile valley that the general protective forces of the most powerful amulets against dangers of every kind (e.g. the udjat-eye) are also beneficial to women and children; that means within the sphere of health and fertility in a broader sense.

Of course, we are not allowed to refer all Egyptian scarabs and figurines of steatite and faience, without exception, to fertility. In Cyprus, for example, it may be that the Egyptian significance of the Ptah-Pataikoi for minerals and the exploitation of metals was present too (Clerc *et al.* 1976: 117-118, 125). Moreover the Phoenician Pataikoi, with whom the Egyptian Pataikoi were identified, or could be identified, were navigation gods (Hölbl 1979, I: 121-125). Thus, in a certain framework, we have to concede that the Egyptian-type amulets had their protective powers for the sailor. In the Greek area, perhaps, the scarabs in the Poseidon temple of Sounion may give an example of this case, unless they refer to Poseidon as impregnator of earth.[7] However, far more dominant is the importance of the amuletic Aegyptiaca as evidence for fertility magic in the Mediterranean world. Although this paper concerns the Phoenician and Punic culture, we have to include also the Greek area. The Greeks got in touch with Aegyptiaca from the 10th and 9th centuries onwards via the Middle East[8] and took over the significance for woman and child as well (De Salvia 1978; 1983b: 209-211). This is proved especially by the tombs at Lefkandi (on the island of Euboea) of the early 9th cent. B.C.[9] From the 8th to 6th centuries certain places of the Greek world, favoured by overseas relations, were flooded with amuletic Aegyptiaca — and here too, the temples of female deities as well as the graves of women and children provide us with most material (De Salvia 1983b). In this respect, in the west, one must mention above all Pithekoussai (on Ischia), where in the 2nd half of the 8th cent. nearly all graves of children, even the poorest, contain one or more scarabs (De Salvia 1978; Hölbl 1979, I: 153-154, II: 177-196). In this connection the Egyptian significance of the scarab within fertility magic among the Greeks of the East and the transfer of these beliefs to Western Greece have been pointed out (De Salvia 1978). The transmission of Egyptian cultural values to the Greeks cannot be understood without the Phoenicians as mediators, at least at the beginning.

The Sardinian scarabs of jasper and cornelian represent a fascinating group of documents, especially because they carry also scenes from the high Egyptian religion (Hölbl 1986, I: 268-271, 277-278, 283). As for the theme of fertility, we may draw our attention to some of them which show the divine child of Egyptian iconography within a shrine (Fig. 14), or to scenes, in which the divine child is characterised as king who, as in Egyptian representations, can even receive infinite years of reign by means of palm-branches (Fig. 15). Here we are confronted with ideas expressed in Egyptian or Egyptianizing manner, which correspond to the Egyptian birthhouse theology (Daumas 1958); "correspondence", it should be emphasised, and not necessarily "acceptance" of a theology. But the child god within a temple, characterized as king, complements on a more spiritual level the sphere of Egyptian fertility magic on the popular level. It is particularly the Punic scarab glyptic that shows us how closely the two aspects of Egyptian influence are interconnected: I mean, the usage of Egyptian-type amulets in accordance with the Egyptian model and the representation of Phoenician divinities by means of Egyptian iconographies. Isis with Harpocrates (Pl. 31), a very popular type among the amulets, is often represented on the jasper scarabs (Fig. 16) — that is, from the iconographic point of view; but sometimes the engraver marks his Egyptianizing mother goddess with an unmistakable attribute of Ashtart (Fig. 17) (Gubel 1980).

The study of the Egyptian and Egyptianizing objects from Phoenician and Punic Malta and Gozo, now in the the museum of Valletta, has been undertaken quite recently by myself. Unfortunately the archaeological background does not offer anything with respect to our question concerning the significance of the Aegyptiaca within fertility magic. The available amulets give us a small but very representative selection from the spectrum known otherwise in the Phoenico-Punic world (Pls. 32-33). Moreover the scanty material at our disposal seems to come — perhaps without exception — from the east and for the most part from Egypt itself. This is remarkable, because in Sardinia or Ibiza the Egyptian-type faience amulets of Punic manufacture are very numerous (Hölbl 1986, I: 163). As a preliminary result we can perhaps say that the Egyptian cultural values from Malta and Gozo fit in best with the Egyptian element in the remaining Phoenician world, but seems to be connected more with the east than with the west and demonstrates, therefore, in its own way the connexion of Malta with the east. However, there is no reason to doubt that the amuletic Aegyptiaca, i.e. the scarabs and faience figurines, of these islands belong also to the evidence of Egyptian fertility magic within Phoenician and Punic culture.

Notes

1 The latest datable Mycenaean contexts, which yielded Aegyptiaca, are represented by some LH IIIC tombs of the local phase II (1165/60-1100 B.C.) at Perati (Attica): S. E. Iakovides, *Perati*, A, Athens 1969, pp. 93, 141, 294, 304; B, Athens 1970, pp. 314-315, 456. At that time only very few people were in possession of these Aegyptiaca, which testify still Late Bronze Age connections between Egypt and the Aegean. The most ancient Aegyptiacum found in a datable context of the 1st Mill. B.C., which is known within the Greek Area, comes from a rich Early Protogeometric tomb at Fortetsa (c. 970-920 B.C.) — a tomb, in which one woman at least was also buried: J. K. Brock. *Fortetsa*, Cambridge 1957, p. 15, no. 106, pl. 173. It is a finger ring of faience, which in my view carries a much deformed *Mn-ḫpr-Rʿ* pseudo-cartouche and which is obviously of Near Eastern manufacture. The closest parallel to the piece is a similar finger ring found at Hama (Syria) in a context (c. 1075-925 B.C.), which chronologically fits in best with the Cretan: P. J. Riis, *Hama*, II, 3, Copenhagen 1948, p. 159, fig. 202. The next Aegyptiaca of the Greek area belong to the early 9th cent. B.C.: a Sekhmet figurine from a Protogeometric tomb at Fortetsa (Brock, *Fortetsa*, pp. 29-30, pl. 21, 264; J.N. Coldstream, *Geometric Greece*, London 1977, p. 49) and the Aegyptiaca of Lefkandi mentioned below, n. 9.

2 A synopsis of the motif "god upon the lotus" on scarabs of hard stone known from Sardinia shows the following divine figures or symbols represented on or above the lotus: sun, moon, scarab, divine child, "Isis", siren, head of Bes, anthropomorphic divinity with head of horse(?), divinity with ram's head carrying a double crown, falcon, lying and sitting sphinx, couchant lion with double crown: Hölbl 1986, I: 271-277; see *ibid.*, II, n. 200 to chapter VII.

[3] This, in my opinion, is also valid for the Canaanite and Phoenician ivories. Cfr. W. Helck, *Betrachtungen zur Grossen Göttin und den ihr verbundenen Gottheiten,* München 1971, pp. 154, 226; Helck 1979: 171. See Hölbl 1986, I: 14.

[4] For another opinion see E. Acquaro, *Amuleti egiziani ed egittizzanti del Museo Nazionale di Cagliari,* Roma 1977, p. 34.

[5] We think in this connexion of the few *shabtis*, which may have come to the west in Pre-Roman times; the circumstances of discovery do not satisfy almost anywhere; see Hölbl 1986, I: 404; II: n. 145 to chapter VI; Gamer-Wallert 1978: 64-65, 73, 186-187, 195, 231-232. Vercoutter 1945, does not mention a single *shabti*; cf. J. Vercoutter, Une statuette funéraire de Nechao II trouvée à Carthage, *Cahiers de Byrsa,* V (1955) pp. 23-28. Heart scarabs are nearly totally absent: cf. Hölbl 1986, I: 62, II, n. 70 to chapter II. With this the rarity of Osiris figurines fits in.

[6] But the reader should be reminded that there are other Aegyptiaca, which are intended for the after-life, above all the amuletic capsules of metal (mostly of gold or silver), which are distributed all over the Phoenician and Punic world (Hölbl 1986, I: 345-353). In a Punic inscription incised on a silver leaf of such an amuletic capsule found in Sardinia we read explicitly of "the Lords of the balance" with reference to the Egyptian Judgement of the Dead: G. Garbini, Iscrizioni funerarie puniche di Sardegna, *Annali dell'Istituto Orientale di Napoli* XLII, (1982) pp. 462-463.

[7] Cf. W. Pötscher, *Der Kleine Pauly* IV (1975) col. 1076 (s.v. Poseidon). — The Aegyptiaca of Sounion: Pendelbury 1930: 83-84.

[8] Apart from the items indicated in n. 1 and 9 cf. the two steatite scarabs of the Tekke Tholos near Knossos, which during the late 9th cent. were in possession of a goldsmith's family of Near Eastern provenance living there, and which were deposited in the tomb together with the very precious stock-in-trade: R.W. Hutchinson, J. Boardman, The Khaniale Tekke-Tombs, *BSA* IL (1954) pp. 218, 227, n° 22-23; *id.* The Khaniale Tekke Tombs, II, *BSA* LXII (1967) pp. 64, 69, pl.8.

[9] For Lefkandi: M.R. Popham *et al.*, *Lefkandi,* I, text: London 1980, plates: London 1979; M.R. Popham *et al.*, Further excavations of the Toumba cemetery at Lefkandi, 1981, *BSA* LXXVII (1982) pp. 213-248, pl. 15-34. The tombs containing Aegyptiaca (including faience beads) are the following in chronological order from Early Protogeometric to Sub-Protogeometric: S 16, P 25B, T 12A, T 14, T 39, PP 42, T 1, T 15, T 22, T 42, PP 21, T 5, T 13, T 32, T 36, S 59, T 27, T 33. Whenever an anthropological examination was made, these tombs turned out to belong mostly to children, some to women.

Summary.

Egyptian type objects of magical nature (scarabs and amulets in form of Egyptian divinities and powerful symbols, commonly made of steatite and faience) are found all over the Mediterranean during the earlier 1st mill. B.C.: as votive offerings in temples of fertilty deities — in the Phoenician sphere, e.g. at Byblos, Sarepta, Kition etc.; in graves, but almost exclusively in those of women and children (e.g. in a grave at 'Atlit, a Phoenician cemetery in northern Palestine, between the legs of a woman); as well as in Punic *Tophets* (Carthage, Sulcis, Tharros). These archaeological circumstances show that the genuine Egyptian amuletic force of the small objects concerning the protection of women and children as well as female fertility was taken over by the Phoenicians more or less unaltered. The known Aegyptiaca from Malta and Gozo fit in best with the picture of the remaining Phoenician world by their typology.

Bibliography

BUHL, M. -L.

1983 — L'origine des sarcophages anthropoides Phéniciens en pierre, *Atti del I Congresso Internazionale di Studi Fenici e Punici, Roma 1979,* I, Roma (Consiglio Nazionale delle Ricerche), pp. 199-202.

CLERC, G. *et al.*

1976 — *Fouilles de Kition,* II: *objets égyptiens et égyptisants,* Nicosia (Department of Antiquities, Cyprus).

DAUMAS, F.

1958 — *Les mammisis des temples égyptiens,* Paris (Société d'Edition "Les Belles Lettres").

DE SALVIA, F.

1978 — Un ruolo apotropaico dello scarabeo egizio nel contesto culturale greco-arcaico di Pithekoussai (Ischia), *Hommages à Maarten J. Vermaseren,* III, Leiden (Brill), pp. 1003-1061.

1983a — Un aspetto di *MISCHKULTUR* ellenico-semitica a Pithekoussai (Ischia): I pendagli metallici del tipo a falce, *Atti* (see Buhl), pp. 89-95, pl. VII-X.

1983b — La problematica della reazione culturale egea all'influenza della civiltà egizia durante l'età arcaica, *Orientalia,* LII, pp. 201-214.

DOTHAN, T.

1982 — *The Philistines and their material culture,* Jerusalem (Israel Exploration Society).

DUNAND, M.

1937-39 — *Fouilles de Byblos,* I: Atlas = 1937, Texte = 1939, Paris (Geuthner).

FREIJEIRO, A.B., SÁNCHEZ, R.C.

1981 — Der neue anthropoide Sarkophag von Cádiz, *Madrider Mitteilungen*, XXII, pp. 236-243, pl. 17-22.

GAMER-WALLERT, I.

1978 — *Ägyptische und ägyptisierende Funde von der Iberischen Halbinsel,* Wiesbaden (Reichert).

GARBINI, G.

1983 — Chi erano i Fenici? *Atti* (see Buhl), pp. 27-33.

GUBEL, E.

1980 — An essay on the axe-bearing Astarte and her role in a Phoenician "triad", *Rivista di Studi Fenici,* VIII, 1. pp. 1-17, pl. I-II.

HELCK, W.

1979 — *Die Beziehungen Ägyptens und Vorderasiens zur Ägäis bis ins 7. Jh.v.Chr.,* Darmstadt (Wiss. Buchgesellschaft).

HÖLBL, G.
1979 — *Beziehungen der ägyptischen Kultur zu Altitalien*, 2 vol., Leiden (Brill).
1986 — *Ägyptisches Kulturgut im phönikischen und punischen Sardinien*, 2 vol., Leiden (Brill).

JOHNS, C.N.
1933 — Excavations at 'Atlît (1930-1), *Quarterly of the Department of Antiquities in Palestine*, II, pp. 41-104, pl. XIV-XXXVII.

KUKAHN, E.
1955 — *Anthropoide Sarkophage in Beyrouth*, Berlin (Mann).

PENDLEBURY, J. D. S.
1930 — *Aegyptiaca*, Cambridge (Univ. Press).

POPPA, R.
1978 — *Der eisenzeitliche Friedhof von Kamid el-Loz*, Bonn (Habelt).

PRITCHARD, J.B.
1975 — *Sarepta, a preliminary report on the Iron Age*, Philadelphia (The Univ. Museum).
1978 — *Recovering Sarepta, a Phoenician city*, Princeton (Univ. Press).

STAGER, L.E.
1982 — Carthage: a view from the Tophet, *Phönizier im Westen*. Die Beiträge des Int. Symposiums über "Die phönizische Expansion im westlichen Mittelmeerraum" in Köln vom 24. bis 27. 4. 1979, hrsg. v. H.G. Niemeyer, Mainz (Zabern), pp. 155-166, pl.17-18.

TORREY, Ch.C.
1919-20 — A Phoenician necropolis at Sidon, *The Annual of the American School of Oriental Research in Jerusalem*, I, pp. 1-27.

VERCOUTTER, J.
1945 — *Les objets égyptiens et égyptisants du mobilier funéraire carthaginois*, Paris (Geuthner).

FERTILITY CULT IN ANCIENT UGARIT

E. Lipiński

The sacred marriage is likely to have been one of the main manifestations of the fertility cult in Ugarit as well as in other regions of the ancient Near East. Our written Ugaritic sources go back to the Late Bronze age, mainly to the 14th and 13th centuries B.C., but the myth and the ritual embodied in the text we are going to examine must be more ancient. In fact, the god El plays the vital role in it, while the god Baal is not even mentioned.

Basing themselves on this mythological and ritual text, known as the Poem in honour of the gods Shachar and Shalim, or Poem on the Gracious Gods (*KTU* 23 = *CTA* 23)[1], some authors assume that the rite of the sacred marriage was performed by the king at the close of the New Year festivities constituting the feast of first-fruits. Accordingly, the concerned text would be the libretto of a cultic play or "ritual pantomime"[2], in which the roles of the Head of the Pantheon, the god El, and of his wife, the goddess Aṯirat, were played by the king and the queen of Ugarit.

Apparently, the first part of the text refers to the preparatory rites performed before the sacred marriage took place. Horizontal lines drawn across the tablet divide the text, separating hymnal and mythological passages from rubrical parts which contained directions of a liturgical or ritual character. The absence of any evident connection between the poetical and the rubrical sections constitutes the main difficulty for the interpretation of this part of the text.

The second part of the composition (lines 30-76) contain the narrative account of the conception and birth of two successive groups of divine children, *viz.* of Shachar and Shalim, who are essentially astral deities, and of the so-called "gracious gods". At the beginning of this narrative, the supreme god El, who lived "at the sources of the rivers, amidst the springs of the two oceans"[3], went out to "the chasm of the sea and advanced to the chasm of the ocean"[4], and saw there two girls or young women moving up and down, next to a basin. When a girl moved upwards, the other one moved downwards in a rocking motion, as if they stood at each extremity of a board balanced on a central support, and made each other go up and down alternatively. This seesaw movement does not seem to have been simply a game, for it took place next to a high basin and aimed at reaching its top.

The chasm, next to which the events narrated in the text took place, is called *gôpu* in Ugaritic,[5] and the expression is attested also in Greek literature; χάσμα πελάγεος, "the chasm of the sea".[6] *Gôpu* could be compared to the chasm seen by Lucian under the temple of Hierapolis. According to the aetiological legend reported by him, all the water of the deluge had run down this chasm, and this event was commemorated twice a year through the rite of hydrophory: water from the sea — probably the Euphrates — was brought to the temple and poured into the chasm.[7] A ceremony similar to this one, also commemorating the great flood, took place at the precinct of the Olympian Earth in Athens. Pausanias relates having seen there a cleft in the ground, a cubit in width, and says he was told by the guides that the waters of the deluge had run down that cleft.[8] Since the festival recalling this event was called ὑδροφορία [9], the Festival of Water-bearing, we can assume that water was poured down the cleft into the ground to slake the thirst of the ghosts dwelling in the nether world.[10] According to Plutarch,[11] the festival took place at the new moon, during the month of Anthesterion, i.e. in February-March.[12] A similar ceremony took place in the postexilic temple of Jerusalem. There, the rite of water pouring was performed during the full moon of Tishri, i.e. in September-October, on the opening day of the great vintage feast, now called the Feast of Sukkoth or of the Tabernacles.[13]

The rite of water pouring is the primitive ritual for rain. It is a common custom all over the world among primitive peoples for the 'rain-makers' to induce rain imitating the falling rain, either by sprinkling water or by pouring it into the ground. Frazer gave numerous instances from various countries, including European ones.[14] For example, we read of naked women and girls from the Russian village of Ploska who poured water into the ground at night, all along the boundaries of their village. These practices aimed at obtaining the rainfall, of which the people were in such dire need, by simulating the falling rain.

Thus, if we apply ethnography to the Ugaritic text under examination, we can assume that the two young women seen by El were neither performing their ablutions over the basin, as some authors surmise, nor washing their clothes, as others suppose; they were simply accomplishing the final rite of hydrophory and pouring into the basin the water brought from the sea, the river or the spring.

This basin is designated by the term *'agannu*, both in the passage we are interested in, and in a rubrical section of the first part of the text, prescribing to incense the basin seven times (line 15).

This *'agannu* or basin is likely to have been made out of copper, bronze or stone and to have been situated in the precinct of the temple, as a symbol of the sea. One could refer to the "sea of cast metal", placed in the temple of Solomon (I Kings 7,23-26)[15] , or to the colossal stone basin from Amathus in Cyprus, now in the Louvre (AO 22897), which measures 3.19 m in diameter and is 1.87 m high, with four false handles in relief encircling bull figures[16]. The original location of this basin and large fragments of a similar one, preserved up to 1.49 m in height, were found in 1976 on the acropolis of Amathus, near the main entrance of the temple dedicated to Κυπρία, the great Cypriot goddess assimilated to Aphrodite.[17] There is no doubt, therefore, that these basins had a cultic function. According to II Chron. 4,6, the "bronze sea" of the Solomonic temple was used for the priests' ablutions, but being over 2.50 m high, it must have been very unpractical for this purpose.

It is true that a staircase flanks a miniature basin similar to the one of Amathus and kept also in the Louvre (MNB 96)[18]. The question is whether the staircase was intended to enable priests to perform ritual ablutions over the water-holder or to make the temple servants' task of pouring water into the basin easier. An element of the answer may be provided by a smaller vessel, 2.13 m wide and 0.41 m high, found by Cesnola next to the eastern entrance of the temple of Golgoi, also on Cyprus[19]. Although this basin was already broken at the moment of its discovery, it was possible to ascertain that its bottom was perforated by a hole measuring 5 cm in diameter. This hole may have some connection with the rite of water pouring and slaking the thirst of the earth, as reported by Pausanias. In any case, the Solomonic "bronze sea" and the Amathus basin in the Musée du Louvre must be related to the fertility cult, as strongly suggested by the symbolic meaning of the twelve oxen sustaining the "sea" and of the bulls sculptured on the four handles of the Amathus basin. With regard to this symbolism and to the religious meaning of a cultic water-holder one could also quote a smaller Syrian vessel flanked by two bulls[20], as well as a scene represented on an unpublished Sidonian sarcophagus kept in the Museum of Istanbul. This scene figures two women standing at the sides of a large vessel in a ritual attitude which has been described as the "worshipping of the fertilizing water"[21].

Considering the cultic implications of the objects described, the "sea" or *'agannu* of our Ugaritic text must have had a similar symbolic significance, as the story itself would seem to suggest[22]. The women mentioned in it are called *mušta'lûtâm* or *mušta'allûtâm la-ri'ši 'aganni*, literally "those raising themselves as high as the top of the basin". This meaning results from the parallel use of the expression in an Amarna letter in which Tušratta, king of Mitanni, reminds Akhenaton of the rich bridal gifts sent by Amenophis III, and which "reached as high as heaven and earth"., *šamê u erṣeta uštelli* [23]. Other translations suggested for the Ugaritian expression do not have any philological basis[24] and neglect an essential point of the narrative, *viz.* that the two women mentioned in the text were filling the "sea" of the temple[25].

The relationship of these women with the sea is confirmed by the 'surnames' *'agzr ym* and *bn ym*, something like "progeny of the sea" and "children of the sea", by which the children to be conceived from El will be called. We assume, in this case, that *'agzr* is identical with the Hurrian term (d) *a-ga-aš-ša-ri,* a divine epithet[26]. In the first part of the text we are dealing with, these children are described as sucking the breasts of *Aṯirat*, El's wife, and of Raḥmay, "the one with the womb" or "the pregnant one", undoubtedly a hypostasis of Aṯirat, personifying the pregnancy of the Mother of the Gods. It is almost certain, therefore, that the two unnamed women represent Aṯirat and her double Raḥmay. Now, in the texts from Ugarit, Atirat's full name is given as *'Aṯirat yammi,* "Aṯirat of the sea" or even "the one treading on the sea"[27]. Consequently, the goddess seems to be related to the sea, and so do the two women of our text.

At this point, it would be tempting to refer to the Near Eastern representations of two goddesses with "flowing vases"[28] or to the "naked woman" with streams of water flowing from her shoulders[29]. One could even refer to the birth of Aphrodite from the sea, and eventually quote Hesiod's popular etymology of her name, derived from ' ἀφρός , "foam"[30]. This comparison is all the more evocative if we consider that Aphrodite is precisely a goddess of birth and fertility, and often seems to be little more than the personification of sexual instincts.

Whatever the relationship between Aphrodite and the two women of the Ugaritic text, the narrative relates that, at their sight, the god El's manhood was aroused despite the fact that in other texts, probably later ones, he is described as an old man with white hair[31]. His organ becomes "as long as the sea", perhaps a designation of the cultual basin, like the one in Solomon's temple, and not of the Mediterranean sea or of a mythological Ocean. Still, if we consider that the given diameter of the "sea" in Solomon's temple amounts to 5 m and that the first stone basin from Amathus measures 3.19 m in diameter, the picturesque expression of the Ugaritian poet gives El a Priapic phallus indeed. The supreme god El brings the two women to his house, — continues the narrative, — then he shoots down a bird, he plucks it and sets it to roast on the fire. Undoubtedly, this action symbolizes a rite of sympathetic magic supposed to heal impotence, as in Babylonian rituals[32], or at least to induce the two women to make love with El. While the bird browns on the coal, magically inflaming the two women with passion for El, an ominous formula, introduced by the verb *patû*, "to charm" or "to bewitch", rather than "to seduce" or "to entice", is "recited by a priest in explanation of the action"[33]: "If the two women cry out 'O sir, sir (*mutu*)', ... the two women are wives of El...But if the two women cry out 'O daddy, daddy (*'adda*)',...the two girls are daughters of El..."

Now, once the bird has browned, the two women cry out "O sir, sir", as was to be expected, and become El's wives. The term *mutu*, in fact, is ambivalent and can mean either "man", "sir", or "husband".

Then El bends over the two women and, after he has laid with them, they conceive and give birth to two children called Shachar and Shalim, "Dawn" and "Sunset".

Then El embraces the two women again, repeating the process of copulation several times, and they conceive the "gracious gods". According to most authors[34], a rubric states at this point that the passage in question should be recited up to five times, *viz*: "He stooped, kissed their lips. Behold! their lips were sweet. While (he was) kissing, there was conception; while (he was) embracing, there was orgasm".

The newly born deities had an enormous appetite. They searched and hunted for food until they came upon "the guardian of the sown-land", who let them enter the fields sown with corn and the orchards planted with vines. There they found the food and the wine they needed. Undoubtedly, this part of the text constitutes the peak of the narrative and the materialization of the results expected from the performed ritual.

However, the question is whether we are really dealing here with a sacred play or "ritual pantomime", or only with a *hieros logos*, a mythological account read by a priest. The rubrical passage prescribing the five-fold recitation of the section that describes El's love-making and the songs to be sung by the assembly would seem to leave enough time for a cultic action to take place, eventually for the sacred marriage to be performed at this moment. Then the narrator continues and announces: "Both of them were in labour and gave birth, they gave birth to the gracious gods".

If we admit that the sacred marriage was actually performed at that moment, it is likely for the god El to have been represented by the king of Ugarit[35].

This eventuality seems to be suggested by the Sumerian parallels[36] and by the role played by the Assyrian king in the ritual of the New Year festival, as well as by the epithet of "king" often apposed to El's name in mythological texts from Ugarit[37]. In fact, the king of Ugarit was present at the ceremony and he is greeted in the first part of the text (line 7).

It is more difficult to say who represented the two women mentioned in the text. It has been assumed that the queen and a high priestess, probably a princess, played this role. However, this is by no means certain, and the two women — supposed also to cry out "Father, Father" or "Mother, Mother" — could quite as well have been young hierodules, like the Babylonian *nadītu*-priestesses who entered the cloister upon reaching their puberty; they were regarded as the wives of their god and were initiated at his festival.

Since the narrative part of the text culminates in quenching with wine the thirst of the gracious gods and since wine played such an important role in the celebration of the New Year festivities, it is likely that the sacred marriage was followed by a banquet, to which only a limited number of initiated persons was allowed to participate. The mention of wine, the allusion to hydrophory, and some other elements which go beyond the scope of the present paper, indicate that the celebration took place in autumn and aimed at providing the autumnal rain-like dew and the winter rainfalls which were of vital importance to the sown soil and to Syrian agriculture in general.

A probable allusion to the king's sacred intercourse with the representative of a goddess is attested also in another ritual text found at Ugarit[38]. This text, however, is more recent and the hierodule personifies there the goddess Astarte-at-the-window[39]. There seems to be no connection between this later text and the more ancient ritual dealt with in this paper.

Notes

1 An annotated bibliography of works pertaining to this text, down to 1971, can be found in D.T. Tsumura, *The Ugaritic Drama of the Good Gods – A Philological Study*, dissert. Brandeis University 1973, pp. 228-239. Another overview is given by R.J. Clifford, Recent Scholarly Discussion of CTCA 23 (UT 52), *SBL Seminar Papers* 1 (1975), pp. 99-105. At least the main recent translations have to be added: J.C. de Moor, *New Year with Canaanites and Israelites*, Kampen 1972, Vol. I, pp. 6-8: Vol II, pp. 17-24; A. Caquot - M. Sznycer - A. Herdner, *Textes ougaritiques I. Mythes et légendes*, Paris 1974, pp. 353-379; J.C.L. Gibson, *Canaanite Myths and Legends*, Edinburgh 1978, pp. 28-30 and 123-127; G. Del Olmo Lete, *Mitos y leyendas de Canaan*, Madrid 1981, pp. 427-448.

2 Thus G.R. Driver, *Canaanite Myths and Legends*, Edinburgh 1956, p. 23b. Cf. Th. H. Gaster, *Thespis*, 2nd. ed., Garden City, N.Y., 1961, pp. 406-417.

3 On El's abode, see E. Lipiński, El's Abode: Mythological Traditions related to Mount Hermon and to the Mountains of Armenia, *Orient. Lov. Per.* 2 (1971), pp. 13-69, here in particular pp. 65-69.

4 Lines 30-31.

5 The term *gp* used here is related to Arabic *ǧauf*, "hollow, cavity, depression". Cf. E. Lipiński, *La royauté de Yahwé dans la poésie et le culte de l'ancien Israël*, 2nd ed., Brussels 1968, p. 205, n. 3.

6 Herodotus, *Histories* IV, 85, where the expression is applied to the Aegean Sea.

7 Lucian, *The Syrian Goddess* 13.

8 Pausanias, *Description of Greece*, I, 18, 7.

9 Plutarch, *Sulla* 14; *Etymologicum Magnum*, ed. T. Gaisdorf, p. 774, *s.v.* ὑδροφορία Hesychius, *Lexicon*, *s.v.* ὑδροφορία

10 The "great chasm" of the Greek literature, χάσμα μέγα (Hesiod, *Theogony* 740), was Tartarus. Euripides, *The Phoenician Maidens*, 1604-1605, speaks even of the "bottomless chasms of Tartarus", Ταρτάρου....ἄβυσσα χάσματα

11 Plutarch, *Sulla* 14.

12 Compare the Scholiasts on Aristophanes, *Acharnians* 1076, and on *Frogs* 218.

13 Mishnah, *Sukkah* IV, 9. Cf. N.H. Snaith, *The Jewish New Year Festival. Its Origin and Development*, London 1947, pp. 85-88. The practice would go back to the First Temple period according to R. Dussaud, *Les origines cananéennes du sacrifice israélite*, Paris 1921, pp. 203-207; *id.*, *Les découvertes de Ras Shamra (Ugarit) et l'Ancien Testament*, Paris 1937, p. 74.

14 J.G. Frazer, *The Golden Bough*, one vol. ed., London 1923, pp. 63-83.

15 See C.C. Wylie, On King Solomon's Molten Sea, *Biblical Archaeologist* 12 (1949), pp. 86-90; M. Noth, *Könige* I (BKAT IX/1), Neukirchen-Vluyn 1968, pp. 155-156. The motif of the "bronze sea" in art history has been studied by M. Trokay, Compositions monumentales du Proche-Orient ancien et représentations mosanes de fonts baptismaux, *Clio et son regard. Mélanges d'histoire, d'histoire de l'art et d'archéologie offerts à Jacques Stiennon*, Liège 1982, pp. 639-652. I owe this reference and the ones of the following two notes to the kindness of Dr Robert Laffineur, University of Liège, whom I warmly thank.

16 A. Hermary, *Amathonte II. Testimonia, deuxième partie: les sculptures découvertes avant 1975*, Paris 1981, pp. 83-84, pl. 19-20, no. 81, with earlier literature. One could add to it A. Parrot, *Le temple de Jérusalem*, Neuchâtel 1954, p. 34.

17 P. Aupert, etc., Rapport sur les travaux de la mission de l'École française à Amathonte en 1976, *BCH* 101 (1977), pp. 781-815 (see pp. 800-803): *id.* - A. Hermary, etc., Rapport sur les travaux de la mission de l'École française à Amathonte en 1979, *BCH* 104 (1980), pp. 805-822 (see p. 806, plan of fig. 1); *id-id.*, Amathonte: Rapport préliminaire sur les travaux de l'École française d'Athènes (1975-1979), *RDAC* 1980, pp. 217-238, pl. XXV-XXIX (see pp. 231-238 referring to the sanctuary of Κυπρία); A. Hermary, Les fouilles de la Mission française à Amathonte (1980-1983), *RDAC* 1984, pp. 265-277 and pl. LX-LXII (see pp. 269-276). — According to the accounts of 19th century travellers, scattered fragments of the second basin were visible on the acropolis of Amathus at the time when the first basin was taken away and transported to the Musée de Louvre. These generally anecdotic reports have been collected in P. Aupert - M.-Ch. Hellmann, *Amathonte I. Testimonia, première partie*, Paris 1984.

18 G. Perrot - Ch. Chipiez, *Histoire de l'art dans l'antiquité* III, *Phénicie, Cypre*, Paris 1885, p. 281, fig. 212, of unknown provenience.

[19] L. Palma di Cesnola, *Cyprus: Its Ancient Cities, Tombs, and Temples,* London 1877, pp. 144-145; J.L. Myres, *Handbook of the Cesnola Collection of Antiquities from Cyprus,* New York 1914, no. 1863; O. Masson, *Les inscriptions chypriotes syllabiques,* Paris 1961, no. 291, pl. 51, 1. A similar vessel was found next to the northern wall of the temple of Golgoi: L. Palma di Cesnola, *op. cit.*, p. 145; J. Doell, *Die Sammlung Cesnola* (Mémoires de l'Académie de S. Pétersbourg VII, sér. XIX, no. 4, 1873), S. Pétersbourg 1873, pl. XIII, 11; J.L. Myres, *op. cit.*, no. 1380.

[20] B. Soyez, Note sur le culte du vase en Syrie, *Berytus* 24 (1975-76), pp. 43-45.

[21] B. Soyez, L'adoration de l'urne (à propos d'un sarcophage sidonien du Musée d'Istanbul), *MUSJ* 49 (1975-76), pp. 543-547, pl. I.

[22] These ritual "seas" may have prompted comparisons like those in the Etana Epic, where Etana tells the eagle that "the wide sea is just like a tube" or "like a bread basket"; cf. *ANET*³, p. 118b.

[23] *EA* 29, 24. The usual Akkadian construction is *šutēlû ana,* "to reach as high as" (*CAD*, E. p. 135b), which corresponds exactly to Ugaritic *št ʿly l.*

[24] They are resumed by D.T. Tsumura, *The Ugaritic Drama of the Good Gods,* pp. 60-63, with a conclusion based on a wrong interpretation of *ʾagannu.*

[25] The comparison drawn by J.R. Porter, Genesis XIX: 30-38 and the Ugaritic Text of ŠḤR & ŠLM, *Proceedings of the Seventh World Congress of Jewish Studies. Studies in the Bible and the Ancient Near East,* Jerusalem 1981, pp. 1-8, between the two women in *KTU* 23 and the two daughters of Lot in Gen. 19, 30-38 does not really help us in understanding either the biblical tale or the Ugaritic myth.

[26] E. Laroche, Glossaire de la langue hourrite, *RHA* 34, 1976, p. 37, referring to *KUB* XLV, 47, III, 6 and IV, 17.

[27] Compare W.F. Albright, *Yahweh and the Gods of Çanaan,* London 1968, p. 105.

[28] A. Parrot, *Mission archéologique de Mari,* Vol. II/2 (BAH 69), Paris 1958, pl. X-XI; Vol. II/3 (BAH 70), Paris 1959, pl. IV-VI; *The Cambridge Ancient History. Plates to Vol. I and II,* new ed., Cambridge 1977, pl. 66.

[29] F. Digard, *Répertoire analytique des cylindres orientaux,* Paris 1975, no. 4452; U. Winter, *Frau und Göttin* (OBO 53), Freiburg-Göttingen 1983, fig. 126.

[30] Hesiod, *Theogony* 188-206.

[31] *KTU* 1. 3, V, 2. 24-25; 1. 4, V, 4; 1. 18, I, 11-12 = *CTA* 3, E, 10. 32-33; 4, V, 66; 18, I, 11-12.

[32] R.D. Biggs, *ŠÀ.ZI.GA. Ancient Mesopotamian Potency Incantations* (TCS 2), Locust Valley 1967, pp. 49ff.

[33] Thus Th. H. Gaster, An Ancient Semitic Mystery-Play, *SMSR* 10 (1934), pp. 156-164 (see p. 156).

[34] Despite some interesting observations, we cannot agree with the recent attempt by D.T. Tsumura, Ritual Rubric or Mythological Narrative? — CTA 23 (UT 52): 56-57 Reconsidered, *Proceedings of the Seventh World Congress of Jewish Studies. Studies in the Bible and the Ancient Near East,* Jerusalem 1981, pp. 9-16, who tried to explain these lines as part of the mythological narrative. See already *id.*, *The Ugaritic Drama of the Good Gods,* pp. 78-81. In particular, Tsumura's translation of *pḫr klʾat* as "total completion" ascribes an unattested meaning to the Ugaritic words, and the term *yrḫ,* "month", does not appear in the text, as would be expected if El was to count the months of pregnancy. Compare *KTU* 117, II, 43-44 = *CTA* 17, II, 43-44 and W.G. Lambert - A.R. Millard, *Atra-ḫasīs*, Oxford 1969, p. 62, lines 278-281.

[35] See already R. Dussaud, Les Phéniciens au Négeb et en Arabie d'après un texte de Ras Shamra, *RHR* 108 (1933), pp. 5-49, in particular pp. 10-11: "Il peut s'agir simplement de prostitution sacrée, comme Lucien le prétend pour Byblos, mais aussi de rites plus solennels caractérisés par l'intervention du dieu lui-même ou du roi divinisé qui s'unit à la déesse de la fécondité", the goddess represented then by "la grande prêtresse".

[36] J. van Dijk, La fête du nouvel an dans un texte de Šulgi, *BiOr* 11 (1954), pp. 83-88; W.H. Ph. Römer, *Sumerische 'Königshymnen' der Isin-Zeit,* Leiden 1965, pp. 128-208; S.N. Kramer, *The Sacred Marriage Rite,* Bloomington 1969; J. Renger - J.S. Cooper, Heilige Hochzeit, *RLA* IV, Berlin - New York 1972-75, pp. 251-269. Compare also the later Tyrian ritual: E. Lipiński, La fête de l'ensevelissement et de la résurrection de Melqart, *Actes de la XVIIe Rencontre Assyriologique Internationale,* Ham-sur-Heure 1970, pp. 30-58.

37 W. Schmidt, *Königtum Gottes in Ugarit und Israel* (BZAW 80), Berlin 1961, pp. 18-20.

38 *KTU* 1. 43 = *CTA* 33, in particular lines 1-2.

39 E. Lipiński, Vestiges phéniciens d'Andalousie, *Orient. Lov. Per.* 15 (1984), pp. 81-132 and pl. XI-XV (see p. 115-116).

Summary

The sacred marriage was the main manifestation of the fertility cult in Ugarit, as well as in the other regions of the ancient Near East. The authors assuming that this rite was performed by the King at the close of the New Year festivities, base themselves on the mythological and ritual text *KTU* 1. 23, allegedly a libretto of a cultic play in which the roles of Head of the Pantheon, El, and of his wife, Aṯirat, were played by the King and the Queen of Ugarit. A series of preparatory rites took place before the sacred marriage, which constituted the peak of the ceremony. The offspring born from this union were called the "gracious gods".

The aim of this contribution is to comment upon the above mentioned composition, of which different interpretations have been given, and to determine to what extent it can be considered a reliable basis for the study of the fertility cult in Ugarit. The sacred marriage reported by a *hieros logos* or even performed in a sacred play, the allusions to hydrophory, which aims at providing dew and rainfalls, and the mention of wine, that played an important part in the New Year festivities, constitute indeed various aspects of a fertility ritual enacted in autumn.

Résumé

Le mariage sacré était l'expression privilégiée du culte de fertilité à Ugarit comme dans les autres régions de l'ancien Proche-Orient. On suppose que ce rite était accompli par le roi à la fin des festivités du Nouvel An et on se réfère, en l'occurrence, au texte mythologique et rituel *KTU* 1. 23, qui contiendrait le scénario d'un drame cultuel dans lequel le roi jouait le rôle du dieu El, le chef du panthéon, et la reine, celui de la déesse Aṯirat, la parèdre de El. Divers rites préparatoires auraient précédé le mariage sacré qui devait constituer l'apogée de la cérémonie. Les enfants nés de cette union portaient le nom de "dieux grâcieux".

Le but de la présente contribution est de commenter le texte en question, dont on a proposé diverses interprétations, et de voir dans quelle mesure il peut servir de base à l'étude du culte de fertilitè à Ugarit. Le mariage sacré, relaté dans un *hieros logos* ou accompli sous la forme d'un drame sacré, les allusions au rite d'hydrophorie destiné à provoquer une rosée abondante et des chutes de pluie, la mention du vin, qui jouait un rôle important lors des fêtes du Nouvel An, voilà autant d'aspects divers d'un rituel de fertilité qui devait effectivement être mis en oeuvre au début de l'automne.

AN UGARITIC TEXT RELATED TO THE FERTILITY CULT (*KTU* 1. 23)

Stanislav Segert

At this conference on archaeology the opinion was expressed that it is possible to separate the objective description of archaeological finds from their interpretation, which may involve some subjective elements. Such a separation cannot be applied to written texts, whether found by archaeological excavation or transmitted by copying. This interdependence of description and interpretation is evident in ancient non-vocalized Semitic texts. A combination of three consonant letters can indicate either a noun or a verbal noun — infinitive or participle — as well as a finite verbal form such as certain persons of the perfect or imperative. Only interpreting in context can indicate the category, the morphological characteristics and the syntactic function of such a word.

This applies to the ancient North Canaanite literary and liturgical texts excavated at Ras Shamra — ancient Ugarit — in Northern Syria on the shore of the Mediterranean. These cuneiform alphabetic tablets were written mostly in the 14th century B.C., but traditions reaching several centuries back had been preserved on them.

The alphabetic cuneiform tablet containing a fertility ritual was found during the second excavation season directed by Claude Schaeffer in 1930, and published by Charles Virolleaud in 1933. Only about one half of the 76 lines of this tablet inscribed on both sides is completely preserved, but at the end probably no more than one line is missing (ample bibliographies in Caquot et al. 1974: 367-368 and Del Olmo Lete 1983: 427, n. 1).

The title used in modern literature, "Birth of Gracious Gods", is taken from the tablet (cf. lines 1-2, 23, 58). Its first part contains ritual instructions, the second part presents a mythological epic poem related to the ritual.

The first, liturgical part (lines 1-29) is divided by eight horizontal lines into nine sections, while the narrative continues in the second part (lines 30-76) without interruption. The parallelistic cola and verses of this epic poem only occasionally coincide with the graphic lines (previous research discussed by Xella 1973: 12-24; Caquot et al. 1974:

357-358, 360-364; Del Olmo Lete 1983: notes to pp. 427-439; various translations in notes to pp. 440-448).

The first liturgical part begins with an invocation: / 'iqra'a 'ilīma na ʿīmīma/ "I will invoke gracious gods" (line 1). A similar introductory formula opens the eighth liturgical section (line 23).

The liturgical character of the first part is indicated by objects and agents related to the cult — such as Prince Mot sitting with a scepter (lines 8-9) — as well as by instructions for ritual actions, such as eating bread and drinking wine (line 6), repeating of liturgical formulas (line 12), boiling of fat milk with herbs (line 19).

The agricultural function of this ritual is indicated by products and actions: / laḥm-/ "bread", / ḫamr-/ and / yēn/ "wine" (line 6), care of vine (lines 9-11) and grapes (line 26), vineyard terraces (line 10), fields of gods and goddesses (lines 13 and 28).

The poetic narrative (lines 30-76) describes actions bringing fertility or related to it: The old supreme god Il overcame his impotence, the weakness of his member (lines 37-40), by shooting down a bird and roasting it on charcoal (lines 37-39). Then he was able to impregnate two wives of his. No names of wives are given in the narrative: they may be supplied from the introductory section (lines 13, 28) as aṯrt wrḥm (y)/ 'aṯirat-) and / raḥmay-/ (?). They gave birth to two gods, Šaḥar "Dawn" and Šalim "Dusk" (lines 42-53).

Afterwards, Il's wives gave birth to gracious gods (lines 58-61). Their names are not given, their number may be related to the instruction requiring to recite the story five times (line 57) as five or rather twice five: ten. These young gods devoured with wide open mouths birds of heaven and fish of the sea (lines 62-63). Then stones and woods of the holy desert are mentioned (lines 65-66). After seven years, poetically equal to eight cycles (lines 66-67), the gods came to the guardian of cultivated land (line 69) and asked for bread and wine (lines 71-72). The guardian provided what was requested (lines 73-74).

Two aspects of fertility, procreation and provision of food, appear in this Ugaritic text. Its use in the cult is indicated in the introductory sections. But the text itself does not give specific information for what festival in which agricultural season it had to be used. On the basis of some hints in the text various interpretations were put forward by modern scholars: festival at the beginning or at the end of grain harvest, festival connected with wine and grape gathering, ritual which had to provide abundant rain. Both spring and fall terms have been considered, the last one in connection with the New Year festival (cf. Caquot et al. 1974: 359; Del Olmo Lete (1983: 436-439).

Among analogies which could help to better understand this Ugaritic text, *hydrophoria* and *hieros gamos* were mentioned. These terms point to Greece, but both these rites were performed in East Mediterranean areas as well.

The connection of *hydrophoria* with the Ugaritic ritual text seems to be tenuous, since it is based on two fragmentary and problematic lines (30-31) where "sea shore" is mentioned. (Cf. Gaster 1966: 427-428; Caquot et al. 357. — A new interpretation of these lines: Del Olmo Lete 1984: 143-146). The comparison with better preserved similar lines 35-36 does not support this interpretation.

According to some interpretations two women are lifting / mušta-'alatēma/(?) water — which is not expressly indicated in the preserved text — to the top / lē-ra'ši/ of a vessel / 'aggān-/. This interpretation of *agn* supported by Hebrew *'aggān* (cf. Caquot et al. 1974: 357) is more appropriate than that proposed by Segert and Zgusta (1953: 274-275), "fire" with reference to Indo-European agni-(cf. Gordon 1965: 351; Xella 1973: 55). Insofar as *hydrophoria* at the Jerusalem temple — as described in post-biblical traditional literature (Mishnah, *Sukkah* 4, 9-10) —was supposed to assure abundant rain by imitating it, by pouring water down, it perhaps can be related to fertility cult. The other kind of *hydrophoria*, attested by Lucian (*De Syria dea,* 13, cf. 48) for Hierapolis in Northern Syria, was connected to the tradition of the flood, as was the rite performed in Athens (Nilsson 1955: 595-596).

The sacred marriage, *hieros gamos*, is well known from the ancient Near East (Jacobsen 1976: 32-47) as well as from ancient Greece (Nilsson 1955: 121-122). In some of these rites the king and queen acted. The use of sacred marriage in fertility rites is based on imitative magic: human fertility may assure fertility of animals and plants. Some relics of sacred marriage rites survived until recent times in agricultural rites performed in the Ukraine, Germany (Frazer 1964: 126-127), and Lithuania (Marija Gimbutas in the discussion of this paper).

The major part of the Ugaritic epic "Birth of Gracious Gods" (lines 33-61) describes in detail the intercourse of god Il with his two wives. No connection with a ritual action is indicated. The greetings / šalāmu/ to the King and the Queen in the introductory part (line 7) point to the participation of the royal couple in the ceremony, but do not give any direct hint to sacred marriage. If the narrative had to serve as model for a rite, two women and one man were expected to participate in it.

The sequence of various kinds of foods which were eaten by the young gracious gods was used as basis for an aetiological interpretation: The gods were first fed from the breast of the lady (line 61). Then they devoured birds and fish (lines 61-63). Only later, after seven or eight years, they moved from the desert to cultivated, sown land /madraʿ/ (lines 66-69), where they obtained from its guardian bread and wine (lines 69-76).

This sequence may reflect the progress of the human society, from living on meat of animals, birds and fish, to organized agriculture that could provide bread and wine (Caquot et al. 1974: 363-364).

The exact location and function of the Ugaritic liturgical text "Birth of Gracious Gods" remains in many aspects uncertain, even after respectable efforts of two generations of competent scholars. In fifty years since the *editio princeps*, consensus on a general understanding was reached. However, many details, especially in the first part, are still waiting for their exact interpretation. The fragmentary state of preservation and lack of close analogies may explain this situation.

Two features requiring further study may be mentioned: the meaning of the number of years, seven or eight, and the role of twins.

The words /šabʿ- šanāt-/ "seven years" are followed by the parallel expression /ṯamānī n-qapat-/ "eight cycles" (lines 66-67). In this parallelistic poetic style the number functionally synonymous with sacred "7" is "7+1", i.e. "8" (cf. Segert 1983: 304). This parallel seems to weaken the relationship of the Ugaritic number "7" to other instances of the number "7", such as sabbatical years of ancient Israelites and 7+7 years in Joseph's story (Genesis, c. 41). In Ugaritic texts the number "7", especially if it is followed by the poetically functional synonym "8", indicates a considerable interval of time between two actions, rather than an exact number.

This interval of 7 years appears several times in the epic cycles. In Baal epics it follows mention of fields (1. 12: II: 44-45), in Aqhat epics it gives the length of drought caused by the murder of young prince Aqhat (1. 19: I: 42-43). The length of seven or eight years in the poem on gracious gods indicates their stay in the desert: the relationship of this interval to agricultural rites is not mentioned.

Among the details which may help a better understanding of this Ugaritic ritual text, the role of *two* gods deserves attention. Šaḥar and Šalim — "Dawn" and "Dusk" — were not twins, they were sons of different mothers. But they were fathered by the same god, conceived and born in the same time. They always appear together and can be considered functional twins.

To quote James Frazer (1964:71): "There is a widespread belief that twin children possess magical powers over nature, especially over rain and the weather". Some North American Indians used to spill water from baskets to produce rain. Mothers of twins — and even graves of twins — were considered instrumental for securing rain by Bantus in Southeastern Africa. The Heavenly Twins, Dioscuri, were credited by ancient Greeks with the power of allaying storms (Frazer - Gaster 1964: 71-73, 177).

In the Ugaritic myth, god Il by impregnating two women at the same time produced two sons, who were functionally twins. The birth of twins, important as a symbol in a fertility cult, was more likely if two wives were impregnated, than if the birth of natural twins were left to chance.

The Ugaritic text "Birth of Gracious Gods" contains substantial data about the fertility cult. Further analysis of the text itself combined with sound use of structural analogies may extract more information from this relatively short and fragmentary document of the ancient Canaanite beliefs and practices.

Summary

A contextual interpretation is applied to a tablet in alphabetic cuneiform from the 14th cent. B.C., found at Ras Shamra-Ugarit in Northern Syria, published in 1933. This ancient Canaanite text "Birth of Gracious Gods" contains a liturgical introduction and an epic poem: The god Il fathered sons from two wives. This fertility ritual was compared to other rites, such as *hydrophoria* — this connection is rather tenuous — and sacred marriage. It was also explained as a reflection of the progress of human society toward agriculture. Even after successful efforts in general interpretation, further studies of details are needed. The parallel expressions "seven years" — "eight cycles" indicate not an exact, but a considerable interval of time. Two gods "Dawn" and "Dusk" were sons of different mothers, but they were born from the same father at the same time; thus they may — as functional twins — be helpful in assuring abundant rains.

Résumé

Un texte ugaritique concernant le culte de fertilité (*KTU* 1. 23).

Une interprétation en contexte est appliquée à une tablette en cunéiformes alphabétiques du 14ème siècle avant J.-C., trouvée à Ras Shamra-Ugarit en Syrie du Nord, publiée en 1933. Cet ancien texte cananéen "La naissance des dieux gracieux" contient une introduction liturgique et un poème epique: Le dieu Il est devenu père des fils nés de deux épouses. Ce rituel de fertilité était comparé à d'autres rites, comme l'hydrophorie — ce rapport est très ténu — et le mariage sacré. Il était aussi expliqué comme réflexion du progrès de la société humaine vers l'agriculture. Même après des efforts réussis en interprétation générale, des études supplémentaires des détails sont nécessaires. Les expressions parallèles "sept années" — "huit cycles" dénotent un intervalle de temps, non exact, mais considérable. Les dieux "Aube" et "Crépuscule" etaient fils des mères différentes, mais ils étaient nés du même père au même temps; ainsi ils pouvaient — comme jumeaux fonctionaux — aider en assurant des pluies abondantes.

Bibliography

Text editions (some with translations and commentaries):

DEL OLMO LETE, G.
1983 — *Mitos y Leyendas de Canaan según la tradición de Ugarit,* Madrid. [Text, Spanish tr., notes, introd.; pp. 427-448].

DIETRICH, M., LORETZ, O., SANMARTIN, J.
1976 — *Die keilalphabetischen Texte aus Ugarit,* 1, Kevelaer/ Neukirchen-Vluyn. [Abbr.: *KTU.*] [Nr. 1. 23].

GIBSON, J.C.L.
1978 — *Canaanite Myths and Legends*, Edinburgh. [Text, Engl. tr., notes; pp. 123-127, cf. pp. 28-30].

GORDON, C.H.
1965 — *Ugaritic Textbook,* Rome. [Nr. 52].

HERDNER, A.
1963 — *Corpus des tablettes en cunéiformes alphabétiques découvertes à Ras Shamra-Ugarit de 1929 à 1939,* Paris. [Nr. 23].

RIN, S.
1968 — *Acts of the Gods* [Hebr.] Jerusalem. [Text, Hebr. tr., notes].

VIROLLEAUD, Ch.
1933 — La naissance des dieux gracieux et beaux, *Syria,* XIV, pp. 128-151. [Editio princeps, French tr., notes].

XELLA, P.
1973 — *Il mito di ŠḤR e ŠLM: Saggio sulla mitologia ugaritica,* Roma. [Text, Ital. tr., commentary].

Translations:

CAQUOT, A., SZNYCER, M., HERDNER, A
1974 — *Textes ougaritiques,* I: Mythes et légendes, Paris. [Paris tr., notes, introd.; pp. 353-379].

GASTER, Th. H.
1950/1966 — *Thespis: Ritual, Myth and Drama in the Ancient Near East,* New York. [Engl. tr., notes; pp. 418-435; cf. pp. 406-417].

Other Literature:

DEL OLMO LETE, G.
1984 — *Interpretación de la mitología cananea,* Valencia.

FRAZER, J.G. (GASTER, Th. H., ed.)
1964 — *The New Golden Bough*, New York.

JACOBSEN, Th.
1976 — *The Treasures of Darkness: A History of Mesopotamian Religion*, New Haven.

MACLEOD, M.D., ed.
1980 — *Luciani Opera,* III, Oxford.

NILSSON, M.P.
1955 — *Geschichte der griechischen Religion*, I, München.

SEGERT, S.
1983 — Parallelism in Ugaritic Poetry, *Journal of the American Oriental Society,* 103, pp. 295-306.

SEGERT, S. - ZGUSTA, L.
1953 — Indogermanisches in den alphabetischen Texten aus Ugarit, *Archiv Orientální,* 21, pp. 272-275.

FERTILITY AS BLESSING AND INFERTILITY AS CURSE IN THE ANCIENT NEAR EAST AND THE OLD TESTAMENT

H.F. van Rooy

1. INTRODUCTION

The subjects of fertility and infertility on the one hand and of blessing and curse on the other are both of such importance in the Ancient Near East and the Old Testament that justification for the study of the relation between the two subjects is hardly necessary. Pederson, who drew attention to the importance of the blessing in Israel, stated that the power to multiply was the premier way in which the blessing manifested itself (Pederson 1926: 204). It was regarded as the most important blessing that a woman could receive (*Ibid.*, 207-208). The curse was the opposite of the blessing, with one of the gravest curses being the failure of a person to create posterity (*Ibid.*, 440).

Curses and blessings are of frequent occurrence in the Ancient Near East. Important written documents or inscriptions were protected by shorter or longer curse-formulae (Fensham 1962a: 2). Curses were used in treaty texts to ensure the keeping of the treaty or the protection of the treaty text. They were associated with oaths and used for the protection of property and institutions (Scharbert 1958: 16). The blessing of God in the Old Testament extended to animals, the patriarchs, humanity as a whole, the ancestors of Israel, individuals, the believers in general, posterity and family, Israel and the tribes, even gentiles (*Ibid.*, 20, 21). Without God's blessing no undertaking could be successful (Psalm 127).

Fertility was especially linked with three spheres: bumper crops, thriving livestock and a growing family (Hoffner 1966: 326). The most important of these was human fertility. Prosperity with regard to crops and livestock would be small compensation to a person without offspring (*Ibid.*, 327). A person without children was therefore regarded as being less than a complete human being.

In Israel many children were an honour and infertility was seen as a trial or chastisement from God, or even as a disgrace (De Vaux 1976: 41). The longing for offspring played an important part in the history of Abraham, Isaac and Jacob in Genesis. Hanna's vow to consecrate her son to God must also be understood in the light of her desire to have a son *(Ibid.*, 465). This paper will discuss the relation between blessing and curse and fertility and infertility in treaty and covenant texts, with regard to the protection of documents, inscriptions and buildings and in historical, mythological and legendary texts.

2. TREATY AND COVENANT TEXTS

Since the publication of Mendenhall's articles in 1954 (1954a and 1954b), a vast number of studies have appeared dealing with the structure of the treaties from the Ancient Near East, their contents and the possible relation between the treaties and the covenant in the Old Testament. The best survey of this material, with an extensive bibliography, is given by McCarthy (1978). Although the treaties do not have a uniform structure, the genre presents certain basic elements that occur in all the extant treaties. This includes an introduction naming the parties to the treaty, the stipulations of the treaty, a list of the gods that were involved as witnesses to the treaty and curses that were pronounced upon the violator of the treaty. In addition to these basic elements some of the treaties exhibit some non-essential elements. The most important of these were an historical prologue and blessings — next to the curses — in the Hittite treaties (Korosec 1931: 12-14). The precise form of the different elements in the structure may also vary in different periods. While the curses in the Hittite treaties from the second millennium B.C. usually consisted of a relatively short, standard formula, the Assyrian and Aramaic treaties from the first millenium contained elaborate curses. In these curses (and in the blessings of the Hittite treaties) fertility and infertility played no minor role.

This can clearly be seen in Fensham's exposition of common trends in Ancient Near Eastern curses (Fensham 1963). Amongst curses directed against the person of the violator of a treaty or another kind of agreement curses pertaining to the death of the cursed person and to the lack of offspring are the first to be defined (*Ibid.*, 158). These curses include the following: the seed of the transgressor will be snatched away, his name will be destroyed, his name and seed will not endure or be named, he will have no son and his name and seed will vanish (*Ibid.*, 159). In the Hittite treaties with the short curse and blessing formula the subject of fertility as such is not mentioned. It is, however, stated that the son of the king that violates the treaty, will die while the gods will protect the son of the king that keeps the treaty. A typical example of such a curse and blessing formula is the one in the treaty between the Hittite king Mursilis and Duppi-Tessub of Amurru:

The words of the treaty and the oath that are inscribed on this — should Duppi-Tessub not honor these words of the treaty and the oath, may these gods of the oath destroy Duppi-Tessub together with his person, his wife, his son, his grandson, his house, his land, and together with everything that he owns.

But if Duppi-Tessub honors these words of the treaty and the oath that are inscribed on this tablet, may these gods of the oath protect him together with his person, his wife, his son, his grandson, (and) his country (Pritchard 1969: 205).

In some of the texts the subject is touched on more directly, though still briefly, as in the treaty between Muwatallis and Alaksandus of Wilusa. In both the curses and the blessings direct reference is made to the seed of the vassal (McCarthy 1978: 2). In the treaty between Tudhaliyas IV and Ulmi-Teshub of Dattasa mention is made not only of the king's son, but also of children in general. The reference to house and country is expanded to include the king's threshing floor, garden, field, orchard, cattle, crops and prosperity (*Ibid.*, 305, 306). The curses and blessings of the treaty between Suppiluliumas and Kurtiwaza are very elaborate. The curses include that Kurtiwaza should have no children even from a second wife and that the Hurri men with their wives, children and country should have no seed if they violate the treaty. The seed and name of the king would be exterminated (Pritchard 1969: 206).

The curses of the Assyrian treaties dating from the first millennium B.C. were much more elaborate, often with individual gods associated with specific curses. In the treaty between Ashurnirari V and Mati'ilu of Arpad the extant curses in the damaged text deal mainly with the fertility of animals and of the land, with famine as the result of violating the treaty. The young of oxen, asses, sheep and horses would all suffer because of a lack of milk. The land would be destroyed by Adad through hunger, want and famine. The people would have to eat the dust as rain would cease. The farmers would not be able to sing a harvest song, there would be no vegetation on the lands nor water in the springs. In a rather damaged portion of the text mention is also made of infertility amongst Mati'ilu wives (*Ibid.*, 533; cf. also Weidner 1932).

Extensive curses relating to infertility appear in the vassal-treaties of Esarhaddon (cf. Wiseman 1958). They concentrate on human infertility and infertility of the land. There are basically two groups of curses in these treaties, namely curses dealing with the alteration or destruction of the tablet (lines 410-493) and curses pronounced upon a violator of the treaty's stipulations (lines 513-668). In the first group Ashur is called upon to deny fatherhood to the king (415-416, *Ibid.*, 60), Zarpanitu to destroy his name and seed (435-436, *Ibid.*, 60) and Belet-ili to put an end to birth in the land (437-438, *Ibid.*, 62; Pritchard 1969: 538). In the second group Girra is called upon to incinerate the king's descendants (524-525, Pritchard 1969: 539). The king's descendants must disappear from the land (537-544, 663-664, *Ibid.*, 539, 541). Infertility in the land is dealt with extensively (440-452, *Ibid.*, 538). Adad is called upon to put an end to vegetation, to destroy the land through storms and locusts, resulting in want and famine (*Ibid.*, 538). Rain and dew must also stay away from the land (530-533, *Ibid.*, 539).

Curses with the same intent as these in the treaties mentioned appear in the Sefire treaties. In the treaty between Assurnirari and Mati'ilu there is a curse stipulating that there would not be enough milk for the young of the oxen, asses, sheep and horses. This same theme appears more extensively in the Sefire treaties with regard to man, cattle, sheep and horses. It is expressed as follows with regard to man: If seven wet-nurses should anoint their breasts and suckle a boy, may he not be satisfied. With regard to animals: If seven mares/cows/ewes should feed a foal/calf/lamb, may he not be satisfied (I Sefire A21-24, Van Rooy 1977: 73). Animal infertility is also mentioned at the end of a damaged part in I Sefire A21. The common curse that the descendants of the violator of the treaty would not inherit a name does also occur in I Sefire C24-25, in the section of the treaty dealing with the protection of the inscription (*Ibid.*, 83). The infertility of the land is the subject of a series of curses in I Sefire A25-29, where Hadad (just as in the vassal-treaties of Esarhaddon) is called upon to destroy the vegetation through hail. To this is added that locusts and other pests must transform the land into a desert so that no vegetation should be visible (*Ibid.*, 73). That Hadad would sow salt in Arpad and its vicinity also relates to infertility (I Sefire A36). Salt causes infertility of the soil and the pronouncement of the curse of infertility is here accompanied by the sowing of salt as a ritual act (Fensham 1962b: 50).

As regards the Old Testament, the distinction between two types of covenant between God and his people or an individual must be kept in mind. There are covenants in which God undertakes obligations and covenants in which He stipulates obligations for his people (Mendenhall 1962: 717-721, Weinfeld 1970). In the former blessings are promised to man and the latter has structural similarities with the vassal treaties, including curse and blessing formulae relating to the keeping or violating of the covenant. An example of the former is the covenant with Abraham (Genesis 12, 15 and 17), in which the subject of Abraham's descendents is of utmost importance. It is a central part of God's promise to Abraham (cf. Gen. 12:2; 15:4-5; 17:2, 4-6). The promise that his son will sit on his throne is also an important part of the covenant with David (II Sam. 7:12-16).

As regards the other type of covenant the curses and blessings of Deuteronomy 28 are of great importance (cf. McCarthy 1978: 179-180 for the structure of this chapter). The blessings are enumerated in 28:1-14 and the curses in 15-68. Two groups of blessings can be distinguished, namely those with the formula *barûk 'attâ* (blessed are you) with the agent unmentioned (3-6) and those with the Lord as subject (7-14). Amongst the first group blessings relating to fertility have an important part: Blessed shall be the fruit of your body, and the fruit of your ground, and the fruit of your beasts, the increase of your cattle, and the young of your flock (4, RSV). The same is true of the second group: And the LORD will make you abound in prosperity, in the fruit of your body, and in the fruit of your cattle, and in the fruit of your ground, within the land which the LORD swore to your fathers to give you (11, RSV). Even the rain, without which the vegetation can not flourish, comes from the Lord (12).

The curses in Deuteronomy 28 are much more elaborate than the blessings. A number of curses are formulated with the formula *'arûr 'attâ* (16-19). Then there are curses with the Lord as subject (20-29, 35-37, 48-49, 59-68) and curses that will be executed by men or animals (30-34, 38-44 and 49-57). Amongst the curses with the formula *'arûr 'atta* is one corresponding closely to the blessing in verse 4, omitting only the reference to "the fruit of your beasts" (18). In this curse and the corresponding blessing the three main aspects of fertility —human, animal and botanical— are summarised in one sentence. This is also true of the blessing of verse 11.

In the curses with the Lord as subject or executed by men or animals, these three aspects occur again, but are more elaborate. Reference is also made to the life-giving rain. The rain will stay away, resulting in drought if the people violate the covenant (22-24). In spite of much exertion the crops of the cultivated lands, vineyards and olive groves would be poor (38-40). Enemies sent by God will destroy the fruit of beasts and the fruit of the land (51). Even the numerous people will decrease in number (53, 62). Many of these curses have strong similarities to curses in the vassal-treaties of Esarhaddon (cf. Frankena 1965: 144-150 for these and other correspondences between Deut. 28 and the vassal-treaties of Esarhaddon). These similarities point to the relation of the covenant curses in the Old Testament to an extensive tradition of curses in the Ancient Near East. Many other curses of a similar character occur in the Old Testament, in contexts relating to the covenant (cf. Deut. 11:3-17; 29:22-23; 30:5, 9) and in the writings of the prophets (Hag. 1:1-11; 2:15-19; Is. 4:2; 5:10; 24:1-7; 30:23-25; 32:9-29; Jer. 3:3; 9:10; 12:10-13; 23:3; Ezek. 36:7-12; 29-30; Hos. 2:21-22; Joel 1:16-20; 2:14, 19, 21-26).

3. CURSES AND BLESSINGS IN INSCRIPTIONS AND DOCUMENTS

Reference has already been made to the practice of protecting inscriptions and important documents with a series of curses. This was a common practice for a long period of time in the Ancient Near East. One of the best-known examples is in the Codex Hammurabi's epilogue, consisting of the last five colums of the codex. This has a relatively short blessing formula pronounced over the man who keeps the laws and does not alter them (about 16 lines). This is followed by an extensive series of curses against the man who does not keep the laws, but abolishes, distorts or alters them, or who destroys the name of Hammurabi (more than 270 lines from rev. col. xxvi 17 till the end of rev. col 28).

Amongst the curses famine appears, as well as the disappearance of the cursed person's name and memory. Enki is called upon to dam up the waters so that there will be no grain. The damming up of the rivers in Mesopotamia would have had same result as drought in Syria and Palestine, but still Adad is called upon to keep the rains back and to dry up the fountains. Nintu must deny the violator an heir, not let him receive a name or let him beget a male descendant (cf. Pritchard 1969: 177-180). The same kind of curses occurs often in Mesopotamian inscriptions. In the long introduction to some of Adad-Nirari I's inscriptions curses pronounced on the violator of the inscription include the destruction of that person's seed and the injunction that want, famine, hunger and drought will plague his country (Luckenbill 1968: 28-29).

In his study of the origin of apodictic laws in the Old Testament Gevirts (1961) paid attention to quite a number of curses relating to the protection of the inscriptions in West Semitic inscriptions. These curses are not as elaborate as those mentioned above, but there are quite a few references to the destruction of a man's seed (Yehawmilk 15, Selim-sezib 14, DNL 5 - cf. Gevirts 1961: 145-146). The same appears on funerary inscriptions (Sin-zer-ibni 11, Tabnit 7-8, Esmun'azar 8-9 - cf. Gevirts 1961: 148-149). To this can be added a few other Aramaic inscriptions (Zakir B27-28, Nerab ii 10, Tema i 13-15 and Guzneh 4-5 - cf. Gibson 1975: 12-13, 97, 149-150, 154).

The Phoenician inscription of Karatepe (cf. Gevirtz 1961: 142-143) has unfortunately been damaged at the section dealing with the curses, but in other places reference is made to fertility, especially as a blessing from the gods (cf. Ai 5-6, Aii 7-8, 11-13, Aiii 7-9, Civ 6-10 - cf. Gibson 1982: 46-55). The last two examples named above are important as they refer to the fertility of men, animals and plants.

4. HISTORICAL, MYTHOLOGICAL AND LEGENDARY TEXTS

As regards the material from the Ancient Near East attention is only given to the texts from Ugarit, in which in a special way something remained extant "of the religious life and thought of the early western Semites" (Caquot and Sznyzer 1980: 7). The religion of Ugarit was mainly a fertility cult with a direct link between the fertility of the gods and the fertility of the land (Craigie 1983: 35). The fact that the Anat-Baal cycle is related to a cultic festival and especially to an autumnal new year festival is well-known (cf. Hvidberg 1962: 52-55; De Moor 1972: 4-16). In the fertility cycle Baal played a prominent part in relation to human procreation, the fertility of flocks (Cassuto 1962: 84-85) and the outpouring of rain. This can be seen in the link between the request that a house must be build for Baal and his sending of the rains at the right time (KTU 1.4 V:6-9).

In El's dream after Baal's death he saw the rain coming again and deduced from this that Baal must be alive again (KTU 1.6 III: 1-21). Gray's comment that "Baal (was) 'the lord' *par excellence* of the fertility-cult of Canaan" (1964:122) is to the point.

The importance of human fertility is at the heart of the legends of Keret and Aqhat. In the Keret texts fertility is clearly regarded as a divine blessing, with the obtaining of a male descendant directly related to the blessing of El (KTU 1.15 II:11-28; cf. also KTU 1.15 III:2-21 and Hempel 1961: 55 n. 118). Daniel, who did not have a son, received El's blessing through the mediation of Baal whereafter a son was born to him (KTU 1.17 I: 15-37). After Aqhat's death seven infertile years were part of the curse pronounced upon the land (KTU

1.19 I: 38-46). Amongst the curses pronounced by Daniel upon the towns that he held responsible for his son's death, is one pertaining to the descendants of one of the towns (KTU 1. 19 III: 53-54).

In Israel fertility was also linked to the blessing of God. He gives blessings in offspring for man and beasts, in the produce of the soil, grain, wine and oil (McKenzie 1952:124). What Israel shared with its neighbours was the relationship between divine beneficence and nature's blessing on the one hand and divine hostility and nature's hostility on the other (*Ibid.,* 132). The difference is, however, the important recognition that blessings are bestowed upon those who keep the covenant and punishment upon those who break it (*Ibid.,* 134). Obedience and fertility go hand in hand. It is often repeated that if Israel keeps God's command, He will send the rain in its time, with subsequent blessings in the realm of nature (Deut. 11:13-15; Lev. 26:3-5). A good example can be found in Deut. 7:12-14: And because you hearken to these ordinances, and keep and do them, the LORD your God will keep with you the covenant and the steadfast love which he swore to your fathers to keep; he will love you, bless you, and multiply you; he will also bless the fruit of your body and the fruit of your ground, your grain and your wine and oil, the increase of your cattle and the young of your flock, in the land which he swore to your fathers to give to you. You shall be blessed above all peoples; there shall not be male or female barren among you, or among your cattle (RSV).

This blessing was also requested in prayer by men to men, as was the case with Rebecca by her brothers (Gen. 24:60), Jacob by Isaac (Gen. 27:28; 28:1-4) and Joseph by Jacob (Gen. 49: 25-26). It was promised by God to men (Gen. 1:28; 9:1-7 - cf. Hempel 1961: 32). In contrast with this, infertility was a punishment for sins (Hos. 9:14; Jer. 5:23-25; Gen 4:11-12). A whole country could even suffer in this way for the sins of individuals (cf. I Sam. 21:1-14), as happened in the legend of Aqhat.

CONCLUSION

This study demonstrates to what extent the subject of fertility as blessing and infertility as curse lived in the hearts and minds of the people of the Ancient Near East. Without this much of the myth and ritual of the Ancient Near East can not be understood precisely because it was directed to fertility, while in Israel petition and sacrifice often had the same aim.

Summary

Fertility and infertility are amongst the most important subjects in curses and blessings in the Ancient Near East and in the Old Testament. Fertility was especially linked to three spheres: bumper crops, thriving livestock and a growing family. This paper treats the subject in treaty and covenant texts, in curses and blessings in inscriptions and documents and in historical, mythological and legendary texts to demonstrate to what extent the subject lived in the heart and minds of the people of the Ancient Near East. This lies at the background of much of the myth and ritual of the Ancient Near East and of petition and sacrifice in Israel.

Résumé

La fécondité et la stérilité figurent parmi les sujets les plus fréquents sur le plan des malédictions et bénedictions aux pays du Proche-Orient antique et dans l'Ancien Testament. La fécondité touchait à trois domaines: des recettes abondantes, un bétail croissant et une famille nombreuse. Cette étude traite le sujet comme il paraît dans les textes de traité et d'alliance au sujet des malédictions et des bénédictions dans les inscriptions et les documents, dans les texts de nature historique, mythologique et légendaire. Le but de cette étude sera donc de démontrer à quelle mesure ce sujet était vivant aux coeurs et aux pensées des gens du Proche-Orient antique. C'est ce qui est à la base de beaucoup de mythes et de rites du Proche-Orient antique et de beaucoup de requêtes et d'offrandes en Israel

Bibliography

CAQUOT, A. & SZNYCER, M.
1980 — *Ugaritic religion,* Leiden (Brill) (Iconography of Religions XV, 8).

CASSUTO, U.
1962 — Baal and Mot in the Ugaritic texts, *Israel Exploration Journal* 12:77-87.

CRAIGIE, P.C.
1976 — *The book of Deuteronomy,* Grand Rapids (Eerdmans) (New International Commentary on the Old Testament).
1983 — *Ugarit and the Old Testament,* Grand Rapids (Eerdmans).

DE MOOR, J.C.
1972 — *New Year with Canaanites and Israelites,* Part one: *Description,* Kampen (Kok) (Kamper Cahiers).

DE VAUX, R.
1976 — *Ancient Israel. Its life and institutions,* London (Darton, Longman & Todd).

FENSHAM, F.C.
1962a — Maledictions and benedictions in ancient Near-Eastern vassal-treaties and the Old Testament, *Zeitschrift für die alttestamentliche Wissenschaft* 74:1-9.
1962b — Salt as curse in the Old Testament and the ancient Near East, *The Biblical Archaeologist* 25:48-50.
1963 — Common trends in curses of the Near Eastern treaties and kudurru-inscriptions compared with maledictions of Amos and Isaiah, *Zeitschrift für die Alttestamentliche Wissenschaft* 75:155-175.

FRANKENA, R.
1965 — The vassal-treaties of Esarhaddon and the dating of Deuteronomy, in De Boer, P.A. *red., Oudtestamentische Studiën* 14:122-154.

GEVIRTZ, S.
1961 — West Semitic curses and the problem of the origins of Hebrew law, *Vetus Testamentum* 11:137-158.

GIBSON, J.C.L.
1975 — *Textbook of Syrian Semitic Inscriptions,* volume II: *Aramaic inscriptions,* Oxford (Clarendon Press).
1982 — *Textbook of Syrian Semitic Inscriptions,* volume III: *Phoenician inscriptions,* Oxford (Clarendon Press).

GRAY, J.
1964 — *The Canaanites,* London (Thames and Hudson).

HEMPEL, J.
1969 — *Apoxysmata,* Berlin (Töpelman) (Beihefte zur Zeitschrift für die alttestamentliche Wissenschaft 81).

HOFFNER, H.A.
1966 — Symbols for masculinity and femininity. Their use in ancient Near Eastern sympathetic magic rituals, *Journal of Biblical Literature* 85: 326-334.

HVIDBERG, F.F.
1962 — *Weeping and laughter in the Old Testament. A study of Canaanite-Israelite Religion,* Leiden (Brill).

KOROSEC, V.
1931 — *Hethitische Staatsverträge. Ein Beitrag zu ihrer juristischen Wertung*, Leipzig (Weicher) (Leipsiger rechtwissenschaftliche Studien 60).

LUCKENBILL, D.D.
1968 — *Ancient records of Assyria and Babylonia I,* New York (Greenwood Press).

McCARTHY, D.J.
1978 — *Treaty and covenant,* 2nd edition, Rome (Biblical Institute Press), (Analecta Biblica 21A).

McKENZIE, J.L.
1952 — God and nature in the Old Testament: Fertility cults, *Catholic Biblical Quarterly* 14:124-145.

MENDENHALL, G.E.
1954a — Ancient Oriental and Biblical law, *Biblical Archaeologist* 17:26-46.

1954b — Covenant forms in Israelite tradition, *Biblical Archaeologist* 17:50-76.

1982 — Covenant (in *The interpreter's dictionary of the Bible* 1:714-723).

PEDERSON, J.
1926 — *Israel* I-II, London (Humphrey Milford).

PRITCHARD, J.B. *ed.*
1969 — *Ancient Near Eastern texts relating to the Old Testament,* 3rd ed., Princeton, N.J. (Princeton University Press).

SCHARBERT, J.
1958 — "Fluchen" und "Segnen" im Alten Testament, *Biblica* 39: 1-26.

TAWIL, H.
1977 — A curse concerning crop-consuming insects in the Sefire treaty and in Akkadian: a new interpretation, *Bulletin of the American Schools of Oriental Research* 225:59-62.

VAN ROOY, H.F.
1977 — *'n Vergelyking van die struktuur van die buite-Bybelse staatsverdrae - met besondere aandag aan die Sefire-verdrae - met die struktuur van Deuteronomium,* Potchefstroom (Thesis (D. Litt.) PU for CHE).

WEIDNER, E.
1932 — Der Staatsverträge Assurnirari VI von Assyrien mit Mati'ilu von Bit-Agusi, *Archiv für Orientforschung* 8:17-34.

WEINFIELD, M.
1970 — The covenant of grant in the Old Testament, *Journal of the American Oriental Society* 90: 184-203.

WISEMAN, D.J.
1958 — *The vassal-treaties of Esarhaddon,* London (British School of Archaeology in Iraq).

THE ISRAELITE RELIGIOUS CENTRE OF KUNTILLET 'AJRUD, SINAI

Zev Meshel

THE SITE

Kuntillet 'Ajrud (Horvat Teiman) is located about halfway between the Mediterranean and the Red Sea (Gulf of Eilat), forty miles south of the Biblical Kadesh Barnea (Fig. 18). It sits on a flat hill which rises beside the water wells of Wadi Quraiya.

Old maps reveal that the site is a crossroads of desert tracks: one leads from Gaza to Eilat; another traverses the Sinai along the Wadi Quraiya; and the third branches off to the south, to the centre of southern Sinai.

The site was discovered by the famous English explorer Edward Palmer who surveyed the Sinai in the 1860s and visited 'Ajrud in 1869. There he carried out a small sounding into the ancient remains and subsequently identified the site as Gypsaria, a site known from Roman sources as a station on the Roman road from Gaza to Eilat.

Our excavation revealed that the ruin is a one-period site. All the remains belonged to one phase in the Iron Age — about 800 B.C.

The site contains the remains of only two structures (Meshel 1978: 9′ - 12′): a main building at the western extremity of the plateau and a smaller building east of it (Fig. 19). The two buildings are in a very different state of preservation. Almost nothing is left of the latter. The main building, whose walls have survived to a height of five feet, measures approximately 75×45 feet, and takes up the whole width of the narrow plateau (Pl. 34).

The entrance to this building is from the east, through a small court with stone benches along the walls. Fragments of frescoes found amidst the debris on the floor of the entrance indicate that parts of the walls were painted with colourful floral motifs and linear designs. An entryway led from the small entrance court to a long, narrow room, which we named the "Bench-room". Both the Bench-room and the entry had benches along the walls and were plastered all over with white, shiny plaster.

The Bench-room extends across the width of the building. The benches along the walls on each side of the entryway take up most of the floor space, leaving only a narrow passage between them. The inner courtyard was empty except for three ovens found in each of the southern corners, indicating that this was probably the cooking area. Steps were found in the same corners. They probably formed part of staircases leading to the roof.

To the south and west of the courtyard were two long rooms. In the floor, bases of pithoi, or storage jars, were firmly embedded and so closely spaced that it must have been difficult to pass between them. There is no doubt that these rooms were used for storing food.

THE INSCRIPTIONS

The most remarkable finds of the excavations were the inscriptions and drawings. Most of these were found in the Bench-room and in the two side rooms entered from the Bench-room. Most of the inscriptions were fragmentary and incomplete, but the written word always has a special significance, particularly in such a remote site. The inscriptions, most in early Hebrew and some in Phoenician script, can be divided into several categories (Meshel 1986): 1) Letters or words incised on stone bowls and pottery before firing. These are Sighn Tithe and offerings which were sent to the priests who inhabited the site and vessels which were dedicated to this place by donors, who asked for divine blessing. 2) Inscriptions written in black or red ink on plaster. — These consist of requests, prayers and blessings to and by "Yahweh of Teiman and his Ashera", "El", "Ba'al" (Meshel 1979: 31). 3) Inscriptions incised or written in ink on pottery vessels after firing. — These are accompanied by drawings and reflect a formula of blessing 'By Yahweh of Samaria and his Ashera".

The inscriptions (and other finds) shed important light on the nature of the site as a kind of religious centre or a way-side shrine.

THE DRAWINGS

Due to its plan and the absence of any cultic vessel we do not think that the building was a temple. But the meaning of the inscriptions, as we saw, is very clear. Some of them were written beside many drawings. Do they have the same meaning? Do they have a religious or cultic significance?

The drawings and decorative designs can be distinguished in the following categories (Beck 1982: 3-64): 1) Coloured fresco designs. — These are fragments of decorated plaster which were found in the debris of the eastern building and at the entryway of the main building. Most of them are of geometrical patterns but there is a scene of a figure seated on a throne holding a lotus flower, and another one showing two figures on a city wall. These two scenes of the wall-paintings may have a religious meaning. 2) A coloured scene of a human head, goat and lotus flower on one of the stones in the jamb of the central opening to the southern store-room. 3) Drawings on various pottery vessels, particularly on two large pithoi, many of which (unpainted) were found in the store-rooms. These two were found in and near the Bench-room (Figs. 20-21). The main scenes, painted in red ink, are: cow-and-calf, ibexes flanking a tree-of-life, a lion, a procession of animals, two Bes figures and a lyre player, procession of worshippers, a boar, a seated figure and some more (Beck 1982).

The drawings were painted by three or four painters. At least one of them was familiar with the most common motifs prevailing in the Near East. The iconographic sources of inspiration lie in the Phoenician world and the regions of north Syria. Do they have a cultic meaning?

CONCLUSION

The drawings cannot be separated from the inscriptions and other finds of the site. They parallel and complement each other. They do have, in our opinion, a cultic significance, in the general wide meaning of this concept. The exact symbolism of each scene is a subject of another paper.

Summary

Kuntillet 'Ajrud, on the Negev-Sinai border, is a religious centre or a way-side shrine from about 800 B.C. The site contains a main rectangular building with a white plastered Bench-room, in which most of the finds were made. The most important of these are inscriptions and drawings on pottery vessels, on wall plaster and stones. The motifs of the drawings are closely connected with the inscriptions and other finds which clearly have a religious character. They too have, in our view, a cultic meaning.

Bibliography

BECK, P.

1982 — The drawings from Horvart Teiman, *Tel Aviv*, 9, no. 1, pp. 3-68.

MESHEL, Z.

1978 — *Kuntillet 'Ajrud, a Religious Centre from the time of the Judaean Monarchy on the Border of Sinai,* The Israel Museum, Cat. no. 175, Jerusalem.

1979 — Did Yahweh have a consort?, *BAR* V, no. 2, pp. 24-35.

1986 — The finds of Horvat Teiman (in Hebrew), *Sinai,* Tel Aviv (forthcoming).

SECTION IV:
THE GRECO-ROMAN WORLD

LES CULTES DE LA FÉCONDITÉ/FERTILITÉ DANS LA GRÈCE DES CITÉS

Pierre Lévêque

L'ambition de notre colloque est grande, qui est de suivre sur des millénaires l'évolution des cultes de la fertilité. Elle est dans le droit fil des interrogations incontournables qui sont actuellement celles des historiens des religions de la Préhistoire et de l'Antiquité: ils veulent suivre les continuités et permanences en même temps que constater les mutations, évolutions ou simples bricolages des idéologies religieuses, en partant, dans le cas présent, d'un thème qui est une des génératrices principales de ces systèmes de pensée: la fertilité. Comme le dit Mircea Eliade , "la végétation est la manifestation de la *réalité vivante,* de la vie qui se régénère périodiquement. La végétation incarne (ou signifie, ou participe à) la *réalité* qui se fait vie, qui crée sans se tarir, qui se régénère en se manifestant en formes sans nombres, sans s'épuiser jamais." Si les questionnements des hommes sur les réalités menaçantes de la nature qui les entoure et les cerne contribuent tout particulièrement à l'élaboration de l'imaginaire, il n'est aucune réalité naturelle qui ait pour eux l'importance de la végétation, dont ils tirent une grande partie de leur nourriture à partir de la révolution néolithique, d'où l'importance primordiale des puissances de fertilité qui sont censées en être les promotrices.

Mais nous sommes presque à la fin de notre parcours, dans la Grèce des cités où tant d'activités autres qu'agro-pastorales se sont développées. Or, les divinités de fertilité dominent encore le panthéon et le vécu religieux des citoyens. A telle enseigne qu'elles restent primordiales jusque dans l'Athènes classique, qui vit de ses productions artisanales, des échanges, de l'exploitation de son empire et où la dure expérience de la guerre du Péloponnèse montre bien qu'elle peut même survivre très forte aux ravages de sa campagne par les troupes péloponnésiennes et à la quasi-disparition de ses activités rurales...

Quelques constations d'abord pour délimiter nos possibilités d'analyse. D'une part, il faut tenir grand compte de la diversité des cités, dont les cultes sont bien spécifiques, même s'ils entrent dans le cadre plus générique de la religion grecque. D'autre part, il est impossible de traiter en Grèce de la fertilité sans évoquer *ipso facto* la fécondité qui lui est indissolublement liée, ce depuis des millénaires. Je n'hésiterais dons pas à parler constamment sans scrupule des cultes de fécondité/fertilité, qui sont au fond ceux de l'*élan vital*, pour parler en termes bergsoniens.

L'analyse des cultes de la Grèce du 1er millénaire nous place dans une évidente continuité. Le déchiffrement du linéaire B des tablettes mycéniennes et les progrès des fouilles ont permis de bien confirmer ce qui n'était jusque-là que forte présomption: que les linéaments essentiels de la religion grecque sont posés dès les royaumes achéens, quand se constitue un étonnant syncrétisme, dit improprement créto-mycénien, qu'il n'est plus possible de révoquer en doute. De la rencontre entre l'idéologie indo-européenne très socialisée des migrateurs grecs et la vieille idéologie naturiste de la Méditerranée orientale naît un imaginaire spécifique où les cultes des forces vives de la nature, incarnées dans les déesses et leurs parèdres, demeurent au premier plan, au détriment de la trifonctionnalité.

Cette continuité n'est pas véritablement entamée par les quatre siècles des Ages Sombres, où d'importantes mutations transforment toutefois l'imaginaire créto-mycénien. Il y a là un problème délicat et que j'ai déjà largement évoqué ailleurs. Il est clair, en tout cas, que quand, au tournant des 9e et 8e siècles, émerge cette forme d'Etat ou mieux de société qu'est la *polis* ("cité-Etat"), le passé est très largement pris en compte.

Les dieux que nous appelons poliades et qui, installés sur les acropoles, protègent la cité sont presque toujours des divinités topiques fixées sur place depuis au moins des siècles: tels Poseidon à Pylos, Héra à Argos, Athéna à Tirynthe et à Athènes, cette dernière portant au reste le nom de la déesse. Même Sparte, pourtant fondée sur un sol vierge, honore des déesses héritières du passé le plus créto-mycénien, Athéna encore sur l'acropole et Artémis Orthia dans les marais de l'Eurotas, dont les représentations figurent une vraie Dame achéenne. On remarquera au passage l'importance d'Athéna en tant que déesse poliade: déjà gardienne armée des palais fortifiés des *wanakes* mycéniens, elle conserve maintenant la même fonction pour protéger la ville des citoyens.

Cette première analyse permet une constatation importante. Ces divinités poliades que nous venons de rencontrer et qui jouent un rôle de premier plan dans l'émergence des cultes civiques sont des divinités fécondantes et fertilisantes bien attestées à l'époque mycénienne, notamment dans les tablettes, mais elles apparaissent ici dans une fonction politique et militaire de protection. Il doit être clair dès le début qu'en Grèce les dieux des forces vives de la nature remplissent en même temps d'autres rôles, très différents, et que leurs attributions s'étendent largement au-delà de la sphère fécondité/fertilité, ce qui dénonce au vif leur situation prépotente.

Si nous voulons maintenant entrer plus loin dans l'analyse des cultes de fertilité dans ce nouveau cadre socio-politique de la cité, nous devons aborder un problème fondamental, qui est de théologie: *comment se structure le panthéon grec,* d'où découlent deux questions: *comment s'organise-t-il comme un ensemble*, en échappant à la simple juxtaposition de dieux, et *quels sont les vecteurs qui constituent les lignes de force de son fonctionnement.*

Réponses difficiles, la religion grecque, au moment où émergent les cités, étant déjà un ensemble complexe et contradictoire où se distinguent des strates superposées. Le syncrétisme créto-mycénien a joué un rôle considérable dans sa constitution (on se rappelle que la plupart des noms des grands dieux grecs figurent dans les tablettes mycéniennes), mais son action même a été aléatoire dans un rapport de force qui a eu tendance, dans les petites monarchies despotiques des Achéens, à briser les structures indo-européennes et à conforter les structures méditerranéennes: il y a eu à la fois net éclatement du tripartisme des migrateurs et flottement dans les vieux cultes indigènes, puisque le syncrétisme a amalgamé les forces idéologiques en présence, juxtaposant les dieux ou les mixant à l'intérieur de personnes divines nouvelles, conservant leurs noms ou les rhabillant de noms grecs. C'est le cas de Zeus, sur lequel nous reviendrons, ou de Coré qui porte un double nom, étant aussi la Crétoise Perséphone. Sur ce fond ancien ont joué les facteurs qui marquent les siècles passablement obscurs des Ages Sombres, les migrations doriennes qui n'ont pas pu ne pas renforcer les éléments indo-européens (sans pour autant réintroduire la trifonctionnalité), mais aussi les apports en provenance d'Orient, très nettement en faveur des cultes de la fécondité/fertilité, qu'il s'agisse de divinités féminines comme Léto, Aphrodite, Cybèle, Hécate ou d'un jeune dieu-fils comme Apollon.

Malgré toutes ces difficultés d'analyse, on peut discerner deux facteurs d'organisation dans le panthéon hellénique: une société globale et des systèmes de forces primitives exprimant la vitalité et la reproduction du *cosmos*.

1. Les dieux ne sont pas de petites forces atomisées; ils sont organisés dans une société globale, bien localisée sur le lointain et inaccessible mont Olympe. C'est Zeus qui y excerce le pouvoir: même si

l'on ne doit pas minimiser ses aspects naturistes qui forment un ensemble cohérent autour du ciel lumineux et orageux (voir l'étymologie de son nom), de la foudre, de la pluie fécondante, il est essentiellement un père (Zeus Pater, comme Dyaus Pitar ou Jupiter) et un roi assumant la fonction de souveraineté. Certes son autorité est loin d'être assurée, traversée et contrariée qu'elle est de contradictions, de révoltes, de jalousies, de violences, d'adultères, comme il appert déjà dans les épopées. Société qui n'est en rien despotique et dont les origines indo-européennes sont peu discutables, même si elle est en constante évolution, admettant de nouveaux venus, faisant taire les rivalités qui débouchent sur des compromis, ou se rationalisant peu à peu, comme lorsque se dégage le concept, ionien sans doute, des douze dieux, dont au reste plusieurs listes très divergentes nous ont été transmises.

2. Au sein de cette société (et la débordant quelque peu, car Olympe et Enfers forment deux espaces fantasmatiques distincts, mais complémentaires) l'analyse permet de distinguer des systèmes de forces primitives, exprimant la vitalité et les possibilités de reproduction de l'univers et organisés autour de divinités de la fécondité/fertilité (et parfois vie éternelle), directement héritières des déités du type néolithique oriental (et surtout anatolien) *via* la Crète et *via* Mycènes. Une typologie paraît possible, sinon aisée.

21. D'abord des divinités féminines, par excellence dispensatrices de fécondité et fertilité et qui jouent un rôle considérable comme kourotrophes, veillant à la conception, à la naissance, à l'allaitement, à la première enfance et à l'éducation des filles et des garçons par le biais des initiations dites couramment pubertaires.

211. Dans la suite d'un long héritage néolithique qui a traversé l'âge du Bronze, elles se présentent sous deux formes, l'une matronale, l'autre virginale. Deux cas de figure doivent être distingués.

Primo, de la manière la plus obvie, il y a deux générations de déesses: celle des soeurs-épouses de Zeus, Déméter et Héra, et de divinités analogues comme Léto dont les
divinités analogues comme Léto dont les origines renvoient aux origines du monde divin; celle des filles de cette première génération, telles Athéna, Artémis, Coré, Aphrodite...

Une autre grille de lecture permet de discerner les déesses-vierges des autres: elles sont trois et appartiennent à la première génération (Hestia) et à la seconde (Artémis, Athéna). Il est bien clair qu'il faut distinguer soigneusement déesse-fille et déesse-vierge (comme nous y incitent par exemple les cas de Coré ou d'Aphrodite). Non moins clair que les facteurs vitaux de fécondité/fertilité ne sont en rien moins présents dans les vierges que dans les mères: ainsi Artémis et Athéna sont parmi les initiatrices et kourotrophes les plus actives. Au reste la distinction peut être moins marquée qu'on ne le croirait au premier abord: à Nauplie (Pausanias, 2, 38, 2), Héra retrouve périodiquement sa virginité en se trempant dans la source Carrathos (le retour annuel de la végétation coïncide avec la revirginisation de la déesse); dans le grand mythe athénien d'Erichthonios, Athéna préside maternellement à l'éducation de l'enfant né du sperme d'Héphaistos, tombé sur la terre et la fécondant après avoir souillé la cuisse de la jeune fille: produit des ardeurs excessives du dieu qui n'arrive pas à posséder sa demi-soeur, mais dont la semence est néanmoins féconde.

Secundo, dans certains cas, il s'agit plus clairement d'une dyade mère/fille, dont les exemples les plus frappants sont ceux de Déméter/Coré à Eleusis ou de Déméter/Despoina en Arcadie. Au contraire, la mère biologique d'Athéna est éliminée dans le processus final de la gestation et, dans l'une des deux formes que revêt le mythe de sa naissance, Aphrodite naît sans le secours de l'élément maternel, directement du sperme des bourses tranchées de Cronos: ces deux cas, qui ne sont certainement pas atypiques, représentent l'inverse d'une parthénogénèse et transcrivent des phantasmes d'une naissance quasi sans mère. Mais revenons aux dyades féminines: l'élément maternel y est en revanche poussé à son paroxysme; Déméter et Coré notamment sont appelées, au duel, "les deux déesses" et forment une indissoluble unité, sentimentale autant que biologique, qui joue à plein dans le vécu religieux et où les analystes décryptent comme les deux pôles successifs et complémentaires de la féminité.

Cette structure très directement mère/fille n'est pas isolée. Dès l'époque crétoise ou créto-mycénienne on voit, dans la grotte d'Amnisos, Héra et sa fille Ilithyie, figurées par des idoles naturelles doubles (stalagmites ou stalactites grossièrement retaillées). Léto et sa fille Artémis, des Asianiques, sont unies dans le mythe par une extrême affection et, dans certaines de ses formes, on voit la jeune déesse aider sa mère à accoucher du petit frère Apollon. Gé et Thémis jouent un rôle capital à Delphes aux origines de la divination et ne sont pas négligeables à Olympie, où l'autel de cendres de Gé, siège d'une antique mantique, jouxte celui de sa fille Thémis édifié sur une bouche (Pausanias, 5, 14, 10).

212. Le fonctionnement des divinités féminines dans la Grèce des

cités est relativement clair. Essentiellement, les vierges mises à part, elles sont des puissances hiérogamiques, comme on le voit bien pour Héra sur le Gargaros dans l'*Iliade* et pour Aphrodite sur l'Ida troyen dans l'*Hymne homérique* qui lui est consacré. Elles participent donc au renouvellement annuel du printemps et se posent ainsi comme indissolublement génératrices de fécondité et de fertilité: on notera par exemple qu'Aphrodite, une divinité qui semble spécialisée dans l'élan sexuel, embrayeur de la reproduction des espèces, est en même temps Antheia, la déesse des fleurs...; l'élan végétal germinatif est très net dans l'union sacrée d'Héra et de Zeus sur le Gargaros: "sous eux, la Terre divine fait naître un tendre gazon, lotus frais, safran et jacinthe, tapis serré et doux dont l'épaisseur les protège du sol" (*Iliade*, 14, 292 sq.).

En second lieu, les vierges, elles—mise à part Hestia qui doit représenter une ancienne déité indo-européenne du foyer, donc la pureté du feu — ne sont pas moins promotrices de fécondité/fertilité (ainsi Athéna est la généreuse donatrice de l'olivier, Artémis est Kédréatis...), mais elles ont une fonction spécifique, qui est de présider aux initiations des jeunes, j'entends aux initiations de classes d'âge: ainsi en Attique Athéna et Artémis se partagent les rôles, Athéna sur l'Acropole avec notamment les Panathénées (dont on faisait remonter la création à Erichthonios ou à Erechthée) et Artémis sur les bordures côtières avec les Brauronies qui voient la retraite de fillettes consacrées, travesties en oursonnes au service de la déesse. Le vase de Brauron où figure leur course éperdue en présence d'un prêtre-ours montre que les fillettes ne sont pas les seules à "faire l'ours" et que la rencontre avec le mâle sublimé sous forme de prêtre-ours simule et dramatise une sorte d'initiation sexuelle, bien normale dans ce type de cérémonies. On se rappelle d'autre part à Sparte le rôle d'Artémis Orthia ("celle qui redresse" [les sexes]) dans le cursus initiatoire des jeunes.

Un troisième mode de fonctionnement met en présence d'un autre type d'initiation, initiation de salut pourrait-on dire: il en est ainsi de Déméter/Coré à Eleusis (et ailleurs dans des sanctuaires-succursales éleusiniennes) ou de Déméter/Despoina en Arcadie. Au couple mère/fille sont liés des mystères — beaucoup plus complexes à Eleusis, mais peu importe — qui sont garantie de salut *post mortem*. Ceux d'Eleusis s'appuient sur le mythe du rapt de la jeune déesse, mythe végétatif et infernal à la fois, mythe de renouvellement périodique et/donc de survie bienheureuse. Mais ce n'est pas le cas en Arcadie, où la péripétie mythique essentielle est celle de la Mère terrible, emportée dans une colère démesurée par le viol qu'elle a subi de son frère Poseidon. Enlèvement et viol, c'est-à-dire actes sexuels imposés à la fille ou à la mère, semblent former le fond de ces drames, qui entraînent d'abord malheur et famine, puis, acceptés et régularisés, engendrent bonheur, abondance, salut.

213. De tels schémas propres aux divinités féminines ont une cohérence interne qui remonte loin dans un passé immémorial. Dès les cavernes du Paléolithique supérieur, la femme est abstractisée dans une déité de fécondité et de chasse, la Grande Déesse. Bien que quasiment jamais dans une représentation concrète, l'acte de fécondation est partout présent, au moins symbolisé dans des signes de bipolarité sexuelle, et il est depuis longtemps patent que la chasse est sexualisée, que l'épieu des chasseurs ouvre des blessures en forme de vulves: la puissance qui domine l'univers surnaturel, autour de laquelle s'organise le double fantasmatique de la nature, est ainsi garante et maîtresse de fécondité et de chasse; elle assure donc la reproduction biologique de la communauté en favorisant les naissances et la dure conquête de la nourriture.

Au Néolithique s'opèrent des mutations fondamentales dans l'habitat et dans le mode de production de la nourriture: sédentarisation, création de l'agriculture céréalière et de l'élevage des animaux domestiques. La divinité féminine de fécondité s'avère alors aussi comme promotrice de fertilité: elle assure la productivité de la terre ouverte par le bâton fouisseur — et ensuite par la houe ou l'araire — comme le ventre féminin l'est par le membre du mâle. Elle devient elle-même une Terre-Mère, une puissance qui assure à la fois les naissances et les moissons, donc la reproduction de la communauté villageoise sous des formes nettement plus complexes qu'au Paléolithique.

Il y a, je le répète, une cohérence profonde de ces représentations analogiques élaborées au fur et à mesure que se développent les puissances du cerveau humain et la complexité des sociétés et qui rassurent les producteurs en mettant toutes leurs activités sous la protection des Grandes Mères devenues aussi des Terres-Mères: elles assument la survie du groupe en accomplissant le rite créateur le plus élémentaire et le plus essentiel — l'hiérogamie qui abstractise l'acte sexuel dans l'ambiance du renouveau annuel — et elles perpétuent aussi leurs bienfaits sur les individus au-delà de la mort, d'où les idoles de déesses qui apparaissent si souvent dans les tombes. Tout le fonctionnement des divinités féminines hiérogamiques des cités grecques est donc dans cette suite millénaire, au sein d'une cohérence d'autant plus forte que le fantasmatique y est directement mis en liaison avec les réalités naturelles de la biologie animale et végétale:

reproduction sexuée de l'homme et des animaux domestiques, renouvellement annuel de la végétation.

Quant aux déesses vierges, peu nombreuses, mais d'une rare importance dans les mythes et les cultes, elles ne représentent pas une première étape de la vie des déesses dans le temps quasi arrêté du panthéon; elles sont résolues à rester telles et elles poursuivent de châtiments farouches leurs compagnes qui acceptent l'étreinte, voire les imprudents qui s'attaquent à elles ou portent des regards sur leur nudité.

On a tendance à les interpréter comme gardiennes du tabou de la virginité qui s'impose avec rigueur dans les communautés néolithiques sédentarisées: lorsque des mariages réguliers s'instituent entre groupes voisins liés par des pactes d'intermariage, les filles doivent rester intactes de manière à constituer un produit frais d'échange. Une telle contrainte sur la nature n'est possible que si elle se surnaturalise dans des déesses vierges et dans des mythes exaltant la virginité.

Cette explication n'exclut au reste pas que d'autres facteurs aient joué, d'ordre démographique: y a-t-il eu une nécessité fondamentale à retarder l'âge du mariage, pour diminuer le nombre des naissances dans des millénaires où le problème de la nourriture reste aigu (on sait que la sédentarisation a de loin précédé la céréaliculture)? Est-ce dès ce moment qu'apparaissent des prêtresses ou des collèges de prêtresses connotées essentiellement par leur virginité? Ce sont des questionnements importants, auxquels il me paraît pour l'instant difficile de donner une réponse nette.

Dans le cas d'Athéna et d'Artémis, il s'agit au reste d'une virginité très positive, qui leur confère de grandes puissances de promotion en tant que kourotrophes et une vitalité exceptionnellement opératoire, par exemple dans les domaines de la production artisanale, de la musique, de la danse, de la chasse...C'est-à-dire dans des secteurs où l'imagination créatrice et l'habileté technicienne jouent un rôle qui dépasse de loin le monde de la fécondité/fertilité.

22. A côté des divinités féminines, figurent bien souvent des enfants-dieux, dont le schème de fonctionnement se dégage aisément: l'enfant divin, fils de la Grande Déesse, a des enfances difficiles, parsemées d'épreuves dont il ne se tire qu'avec l'aide généreuse de divinités féminines; adolescent, il connaît l'amour de la Déesse qu'il féconde et meurt, d'une mort suivie de résurrection qui est pour les fidèles le gage de leur propre résurrection. Ce thème du fils-amant de la Mère est largement présent dans le mythe grec, mais rarement dans sa totalité.

221. Il y a des dieux-fils qui ont avec leur mère de solides attaches, comme on le voit dans des cas aussi différents que celui d'Apollon (intégré avec Léto et sa soeur Artémis dans la triade des Létoïdes) ou celui d'Héphaistos (rejeton de la seule Héra, d'après Hésiode, et rendu infirme par Zeus qui le précipite de l'Olympe, parce qu'il avait voulu défendre contre lui sa mère, selon le chant 1 de l'*Iliade*); mais leur vie ne s'organise pas sur le modèle épreuves / fécondation de la mère / mort et résurrection.

Mais, dans bien des mythes, une partie au moins du schéma est aisément décryptable. Il en est ainsi de Dionysos (dont le nom semble au reste signifier "enfant divin"), des Dioscures ("des jeunes divins") à la naissance ambiguë et à la mort alternative, d'Hyakinthos, le jeune dieu de la végétation bulbeuse d'Amyclées, tué par la maladresse de son ami Apollon à moins qu'il ne s'identifie à lui, des divers enfants divins qui sont les partenaires de Déméter à Eleusis... Mais deux cas peuvent apparaître particulièrement signifiants. Celui de Jasion, foudroyé après avoir (pour avoir) joui de Déméter sur la jachère trois fois labourée de Crète: de cette hiérogamie naît Ploutos "bienfaisant, qui va parcourant toute le terre et le vaste dos de la mer et du premier passant aux bras de qui il tombe, il fait un riche et lui octroie large opulence" (Hésiode, *Théogonie*, 969 sq.). Celui de Zeus qui, dans ses enfances crétoises incorporées à sa personne de dieu père et roi, apparaît en proie aux pires difficultés aprés sa naissance tumultueuse et les persécutions de son père, ne s'en tire qu'avec de multiples concours, connaît l'amour de la Mère (Héra), meurt et est enterré sur le mont Iouktas où l'on montrait son tombeau, au grand étonnement d'un Callimaque (*Hymne à Zeus*, 8-9) qui ne pouvait admettre le trépas d'un Immortel...

Dans certains cas, la structure est plus complexe, l'enfant divin apparaissant avec un couple mère/fille dans une "sainte famille" du type néolithique anatolien. Ainsi de Zeus en Crète à Amnisos, dont nous verrons le culte devant la caverne d'Héra/Ilithyie. Ainsi des enfants divins d'Eleusis avec Déméter et Coré. Ainsi d'Hyakinthos avec sa mère Diomédé et sa soeur Polyboia. Ainsi des Létoïdes.

222. Les témoignages sur ces enfants divins dans le culte et le mythe en Grèce peuvent être multipliés, à condition de noter que la structure est en désagrégation. D'où les difficultés que nous rencontrons à bien cerner son fonctionnement.

Les jeunes dieux qui n'ont pas les caractères de l'enfant divin méritent de retenir un instant notre attention. L'exemple typique est celui d'Apollon: il porte en lui jeunesse, beauté, éclat (mais pas tellement séduction amoureuse et ses amours sont bien souvent décevantes), et il possède toutes les forces d'inspiration, prophétique, poétique, chorégraphique et musicale, qui sont celles de la Terre. Sa liaison est claire avec les forces fécondantes et fertilisantes, comme il est naturel pour un dieu-fils qui partage avec la déesse-fille le privilège d'être le meilleur témoignage de la fécondité de la Mère, le fruit même de la Maternité.

Dans le modèle de l'enfant-dieu, le fonctionnement, plus complexe, est à analyser à plusieurs niveaux. Bien entendu, il est d'abord la Maternité en acte. Mais aussi il se révèle acteur d'un vaste processus cosmique qui renouvelle l'univers d'une double manière: fécondation de la Mère par son fils dans un système clos indéfiniment renouvelable, donc en dehors des astreintes du temps; mort du jeune dieu qui ressuscite, dramatisation violente du cycle végétatif.

Le cas de Dionysos est sans doute le plus expressif: il est au reste d'autant plus intéressant que ses liens avec la Crète sont considérables, tant par le mythe d'Ariane que par les allégations des Crétois qui le faisaient naître en Crète de Zeus et de Perséphone et par la localisation en Crète du dépècement de l'enfant-dieu par les Titans (Diodore, 5, 75). C'est un dieu dont les connotations fécondantes sont immenses (voir par exemple le rôle du *phallos* dans ses cérémonies), mais pas plus que ses connotations végétales: dieu du lierre, du pin, de la vigne, il est le donateur par excellence du *ganos*, cette humidité créatrice, ce scintillement de joie qui est dans la végétation et dans les liquides vivifiants, rosée, ruisseaux, lait, vin. Or, dans leur arrangement grec, les mythes qui touchent ses rapports avec sa mère sont particulièrement signifiants et émouvants: s'il lui a coûté la vie par suite du voeu imprudent qu'elle avait fait, il va la lui redonner avec l'éternité en la faisant pénétrer dans l'Olympe, symbole du salut par l'amour, dit-on non sans raison, mais aussi de ses relations avec une Grande Déesse, sa mère, dont le nom de Sémélé a toute chance de signifier "la Terre".

De même que certaines déesses très engagées dans la fertilité — telle Déméter qui est à l'origine de la céréaliculture — sont en même temps donatrices essentielles du salut, de même les enfants divins sont au coeur des mystères. Dans la grotte de l'Ida, l'enfant Zeus renaît chaque année de la Mère dans des cérémonies d'un réalisme émouvant, le sang de la naissance bouillonnant dans ses couches. A Eleusis, outre les diverses formes d'enfant divin (Démophon, Triptolème...), il y a Brimos "le Fort" qui naît de Brimo "la Forte", dans la dernière scène de l'époptie, des embrassements mystiques de Zeus et de Déméter représentés par leurs prêtres et le peuple saint chante la naissance et psalmodie "Pleus et conçois". On en arrive à la très forte présomption que, dans ces liturgies immémoriales, le fidèle s'identifie au nouveau-né, fruit de l'hiérogamie, et que c'est ainsi qu'il devient en partie divin et qu'il peut survivre comme un Bienheureux *(olbios)* tandis que les non-initiés d'Eleusis croupissent après leur mort "dans les moites ténèbres".

223. Certes la religion grecque ne nous donne pas de cas d'enfant-dieu révélant la totalité du schéma, aussi net par exemple qu'Attis, Adonis ou Osiris, mais la multiplicité des vestiges est en soi signifiante. Ici également c'est tout un passé immémorial, remontant sans doute jusqu'au Néolithique, qui s'exprime: l'adolescent qui meurt et ressuscite, après avoir fécondé la Mère, dramatise le renouveau du cycle végétatif tout autant que le rapt de la jeune déesse et les aller-retour qui en dérivent. Ils représentent l'un et l'autre des passages: mort d'un côté et de l'autre soumission par la force à la première possession sexuelle. Le premier est plus brutal, plus traumatisant, il contraint davantage à une méditation sur la vie et la mort, sur la mort et la survie, sur la vie triomphant de la mort qui est au fond de tous les cultes de fertilité, tant est aisée et féconde en consolations l'analogie entre mort de l'individu et mort annuelle de la végétation, entre résurrection de l'homme et éternel retour de la Nature végétale.

* * *

Nous sommes parti de la constatation que le panthéon grec révèle deux types de structures: la société globale de l'Olympe et de petits ensembles qui lui donnent sa vraie cohérence, constitués qu'ils sont de systèmes de forces organisés autour des puissances féminines de fécondité/fertilité et des jeunes dieux leurs parèdres. L'analyse que nous en avons faite permet peut-être maintenant d'apporter des solutions aux deux questions que nous nous posions.

La très puissante construction de l'Olympe autour de la personne de Zeus donne les plus fortes présomptions qu'il s'agit d'une structure indo-européenne, commode à l'origine pour organiser la trifonctionnalité (encore que bien des panthéons orientaux soient organisés eux aussi comme des cours célestes, mais sans tripartisme). En fait, l'Olympe ne conserve que des restes très évanides de trifonctionnalité et, d'autre part, il ne joue aucun rôle dans le culte. C'est un espace structurant qui permet de réunir tous les dieux (sauf ceux des Enfers) dans un lieu unique, au sein d'une certaine harmonie personnifiée dans Hébé ("Puberté, Jeunesse") qui leur fournit leur nourriture/boisson spécifique, sans que disparaissent pour autant ni leurs contradictions et les sentiments mesquins qu'ils nourrissent les uns pour les autres, ni une certaine chronologie qui permet l'accession de nouvelles divinités, tels Dionysos ou Héraclès. C'est un espace de luttes et de conciliation, qui récupère tous les dieux du vécu religieux, quelle que soit leur origine, méditerranéenne, grecque ou orientale. Et c'est le cadre de tant de chatoyantes fictions, comme dans l'*Iliade*, des fictions qui me paraissent plus littéraires que vraiment religieuses.

Les structures vivantes, vécues, qui organisent le panthéon autour des puissances de l'élan vital — et qui sont naturellement intégrées dans l'ensemble Olympe — se révèlent d'une autre importance. Elles correspondent aux besoins des hommes — consommateurs de fantasmatique, à telle enseigne que, dans les cas les plus nombreux, ce sont des divinités de fécondité/fertilité qui se sont imposées depuis le IIe millénaire comme divinités topiques et qui continuent à patronner la religion poliade: considérable extension de leurs pouvoirs primitifs.

Peu de temps après la composition définitive des épopées, Hésiode, dans un prodigieux effort de rationalisation, organise sa *Théogonie* autour de trois principes constructeurs: remonter au passé le plus lointain, au Chaos initial, bien antérieur à la constitution de l'Olympe, en suivant d'incontestables modèles orientaux; montrer les luttes de générations et de puissances (dont beaucoup sont de monstrueuses puissances du mal); organiser le *planning* d'ensemble du monde surnaturel autour des *impetus* de la sexualité qui permettent les enfantements successifs, à partir d'une phase première de parthénogénèse, à telle enseigne que l'ensemble du poème peut se résumer dans un tableau généalogique démesuré. Ce que nous y voyons vivre et agir, ce sont ces forces profondes de l'élan vital productrices de toutes les émergences de dieux, monstres ou héros: telle est bien la vraie logique de la pensée religieuse des Grecs. Un mot-clef de la *Théogonie* est au reste *eros*, l'amour, qui, malgré sa polysémie, désigne essentiellement l'élan génésique auquel ni dieux ni hommes ne peuvent résister. Il ne me paraît pas sans intérêt de noter que le vocable, pour lequel on cherche en vain des étymologies indo-européennes vraisemblables, ait toute chance d'être méditerranéen, crétois.

Ainsi s'explique la tonalité très spécifique de la théologie hellénique au reste si souple. Les dieux y jouent un rôle beaucoup moins important que les déesses. Des trois frères Cronides, Hadès a une union stérile avec Coré en tant que prince des Enfers, Poseidon — dont le nom fait pourtant un "Maître ou Epoux de la Terre" — a essentiellement des amours malheureuses et une postérité de monstres. Zeus apparaît ainsi comme le géniteur universel, par ses épouses légitimes multiples[1], dont Héra n'est que la dernière, et par ses innombrables liaisons ou aventures. C'est le vrai reproducteur du monde divin et il révèle bien ici sa dualitè fondamentale. En effet, dieu indo-européen par l'essentiel de sa stature et de ses fonctions, il est, en tant que Téleios — et avec Héra Téleia — le protecteur du mariage et le garant de sa consommation, mais déjà les enfants qu'il a d'elle sont peu nombreux et disparates (avec des relents de parthénogénèse pour Héphaistos). L'essentiel de ses activités de procréation s'accomplit hors du mariage. De fait, il conserve beaucoup de l'enfant divin crétois qui s'est amalgamé en lui avec le dieu père et roi, maître de la foudre, qui représente son héritage indo-européen: la multiplicité des métamorphoses animales sous lesquelles il possède ses partenaires (surtout sous forme de taureau et de divers volatiles), ses amours adolescentes — bien connues d'Homère (*Iliade*, 14, 295) — avec sa soeur Héra, vers qui il volète en coucou d'après une tradition ultérieure, ses enlèvements de nymphes ou héroïnes en taureau...

On ne peut pas non plus ne pas être frappé par son étrange association, à la grotte d'Amnisos, avec la dyade Héra-Ilithyie. Il est honoré, sur une petite butte devant la caverne, comme un dieu nourrisson: c'est là qu'a été consacré son cordon ombilical et que les femmes, après d'heureuses couches, viennent offrir celui de leur nouveau-né. Structure patente de "sainte famille" où la topographie même est signifiante: devant le sanctuaire rupestre le *divine child* sert d'introducteur, d'agent nécessaire au fonctionnement de la dyade. Mais ce qui retient l'attention, c'est qu'ailleurs Zeus n'est pas l'enfant d'Héra, mais son frère, son jeune amant, son époux, de même qu'Ilithyie est ensuite considérée comme sa fille...La confusion est ici d'autant plus signifiante que, dans la grotte de sa naissance, sur l'Ida, il est tout simplement mentionné dans les mystères comme le fils de la Mère.

C'est dire la richesse prégnante des cultes de fécondité/fertilité qui continuent à répondre pleinement en Grèce aux questionnements et aux angoisses des hommes concernant leur vie sur terre et leurs possibilités de survie, malgré la forte socialisation et la diversification des activités entraînées par l'émergence des cités, malgré la rationalisation de la philosophie qui cherche une autre *physis*, un autre principe d'évolution du monde que les étreintes et enfantements des dieux. Les puissances de la germination et de la fécondation, de la fructification et de l'enfantement gardent leur force d'exégèse et de persuasion et permettent de satisfaire tous les besoins: ces déités qui sont celles de l'expansion et du renouvellement de l'univers, qui portent en elles les secrets qu'elles dévoilent aux initiés dans les mystères pour vaincre la mort, sont aussi désormais celles qui protègent citoyens, acropole, cité...

Encore faudrait-il pouvoir, au-delà de cette analyse des génératrices du panthéon, suivre l'évolution de ces cultes qui ne cessent de se renforcer: à l'époque archaïque, avec l'intégration de Dionysos et de Déméter-Coré dans la religion poliade dont ils étaient quasiment exclus — et ce souvent grâce aux efforts des tyrans soucieux de promouvoir les divinités chères au peuple paysan — ou, dès la fin du 5e siècle, avec l'orientalisation de la religion qui conforte les Mères et leurs jeunes parèdres.

Note

1 Il est intéressant de suivre Hésiode, *Théogonie,* 886, sq. dans l'évocation des épouses de Zeus jusqu'à Héra. Mises à part Déméter et Léto qui sont des figures divines à la forte personnalité, les voici avec leur descendance: Métis (Athéna), Thémis (Heures et Moires), Eurynomé (Grâces), Mnémosyne (Muses). Apollon excepté, il n'engendre que des filles, et bien souvent de véritables collèges de déesses de fécondité/fertilité.

Bibliographie

Je donne ici les titres de mes articles antérieurs que j'ai utilisés dans ce rapport de synthèse.

1981 — Contribution à une théorie historique de la production de la pensée religieuse..., *Dialogues d'histoire ancienne*, p. 53 sq.

1981 — La pensée des chasseurs archaïques, *ibidem*, p. 41 sq.

1984 — La dépendance dans la structure trifonctionnelle indo-européenne, *Dialogues d'histoire ancienne,* p. 51 sq.

1972 — Formes et structures méditerranéennes dans la genèse de la religion grecque, *Praelectiones Patavinae*, Rome, p. 23 sq.

1975 — Le syncrétisme créto-mycénien, dans. F. Dunand et P. Lévêque, *Les syncrétismes dans les religions de l'Antiquité,* Leyde, p. 19 sq.

1985 — I Dori e la religione della età buia, dans D. Musti, *Le origini dei Greci,* Rome, p. 259 sq.

1984 -- La genèse d'Aphrodite à Chypre, *Mélanges Roland Fiétier,* Paris, p. 419 sq.

1984 — Astarté s'embarque pour Cythère, *Hommages à Lucien Lerat,* Paris, p. 451 sq.

1973 — Continuités et innovations dans la religion grecque de la première moitié du 1er millénaire, *Parola del Passato,* p. 23 sq.

1982 — *Olbios* et la félicité des initiés, *Hommages à Charles Delvoye,* Bruxelles, p. 113 sq.

1984 — Genèse de la cité, contradictions sociales et mutations religieuses, *Centro ricerche e documentazione sull'antichità classica, Atti 1980-1981,* Rome, p. 347 sq.

LE TOMBEAU D'AMPHION ET DE ZÉTHOS ET LES FRUITS DE DIONYSOS

Maria Rocchi

Pausanias raconte que le tombeau d'Amphion et de Zéthos à Thèbes de Béotie était un "tumulus pas grand" et il s'étend sur le récit de ce que, chaque année, Thébains et Tithoréens auraient fait autour de ce tombeau pour appeler la fertilité sur leurs champs respectifs.[1]

Toujours selon Pausanias, quand le soleil se trouvait dans la constellation du Taureau, les habitants de Tithorée en Phocide projetaient de dérober de la terre au tumulus thébain d'Amphion et de Zéthos pour la porter sur la tombe d'Antiope dans leur propre cité, et ceci afin d'obtenir une bonne récolte au détriment des Thébains qui, de leur côté, devaient surveiller leur tumulus.

Le comportement des uns et des autres se baserait sur un oracle de Bakis dont Pausanias nous rapporte le texte et il ajoute qu'Antiope, la mère des deux héros, était ensevelie à Tithorée avec Phokos, son dernier époux.[2]

De nombreux savants ont interprété le récit de Pausanias, mais leurs hypothèses ne nous semblent pas tout à fait convaincantes.

J.G. Frazer, commentant le texte de Pausanias, avance l'hypothèse que la période indiquée pour la démarche des Tithoréens correspondait à l'époque des semailles et il rappelle à ce propos que, dans la Rome antique, les Lois des Douze Tables interdissaient, entre autre, de dérober par des pratiques magiques la récolte du champ d'autrui.[3]

F. Vian voit, dans ce qu'il définit comme un "curieux rite agraire", une confirmation des prérogatives qui situeraient les jumeaux Amphion et Zéthos, bergers et bâtisseurs de murailles, dans la "troisième fonction" dumézilienne de la civilisation indo-européenne.[4]

W. Burkert pense, lui, à une forme résiduelle d'un rite de passage transposée sur le plan magique et il la met en relation avec un autre rite nocturne, celui célébré par les Hipparques thébains près de la tombe de Dirké, au moment de la passation des pouvoirs.[5]

A. Schachter, de son côté, pense que Pausanias ne se réfère pas à un rite effectivement célébré de son temps, mais qu'il aurait inventé cette histoire à partir du texte de Bakis.[6]

Il nous semble donc nécessaire d'analyser de près les témoignages des Anciens afin de mieux comprendre la situation cultuelle, objet de notre étude.

L'oracle de Bakis dit textuellement: "mais quand un homme de Tithorée offre des libations pour Amphion et Zéthos, des prières et des offrandes propitiatoires, dans la période où le Taureau est ensorcelé par la force du glorieux soleil, alors toi, prends bien garde qu'un grand mal ne s'abatte sur la cité car, en effet, les fruits s'abîmeront ici si les Tithoréens partagent la terre et s'ils la transportent sur le tombeau de Phokos".[7]

On appelait communément, "bakides" les thaumaturges et les devins possédés par les dieux[8] et parmi eux la tradition et Pausanias en indiquaient un de Béotie.[9]

On peut aussi attribuer à un devin béotien l'oracle qui nous intéresse étant donné qu'il est adressé à un homme de Thèbes, qu'il concerne le tombeau des Dioskouroi de cette cité et qu'il est prononcé dans le but de ne pas laisser les Thébains perdre les fruits de leur terre.

Selon Bakis il s'agit d'un danger menaçant dont, à cette époque précise, les Thébains doivent se garder: un homme de Tithorée donne des offrandes sur le tombeau d'Amphion et de Zéthos et les Tithoréens partagent (δασσαμένων)[10] la terre du tumulus pour emporter leur part sur le tombeau de Phokos.

Dans sa description de Thèbes, Pausanias cite le texte de l'oracle de Bakis et l'enrichit de détails.

Dans le récit de Pausanias, il convient avant tout de noter que le danger annoncé par l'oracle n'avait pas un caractère exceptionnel mais qu'il se répétait chaque année, chaque fois que le soleil dans sa course à travers la Zodiaque qui détermine la succession des mois, revenait dans la constellation du Taureau. L'action des Tithoréens devait consister à dérober en cachette, contre la volonté des Thébains (ὑφαιρεῖσθαι δὲ ἐθέλουσιν), de la terre du tumulus pour la répandre autour (περιάψωσι)de la tombe d'Antiope et de Phokos, et rendre ainsi plus féconde leur récolte. Tout ceci au détriment des Thébains qui, de leur côté, auraient dû surveiller le tumulus, suivant "à la lettre" l'ordre de Bakis.[11]

Il ne ressort, ni du texte de Bakis ni de celui de Pausanias, que les habitants des deux cités se soient jamais réellement affrontés autour du tumulus.

Il apparaît invraisemblable que pour célébrer un rite l'on ait pu chaque année, voler de la terre à un tumulus "pas grand" et courir le risque d'irriter les héros et même celui de les faire revenir puisque, en enlevent de la terre, on amincit le diaphragme qui separe les morts du monde des vivants.[12]

A notre avis, l'hypothèse la plus probable est que les Tithoréens avaient l'intention de partager le tumulus d'Amphion et de Zéthos avec les Thébains et, une fois parvenus à leurs fins, d'en répandre, une fois pour toutes, la terre en cercle[13] autour de la tombe d'Antiope et de Phokos, réunissant ainsi les fils avec la mère, ce qui leur aurait valu en échange une fertilité accrue de leurs champs.

A notre avis, en outre, l'oracle de Bakis, qui s'adresse aux Thébains, n'aurait servi qu'à repousser avec autorité les intentions des Tithoréens. En montant simplement bonne garde autour du tumulus, les Thébains auraient conjuré le danger d'être dérobés, d'être frappés par la colère d'Amphion et de Zéthos et de voir dépérir les fruits de leur terre.[14]

Il arrive souvent dans le monde grec que des héros soient ensevelis dans plusieurs endroits; que des cités se disputent les tombes de morts illustres[15] ou que l'une d'elles, se conformant à la volonté des dieux exprimée par un oracle, réussisse même à transférer les os d'un héros sur son propre territoire.[16]

Il se pourrait que dans notre cas il s'agisse aussi d'une controverse pour la possession d'une tombe. On attribuait, en effet, plusieurs demeures aux morts Amphion et Zéthos. On disait qu'ils étaient ensevelis à Thèbes près des portes Proitides, hors des murailles[17] qu'ils avaient eux-mêmes bâties; ou encore que, nés de Zeus et d'Antiope, ils étaient un couple de jumeaux dioscuriques[18], c'est à dire en mesure, comme Kastor et Polydeukes, d'aller et de venir entre leur demeure souterraine et celle qu ils auraient eue parmi les étoiles[19]; ou, enfin, qu'ils avaient une tombe à Tithoraia.[20] Cette dernière information, même si elle n'était que construite par Stephanos de Byzance à partir du texte de Pausanias, confirmerait notre hypothèse sur l'origine du récit du Périégète, à savoir un conflit entre deux cités pour la possession d'une tombe.

Il nous reste à voir pourquoi l'état d'alerte se vérifiait autour du tombeau des héros à une certaine période de l'année et quels étaient les fruits menacés.

La période pendant laquelle le soleil se trouve de nos jours dans la constellation du Taureau s'étend du 21 avril au 21 mai.[21]

Deux groupes d'étoiles forment dans le ciel la figure ouranienne du Taureau: les Hyades représentent le bucrane et les Pléiades la partie terminale, étant situées près de la queue ou à mi-dos là ou le corps de l'animal, visible dans sa seule partie antérieure, est coupé.[22]

Les deux groupes d'étoiles étaient mis en relation avec Dionysos. Les Hyades auraient été les nourrices du dieu[23]; et elles auraient donné la vigne aux hommes.[24] Les Pléiades, elles aussi nourisses du dieu, apparaissaient dans le ciel comme un "botrys", une grappe de raisin.[25]

Pour comprendre à quels fruits se référait l'oracle, il est nécessaire de se reporter aux travaux agricoles qui occupaient les Thébains quand le soleil se trouvait dans la constellation du Taureau.

J.G. Frazer (*loc. cit.)* pensait qu'il s'agissait des semailles de printemps car on disait, en effet, que le paysan devait labourer pendant cette période.[26]

Il semble toute fois qu'il faille écarter les "fruits de Demeter" qu'ils vont être moissonnés quand le soleil se trouve dans les Didymoi.

Par contre, c'est aux vignes qu'il faut consacrer un grand soin en avril-mai à cause de la floraison et pour aider la formation des fruits.[27]

Hésiode dans "Les Travaux" donne à ce propos un précepte qu'il introduit par une formule oraculaire (cfr. West *ad* 571) à la manière de Bakis: "Mais, quand le porte-maison monte de la terre à l'escalade des arbres fuyant devant les Pléiades, ce n'est plus le temps de piocher les vignes. Aiguisez les faucilles et éveillez vos serviteurs...au temps de la moisson, quand le soleil sèche la peau. C'est l'heure de faire vite, de ramasser votre récolte." (trad. Mazon vv. 571-575; cfr. 383 ss.).

La scholie à ces vers fournit les motifs techniques de l'exhortation d'Hésiode: après le "lever matinal" ou *epitolé* des Pleiades quand le soleil entre dans la constellation des Didymoi, il ne faut plus piocher la vigne; la terre, en effet, est desséchée et les racines, exposées au soleil, seraient abîmées par la chaleur de l'astre et il ne faut plus tailler la plante mais la laisser nourrir en paix ses fruits.[28]

L'*epitolé,* c'est à dire l'apparition des Pleiades dans le ciel quelques instants avant l'aube, a lieu au mois de mai[29] quand le soleil se trouve dans la constellation du Taureau.[30]

L'exhortation d'Hésiode de ne pas travailler la vigne est donc motivée, non seulement par le fait que, à cette époque, c'est la fauche du blé qui doit occuper les ouvriers aux champs, mais aussi par les conditions particulières des vignes.

C'est à peu près au "lever matinal" des Pleiades qu'ils arrivent dans les vignobles les jours de la floraison.[31]

On apprend à ce propos que les vignerons chargés d'émonder les pampres, s'abstenaient de ce travail au mois de mai pendant la floraison.[32] On empêchait même d'entrer dans les vignobles pour éviter d'abîmer les plantes.[33] On prenait les mêmes précautions pour le piochage des vignes, pour ne pas risquer d'abîmer les fruits.

Par contre, à qui n'avait pas coutume de piocher souvent la vigne à chaque période de l'année,[34] on recommandait de le faire au moins trois fois par an dont l'une, précisément, dans la période qui nous intéresse. Le remuage de la terre en avril-mai[35] avant la floraison ou le "lever matinal" des Pléiades,[36] avait pour but d'assurer une nourriture supplémentaire à la plante pour l'aider dans la formation des fruits.

On peut donc déduire, de tout ce qui précède, qu'aux environs de l'apparition des Pléiades, lorsque le soleil se trouvait dans la constellation du Taureau, on arrêtait de travailler les vignes à cause de la floraison et que le passage du soleil de la constellation du Taureau à celle des Gémeaux coïncidait avec la phase critique liée à la formation des nouveaux *karpoi*.

La relation qui existait entre Antiope et ses fils et Dionysos — que les Thébains appelaient "ampelos" c'est-à-dire "vigne"[37] — peut expliquer pourquoi ces personnages mythiques étaient précisément mis en cause dans cette période critique pour la viticulture.

C'est Pausanias[38] qui fait de Dionysos l'arbitre de leur vicissitude. Antiope, dit-il, aurait été ensevelie à Tithorée parce que c'est là qu'elle serait arrivée après que Dionysos l'aurait frappée de folie et fait errer à travers l'Hellade pour la punir de la peine excessive infligée à Dirké qui, à Thèbes, l'aurait eu en grand honneur parmi tous les dieux. Antiope, accueillie et guérie par Phokos, l'aurait épousé et aurait partagé sa tombe une fois morte.

Il convient de résumer ici les traits essentiels du mythe auquel se réfère Pausanias pour comprendre le rôle de Dionysos.

On disait qu'Antiope, mère d'Amphion et de Zéthos, était fille d'Asopos ou de Nykteus et qu'elle avait comme ancètre Alkyone une des Pléiades[39] que nous avons vu former le corps du Taureau ouranien.

Zeus l'aurait séduite sous le traits d'un satyre[40] ou d'un taureau,[41] c'est-à-dire sous une apparence dionysiaque

Antiope donna le jour à deux jumeaux à Eleuthère, dans une grotte qu'on indiquait près du temple de Dionysos au pied du Citheron, la montagne où les Thébains célébraient les rites dionysiaques.[42]

Abandonnés sur le Citheron par Antiope après leur naissance, les jumeaux auraient été élevés par des bergers et ils n'auraient revu leur mère qu'à l'occasion des faits dont parle Pausanias.

Antiope, prisonnière du roi de Thèbes, Lykos et de Dirké, serait parvenue à s'echapper miraculeusement et à rejoindre le Citheron[43] où elle aurait demandé aide à ses fils. Ceux-ci auraient fait périr Dirké en l'attachant aux cornes d'un taureau, c'est-à-dire de la même façon dont Dirké aurait eu l'intention de tuer elle-même Antiope,[44] ou de la faire tuer par Amphion et Zéthos, bouviers à son service.[45]

Ce qui nous intéresse plus particulièrement, ce sont les conséquences que cette histoire légendaire a pu avoir pour les Thébains et les Tithoréens.

La mort de Dirké et de son époux Lykos, roi de Thèbes, tué lui-aussi par Amphion et Zéthos ou depouillé de son royaume, permit aux fils d'Antiope de devenir rois à leur tour, d'entrer enfin dans la cité et d'avoir l'honneur de ce tombeau.

Un fragment de l'Antiope d'Euripide souligne l'incertitude qui suivit la mort de Dirké: à ce moment-là, Amphion ignore encore s'il va être puni pour l'avoir tuée ou si, avec l'aide de Zeus, son père, il va réussir à vaincre Lykos et à s'emparer du royaume avec son frère.[46] Hermès intervient alors et explique comment l'ordre fixé à l'avance par Zeus doit être exécuté à Thèbes: Amphion et Zéthos deviendront rois de la cité et seront honorés comme Dioscures[47]; le cadavre de Dirké doit être jeté dans une source qui prendra son nom.[48]

Après sa mort, Dirké continue donc à jouer un rôle pour les Thébains: c'est dans sa source que naît l'un des deux fleuves qui entourent la cité[49] et où Zeus aurait trempé Dionysos pour le sauver des flammes qui consumaient Sémélé, sa mère.[50]

Quant au destin d'Antiope, lié à la mort de Dirké, il intéresse surtout les Tithoréens. Contrainte par Dionysos à abandonner Thèbes, elle épouse Phokos et en partage la tombe à Tithorée. Cette vicissitude d'Antiope quittant la métropole des Bacchantes pour le Parnasse, autre lieu dionysiaque, [51] pourrait témoigner du rôle joué par la cité de Thèbes dans la diffusion du culte du dieu.[52] Mais du fait qu'Antiope, une fois guérie de sa folie momentanée, s'établit définitivement auprès du héros qui a donné son nom à la Phocide,[53] il nous semble que son destin est plutôt semblable à celui des Proitides.[54]

A la fin de cette analyse, on peut donc penser que le danger qui menaçait les Thébains dans la période avril-mai, qu'ils appelaient "*Thyios*",[55] était le suivant: si les Tithoréens, au nom de cette Antiope qui était arrivée chez eux frappée de folie "*thyia*",[56] étaient parvenus à s'approprier du tumulus d'Amphion et de Zéthos, l'ordre voulu pour Thèbes par les dieux aurait été renversé. Pour conjurer ce danger, les Thébains, obéissant à l'oracle, montaient bonne guarde chaque année pour empêcher que l'on outrageât leurs Dioscures just'avant que le soleil entre dans le signe zodiacal dans lequel on les reconnaissaient dans le ciel[57] et que Dionysos ne se venge sur les fruits de leur terre, dans son courroux contre Antiope qu'il avait bannie de Thèbes.

Notes

Je remercie le Professeur Pierre Lévêque pour l'intérêt qu'il a bien voulu manifester à mon étude, ainsi que pour les précieux conseils et suggestions qu'il m'a aimablement donnés.

1 Paus. 9, 17, 3-7; cf. pour les fouilles archéologiques sur le "tumulus d'Amphion" Th. G. Spyropoulos, *Ampheion,* Sparte 1981.

2 Pausanias mentionne de nouveau le tombeau (10, 32, 8-11) à propos de Tithorée ville phocidienne dejà en déclin de son temps, située au sommet du Mont Parnasse dont elle tirait son nom (cf. Hdt. 8, 32).

3 J. G. Frazer, *Pausanias's Description of Greece,* V, London 1898, p. 57 s.; H. Hitzig - Bluemner, *Pausaniae Graeciae Descriptio* III, Lipsiae 1907, p. 438.

4 F. Vian, *Les Origines de Thèbes,* Paris 1963, p. 135.

5 W. Burkert, *Homo necans*, Berlin-New York 1972, p. 210; *id. Griechische Religion der archaischen und klassischen Epoche,* Stuttgart 1977, p. 325.

6 A. Schachter, Cults of Boiotia, *BICS Supplement* XXXVIII, 1981, p. 29.

7 Paus. 9, 17, 5.

8 Cf. Pla. *Thg.* 124 D; Arist. *Pr.* 30, 1 (954a); Plu. *De Pyth. or.* 10.

9 Paus. 10, 12, 11; Theop. *F.* 78 (Grenfell-Hunt).

10 Cf. par exemple Zeus et les dieux qui se partagent la terre (Pi. *O.* 7, 55 et Sch. *ad loc.*); St. Byz. *s.v.* δατέομαι 'divido, partior"; Liddell-Scott-Jones, *s.v.* "divide among themselves".

[11] Pausanias: φρουράν ἔχουσι Bakis: πεφυλάξο φρουρά Hsch. *s.v.* φυλακή στρατός Suid. *s.v.* φρουρά φυλακή.

[12] A. Schnauter, *Frühgriechische Totenglaube. Untersuchungen zur Totenglaube des mykenischen und homerischen Zeit,* New York 1970, p. 18 s.

[13] Cf. à propos du cercle qu'ils décriraient autour de leurs morts S. Eitrem, *Opferritus u. Voropfer der Griechen und der Römer,* Kristiania 1915, p. 9-12; A. Schnaufer, *op. cit.*, 19. Il faut remarquer à ce propos, que diverses lectures nous sont proposées par les editeurs du texte de Pausanias: Hitzig-Bluemner conjecture avec Frazer περιτιθῶσιν Spiro lit dans les codices περιάφωσι ; Rocha-Pereira prefère indiquer une lacune.

[14] On lit dans les malédictions funéraires que la terre ne doit plus donner de fruits aux violateurs de tombeaux cf. A. Parrot, *Malédiction et violation des tombes*, Paris 1939, p. 141-143; 151; L. Robert, Malédictions funéraires grecques, *CRAI* 1978, p. 262 note 117; 270 note 5; 283.

[15] Cf. F. Pfister, *Der Reliquienkult im Altertum*, Giessen 1909, p. 193-211; 218 ss; et à ce propos aussi C. Bérard, Récuperer la mort du prince; héroisation et formation de la cité, dans *La mort. les morts. dans les sociétés anciennes*, G. Gnoli et J.P. Vernant, Cambridge-Paris 1982, p. 98; F. Hartog, La mort de l'autre, *ibid.* 143 s.

[16] Cf. les cas de Hektor (Lyc. 1204 ss. *Sch. ad loc.* 1208; Aristodem *F.* 7 (*FGrH*); Paus. 9, 18, 5); Rhesos (Polyaen. 6, 53): Hesiodos (Arist. *F.* 565 Rose) Arkas (Paus. 8, 9, 3-4; 36, 8) Aristomenes (Paus. 4, 32, 3). La confrontation est dejà suggérée par Weniger, Roscher *s.v. Phokos* 2412.

[17] Paus. 9, 16, 6; Sch. E. *Ph.* 145; ou Borrhaiai "du Nord" A. *Th.* 527 s.

[18] Cf. pour Amphion et Zéthos "Dioscures"; Pherecyd. *F.* 124 (*FGrH*); Pi. *P.* 9, 38; *Sch. ad loc.*; E. *HF.* 29 s.; *Ph.* 606; *Antiop. F.* 48 (Kambitsis) 98 s.; Hsch. *s.v.* Διόσκουροι ; *Sch.* Hom. *Od.* 19, 518; A. Schachter, *Cults of Boiotia, loc. cit.*

[19] Hyg. *Astr.* 2, 22; Ov. *Fast.* 5, 719 s.; cf. G. Piccaluga, I Dioskouroi: la morte come libera scelta, *Il senso del culto dei Dioscuri in Italia, Atti del Convegno di Taranto 1979,* Supplemento: Produttività Ionica X, 43 s.

[20] St. Byz. *s.v.* Τιθοραία

[21] Cf. Eudox *F.* 245; 258a (Lasserre); 22 avril-21 mai; Gem. *Calend.* p. 107 (Aujac): 23 avril-24 mai: Ov. *Fast.* 4, 713-720; 20 avril-19 mai; Colum. *Rust.* 11, 2, 36; 43.

[22] Eratosth. *Cat.* 14; 23; Hyg. *Astr.* 2, 21; *Exc. Tzetz. de Pleiadibus* p. 551 (Martin); Sch. Hom *Il.* 18, 486; Sch. Arat. 172.

[23] Hyg. *Astr.* 2, 21; Sch. Arat. 174; Serv. *Aen.* 1, 744.

[24] Pherecyd. *F.* 90b (FGrH).

[25] Sch. Hom. *Il.* 18, 486; Sch. Arat. 254 (p. 201 Martin).

[26] Manil. 4, 140-149, 380; 518-524.

[27] Cf. pour les *karpoi* "fruits de la vigne": Hom. *Il.* 3, 246; 18, 561-568; Hdt. 1, 212.

[28] Sch. Hes. *Op.* 571-577 (Pertusi).

[29] Cf. les jours de mai indiqués par les auteurs: 5 (Gem. p. 107 Aujac); 10 (Colum. *Rust.* 11, 2, 40); 11 (West *ad* Hes. *Op.* 383 ss.); 13 (*Excerpt. Tzetz de Pleiadibus* p. 548 Martin); 14 (Eudox. *F.* 254 p. 204 Martin); H. Gundel, in *RE s.v.* Pleiaden 2511-2514; chez les Latins la datation varie entre le 22 avril et le 11 mai, cf. A. Le Boeuffle, *Le nom Latin d'astres et de constellations,* Paris 1977, p. 272.

[30] Sch. Hes. *Op.* 383-387 (p. 130 Pertusi); 385a; 571-577; Sch. Arat. 254 (p. 204 Martin).

[31] La floraison de son début à la chute des fleurs, dure 10-20 jours dans les vignobles, selon l'espèce des plantes (cf. B. Pastena, *Trattato di viticoltura italiana,* Bologna 1981, p. 199) et sa durée est fonction des conditions climatiques. Pour évaluer à peu près la durée de la floraison dans les vignobles thebains, il peut être utile de savoir que, dans la région de Palermo c'est à dire environ à la même latitude, de nos jours, les vignes les plus précoces commencent à fleurir début mai (2-13) et, exceptionnellement, fin avril; les autres vignes vers le 10-21 mai et les vignes tardives le 14-26 mai; et que les grappes commencent à se former fin mai/début juin ou au plus tard vers la mi-juin, (cf. B. Pastena, *loc. cit.* p. 199; 217; 219; 957 s.).

[32] Thphr. *CP* 3, 16. Pli. *NH.* 17, 190 *Pampinatio verna in confesso est ab idibus Maiis,* (15V) *intra dies X, utique antequam florere incipiat.* Colum. *Rust.* 11, 2, 44. *Ab idibus usque in calendas Iunias* (15 V-1VI) *veteranam vineam prius quam florere incipiat iterum fodere oportet eandem et ceteras et omnes vineas identidem pampinare,*; Gp. 3, 5, 7; Colum. *Rust.* 11, 2, 37-38; Pallad. 6, 2, 1.

33 Colum. *Rust.* 4, 28, 1, *Tempus autem pampinationis antequam florem vitis ostendat maxime est eligendum sed et postea licet eandem repetere. Medium igitur eorum dierum spatium, quo ' acini formantur, vinearum nobis aditum negat quippe florentem fructum movere non expedit.*

34 Colum. *Rust.* 4, 5; *Arb.* 12, 2.

35 *Gp.* 3, 4, 5; 5, 4; cf. B. Pastena, *loc. cit.*, p. 923.

36 Thph. *CP.* 3, 16, 1-2 (*cit.*). Gp. 3, 5, 7. Une inscription de l'île d'Amorgos (IG XII, 7, 62 vv. 8-10) exhortait de piocher les vignes avant les vingt derniers jours du mois du Taureau. Pli. NH. 17, 188-189 *satis esse ter anno confodi ab aequinoctio verno ad Vergiliarum exortum et canis ortu et nigrescente acino quidam ita determinant:...iterum ab idibus Aprilibus antequam concipiat hoc est in VI idus Maias dein prius quam florere incipiat et cum defloruerit et variante se uva.;* Colum. *Rust.* 4, 28, 2 *Nec infitior plerosque ante me rusticarum rerum magistros tribus fossuris contentos fuisse; ex quibus Graecinus qui sic refert: potest videri satis et variante se uva.;* Colum. *Rust.* 4, 28, 2 *Nec infitior plerosque ante me rusticarum rerum magistros tribus fossuris contentos fuisse; ex quibus Graecinus qui sic refert: potest videri satis esse constitutam vineam ter fodere,. Celsus quoque et Atticus consentiunt tres esse motus in vite...unum quo germinet; alterum quo floreat, tertium quo maturescat. Hos ergo motus censent fossionibus concitari.*

37 Clem. Al. *Protr.* 2, 22 P.

38 Paus. 9, 17, 6; 10, 32, 10 s.

39 Hom. *Od.* 11, 260 ss.; Apollod. 3, 10, 1; A.R. 1, 735 s.; 4, 1089s. Sch. *ad. loc.*

40 E. *Antiop. F.* 31 (Kambitsis); Ov. *Met.* 6, 110 ss.: Nonn. *D.* 7, 123; 16, 242; 31, 217; Sch. Stat. *Theb.* 9, 423; Myth. Vat. 1, 204.

41 Myth. Vat. 2, 74; Sch. Stat. *Theb.* 7, 189.

42 Paus. 1, 38, 8 ss.; cf. Hyg. *F.* 7; Myth. Vat. 1, 94; 2, 74.

43 Apollod. 3, 5, 5; Prop. 3, 15, 11; Hyg. *F.* 8; sur le Citheron elle aurait rencontré Dirké venue y célébrer les rites de Dionysos; cf. W. Luppe, Das Neue Euripides Fragment P. Oxy 3317, *ZPE* XLII, 1981, p. 27-30.

44 Suid. *s.v.* Ἀντιόπη

45 Sch. E., *Ph.* 102.

46 E. *Antiop. F.* 48 (Kambitsis) vv. 1-16.

47 E. *Antiop.* (*loc. cit.*) vv. 67-79; 86-103. cf. note 18.

48 E. *Antiop.* (*loc. cit.*) vv. 80-85; Amphion et Zéthos auraient jeté eux-mêmes le cadavre dans la source (Apollod. 3, 5, 5) que l'on disait être jaillie du corps (Sch. Stat. *Ach.* 1, 12) ou du sang de Dirké (Sch. Stat. *Theb.* 3, 205) à l'endroit où le taureau l'aurait transportée (Sch. E. *Ph.* 102). On disait aussi que les eaux de Dirké devenaient rouges pour annoncer un danger imminent aux Thébains (D. S. 17, 10, 4; Ael. *VH.* 12, 57; Stat. *Theb.* 4, 374 s.).

49 E. *Pho.* 101 s.; 825-827.

50 E. *Ba.* 519-525.

51 S. *Ant.* 1115-1151; E. *Ion.* 1125 s.; Paus. 10, 64; 32, 7.

52 À propos d'Antiope prêtresse du temple du Soleil et Bacchante cf. Cephalio *F.* 5 *FGrH*; Georg. Cedr. *Hist. Comp.* 24 C; Weniger, dans Roscher, *s.v.* Phokos, 2412, voit une relation entre le menadisme d'Antiope (Paus. *loc. cit.*) et son arrivée à Tithorée.

53 Paus. 10, 1, 1; 2, 29, 3; St. Byz. *s.v.* Φωκίς

54 L'emplacement de la tombe des fils d'Antiope près des portes Proitides, coïnciderait avec la ressamblance entre leur mère et les filles de Proitos, lesquelles furent guéries d'une folie dionysiaque, et rendirent une source "ennemie de la vigne" et épousèrent Melampous, la guérisseur, et son frère; cf. Apollod. 2, 2, 2; Ov. *Met.* 15, 322, ss.; St. Byz. *s.v.* Ἀζανία ; MK. Massenzio, Xenia dionisiaca, *SMSR* XL, 1969, p. 97-104; P. Scarpi, Melampous e i "miracoli" di Dionysos, *Perennitas. Studi in onore di A. Brelich,* Roma 1980, p. 435-440.

55 *Thyios,* à Thèbes (IG VII 2423) comme dans le calendrier béotien, était le conquième mois de l'année et commençait après le solstice d'hiver; cf. P. Roesch, *Études Béotiennes,* Paris 1982, p. 46; 54.

56 À propos des *Thyiai* "femmes folles du dieu" sur le Parnasse, cf. Paus. 10, 6, 4; 32, 7.

57 Cf. l'identification de la constellation des Didymoi avec les Dioscures dans Eratosth. *Cat.* 10; Hyg. *Astr.* 2, 22; et en particulier avec Amphion et Zéthos dans Sch. Germ. BP68, 6; Anth. Lat. 626, 2 (Riese).

Summary

Pausanias reports that every year when the Sun was passing through the constellation Taurus, Tithoreans planned to steal earth from the tomb of Amphion and Zethos in Thebes of Boeotia.

Bringing this earth in their city and pouring it over Antiope's tomb they would have fąvoured the fertility of their fields. In order to preserve the fruits of their country and following the oracle of Bakis, Thebans kept watch over the tomb of Amphion and Zethos.

An analysis of Pausanias' text suggests that a quarrel divided the two cities, every part claiming the right to have in its land the tomb of Antiope's sons. The involvement of the mythical figures and the peculiar phase in the vineyards' life during that period of the year (April-May) both suggest that Thebans tried to protect the growth of the fruits of Dionysos.

Résumé

Chaques année, quand le Soleil se trouvait dans la constellation du Taureau, les Phocidiens de Tithorée essayaient d'offrir des libations sur le tumulus thébain d'Amphion et de Zéthos, et d'en dérober de la terre afin de la répandre autour de la tombe d'Antiope qui se trouvait chez eux, et ceci pour appeler la fertilité sur leurs champs.

De leur côté, les habitants de Thèbes, suivant en cela l'oracle de Bakis, s'efforçaient d'empêcher l'action des Phocidiens pour préserver les fruits de leurs propres champs.

Le passage de Pausanias laisse envisager l'existence d'une controverse entre les deux cités pour la possession du tumulus, les Thébains repoussant chaque année les prétentions des Tithoréens qui auraient pu bouleverser l'ordre établi par les dieux.

Les références aux personnages mythiques; le mois en question ainsi que les travaux des vignerons à ce moment de l'année, tout porte à croire que les fruits dont on voulait protéger la récolte étaient les fruits de Dionysos.

TWO ALTARS DEDICATED TO DEMETER: THE GODDESS OF FERTILITY

Mükerrem (Usman) Anabolu

The Aegean Coast of the Anatolian peninsula stands out for its vast stretches of fertile land enriched by the rivers which flow into these plains leaving behind their alluvial deposits which fertilize the soil to high standards. On such fertile soil one is not surprised to find out how much importance was given in ancient times to Demeter, Goddess of Fertility.

The altar in Manisa (ancient Magnesia ad Sipylum) Museum (Inv No. 244)[1] and the altar in Selçuk (ancient Ephesos) Museum (Inv No 1728)[2] both dedicated to the goddess Demeter, are the best two of many examples supporting this hypothesis. (Pls. 35-36).

Both altars are made of marble and decorated with bucranion and garland pattern. The first one, which was found in Sardis (Sart), has a cylindrical shape. The second one has the shape of a rectangular prism. Both altars have inscriptions on them. The altar in Manisa Museum bears solely bucrania and relatively thin garlands compared to the altar in Selçuk Museum. The garlands have a uniform thickness and do not become thicker towards the centre. The inscription is not complete due to some breakages.

Ν Ϲ ϽΗΜΟΝΟΣ

ΤΡΙΤϹ Π ΤΡΟΦΟΡΟΣ

ΜΗΤΡΙΣ ΚΕΠΝΟΥ. ΑΝΕΘΗΚΕ

But from the surviving part it is understood that this altar was dedicated to Demeter by "the Priest of the Mother of Gods...OEMON. Due to the epigraphical character of the inscription this altar can be dated back to the late Hellenistic or the early Roman Imperial periods.

The altar in Selçuk Museum, which was found in Ephesos, has another type of bucrania which have preserved their flesh, skin, hair and organs, like eyes and ears. Its garlands, adorned with different kinds of fruit, are thick and become thicker towards the center. According to its inscription

[Θ Ε Α] Κ Α Ρ Π Ο Φ Ο Ρ Ω Ε Υ Χ Η Ν

[Δ Ι] Κ Λ Η Σ Ε Υ Β Ι Ο Τ Ο Υ

this altar was dedicated to Demeter Karpophoros (Demeter the Basket Carrier) by Eubiotos, Son of Diokles (?)[3] Again, according to the epigraphical character of the inscription and the artistic style of the garlands, this altar can be dated back to the early Imperial period.

On both altars there are representations of *papaver somniferum* pods which are the attributes of the Goddess. The altar in Selçuk Museum carries spike, torch and basket reliefs which are also symbols of the Goddess. Dr. Cr. H. Greenwalt Jr., from the University of Berkeley, the present director of the Sardis excavations, has recently found a Demeter Karpophoros altar without bucranion and garland pattern. Only the altar in Selçuk Museum shows an empty basket. The altar found in Sardis has a serpent coming out of the basket, which reminds us of the *Cista Mystica* on the Cistophoros type of coins related to Dionysos, god of vintage, wine and drunkenness. As a matter of fact, in most situations the mysteries of Demeter and those of Dionysos are interrelated.[4]

There is a temple dedicated to Demeter in Pergamon (Bergama) constructed in the second half of the III century B.C. by Philetairos, the founder of the Pergamene kingdom, and his brother Eumenes in the name of their mother Boa.[5] There is a monumental altar in front of the temple which must have been set up after the *templum in antis* plan. Later Apollonis, the wife of King Attalos I had a propylon added to this temple. The temple was rebuilt during the II century A.D.

The baseless columns of the propylon had no grooves and their capitals are different from the usual ones. On the left hand side of the entrance to the temple, there is a votive pit for baby pigs and pastry to be thrown in as offerings to Demeter, Persephone and Hades. On the right hand side, there stood a fountain for purification and ritual ablution. This fountain was covered with a half-dome in the shape of an oyster shell. A 20 meter wide area separates the propylon from the monumental altar. On the northern side of this area, which is higher, are placed ten sitting rows. On the southern side of the area, which is lower, is a chain of rooms which are reached by a stairway. These rooms could possibly have a connection with the mysteries of Demeter in the same way as the sitting rows.

Priene (Güllübahçe) has another temple dedicated to Demeter which has an irregular plan and a well preserved votive pit.[6] There should be a Demeter temple in Sardis (Sart), in Nikomedia (Izmit),[7] in Knidos (Reşadiye)[8] and in Amisos (Samsun on the Black Sea Coast).[9]

The symbols of the Goddess Demeter can also be noticed in many sculptural works.

The Demeter statue in the British Museum was found in Knidos. In the Smyrnean Agora (Izmir), a statue of Demeter was uncovered together with another of Poseidon.[10] These beautiful pieces of sculpture are actually on display in Izmir's newly constructed Archaeological Museum.

In Istanbul Archaeological Museum, there is a tripod base[11] and a votive relief representing Demeter with her daughter Persephone.[12] The Museum of Bergama houses another relief representing the Goddess before her own altar holding a torch in her hand.[13] In the same Museum, there are representations of *papaver somniferum* pods.

Roman coins of Erythrai[14] and Smyrna (Izmir),[15] bear figures of veiled Demeter Horia.

The Kharoneion in Akharaka (Salavatlı in Lydia) which was connected to Nysa (Sultanhisar) by a sacred road, must have been related somewhat to the Goddess Demeter.[16]

Akharaka is known to be a prominent health centre of the Roman Imperial period. Much is known about Akharaka from Strabo.[17]

Notes

1 G.M. Hanfmann - N.H. Ramage., *Sculpture from Sardis. The Finds Through 1975*, Harvard 1978, p. 128, no 160, fig. 307; M. Usman Anabolu, Batı Anadolu da Bulunmus Olan Askı (Girland) lı Sunaklar, *E.Ü Edebiyat Fakültesi Yayınları, Arkeoloji - Sanat Tarihi Dergisi* vol. 3, Manisa (Şafak Basimevi) 1984, p. 12, no 25, figs. 1a and 1b.

2 *Ibid.*, p. 5 no 4, figs. 14a - 14c.

3 Demeter is mentioned with the same epithet in another inscription found in Ephesos (*SIG* 820, 5). Dr. H. Malay has just determined that this epithet was also employed for Agrippina in the early Roman Imperial period,

4 G. Gruben, *Die Tempel der Griechen*, Munich 1961, *pp. 210 and 416.*

5 *Ibid.*, pp. 413 - 416, fig. 330; G.E. Bean, *Aegean Turkey*, London (E. Benn) 1966, pp. 78/79. The first structure was a *templum in antis* in the Ionic Order. The Pergamenes converted it into a *prostylos* of the Corinthian Order: (E. Akurgal, *Ancient Civilization and Ruins of Turkey, Istanbul 1978, pp. 92/93, fig 34. For more detailed information see W. Dorpfeld, Die Bauwerke des Bezirkes des Demeter, Jahrbuch des Deutschen Archäolgischen Instituts, Archäologische Anzeiger*, vol. 35 (1910), pp. 537-542; *Berliner Philologische Wochenschrift*, vol. 30 (1910) pp. 1587-1590.

6 G. Gruben, *op. cit.* p. 356, fig. 285; M. Schede, *Priene*, pp. 91-96; G.E. Bean, *op. cit.*, pp. 206/207.

7 C. Bosch, *Die Kleinasiatische Münzen der Römischer Kaiserzeit*, vol. II/1, Stuttgart, 1935, p. 245. Simeon Metaphrastes (Migne, 116, 1073), P.O. Pogodin and O.F. Wullf have met the architectural pieces of the above mentioned temple: see P.O. Pogodin - O.F. Wullf, Nikomedia, *IRAI* vol. 2 (1897) pp. 77-184.

8 I.C. Love, Excavations in Knidos 1971, *Türk Arkeoloji Dergisi* vol XX/2, Ankara 1973, pp. 102-103, fig. 29.

9 M. Usman Anabolu, *Antik Devir Küçük Asya Sikkeleri Üzerindeki Mimarlik Tasvirleri* (in Turkish) (Unpublished thesis presented to the I.Ü. Edebiyat Fakütesi Klâsik Arkeoloji Kürsüsü in 1949 in Istanbul) p. 124.

10 Akurgal, *op. cit.*, pp. 49 and 51.

11 G. Mendel, *Catalogue des Sculptures Grecques, Romaines et Byzantines*, vol. 1, Istanbul (Macon) 1912, pp. 385-390, no. 638.

12 *Ibid.*, pp. 566-568.

13 *Pergamenische Forschungen*, vol. 1, p. 91, fig. 20; *Athenische Mitteilungen* vol XXX, pp. 509-510.

14 B.V. Head, *Historia Numorum. A Manual of Greek Numismatics* p. 579.

15 *Ibid.*, p. 590.

16 H. Pringsheim, *Nysa ad Maendrum Nach Forschungen und Aufnahmen in den Jahren 1907 und 1909* (Jahrbuch des Kaiserliche Deutschen Archäologischen Instituts, X, Ergänzungsheft), pp. 57-61, figs. 27-30.

17 Strabo, xiv. 649.

Summary

Two altars decorated with bucrania and garlands and carrying inscriptions dedicated to Demeter are the subject of this paper. The first one was discovered in Sardis and is housed in the Museum of Manisa (Inv. No. 244). The second altar, dedicated to Demeter Karpophoros (Demeter the Basket Carrier), comes from Ephesos and is exhibited in the Museum of Selçuk. They belong to the late Hellenistic and to the Roman Imperial period respectively. A third altar, from Sardis, is also dedicated to Demeter Karpophoros, but lacks bucrania and garlands.

There are two excavated temples dedicated to Demeter in Western Asia Minor, one in Priene and the other in Pergamon.

Résumé

Des deux autels de Déméter, muni chacun d'une inscription et décorés tous les deux de bucrania et de guirlandes, le premier, découvert à Sardis, est exposé au Museé de Manisa (No. d'Inv. 244), le second, découvert à Ephesos, est éxposé au Musée de Selçuk (No. d'Inv. 1728). Le premier de ces deux autels de l'époque hellénistique tardive et le second de l'époque romaine impériale. Un troisième autel de Déméter muni d'une inscription a été découvert à Sardis, mais celui-ci ne comporte ni burcania ni guirlandes.

Deux temples fouillés, dédiés à Déméter, existent en Asie Mineure occidentale, l'un à Priene et l'autre à Pergame. Déméter fut l'objet de plusieurs oeuvres et fut aussi représentée sur les monnaies.

ARCHÉOLOGIE ET CULTES DE FERTILITÉ DANS LA RELIGION ROMAINE (des origines à la fin de la République)

Marcel Le Glay

Le sacré est défini par Mircea Eliade, *Le sacré et le profane*, p. 27, comme "le réel par excellence, à la fois puissance, efficience, source de vie et de fécondité". Cette définition s'applique-t-elle à la religion romaine? Avant de répondre à cette question, qui est — me semble-t-il — au coeur du sujet, il paraît utile de rappeler quelques évidences.

Il est clair tout d'abord que le mot "fertilité" concerne d'autres domaines que les champs et les travaux agricoles. Il intéresse tout autant les hommes et les animaux. Pour tous, la fertilité met en oeuvre à la fois les forces du Ciel et les forces de la Terre, non seulement dans leurs couches supérieures, mais aussi dans leurs étages inférieurs: les dieux olympiens célestes et les dieux chthoniens infernaux sont les uns et les autres dieux de la fertilité et de la fécondité. Les cérémonies qui visent à obtenir ou à sauvegarder ces dons des dieux sont célébrées aussi bien dans les sanctuaires de hauts-lieux qu'autour du *mundus*.

D'autre part, on sait bien, parce qu'on l'a souvent écrit, que la religion romaine est une religion politique et évidemment aussi sociale et psychologique. On la dit aussi pratique, naturaliste et terrienne. F. Altheim, *La religion romaine antique,* p. 66, a parlé de "primordialité du temporel". Une question se pose alors: a-t-elle toujours eu ces caractères? Ou bien les a-t-elle acquis? Et comment? par quels processus? La religion romaine, bien sûr, a évolué: elle n'est plus à la fin de la République ce qu'elle était dans les premiers temps de Rome.

Troisième évidence. Si notre connaissance de la religion et de la vie religieuse dans ses formes multiples bénéficie toujours d'une analyse plus poussée des textes littéraires, d'une étude plus comparative des données traditionnelles, les grands progrès récents viennent plutôt des découvertes épigraphique et archéologiques.

Ce sont incontestablement les découvertes de l'archéologie qui ont, depuis les travaux de G. Dumézil, enrichi le plus notre perception de la vie religieuse dans la *Rome archaïque*. On connaît les théories duméziliennes sur la tripartition fonctionnelle des sociétés issues du rameau indo-européen, tripartition qui a conduit à distinguer les divinités de la première fonction (Jupiter et la souveraineté), de la deuxième fonction (Mars et la guerre), de la troisième fonction (Quirinus et la production). Même si ces théories ont été vivement attaquées dans leur rigueur, elles dominent encore assez dans le monde des chercheurs pour qu'on les évoque ici. Qu'on les adopte ou qu'on les critique, demandons-nous donc quelle était la place des cultes de fertilité dans la religion romaine archaïque. Très importante, sans nul doute, à considérer, ce qui n'est pas toujours reconnu[1]:

1) *les aspects agraires de la trinité pré-étrusque Jupiter-Mars-Quirinus.*

Au moins selon G. Frazer, pour qui JUPITER, comme *rex* latin aux tâches magico-agricoles, était surtout garant de fécondité. Pour Dumézil, en revanche, Jupiter, dieu du ciel lumineux, n'a nullement ce caractère; il est "chef en toutes choses, d'abord politiquement et jadis, sans doute, religieusement" (*La religion romaine archaïque,* p. 159). Cela dit, même si Jupiter n'est pas un "Jupiter agraire", il faut bien reconnaître que "chef en toutes choses", il intervient aussi dans le domaine agraire, comme *Iupiter Ruminus, Almus, Pecunia.* D'autre part, le rituel révèle qu'il joue un rôle dans les *Vinalia* du 23 avril et du 19 août. Et on sait bien que lui sont attribuées toutes les fêtes qui concernent le vin, le vin ayant un rapport privilégié avec la souveraineté.[2] Ainsi les *Meditrinalia* du 11 octobre, fête de la "médication" du vin nouveau.

MARS était incontestablement d'abord et avant tout le dieu des guerriers, et selon Dumézil, nullement dieu agraire.[3] Il reste qu'il intervient dans les rites de fertilité / fécondité, notamment dans le fameux *uer sacrum.*

Quant à QUIRINUS, il est bien évidemment en relation privilégiée avec les forces de production: il est le dieu qui veille à l'approvisionnement en grains.[4] Et on ne voit son flamine, le *flamen Quirinalis,* intervenir rituellement qu'en trois circonstances: lors des *Robigalia* du 25 avril, fête agraire, lors des *Consualia* d'été (le 21 août), fête des grains en relation de calendrier avec les fêtes d'*Ops*, déesse de l'abondance agricole, enfin lors des *Larentalia* au 23 décembre, en relation de calendrier avec *Saturnus.*

2) *l'importance des divinités de la troisième fonction dans le panthéon et la place des fêtes agricoles dans le calendrier public romain.*

Sans insister, car ce sont là choses bien connues, il faut tout de même rappeler que, dans la liste des 14 divinités qui accompagnent Quirinus — liste des divinités, que d'après Varron, *De l.l.*. 5. 74, Titus

Tatius est censé avoir introduites à Rome — 7 concernent l'agriculture et la vie rurale: *Ops* associée dans le calendrier à *Consus,* dieu des *Consualia, Flora, Saturnus, Terminus, Vortumnus, Volcanus* (à qui on sacrifie le 23 août, en même temps qu'à *Ops/Quirinus*), les Lares, patrons des portions du sol et des carrefours. Deux autres favorisent les naissances: *Lucina* et *Diana.* Deux autres (*Sol* et *Luna*) sont des divinités des astres, pour les Romains régulateurs des saison et des mois. Deux autres (*Vedius* et *Larunda,* variante de *Larenta,* bénéficiaire des *Larentalia*) sont en relation avec le monde souterrain.

3) *les bienfaits attendus du culte domestique et familial.*

Aussi bien en ce qui concerne l'homme vivant, que protège son *Genius*, qui par ailleurs assure le continuité des générations (faut-il rappeler que *genius* dérive de *gignere*, engendrer?), que l'homme mort: on sait que les Mânes sont célébrés quotidiennement dans le culte domestique familial et plus officiellement lors des *Parentalia* de février et des *Lemuria* de mai, où l'on met en cause Pluton, le dieu des morts, des enfers et de la fécondité. On sait aussi que les dieux du foyer et de la maison, les Pénates protègent, quant à eux, les réserves et assurent leur renouvellement.

Mais on voit bien que pour toutes les divinités mentionnées (ou presque), aussi bien pour Jupiter que pour Saturnus, Ops et les autres, se pose toujours une question: quelle est dans leur essence, leur nature et leurs fonctions la part proprement romaine ou italique? la part plutôt méditerranéenne? la part grecque? Et pour celle-ci, *dans quelle mesure l'hellénisation a-t-elle modifié l'état de choses primitif?* Car tout le monde sait bien qu'il faut distinguer deux phases de l'hellénisation:

— d'une part avec les apports grecs et gréco-étrusques des VIe-Ve siècles, parfois dès la fin du VIIe siècle av. J.C.

— d'autre part les apports grecs et hellénistiques, les uns directs, les autres transmis par le canal des peuples italiques.

On ne peut prendre ici que des exemples.

Le premier, sur lequel je passerai vite, parce qu'il est bien connu, est celui de la TRIADE CAPITOLINE qui, au temps de la domination étrusque, se substitue à la triade primitive Jupiter-Mars-Quirinus.

Pour Jupiter, quand il devient *I(upiter) O(ptimus) M(aximus),* sa première qualité, exprimée par sa première épiclèse, est d'être *optimus,* avant même d'être *maximus*, le plus grand des dieux, ou le plus grand de tous les Jupiters. Cicéron, dans le *Pro domo sua*, dit qu'il est *optimus propter beneficia et maximus propter uim.* Mais cette valeur "morale", exprimée par le mot *beneficia* = bienfaits, n'est pas la plus ancienne. La plus ancienne est celle qui se rattache à l'étymologie même du mot *Ops*, la puissance qui engendre, crée les *opes*, c'est-à-dire les richesses, l'abondance. Il s'agit donc d'une valeur très concrète qui fait d'abord de Jupiter le dieu qui pourvoit au bonheur matériel des hommes.[5] Ce qui ne l'empêche pas, bien sûr, d'être le dieu du ciel, maître du panthéon olympien.

Pour Junon, qui est reine (*Iuno Regina*) sur le Capitole, elle est aussi la déesse qui préside aux accouchements (*Lucina*). C'est sous ce nom qu'elle figure, par exemple, sur des tablettes de bronze de Norba.[6] Et la déesse grecque, à laquelle elle fut très tôt assimilée, Héra, est la déesse à la grenade, symbole bien connu de fécondité. Ses fêtes, qui ont un "rapport certain avec la fécondité des femmes et généralement avec la féminité",[7] sont d'ailleurs appelées les *Matronalia.* Ce sont précisément des cérémonies qui célèbrent la fécondité des femmes mariées et des mères.

Quant à Minerve, "déesse des métiers et de ceux qui les pratiquent",[8] déesse des arts et des artisans, si les découvertes récentes de Pratica di Mare (*Lavinium*) ont jeté de nouvelles lueurs sur l'influence directe d'Athéna et de son type iconographique au VIe-Ve s. av. J.C., — on savait déjà notamment par une statuette votive étrusque de Modène[9] qu'au début du Ve s. le type de l'Athéna Promachos était connu en Etrurie — si donc les magnifiques statues de Lavinium accentuent le caractère guerrier de la déesse, on n'oublie pas que d'autres représentations montrent Minerve assise, tenant un enfant sur ses genoux, dans l'attitude bien connue de la déesse-mère.[10]

Le deuxième exemple, particulièrement significatif, est une authentique révélation de l'archéologie. C'est celui des FORTUNAE italiques, déesses de la fécondité. La plus célèbre est la *Fortuna Primigenia* de *Praeneste*, dont le sanctuaire a été révélé dans son ensemble par les fouilles qui ont suivi les bombardements de 1944[11] , avec un premier secteur sacré au centre de la ville (le sanctuaire inférieur) et un second étage à flanc de colline jusqu'à la tholos du sommet (le sanctuaire supérieur). Dans son plein développement architectural, on l'a longtemps attribué à l'époque syllanienne. En fait, si après la reprise de *Praeneste* par les troupes de Sylla, des travaux y furent certainement effectués, les inscriptions retrouvées ont montré que la grande époque de la construction remontait au milieu du IIe s. av. J.C., vers 160-150, fruit de l'évergésie des *negotiatores* d'Italie centrale, pour se développer surtout dans les années 110-100.[12] C'est du moins la chronologie valable pour le sanctuaire du haut. Car le sanctuaire inférieur, lui, renvoie jusqu'au IVe-IIIe s. A ce moment, on y vénérait une *Fortuna,* mère ou fille de Jupiter, on en a beaucoup discuté, en tout cas une déesse courotrophe, qui était en même temps déesse des sorts. Pour J. Champeaux, qui a consacré dernièrement un livre fondamental à *Fortuna,*[13] la déesse de *Praeneste* doit être considérée comme la Première née et la Première mère "à l'intarissable fécondité, qui a enfanté le monde à ses origines et qui, sans cesse, le fait renaître, en une véritable création continue" (p. 38); mère de Jupiter et de Junon, elle est pour ses fidèles la protectrice des mères humaines, le modèle divin de la maternité. Le sol de Palestrina a d'ailleurs livré par centaines des statuettes en terre cuite d'hommes et surtout de femmes, ainsi que des ex-voto anatomiques: offrandes qui ne peuvent convenir qu'à une déesse courotrophe, elle-même représentée comme une femme allaitant un enfant ou tenant une corne d'abondance et coiffée d'un *modius*, autant de traits caractéristiques des divinités de la fécondité. Il n'est donc pas douteux qu'alors la *Fortuna Primigenia* était une déesse toute-puissante dans le domaine des naissances, des accouchements et des premiers temps de la vie des nouveaux-nés.

C'est ensuite qu'elle est devenue surtout célèbre par sa fonction de déesse oraculaire, avant d'être vénérée aux Iers siècles av. et apr. J.C. comme déesse souveraine, dominant de sa tholos supérieure la ville et sa région, la Latium et l'Italie.

Mais au-delà du IVe s.? Il y eut très probablement une première phase dans l'histoire de la déesse de *Praeneste* et de son culte. Un culte de grotte, lié à une Terre-Mère, dont la *Fortuna Primigenia* fut l'héritière. Nous touchons là à un phénomène religieux méditerranéen bien connu. Il est d'ailleurs un autre aspect, très méditerranéen lui aussi, qui a été révélé par les découvertes de la tombe Bernardini: parmi des objets datables du VIIe s. av. J.C., une *potnia thèrôn*[14] qui montre que la déesse détenait alors la puissance d'une maîtresse de la nature.

Parvenus à ce point, demandons-nous ce qu'il en était des autres Fortunes du Latium et de Rome. La *Fortuna* d'*Antium* chez les Volsques est moins bien percue que celle de *Praeneste*. Du moins sait-on qu'elle se présentait d'une manière originale: sous la forme jumelée d'un couple de deux Fortunes, que Martial, à la fin du Ier s. apr. J.C. appelle encore les *Sorores*. Comme à *Praeneste*, elles sont déesses-mères, guérisseuses, et protectrices universelles, donc d'abord d'Antium, dont elles sont devenues divinités poliades. Comme à *Praeneste* encore, elles rendent des oracles.

Si du Latium rural, paysan, nous passons à Rome, dans le cadre de l'*Urbs* naissante — sans oublier que dans ses débuts elle fut aussi une "ville de paysans" — il est particulièrement intéressant de se poser la question de la nature des *Fortunae* romaines: sont-elles, là aussi, des divinités de la fécondité? ont-elles les mêmes caractères que leurs soeurs du Latium? Il est d'autant plus important de se poser cette question que nous touchons là aux origines mêmes de Rome et donc de la religion romaine, si l'on en croit Plutarque dans son traité *De la Fortune des Romains* (*Fort. Rom.,* 5), où il écrit: "Les temples de la Fortune sont illustres et anciens, et ils se confondent presque avec les premières fondations de la Ville."

Rome possédait au moins trois temples importants de *Fortuna.* Le plus ancien était sans doute celui de *Fors Fortuna*, qui se trouvait *trans Tiberim,* le long de la via Campana. On le faisait remonter au roi Servius Tullius, à qui la légende attribuait un attachement particulier à la Fortune. La fête de la déesse, célébrée le 24 juin, au solstice d'été, était marquée par une *Tiberina descensio*. C'était une joyeuse fête populaire avec descente du fleuve et jeux nautiques. Il s'agissait de rappeler et d'honorer les fonctions premières de la déesse, ses pouvoirs sur les eaux et sur la marche du soleil, qui — note justement J. Champeaux, p. 231 — "s'inscrivent au sein d'une même fonction de fertilité". Divinité de la campagne romaine, plus que de Rome, *Fors Fortuna* était chère surtout à la plèbe et aux esclaves.

A Rome même cette fois, la *Fortuna* du *Forum Boarium* nous est devenue assez familière depuis les fouilles de San Omobono, qui ont livré les vestiges des deux temples jumeaux de *Fortuna* et de *Mater Matuta.*[15] Deux déesses dont le *natalis* commun, fêté le 11 juin, fondait déjà l'étroite solidarité. Les découvertes de 1938, complétées à l'occasion des recherches archéologiques reprises après 1959, ont révélé sept niveaux, dont le plus ancien paraît dater du VIe s. av. J.C. (nous ne sommes pas loin de Servius Tullius!). Il s'agit, pour cette haute époque, de deux autels, parents proches des treize autels de Pratica di Mare. Le premier temple se situe entre 500 et 475. Il fut reconstruit plusieurs fois, notamment par M. Fulvius Flaccus, le consul qui s'empara de Volsinies en 264; une inscription de San Omobono, publiée en 1963-64 et interprétée par M. Torelli en 1968, le rappelle.[16] Les restes des victimes, retrouvés au fond d'une fosse à sacrifices, dans l'*area* sacrée, et qui datent de la première phase de l'histoire du site, indiquent clairement que la déesse honorée était une Terre-Mère. Plus tard, vers le IIIe s., *Fortuna* apparaît ici comme une courotrophe, qui préside aux rites matrimoniaux. Tandis que *Mater*

Matuta veille sur la croissance des enfants. Sa fête s'appelait les *Matralia* et le culte était réservé aux matrones *uniuirae*. On y reviendra plus loin, à propos du sanctuaire de *Satricum*.

Vient enfin la *Fortuna muliebris*, dont le sanctuaire se trouvait en dehors de la Ville, au 4e mille de la via Latina. Son nom même suffit à indiquer son caractère matronal. Mais il faut noter qu'au Ve s. elle avait plutôt une nature guerrière, qui s'est atténuée ensuite au profit de son aspect matronal.[17]

Rome a connu plus tard une autre *Fortuna*, la *Fortuna Huius Diei*, dont le temple fut construit vers 101 dans l'*area sacra* de l'Argentina, sur le Champ de Mars, par Q. Lutatius Catulus à la suite de la victoire de Verceil sur les Cimbres. Il y avait d'autres *Fortunae* à Rome, mais moins importantes, semble-t-il.

En bref, nous nous trouvons face à des *Fortunae*, dont les unes sont à la fois poliades et oraculaires, celles de *Praeneste* et d'*Antium*, dont les autres ne le sont pas, celles de Rome. En revanche, toutes sont déesses-mères, déesses de fertilité et de fécondité. Des questions dès lors ne manquent pas de se poser: l'ont-elles toujours été? Ou ont-elles subi une évolution, marquée par une transformation fonctionnelle? Si oui, cette évolution leur est-elle propre? Ou bien est-elle commune aux autres divinités féminines du Latium?

A *Praeneste*, on l'a vu, dans la phase la plus ancienne de l'histoire du sanctuaire, dominait une Terre-Mère, vénérée dans une grotte; et dans la Tombe Bernardini est resté le souvenir d'une *potnia thèrôn*. A Rome, à San Omobono, c'est également vers une Terre-Mère qu'orientent les restes de sacrifices datables du VIe, sinon de la fin du VIIe s. Quant à la *Fortuna muliebris*, l'aspect guerrier qu'elle revêtait au Ve s. ne nous éloigne guère de la conception d'une *potnia thèrôn*. Il y a là manifestement une certaine homogénéité. Qu'en est-il chez les divinités féminines du Latium et de la Campanie?

Parmi les plus célèbres, figure la *Mater Matuta de Satricum,* déesse dont les liens avec *Fortuna* sont particulièrement étroits à Rome. Les fouilles récentes italo-néerlandaises, qui ont livré une inscription très discutée, gravée sans doute en l'honneur de la déesse du lieu, ont réattiré l'attention sur le dépôt votif retrouvé naguère dans le temple, daté du VIIe s. av. J.C. et notamment sur deux plaques à reliefs d'argent qui en faisaient partie: elles figurent toutes deux une maîtresse des animaux flanquée de griffons ailés.[18] C'est plus tard qu'elle est devenue courotrophe.

La nature de la *Diana Nemorensis* est plus complexe. A l'origine, elle apparaît à la fois comme déesse lunaire (de la lumière de la nuit), déesse du lac (où se reflète la lune), et déesse du bois sacré (*potnia thèrôn*). Pour cette raison la statue de culte était triple; elle présentait trois déesses debout: au centre Hécate, associée à Diane à l'arc et à Diane, déesse lunaire au pavot. Ici encore, c'est à une date plus tardive, au IVe-IIIe s, qu'elle est devenue déesse de fertilité, déesse des femmes et accoucheuse.[19]

L'évolution de la *Junon* de *Gabies*[20] est parallèle. C'est sans doute à cause de sa transformation en déesse de fécondité qu'au IVe-IIIe s. le culte de la *Fortuna* de *Praeneste* a été introduit dans son sanctuaire, très probablement par les Oppii, riches *negotiatores* prénestins; les dépôts votifs recueillis dans l'*area* de Gabies l'attestent. A moins que ce ne soit le contraire. C'est-à-dire que l'introduction du culte de *Praeneste* à Gabies ait provoqué ou hâté l'évolution de la déesse locale en courotrophe.

Feronia, pour sa part, possédait trois sanctuaires particulièrement fameux: au *lucus* de l'*ager* capénate, le temple de Terracine et le temple de *Trebula Mutuesca* chez les Sabins. Son culte était d'ailleurs sans doute d'origine sabine. Des découvertes relativement récentes ont permis de préciser la nature de cette déesse, dont le *lucus* de Capène était déjà célèbre à l'époque royale, si l'on en croit Tite Live (I, 30, 5). Sa renommée, en tout cas, était grande et sa richesse considérable — on sait, toujours par Tite Live (XXVI, 2, 8) que les Capénates lui apportaient des présents et les prémices de leurs récoltes — puisque Hannibal en 211 le pilla. Ce qui explique sans doute, comme l'ont noté justement R. Bloch et G. Foti,[21] que dans les *favissae* du sanctuaire n'aient été retrouvées que des inscriptions et, comme matériel, des statuettes en terre cuite, représentant notamment des bêtes de labour ou des parties du corps humain (pieds, mains, têtes, yeux, etc.). Tous ces objets votifs montrent clairement que *Feronia*, devenue protectrice des affranchis, fut d'abord déesse des sources et de l'eau, mais surtout déesse des moissons. C'est là, souligne R. Bloch, "un de ses traits les plus archaïques et les plus profonds" (p. 76). Et c'est parce qu'elle était avant tout déesse de la Terre et de ses fruits qu'on venait lui offrir les prémices des récoltes; l'*ager* capénate était renommé pour son blé et ses vergers. Accessoirement elle est devenue guérisseuse et sans doute accoucheuse, comme le montrent les ex-voto d'enfants emmaillotés.

La *Iuno* de *Capoue* n'était pas moins fameuse, si l'on en juge par le nombre d'ex-voto recueillis dans son sanctuaire, très fréquenté du VIe au IIe s. av. J.C.: plus de 6.000 objets comportant des statuettes de bébés langés et des ex-voto anatomiques. A quoi s'ajoutent quelque 600 figurines en terre cuite d'une déesse courotrophe. Après avoir hésité entre une *Fortuna* et *Iuno*, J. Heurgon[22] s'est finalement prononcé pour une *Iuno*, qui — il faut le souligner — était aussi à ses débuts *potnia thèrôn.*

A Capoue toujours, *Diana Tifatina* a subi, semble-t-il, une évolution différente, mais non moins significative. Déesse de la naissance et de la végétation à l'origine, maîtresse des animaux aussi, elle est devenue sous l'influence hellénique, une Diane chasseresse à l'arc. Mais sans jamais perdre complètement ses fonctions originelles.[23]

Enfin, pour dire un mot de *Cérès*, particulièrement connue dans le Samnium, à une époque ancienne, bien antérieure à la romanisation, notamment à *Corfinium* chez les *Paeligni*,[23] on sait que sur la célèbre tablette de bronze d'Agnone sont nommées quelque 16 divinités de l'agriculture et de la fécondité, groupées autour d'une "Cérès osque".

Si, avant de tirer de cette rapide analyse quelques conclusions, nous opérons un bref retour à Rome pour examiner quelques divinités de la fertilité autres que les Fortunes, certaines constatations s'imposent. D'abord à propos de la déesse *Ops*, déesse de l'Abondance, par l'action de qui on obtient les *opes* (à la fois ressources et richesses). *Ops*, à qui P. Pouthier a consacré un livre récent,[25] est présente à Rome au moins dès le deuxième quart du VIe s. dans le *sacrarium Opis Consiuae*, sous la *Regia* qui fut construite à la fin du VIe s., comme l'ont montré les fouilles de F. Brown. Son importance apparaît en pleine lumière si l'on réfléchit à l'emplacement de ce *sacrarium* près de Vesta, au coeur religieux du premier Forum,[26] et les liens entre Ops et Vesta se précisent, si l'on se souvient que les Vestales et le *pontifex maximus* (successeur du *rex sacrorum* dans la *Regia*) jouent un rôle dans la cérémonie des *Opiconsiuia* du 25 août, les *Consualia* étant célébrées, elles, le 21 août. Le rapport étroit d'Ops avec Consus, le dieu qui veille sur la réserve de grains, paraît clair. Une relation presque aussi étroite l'unissait à *Saturnus*, comme l'indique la deuxième fête d'Ops, les *Opalia* du 19 décembre qui se déroulaient sur une *area* voisine de l'*area Saturni.* Mais ce qui frappe le plus dans l'histoire de cette déesse, c'est son divorce. Vers 250 av.J.C., une double' dissociation se produit: tandis que le temple de Consus reste *in Auentino* et le temple de Saturne au pied du Capitole, où il est implanté depuis le début du Ve s., Ops s'installe à part *in Capitolio.* Elle a acquis son autonomie. Avant de tomber dans un certain oubli sans doute à cause du succès de Cérès. Comme *Saturnus* d'ailleurs, dont il faut dire un mot.

D'autant que son cas constitue une originalité. Alors qu'ailleurs en Italie, les divinités de la fertilité sont essentiellement féminines, tolérant au mieux près d'elles un parèdre de rang inférieur, à Rome les dieux mâles occupent une place particulière. Ainsi *Consus* et *Saturnus.*[27] Avant même la fondation de Rome, il existait, semble-t-il, dans l'Italie centrale primitive et agricole (soumise à l'influence sicule), un grand dieu de la fertilité / fécondité, qui, reçu dans le panthéon romain, s'installa, comme "dieu sabin" de la troisième fonction, au pied du Capitole. Il emprunta beaucoup aux Etrusques, qui avaient leur Satre, notamment son nom et sa valeur de dieu redoutable des profondeurs de la terre. En 497, un temple érigé *etrusco more* sur l'*area* qui lui était réservée aux confins du Forum et du Capitole fut voué à un *Saturnus* à la fois divinité du monde souterrain, chthonienne et agraire, temple dont le haut *podium* abritait le trésor de la Ville, l'*aerarium Saturni.* Marquant bien son caractère agraire, sa fête très ancienne, les *Saturnalia* primitives, était fixée au 17 décembre, après l'achèvement des travaux des champs et juste avant le solstice d'hiver. C'est dire qu'elle reflétait la conception très ancienne qui lie les aspects fécondants au sous-sol de la Terre. Il n'y eut pas de grands changements avant la réforme qui intervint à la fin du IIIe s., en 217 av.J.C., en une occasion bien précise, sur laquelle on va revenir.

De l'examen de toutes ces divinités de Rome et de l'Italie centrale, on peut dire, en conclusion:

— que toutes les divinités féminines de la fertilité ont commencé dans leur phase archaïque par être des expressions de la Terre-Mère méditerranéenne, avant de se présenter, presque partout, comme "maîtresses des animaux", présentation courante dans le monde oriental et, sous l'influence de l' "Artémis orientale", dans le monde étrusque dès le VIIIe-VIIe s.

— qu'au IVe-IIIe s., l'aspect violent, guerrier, dominateur de la *potnia thèrôn* a été oblitéré par le caractère courotrophe et généralement guérisseur de la déesse de fertilité / fécondité. Au point que souvent les divinités perdent même leur individualité pour devenir, comme l'a très justement observé Mme F.H. Pairault,[28] "sous des traits quasi interchangeables, pourvoyeuses d'abondance et de fécondité, divines nourrices et protectrices. Elles sont alors annexées presque exclusivement au service de la société féminine."

— Les cas un peu particuliers d'*Ops* et de *Saturnus* à Rome ne permettent pas de modifier la portée de ces conclusions. On constate même que, si les données initiales sont différentes, les changements qui les affectent interviennent vers les mêmes dates, au IIIe s.

Il y a donc là un fait nouveau et important, qu'il faut tenter d'expliquer. Bien sûr, on sera tenté de faire appel à l'influence grecque. De fait, le rôle d'Héra, bien implantée en Sicile et en Grande-Grèce — on pense par exemple à l'Heraion du Silaris — paraît avoir été considérable. La déesse à la grenade, symbole de fécondité, n'a pas été seulement assimilée à Junon. Son influence a été beaucoup plus large. Elle a affecté plus ou moins toutes les divinités féminines de l'Italie centrale.

Toutefois cette explication ne peut pas suffire. Il faut aussi prendre en compte certaines considérations sociales. A Rome comme en Italie, au IVe siècle on passe d'un monde à un autre: d'un monde dominé par les patriciens à un monde plus plébéien. En simplifiant, abusivement peut-être, on peut tout de même dire que dans le monde patricien dominaient les activités guerrières, violentes, sous la forme militaire ou sous la forme de la chasse (comme succédané); à ce monde violent convenaient bien les divinités "maîtresses des animaux". Le monde plébéien qui commence à le remplacer — c'est le moment où les plébéiens accèdent au pouvoir politique — est un monde dont les préoccupations principales sont davantage liées aux activités rurales (agricoles et pastorales) et à la vie familiale. Faut-il rappeler que les *proletarii* (jusque là *infra classem*) sont par définition ceux qui dans l'Etat ne comptent que par leurs enfants, qui n'ont pas d'autres richesses que leur descendance, leur progéniture? Notons d'ailleurs à ce propos que la réforme des *Saturnalia* en 217, pendant la deuxième guerre punique, à un moment particulièrement dramatique de l'histoire de Rome, fut imposée par la nécessité d'associer tout le *populus* et même les esclaves à un mouvement de salut public destiné à sauver la Ville.[29]

Peut-être comprend-on mieux alors que toutes les grandes déesses à qui s'adressait la "nouvelle" piété des Romains aient au IVe-IIIe s. acquis les pouvoirs de divinités de la fertilité / fécondité, de déesses des femmes, courotrophes et guérisseuses.

Cette mutation profonde s'est prolongée et accentuée à partir du IIIe-IIe s. av.J.C. avec l'introduction dans le panthéon romain — résultat des conquêtes — de divinités de caractères très différents et avec l'influence croissante des doctrines des diverses écoles philosophiques grecques, qui vont entraîner des conséquences multiples. C'est ainsi qu'on voit s'accuser de plus en plus la différenciation des divinités du panthéon dans le sens d'une spécialisation de plus en plus grande. Ce mouvement avait commencé bien avant; l'exemple de Junon qui avait au départ un caractère très polyvalent, vite corrigé, le montre. Du moins a-t-il alors été activé. On le voit avec Cérès, d'abord divinité de la fertilité en général, qui devient avant tout la déesse des moissons. Apparaissent aussi — c'est une autre conséquence — des nouveautés idéologiques: la religion prend un aspect de plus en plus politique (dans le sens étroit), et les dieux et déesses du panthéon commun sont de plus en plus accaparés par les *gentes* ambitieuses qui tentent de les mettre à leur service ou au service de leur cause: ainsi Vénus, puis Isis, par les Metelli. Là non plus l'idée n'est pas tout à fait nouvelle: il y a longtemps, dit-on, que les Aurelii se réclamaient de Sol! Toujours est-il que le développement des cultes gentilices (qui mériteraient une étude spéciale) marque un moment important de l'histoire de la religion romaine. D'autant plus perceptible qu'il s'accompagne d'un essor architectural sans précédent: construire des temples de plus en plus monumentaux, de plus en plus luxueux relève de la *dignitas*. Tous ces changements, qu'accompagne une évolution sensible du sentiment religieux des Romains, conduisent tout naturellement à de profondes déformations — Jean Bayet a employé le mot "détérioration"[30] — des cultes anciens. Le cas des *Cerialia* primitives, "détériorées" sous l'influence des Eleusinies, est très significatif. Celui de *Saturnus* et de *Iuno* sous l'influence de Ba'al et de Tanit du fait de la deuxième guerre punique est tout aussi révélateur.

*　　　　　*　　　　　*

On peut, dans ces conditions, se demander *quelle place occupent encore les cultes de fertilité à la fin de la République et au début de l'Empire?*

Il est essentiel — me semble-t-il — de distinguer à ce moment de l'histoire la situation qui s'offre à Rome et en Italie de celle que présentent les provinces. Encore pour celles-ci ne faudrait-il pas généraliser.

A **Rome**, où la religion subit une double évolution, politique et mystique, on peut très légitimement se demander ce que deviennent, dans une ville qui a perdu la plupart de ses attaches paysannes, les cultes de fertilité. Pour les uns, la religion apparaît comme de plus en plus accaparée, on peut dire manipulée, à des fins politiques. Face aux grandes *gentes* couvertes par les dieux gentilices, les *imperatores* ambitieux, qui ne leur appartiennent pas forcément ou qui s'en détachent volontairement, éprouvent le besoin de se placer sous la protection particulière et personnelle d'une divinité. Ce qui prouve d'ailleurs que, contrairement à ce qu'on croit encore trop souvent, il n'y a pas alors déclin du sentiment religieux. Marius se réclame d'*Honos* et de *Virtus*; Sylla de *Venus felix,* Pompée de *Venus uictrix*, César de *Venus genetrix*, mère d'Enée, donc de Iulus et des Iulii et mère des Romains, Octave d'Apollon, face à Marc Antoine qui invoque Dionysos. Et pour des raisons, évidemment plus idéologiques que religieuses, leurs constructions sacrées sont marquées par un gigantisme ostentatoire de type publicitaire. Il faut bien voir pourtant qu'elles ne sont jamais conçues en dehors du cadre religieux traditionnel.

Pour d'autres, la religion devient plus intellectuelle, plus spiritualiste, voire mystique, sous l'influence des philosophies grecques et gréco-orientales, notamment du néopythagorisme, sous l'influence aussi des cultes hellénistiques. On a cité déjà l'exemple des *Cerialia* envahies par les mystères éleusiniens. On a évoqué aussi le cas de Saturnus, dont le culte proprement dit a quasiment disparu; en restent l'*aerarium Saturni,* les Saturnales, devenues une fête populaire joyeuse, et un *topos* littéraire, celui du dieu de l'âge d'or.

Une troisième déviation se développe dangereusement à la fin de la République et au début du Principat augustéen, au point de provoquer l'intervention répressive d'Auguste et de ses successeurs. Ce sont les pratiques magiques et de sorcellerie qui jusque là ne touchaient que les campagnes et le petit peuple des villes, qui maintenant gagnent le demi-monde des nouveaux riches, gavés de richesses (souvent acquises à l'occasion des proscriptions), que dépeint Horace. Qui pénètrent même dans l'aristocratie sénatoriale.[31] Notons que c'est justement du Ier s. av.J.C. que datent les plus anciennes *tabellae defixionum* en latin.[32]

Dans ces conditions, apparemment bien peu favorables, que deviennent les cultes de fertilité? Leur situation paraît dominée par deux phénomènes qui assurent leur survie:

C'est d'abord la pénétration des religions orientales, en particulier des cultes alexandrins d'Isis et de Sérapis, dont l'aspect de divinités de fertilité n'est pas négligeable. *Isis* parmi ses pouvoirs universels est *Fortune.* Elle est *frugifera.* Elle est Bubastis, la déesse de la naissance et Thermouthis, déesse de fertilité. Sérapis est dieu chthonien, au *modius* orné d'épis de blé et de fleurs. Par Délos, qui a pu servir de relais, ou directement, il s'est implanté à *Puteoli* dès 105 av.J.C., et à Pompéi Isis a un temple dès l'époque de Sylla. De là le culte isiaque a très vite gagné la Sardaigne.[33] Sur la route de Rome, Isis est aussi à *Praeneste.* On a évoqué déjà le rôle des *negotiatores* dans l'extension du sanctuaire de *Fortuna Primigenia.* Or, non seulement l'épigraphie révèle les noms des mêmes familles (les Caltii, les Numitori, les Samiarii) parmi les évergètes de Délos et de *Praeneste*, mais elle atteste l'existence, à Délos, d'une *Isis Tychè Prôtogenia* d'une part et d'autre part l'existence dans le sanctuaire inférieur de *Praeneste* d'un *Iseion*, contemporain de celui de Pompéi et du *Serapeion* de Pouzzoles. N'oublions pas qu'Isis protège le commerce maritime et ceux qui s'y livrent, tout comme *Fortuna*, et qu'on la représente parfois munie du gouvernail de la Fortune. Dans le même temps, ou peu après, à Rome Isis est introduite sur le Capitole par un collège, la corporation des marchands d'esclaves, liés aux *negotiatores*. Dès le début du Ier s. av. J.C. est nommé dans une inscription un *sacerdos Isidis Capitolinae*.[34]

Un autre phénomène, moins religieux, plutôt porteur d'idéologie, a joué vers la même époque un rôle important: le développement du thème de l'âge d'or, du *saeculum aureum* marqué, on le sait, par le triomphe absolu de l'ordre et de la paix, générateurs d'abondance, fruit de la fertilité et de la fécondité. Toutes notions d'autant plus en faveur que Rome était plongée dans l'horreur des guerres civiles avec leur cortège de violences et de misères. Les études d'A. Alföldi en particulier[35] ont montré que ce thème, originaire d'Alexandrie, avait été lancé à Rome en même temps que les thèmes de Victoire par les *imperatores* de la fin de la République. C'est en effet à l'époque de Marius, puis de Sylla, qu'apparaissent sur le monnayage le caducée, les épis et la *cornucopia* (tous emblèmes lagides)[36] qui sont l'annonce, la promesse de la *felicitas*. Mais maintenant, il ne s'agit plus tellement de richesse personnelle, ni d'abondance née de l'accumulation des grains dans les greniers ou des troupeaux dans les bergeries. Bien que cette idée n'ait pas disparu, c'est aussi la *felicitas* de Rome et de l'empire qui est envisagée et annoncée. Ce thème de la *felicitas imperii* conditionnée par la *salus Imperatoris*, exalté par les écrivains augustéens, va devenir un des slogans de la propagande impériale, en fait un de ses éléments favoris, repris, avec l'annonce de l'âge d'or, par chaque empereur à son avènement. Les reliefs de l'*Ara Pacis Augustae* sont à cet égard très significatifs.

Naturellement les choses sont sensiblement différentes en **Italie**, où les derniers siècles de la République ont été fertiles en profonds bouleversements. Au point d'y provoquer une rupture de l'équilibre socio-économique. Des mutations considérables ont affecté la vie des campagnes à la suite des conquêtes, puis des guerres civiles et des proscriptions. La municipalisation et son pendant, l'urbanisation ont fait d'importants progrès, surtout en Italie centrale et en Campanie.[37] Au point de vue social, le développement d'une classe de notables municipaux, détenteurs parfois de fortunes énormes, nées d'activités commerciales (pour les *negotatiores*), mais aussi des proscriptions, a déjà des incidences multiples. Pour ce qui nous concerne, retenons seulement que, parmi eux, on rencontre des évergètes, qui construisent des temples souvent fastueux, embellis de matériaux grecs, d'une ornementation à la grecque, d'un luxe un peu ostentatoire qui exprime et proclame leur récente *dignitas*.[38] Et comme ces gens-là ne perdent jamais de vue leurs intérêts, leurs choix et pourquoi pas leur religiosité les ont portés volontiers vers les divinités protectrices de leur fortune.

C'est ainsi que, tandis que chez les Marses et les Péligniens les fouilles récentes ont attiré l'attention sur le culte d'Hercule: à *Sulmo un Hercule Curinus*, protecteur des troupeaux, ce qui est bien normal dans une région d'économie pastorale, à *Alba Fucens*, à la limite du pays marse, un Hercule plus hellénisé, on trouve à *Tibur*, le même Hercule, qualifié ici de *Victor*, mais il a des liens étroits, un peu surprenants avec le commerce. A Ostie, sur un *podium* unique, à l'intérieur d'un vaste enclos rectangulaire, à l'Ouest du théâtre, on érige dans la première moitié du Ier s. av.J.C. "quattro tempietti", comme les désignent les archéologues italiens: ils sont voués à quatre divinités féminines de la fertilité / fécondité, Vénus, Fortuna, Cérès et Spes, toutes déesses de caractère plébéien, ce qui n'étonne pas dans une ville-port fréquentée par les marins et les négociants.

Comme on le voit — et les exemples pourraient être multipliés — les divinités sont souvent devenues, du moins dans les villes et les bourgs, divinités du commerce, sans perdre pour autant leurs puissances originelles. Il y a là tantôt une extension, un enrichissement de leurs fonctions initiales, tantôt une déviation ou un gauchissement de ces fonctions, qui se sont adaptées à des conditions socio-économiques nouvelles.

On n'observe pas les mêmes transformations dans les **provinces**. La matière est très riche; on ne pourra ici que prendre quelques exemples.[39] La matière est très riche pour plusieurs raisons. D'abord parce qu'il semble bien que dans les provinces se sont en quelque sorte réfugiés les cultes de fertilité; on y trouve en effet des divinités qui à Rome et en Italie sont plus ou moins oubliées (par exemple Janus et Saturnus en Afrique du Nord). Ensuite parce que, sur les cultes de fertilité indigènes partout très nombreux, sont venus se greffer les vieux cultes romains, qui les ont du même coup enrichis et d'une certaine manière ré-activés. Nous touchons là à un problème très complexe d'*interpretatio*, dans lequel il n'est pas possible d'entrer ici (ce pourrait être le thème d'une autre colloque!). Disons, pour simplifier, qu'on entrevoit:

— des cas où les cultes indigènes se sont maintenus sans changement ou presque;

— des cas où ils ont été absorbés par des divinités romaines ou gréco-romaines; dans certains cas, il n'ont fait que disparaître sous un nom latin.

— des cas où leur personnalité s'est enrichie par syncrétisme d'assimilation.

En **Hispania**, ce qui frappe le plus, c'est la quantité innombrable, quasiment inchiffrable, parce qu'elle s'accroît chaque jour, des divinités des eaux, à la fois guérisseuses et puissances de fertilité, parfois en même temps célestes et chthoniennes, veillant aussi bien sur l'au-delà que sur l'abondance terrestre. C'est le cas des deux principales divinités lusitaniennes, *Endovellicus* et *Ataecina.*[40]

En **Gaule** et dans les **Germanies**, où presque toutes les divinités locales sont ou bien des divinités des eaux guérisseuses ou des divinités de la fertilité, l'impression est un peu la même que dans la péninsule ibérique. Peut-être note-t-on cependant quelques différences. Par exemple une plus grande diffusion de certains dieux de caractère plus fonctionnel. On pense à Sucellus, le dieu au maillet, à l'origine dieu des viticulteurs, mais qu'on rencontre vite dans des régions non viticoles parce que sa puissance s'est étoffée. On pense aussi à Epona, déesse des éleveurs de chevaux, qui a connu une certaine faveur hors du milieu hippique. Une autre différence: l'extraordinaire faveur des déesses-mères, appelées ici *Matres,* là *Matronae*, là encore *Matrae*. Faveur particulièrement affirmée dans la région lyonnaise et surtout dans les Germanies, où récemment C.B. Rüger a enfin reconnu "a husband for the Mother Goddesses".[41]

En **Afrique du Nord**, les questions sont peut-être spécialement complexes, du fait de la multiplicité des influences qui au fil des siècles se sont exercées sur le monde divin indigène: influences phéniciennes, puis puniques, influences grecques, puis hellénistiques, influences romaines, puis orientales. Deux exemples suffiront à montrer la complexité des problèmes. Celui de *Cérès*, ou plutôt des *Cereres* — particularité africaine — dont le culte fut introduit au IVe s. av.J.C. dans la Carthage punique à partir de la Sicile, plus précisément de Syracuse, où Déméter et Korè étaient vénérées depuis longtemps. Apparemment il devrait se présenter avec un caractère mystique très accentué. En réalité on constate qu'il revêt surtout un double aspect: d'abord, celui, le moins attendu, de culte poliade, dans la mesure où il s'est trouvé lié à la refondation de Carthage et surtout au sort de la nouvelle colonie, redevenue capitale de la province d'*Africa* unifiée dans les années 40 av.J.C.[42] Ensuite, celui, plus conforme à ses origines, de culte de fertilité, mais ici très tôt lié au culte impérial. Une stèle de *Theveste* montre très bien la double fonction, chthonienne et agraire, des *Cereres*. Tandis que dans le temple qui lui fut voué en haut du théâtre de *Lepcis Magna*, la déesse, qui porte des épis avec la couronne tourelée de divinité poliade, est dénommée *Ceres Augusta*.

Le cas de *Saturnus* est au moins aussi révélateur de la mentalité religieuse des Berbéro-romains. Pour ne pas répéter ce qui a été expliqué ailleurs,[43] qu'il suffise de rappeler que sur de très vieux cultes naturistes berbères s'est greffé aisément le dieu d'origine phénicienne Ba'al-Hammon, dont les Romains ont fait, par captation sur place, *Saturnus*. Cela, sans que soit le moins du monde affecté son caractère de dieu suprême et, en quelque sorte, "national" (le mot ne convient guère dans un pays de structure tribale) des Africains. A la fois chthonien et céleste, dieu de fécondité des familles et des troupeaux, dieu de fertilité des champs, des vergers et des jardins, protecteur des vivants et garant de survie, il est pour tous, mais plus particulièrement pour les petites gens, "le" grand dieu souverain. On l'assimile d'ailleurs à l'occasion, à Jupiter. C'est en tout cas au dieu-providence, pourvoyeur des fruits de la terre, que jusqu'à très basse époque les Africains ont offert leurs offrandes et leurs stèles votives.

* * *

En conclusion, trois remarques s'imposent, me semble-t-il.

1) Si les mythes d'une part, d'autre part les caractères qui définissent la nature des dieux et par conséquent les rites sont en relation étroite et directe avec les préoccupations majeures des hommes, il n'est pas surprenant que les divinités et les rites de fertilité aient occupé une place particulièrement importante dans la vie religieuse de pays tels que Malte ou l'Afrique du Nord, où les conditions climatiques rendaient la vie quotidienne spécialement difficile.

2) L'importance des cultes de fertilité dans la religion romaine très ancienne (parmi les 45 jours de fête du calendrier archaïque, marqués NP — *nefasti puri,* ou *priores,* ou *posteriores*, peu importe ici — sigle qui de toute facon désigne les fêtes les plus anciennes, prennent place toutes les fêtes en rapport avec les divinités de fertilité), incite à aller au-

delà des constatations courantes sur le caractère naturaliste et terrien des rites, sur le caractère pratique de la religion romaine, une religion qu'on présente volontiers comme dénuée de véritable sentiment religieux.

Au vrai, c'est d'*utilitas* qu'il faut parler. Comme le fait Cicéron (*De natura deorum*, III, 61) qui, à propos des abstractions divinisées par les Romains et notamment des statues que les hommes dressent dans les temples qu'ils leur consacrent, souligne que, s'ils agissent ainsi, c'est à cause de leur *utilitas*: *quarum rerum utilitatem uideo*. C'est une idée sur laquelle il insiste ailleurs (II, 61): *Utilitatem igitur magnitudine constituti sunt ei di qui utilitates quasque gignebant*. Des dieux utiles aux hommes de par leur nature: c'est une idée stoïcienne. Elle est exprimée par la bouche du stoïcien Balbus, mais aussi par l'académicien Cotta. Tous deux disent à peu près la même chose: si les hommes ont rangé ces entités abstraites parmi les dieux, c'est en tant que productrices de choses utiles, utiles pour la société et pour la Cité. Est-ce par hasard que l'anniversaire de la fondation de Rome, le 21 avril, correspond à la fête des *Parilia*? A Rome, comme dans toutes les cités antiques, la religion traditionnelle est *liée* au système de la cité. L'*utilitas* ne situe donc pas les relations hommes-dieux sur le plan inférieur de l'obtention, de la satisfaction de bas intérêtes matériels personnels, mais les élève au plan de l'intérêt supérieur de la société et de la Cité de Rome. A ce degré, l'*utilitas* n'est pas exclusive de sentiment religieux. Cicéron d'ailleurs parle de "sentiment religieux pour le bien des cités" (*De legibus*, II, 27).

3) Pour préciser les choses, je veux dire le sens des relations hommes-dieux, il faut encore recourir à Cicéron (*De officiis*, II, 11): *Deos placatos pietas officiet et sanctitas, maxime autem et secundum deos homines hominibus maxime utiles esse possunt*. Le texte est explicite: c'est la *pietas* et la *sanctitas* qui seules peuvent assurer la *pax deorum*; et le fruit de la *pax deorum* est l'*utilitas*.

On retrouve la même idée chez Ovide (*Fasti*, II, 535): *pietas pro diuite grata est munere*. Même s'il inverse les termes! Ainsi la prospérité, l'abondance ne commandent pas, ou ne doivent pas commander la piété. Elles en sont les fruits. La prospérité est le résultat de la religiosité. Et c'est bien pourquoi tout habitant de l'Empire, tout citoyen romain a fortiori doit être *religiosus, pius,* puisqu'il doit vouloir assurer la *felicitas imperii*.

Notes

1 Je n'ai pas trouvé le mot fertilité dans le livre récent de J. Scheid, *Religion et piété à Rome,* Paris, 1985.

2 Voir G. Dumézil, *Fêtes romaines d'été et d'automne,* Paris 1975, p. 87 ss.

3 Selon G. Dumézil, *La religion romaine archaïque,* Paris, p. 215 ss.

4 *Ibid.*, p. 246 ss.

5 Voir J. Marouzeau, *C.R.A.I.,* 1956, p. 347-348 = *R.E.L.*, 34, 1956, p. 40-41. Précisions de R. Schilling, A propos de l'expression Iuppiter Optimus Maximus, *Soc. Acad. Dacoromana, Acta Philologica,* III, 1964, p. 345-348.

6 *C.I.L.*, I², 359-360; *I.L.L. R.P.*, 162-163; *Imagines,* 80-81; *Not. Sc.*, 1903, p. 255-256; *Roma medio repubblicana. Aspetti culturali di Roma e del Lazio nei secoli IV e III a.C.*, Roma 1973, p. 338-339, nos. 489-490, tav. LXXIII.

7 G. Dumézil, *op. cit.*, p. 291. Sur Hera-Uni-Astarte, voir les Tablettes de Pyrgi: M. Pallottino et coll., Scavi nel santuario etrusco di Pyrgi, *Archeologia classica,* XVI, 1964; Pyrgi. Scavi del santuario etrusco (1959-1967), *Not. Sc.,* Supl. II, 1970; A.J. Pfiffig, *Uni-Héra-Astarté* (*Oesterr. Akad. Wissensch., Phil. Hist. Kl., Denkschriften,* 88, 2), Vienne 1965; J. Heurgon, A. propos des inscriptions de Pyrgi, *Bull. Arch. Comité Trav. Hist. et Sc.*, 1968, p. 247-251; R. Bloch, Héra, Uni, Junon en Italie centrale, *C.R.A.I.*, 1972, p. 384-396. Sur toutes ces questions, voir R. Bloch, *Recherches,* 1980.

8 G. Dumézil, *ouv. cit.*, p. 300 ss.

9 *Civiltà degli Etruschi,* a cura di M. Cristofani, Milano 1985, p. 283-284, no. 10.28. Voir R. Bloch, *Recherches,* 1980, p. 351 ss.

10 Voir F. Castagnoli, Il culto di Minerva a Lavinium, *Accad. Naz. dei Lincei,* quad. 246, 1979.

11 G. Gullini et F. Fasolo, *Il santuario della Fortuna primigenia a Palestrina,* Roma 1953.

12 Selon A. Degrassi, plusieurs articles réunis dans *Scritti vari di Antichità,* I-IV, Trieste 1962-1971. Voir aussi *I.L.L.R.P.*, I, p. 79 ss.

13 J. Champeaux, *Fortuna. Recherches sur le culte de la Fortune à Rome et dans le monde romain,* I. *Des origines à Auguste,* Roma 1982.

14 Voir *Civiltà del Lazio primitivo,* Roma 1976, p. 235, no. 34, tav. XLIX A.

15 Voir, avec bibliographie récente, J. Champeaux, *op. cit.*, p. 199 ss. (pour le temple de Fors-Fortuna); p. 249 ss. (pour celui du Forum Boarium).

16 A. Degrassi, *Bull. Comun.*, 79, 1963-64 (1966) p. 91-93; M. Torelli, *Quad. Ist. Top.*, 5, 1968, p. 71 ss.

17 Voir toujours, avec bibliographie récente, J. Champeaux, *op. cit.*, p. 335 ss.

18 Voir *Civiltà del Lazio primitivo,* Roma 1976, p. 329-330, tav. LXXX-VII, 1 et 2.

19 En dernier lieu F.H. Pairault, Diana Nemorensis, déesse latine, déesse hellénisée *M.E.F.R.A.*, 81, 1969, p. 425-471.

20 En dernier lieu *El santuario de Juno en Gabii,* sous la direction de M. Almagro-Gorbea, Roma 1982. Voir M. Le Glay, Les Oppii de Praeneste à Gabies, *Z.P.E.*, 58, 1985, p. 204-206.

21 R. Bloch, G. Foti, Nouvelles dédicces archaïques à la déesse Feronia, *Rev. Philol.*, 27, 1953, p. 65-77.

22 J. Heurgon, *Capoue préromaine. Recherches sur l'histoire, la religion et la civilisation de Capoue préromaine,* Paris 1942, p. 307 ss.

23 *Ibid.*

24 Voir H. Le Bonniec, *Le culte de Cérès à Rome des orgines à la fin de la République,* Paris 1958, p. 40-44 (sur la tablette d'Agnone). Sur une inscription de *Corfinium* mentionnant une *sacaracirix cerfum = sacratrix cerfum = sacerdos Cererum*: A.L. Posdocimi, Le iscrizioni prelatine in Italia, *Atti dei Convegni Lincei,* 39, 1979, p. 176.

25 P. Pouthier, *Ops et la conception divine de l'abondance dans la religion romaine jusqu'à la mort d'Auguste,* Paris 1981.

26 Fouilles de F. Brown de 1935 à 1967. Voir en dernier lieu F. Coarelli, *Il Foro romano: Periodo arcaico*, Roma 1983.

27 Cf. M. Le Glay, *Saturne africain. Histoire,* Paris 1966, p. 449 ss. et surtout Ch. Guittard, Les origines de Saturne romain, dans R. Bloch et coll., *Recherches sur les religions de l'Italie antique*, Genève 1976, p. 43-71.

[28] *Art. cit.*, p. 438-439.

[29] M. Le Glay, *op. cit.*, p. 470 ss.

[30] J. Bayet, La détérioration des Cerialia par le mythe grec, *C.R.A.I.*, 1950, p. 297-303; Les "Cerialia". Altération d'un culte latin par le mythe grec, *Rev. Belge de Philol. et d'Hist.*, XXIX, 1951, p. 5-32; p. 341-366.

[31] Cf. M. Le Glay, La magie et la sorcellerie au dernier siècle de la République, *Mélanges offerts à J. Heurgon: L'Italie préromaine et la Rome républicaine*, I, Roma 1976, p. 525-550.

[32] *C.I.L.*, I², 2520; *Inscr. Délos*, 2534.

[33] Voir M. Le Glay, Isis et Sarapis sur un autel de Bubastis à Porto Torres (*Turris Libisonis*), dans A. Boninu, M. Le Glay, A. Mastino, *Turris Libisonis colonia Iulia*, Sassari 1984, p. 105-116.

[34] Voir F. Coarelli, Iside Capitolina, Clodio e i Mercanti di schiavi, *Alessandria e il mondo ellenistico-romano (Studi in onore di A. Adriani)*, 1984, p. 461-475.

[35] Sous le titre général *Redeunt Saturnia regna*, voir A. Alfoldi, An Iconographical Pattern heralding the Return of the Golden Age in or around 139 B.C., *Chiron*, 3, 1973, p. 131-142; Iuppiter-Apollo und Veiovis, *Chiron*, 2, 1972, p. 215-230; Apollo und die Sibylle in der Epoche Bürgerkriege, *Chiron*, 5, 1975, p. 165-192; Zum Gottesgnadentum des Sulla, *Chiron*, 6, 1976, p. 143-158; From the Aiôn Plutonios of the Ptolemies to the Saeculum Frugiferum of the Roman Emperors, *Greece and the Eastern Mediterranean in the Ancient History and Prehistory, Studies presented to Fritz Schachermeyer*, Berlin-New York 1977, p. 1-30; Frugifer-Triptolemos in ptolemäisch-römischen Herrscherkult, *Chiron*, 9, 1979, p. 533-606.

[36] Voir E. La Rocca, *L'età d'oro di Cleopatra. Indagine sulla Tazza Farnese*, (Doc. e Ric. d'Arte alessandrina, V), Roma 1984.

[37] Voir notamment E Gabra, Considerazioni politiche ed economiche sullo sviluppo urbano in Italia nei secoli II e I a.C., *Hellenismus in Italien. Koll. in Göttingen Juni 1974*, II, Göttingen 1976, p. 315-326; H. Galsterer, Urbanisation und Municipalisation Italiens im 2. und 1 Jh.v.Chr., *ibid.*, p. 327-340.

[38] Cf. P. Gros, *Architecture et Société à Rome et en Italie centro-méridionale aux deux derniers siècles de la République* (Coll. Latomus, vol. 156), Bruxelles, 1978. Voir aussi plusieurs articles de *Les "bourgeoisies" municipales italiennes aux IIe et Ier ac.J.C.*, Paris-Naples 1983.

[39] On trouvera d'autres exemples dans M. Le Glay, Les religions populaires dans l'Occident romain, *Praktika tou H'diethnous Synedriou Ellènikès kai Latinikès Epigraphikès, Athena 1982* (1984) p. 150-170.

[40] Voir. J. D'Encarnaçao, *Divinidades indigenas sob a dominio romano en Portugal*, Lisbonne 1975, p. 181 ss; *Inscriçoes Romanas de Conventus Pacensis*, 1984, 483-565; J.M. Blasquez, *Religiones primitivas de Hispania. Fuentes literarias y epigraficas*, 1962; J.M. Blasquez et coll. *La religion romana en Hispania*, Madrid 1981.

[41] C.B. Rüger, A Husband for the Mother Goddesses. Some observations on the Matronae Aufaniae, *Rome and the Northern Provinces*, 1983, p. 210-219.

[42] En dernier lieu, M. Le Glay, Les religions de l'Afrique romaine au IIe siècle d'après Apulée et les inscriptions, *L'Africa romana* (Atti del I convegno di studio, Sassari, 16-17 dicembre 1983), Sassari 1984, p. 54 ss.

[43] M. Le Glay, *Saturne africain. Histoire*, Paris, 1966.

LES DIVINITÉS FEMININES DE LA FERTILITÉ ET DE LA FÉCONDITÉ EN HISPANIA PENDANT L'ÉPOQUE ROMAINE

Marc Mayer — Isabel Rodà

Nous nous trouvons devant un des aspects qui comptent peu de témoignages dans l'archéologie hispanique, fait que l'on ne doit pas imputer sèulement à des lacunes d'information. Il y a en effet une absence de documents qui remonte jusqu'à l'époque préhistorique. Il suffira de rappeler l'absence totale, même dans la riche zone cantabrique, de "Venus" paléolithiques.[1] Les premieres sculptures féminines ayant les traits sexuels bien marqués, correspondent à des représentations qui datent de la période Enéolithique et gagnent progressivement en réalisme au commencement de l'Age de Bronze; leur localisation coïncide avec le midi péninsulaire avec une plus forte concentration dans le Sudouest.[2] Il s'agit d'images d'une divinité féminine de fécondité arrivées par des filtrations du monde méditerranéen parce que, en plus des parallèlles anatoliques, il semble bien qu'elle corresponde à la même divinité sémite dérivée d'Astarté et vénérée plus tard dans le monde autochtone préromain aussi bien dans la zone celtique (Cerro del Berrueco, Salamanque) que dans l'ibérique.[3] Les premières sculptures féminines de féconditè arrivent, donc, par des contacts méditerranéens.

D'autre part dans les peintures rupestres du Levant espagnol on voit apparaître des répresentations de danses rituelles qui font référence à une divinité féminine qui rend propice l'agriculture, la chasse et surement aussi la fécondité (Grottes de "Los Caballos", "Agua Amarga" et "El Polvorín"). D'autres scènes où apparaissent également des danseuses féminines, comme celle bien connue de Cogul, correspondent plus tôt à des cultes de type phalique.[4]

C'est effectivement quand nous arrivons à la phase préromaine que les cultes à la fertilité deviennet beaucoup plus évidents, phenomène que l'on doit attribuer à l'absortion des cultes exotiques apportés par les colonisateurs, comme ceux de Tanit, de la Potnia Theron, de Déméter et de l'Artemis éphésienne.[5] C'est grâce à ces influences que la divinité métroaque trouverait sa forme définitive, assise ou debout allaitant son enfant, que l'on trouve à plusieurs reprises dans le sudest hispanique, surtout dans des terrecuites.

Que l'on pense, par exemple, à l'impact direct qu'a pu exercer l'importation de statues comme la célèbre Dame de Galera (Grenade) sur la conformation plastique des images des divinités autochtones.[6]

De toute façon il faut tenir compte de la difficulté qu'entraîne le peu de témoignages dans cette zone, bien plus nombreux dans des zones voisines comme la *Gallia*, et le silence des sources classiques en ce qui concerne les aspects de fécondité de la réligiosité préromaine hispanique pour laquelle on peut appliquer la division traditionelle de notre Péninsule en Hispania celtique et Hispania ibèrique. On peut garder cette division au plan général, mais il faut apporter des nuances à la lumière des nouvelles découvertes: dans la zone catalane, par exemple, qui est ibèrique mais avec un fort substrat du premier Age de Fer, nous connaissons au IIIème siècle ap. J.C. des noms de dieux indigènes. Dans tous les cas il s'agit de théonymes nettement celtiques comme *Herotoragus* ou *Herotus-Ragus, Seitundus.*[7]

Il est de plus en plus évident que dans les cultes de fertilité-fécondité, la romanisation trouve un substrat bien défini grâce à la seculaire pénétration d'influences orientales par voie méditerranéene adaptées au monde autocthone. Rome en réalité ne fit autre chose qu'enrichir cette structure préexistente et changer de signe ou d'orientation certains cultes, comme peut-être celui de la Lune qui parmi les habitants préromains aurait eu un sens plus concret en relation à la mort.

Les interpretations romaines reposeraient sur la religiosité indigène impregnée, surtout dans le midi, d'éléments sémites; d'après cet ensemble de données on peut déduire qu'en Bétique le culte à la *Dea Caelestis* aurait eu un grand succés et que précisement les cultes romains les plus étroitement liés à la fécondité-fertilité qui réussirent à avoir une plus grande diffusion furent, comme on verra, les orientaux.[8]

La documentation que nous avons dans ce domaine pour l'époque romaine n'est pas non plus d'une énorme richesse. C'est pour celà que nous préférons d'avance envisager cette problématique dans une vaste perspective et nous croyons qu'il faut être d'accord avec G. Dumézil au moment de débattre les apriorismes et postulats que la vision de M. Eliade entraîne.[9] Quoique lorsque le chercheur se trouve devant un problème comme l'est l'hispanique, où d'autre part les études pré et protohistoriques ont encore à dire leur dernier mot, on est forcé de reconnaître que la vision d'Eliade présente une cohérence et une efficacité qui dans le cas qui nous occupe ne peut pas être ignorée; nous en aurions peut-être un exemple privilégié dans l'ensemble Lune-Pluie-Fertilité-Femme-Serpent-Mort-Régenération périodique. Il est évident que en partant d'un postulat de ce type, le panorama devient plus riche dans le cadre hispano-romain qui délimite notre travail avec seulement des références occasionelles à l'existence antérieure de croyances que les formes romaines et orientales ne font plus que revêtir, interpréter et substituer.

De ce point de vue l'iconographie prend pour notre objectif un interêt primordial. L'épigraphie funéraire nous apparaît dans les zones dans lesquelles la romanisation fut plus pénible, comme un élément révélateur: les représentations lunaires, par exemple, apparaissent dans des monuments autochtones et également dans des monuments romains, pervivence très nette de types antérieurs, phenomène qui a son parallèle dans la Gaule et dans d'autres parties de l'Empire romain[10]. Romaines également mais de caractère manifestement celtisant sont les représentations lunaires sur les urnes oicomorphes de Poza de la Sal et dans les stèles de Lara de los Infantes[11] qui écartent les cultes proprement romains dont le point culminant est indiqué par l'invocation à la Lune Auguste intégrée dans l'apparat du culte impérial (*CIL* II, 4458).

Rappelons maintenant le passage de *Firmicus Maternus (De errore* 4, 1, 1) sur la préponderance de la Lune: *omnia animantium corpora et concepta procreat et generata disoluit*, allégué avec raison dans les études sur ce thème.

Quoique l'apport nouveau de la romanisation pour le cas d'*Hispania* soit la valeur initiatique, non seulement des cultes en relation avec la Lune, mais encore de l'ensemble des cultes en relation avec la fertilité pour lesquels dans certains cas la romanisation se borne à vehiculer des éléments d'organisation et par conséquent rituels à des croyances moins structurées mais déjà existentes. Ce phenomène cristallisera avec l'influence des cultes orientaux qui cachent même les vêtements romains.

Les cultes aux eaux, qui semblent très clairement préromains en *Hispania*, perdurent largement à l'époque romaine, également sous des advocations traditionelles dans des zones thermales très romanisées; nous en avons un exemple typique dans les *Aquae Calidae* de la *Tarraconensis* mises sous le patronat d'Apollon mais avec la parution de Minerva et d'Isis et d'abstractions du type *Salus*.[12]

Il est par ailleurs presque paradoxale dans les zones où la romanisation a pénétré avec plus de difficulté, de constater la présence cultuelle des Nymphes. En éffet dans des zones montagneuses proches à des sources thermales qui partant des Pyrénées (Val d'Aran) s'étendent par la Navarre, la Galice, le nord du Portugal, la Castille-Leon et l'Extremadure, on invoque les Nymphes aussi bien dans leur ensemble (ce qui donne l'impression de cultes aparemment hellénisés, comme on l'entrevoit par les formules de type *ex uisu* qui est écrite dans une inscription du Musée d'Orense, *CIL* II, 2527) que par des épithètes qui dénotent clairement leur caractère préromain. Nous avons de cette façon le témoignage des *Nymphae Caparenses*[13], des *Nymphae Fontis Ameuchi* (*CIL* II, 5084) et des *Nymphae Varcilenae* (*CIL* II, 3067).

Il faut ajouter à cette distribution géographique que la plus grande concentration d'hommages aux *Fontes* coïncide précisément avec l'Extremadure et les zones portugaises voisines, de la même manière que provient du Portugal (Caldas de Monchique) la consécration aux *Aquae Sacrae* et de Salamanque (Retortillo) aux *Aquae Eleate(n)ses.*[14]

Un autre chemin théoriquement bien battu et peut-être archétype à l'excés, lie depuis toujours les divinités chtoniennes avec la fertilité de la terre. Il s'agit évidemment, lorsqu'on se réfère à l'Hispania, et spécialement à la zone qu'on vient de mentionner plus haut, d'un thème polémique qui a opposé de nombreux érudits. Nous faisons allusion au culte d'*Ataecina-Ataegina-Adaegina*, de caractère manifestement infernal, comme nous l'indiquent les inscriptions, surtout une *devotio* de Mérida (*CIL* II, 462). S. Lambrino proposa un couple infernal *Ataecina-Endovelicus* qu'il n'y a pas lieu de développer ici.[15]

Quoi qu'il en soit, il devient évident qu'on ne peut pas s'incliner pour le versant infernal de la divinité parce que cela impliquerait qu'on ignore l'étude comparative des religions et l'aspect de fécondité que comporte une divinité des entrailles de la terre: son *interpretatio* romaine sous la forme de Proserpine en est un signe bien évident comme le sont certains symboles - tel le cyprès - fermement liés à cette déesse.

Quand l'on arriverait à verifier la réalité de certaines formes rituelles préromaines d'inhumation de nouveaux-nés dans des enceintes urbaines, nous serions devant une puissance supérieure à celle qu'on attenderait des cultes de fertilité liés à la terre. Mais dans ce domaine il faut tenir compte du problème de la stratigraphie et des nécropoles amorties qui ont déjà fait problème par exemple dans le cas de la culture de l'Argar.

Liées aussi à cette double caractéristique de l'infernal et de la fertilité il pourrait y avoir d'autres divinités autochtones féminines documentées à l'époque romaine mais la mention purement épigraphique les soutient dans une ambiguité dont même les études d'ensemble n'ont pas réussi à les liberer. Ce serait le cas par exemple de plusieurs formes de *Verora* dont le caractère masculin-féminin n'est pas encore éclairci, et dont le nom reçoit différentes graphies qui ne peuvent révêtir des divinités d'advocation distincte mais qui présentent en même temps la formule *ex uisu* déjà cité.[16]

Le chemin est, donc, difficile qui nous permettrait de relier ce type de divinités avec une iconographie concrète, comme c'est le cas de *Bandua* qui réunit probablement les qualités de *Tyche-Fortuna* et de *Tutela.*[17]

Quelques représentations de *Tellus* et de *Salus* pourraient, peut-être, abriter des cultes préexistents, bien que leur parution revête, malgré leur localisme, des formes absolument romaines, comme celles qui vont dès la *Salus Umeritana* de Santander à la *Salus Augusta.*[18]

D'autre part, puisqu'on a fait allusion au manque d'iconographie, on peut poser d'une manière semblable mais à l'inverse la même question car dans le monde ibèrique du Levant (Sagonte) et du Sud-Est nous avons la représentation d'une divinité masculine parmi les chevaux, un *despotes hippon* de nom inconnu que J.M. Blázquez interprète comme "una parodia de la diosa de la fecundidad venerada por los iberos en el levante ibérico".[19] Des invocations à la déesse Epone apparaissent seulement dans la zone celtique de la Péninsule Ibèrique en Castille et en Alave très précisément.[20]

Pour ce qui concerne la distribution des cultes orientaux en *Hispania* nous avons toujours l'étude globale d'A. García y Bellido publié à Leyden le 1967, mais il faut tenir compte des multiples trouvailles de ces dernières années : la côte de la Tarraconaise, par exemple (qui correspond plus ou moins à la zone catalane actuelle) après avoir longtemps été un vide sur les cartes de distribution d'A. García y Bellido, en constitue aujourd'hui l'un des points les plus intéressantes; en 1979 J.M. Bendala mit en évidence les nombreuses nouveautés, mais sans prétendre en faire un inventaire exhaustif.[21]

Dans la domaine que nous analysons, il y a lieu de mettre l'accent sur les cultes de *Cybèle-Magna-Mater, Dea Caelestis* et sur certains aspects du culte d'Isis.

Les témoignages qui font référence à Cybèle sont concentrès dans l'occident péninsulaire quoiqu'on dècouvre de nouvelles données dans les zones côtières de la Méditerranée, comme par exemple la Cybèle du

Musée de Reus qui est pour le moment parmi les meilleures représentations iconographiques[22] de la divinité la mieux connue dans notre pays grâce aux textes épigraphiques[23]; il faut dire toutefois que les représentations de Cybèle semblent plutôt correspondre à des cercles privés.[24]

D'autre part les représentations de Cybèle dans des mosaïques du thème de jeux de cirque, également de caractère domestique, ne peuvent pas être considérées comme un document sur la diffusion de son culte car elles obéissent à des oeuvres de répertoire, tardives qui plus est, mais elles impliquent à l'évidence une familiarité avec l'image de la divinité.[25]

Le culte de Cybèle en *Hispania* ne se trouve en relation avec celui d'Attis que de manière occasionelle, celui-ci étant représenté couramment dans les régions méditerranéennes dans des monuments funéraires mais seulement comme symbole de la continuité de la vie après la mort.[26]

La répartition plutôt occidentale de Cybèle peut surprendre en première instance mais il faut tenir compte, en outre des prècisions d'A. García y Bellido et d'A. Bendala, que — comme on l'a déjà signalé — les plus anciennes manifestations de sculptures de divinités féminines de fécondité se trouvent localisées dans le S.O. de la Péninsule Ibérique et non pas dans le littoral méditerranéen.

Il faut aussi rappeler le fort impact de la déesse Tanit dans le Sud qui présente une série de plateformes pour la superposition des cultes de la *Dea Caelestis* et à un niveau supérieur d'*interpretatio* de celui de *Iuno* — encore que, dans ce cas, il y a lieu de considérer avec prudence et réserve les hypothèses d'A. García y Bellido parmi lesquelles une des plus suggestives est sans doute celle d'un culte à *Iuno* et Hercule à Grenade qui cacherait peut-être Tanit et Melkart.[27]

Caelestis, enracinée surtout dans la Bétique, presente en *Hispania* des caractéristiques liées à des cultes officiels sous le qualificatif d'Auguste, en relation dans le cas d'*Italica* avec les *uestigia*,[28] ce qui semble éloigner la configuration de la déesse de leurs attributs originaires relatifs aux cultes de la fertilité dans son acception orientale.

Il ne faut pas oublier non plus la séquence *Tanit-Caelestis-Demeter-Diana* qui s'infléchit tout naturellement sur la tradition antérieure, comme on peut le voire très clairement dans l'île d'Ibisse[29] et dont la représentation d'une stèle de Tajo Montero, comme le veut

García y Bellido,[30] pourrait en être une des preuves. Une évidence pareille et très répandue serait les *tymatheria* de terre cuite qui représentent tantôt Tanit, tantôt Demeter, l'un des véhicules les plus communs de popularisation de ce taffetas.[31]

Dans le cas d'Isis-Hathor, le culte féminin le plus répandu dans la Péninsule Ibérique, présente, comme cela est bien connu, malgré son caractère soteriologique, un symbolisme qui ne peut pas être séparé du culte de la fertilité. Cela apparaît d'une manière évidente dans certaines epithètes du fait de leur acceptation parmi les femmes et de leur assimilation à Astarté.[32] Sa valeur comme symbole lunaire la rapproche par ailleurs à *Demeter* et, par conséquent, à Diane.

La distribution géographique du culte à Isis est essentiellement différente de celle de Cybèle; dans la cas d'Isis, semble-t-il, l'armée n'a pas joué un rôle très important comme elle l'a joué dans le cas de Cybèle, et de plus ses témoignages se répandent à la péripherie péninsulaire, formant un cercle qui entoure la Mesète.[33] La date de l'introduction du culte d'Isis est aujourd'hui contestée, mais bien que les témoignages soient surtout romains, il est fort probable la connaissance d'Isis dans la Péninsule dès l'époque des colonisations historiques.[34]

Le problème de l'Artemis éphésienne est une question très débattue et qui reste toujours obscure. Les sources littéraires semblent remarquer que le culte d'Artemis accompagna la colonisation phocéenne qui, dès *Massalia*, irradia vers la côte nord-orientale d'*Hispania*. En fait nous pouvons remarquer la totale absence de témoignages épigraphiques ou iconographiques fait que l'on doit ajouter à leur prèsence ou non dans les monnaies emporitanes.[35]

C'est un fait acquis que, dans les zones de colonisation grecque et également dans les autres, les cultes d'époque romaine postérieurs à Diane ne semblent pas se rattacher à des cultes antérieurs d'ascendence hellénique: rien ne semble indiquer une quelconque distinction par rapport à sa présence dans d'autres zones de l'Empire.

On ne peut tirer aussi que de maigres conséquences de la présence des divinités du sanctuaire d'Eleusis dans sa version romaine. Ceres est très rarement présente et la documentation épigraphique nous l'offre sous une forme absolument officielle avec l'advocation d'Auguste, comme par exemple dans une inscription de Munigua, hommage d'une flaminique.[36] Proserpine, à son tour, garde son caractère infernal — on doit penser au discours sur *Ataecina* — mais malgré tout un certain caractère salutifer n'est pas absent.[37]

Une divinité dont le caractère est susceptible de prendre aussi des formes diverses est *Hecate*. Nous avons un ex-voto de Toledo conservé à Madrid qui represente la divinité avec ses mains aux seins comme symbole de fécondité.[38]

En dernier lieu il faut mentionner le problème des *Matres* que l'on peut envisager sous deux aspects, en les considérant comme un culte autochtone implanté dans les régions les plus celtisées; soit comme un culte importé et tout de suite enraciné qui aurait pris d'épithètes hispaniques. La position la plus claire serait d'accepter la première hypothèse sans écarter le renforcement de ce culte par l'influence des *Matres* germaniques, culte transferé par les militaires dans leurs déplacements: la présence des *Matres Aufaniae* en *Germania* et en *Hispania* peut-être symptomatique dans ce cas.[39] Une fois de plus il est nécessaire de mettre en évidence l'importance, quand il s'agit de témoignages épigraphiques, de l'analyse de l'origine sociale des individus qui rendent tel ou tel culte, avant de commencer à parler d'une géneralisation géographique.

On pourrait alléguer en faveur d'une origine étrangère du culte aux *Matres* sa dispersion dans la moitié occidentale de la Péninsule (Bétique, Galice et Mesète nord spécialement); il coïnciderait donc avec la répartition de Cybèle, culte — comme on l'a déjà dit — répandu sûrement à travers les milieux militaires. De toute façon cela n'empêche pas que parallèlement à son importation, il se serait produit un renforcement d'un culte préexistent.

Pour finir, tout en étant conscients de la précarieté des documents dont nous disposons dans la Péninsule Ibèrique et des risques que l'on encourt à aventurer un panorama global d'après des éléments dispersés, nous croyons qu'il nous est possible d'esquisser une structure qui, plutôt que de réfléchir archétypes, prétende être flexible et mettre en relief les lignes d'ores et déjà aprèciables, tout en permettant de préciser par étapes successives les critères de pertinence qui s'appuient sur des études sociologiques. Ce faisant il serait possible d'ébaucher une vue d'ensemble en fonction des nouveaux témoignages archéologiques et épigraphiques.

Dans l'état actuel, on constate la cohérence du panorama des divinités féminines de la fécondité comme divinités derivées de celles de la Méditerranée orientale avec des éléments anatoliens qui réussirent — il ne faut pas l'oublier — à avoir un grand écho dans l'aire méridionale et sud-occidentale. Ce fait constitue un premier substrat sur lequel les colonisations historiques apporteront de nouveaux cultes de la même origine qui semblent s'imposer sans peine sur ceux qui préexistaient comme s'ils les continuaient. Les cultes de Tanit et d'Astarté dont il y a dans le monde ibérique plusieurs versions iconographiques, illustrent bien, à notre avis, ce procès d'implantation.

Il y a lieu de remarquer enfin la faible vitalité, même dans des zones ayant une plus forte présence hellénique, d'un quelconque type de culte qui ne soit prècisément l'adaption grecque de ces cultes orientaux; rappelons à ce sujet le problème de l'Artemis éphésienne connue seulement grâce à des références littéraires.

L'*interpretatio* romaine ne fit que précipiter le syncretisme qui c'etait déjà produit antérieurement. L'introduction du panthéon romain avec ses propres divinités de la fertilité et de la fécondité, trouva une ambiance propice et qui n'etait pas étrangère. Il va de soit que les abstractions divinisées de ce caractère ne furent moins afavories et son utilisation politique en bénéficia tout en arrivant à une espèce de *koiné* cultuelle de laquelle n'émergent qu'occasionellement les divinités orientales où de divinités dans sa forme simple. L'accumulation syncrétique des noms et d'epithètes constituera le véhicule habituel pour ces idées de la fertilité.

Notes

1 L'art meuble du Nord de la Péninsule préfera toujours les techniques de la gravure et de la peinture à celle de la sculpture; il y a en plus une faible présence des antropomorphes. Voir. E. Jordà, Arte de la Edad de la Piedra, *Historia del Arte Hispánico, I, 1. La Antigüedad,* Madrid 1978, pp. 38 et 45.

2 M.J. Almagro Gorbea, *Los ídolos del Bronce I hispano* (Bibliotheca Praehistorica Hispana, XII), Madrid 1973; F. Jordà, *op. cit.*, pp. 117.121.

3 J.M. Blázquez, *Diccionario de las Religiones Prerromanas de Hispania*, Madrid 1975, pp. 30-32.

4 F. Jordà, Les representaciones de danzas en el arte levantino, *III Congreso Nacional de Arqueologia,* Porto 1974, pp. 43-52; F. Jordà, *op. cit.*, pp. 142-143; M. Almagro, *El covacho con pinturas rupestres de Cogul (Lérida),* Lérida 1952.

5 Cf. M.J. Pena, Artemis-Diana y algunas cuestiones en relación con su iconografia y culto en Occidente. El problema de la Artemis ampuritana, *Ampurias* XXXV, 1973, pp. 121-134; *id.*, Contribución al estudio del culto de Diana en Hispania I. Templos y fuentes epigráficas, *La Religión Romana en Hispania*, Madrid 1981, pp. 47-57. Pour un panorama plus complet, A. García y Bellido, *Les religions orientales dans l'Espagne romaine*, Leiden 1967 (Etd. Prel.s aux Rels. Orientales dans l'Empire romain, t. 5), pp. 18-20. Sur l'important santuaire de *Segobriga*, voir maintenant G. Alföldy, Epigraphica Hispanica VI. Das Diana-Heiligtum von Segobriga, *ZPE* 58, 1985, pp. 139-159, pl. VII-X. Pour un panorama général voir J.M. Blázquez, Aportaciones al estudio de las religiones primitivas de Hispania, *Archivo Español de Arqueología*, XXX, 1957, pp. 15-86.

6 J.M. Blázquez, *Diccionario...*, p. 32 avec bibliographie. Sur l'influence de l'image d'Astarté dans la Péninsule voir aussi pp. 30-39. Il faut tenir compte qu'on a trouvé en *Hispania* des têtes de Venus gravées sur des images d'Astarté (J.M. Blázquez, *Aportaciones...*, pp. 23-24).

7 Cf. G. Fabre - M. Mayer - I. Rodà, *Inscriptions romaines de Catalogne I. Barcelone* (*sauf Barcino*) Paris, 1984 (=*IRC*I), pp. 93-94; *eid.*, dans *Fonaments,* 5, 1985, pp. 181-182 pour *Seitundus.* Sur les sources littéraires, v. J.M. Blázquez, El sincretismo en la Hispania romana entre las religiones indígenas, griega, romana, fenicia y mistéricas, *La Religión romana...*, pp. 192-200.

8 Voir A. García y Bellido, *Les religions orientales...*, pp. 140-141. Sur la présence à Fontes (Portugal) de la déesse grecque *Auge*, déesse de la chaleur et de la fécondité, cf. J.M. Blázquez, *Diccionario...*, p. 42 avec bibliographie. Sur les sculptures de Tajo Montero, cf. maintenant M. Blech, Esculturas de Tajo Montero (Estepa). Una interpretación iconografica, *La Religión romana...*, pp. 99-109 où l'on met en rélief les survivances puniques.

9 G. Dumézil, préface dans M. Eliade, *Traité d'histoire des religions,* Paris 1970 (nouv. éd. rev), pp. 5-9; voir pour la théorie de M. Eliade especiallement, chap. IV-V, pp. 139-187, VII, pp. 208-309, et XI-XII, pp. 326-366.

10 F. Cumont, *Recherches sur le symbolisme funéraire des romains*, Paris 1969 (nouv. éd.), pp. 293-9, et 234-9; J. Taboada, O Culto da Lua no Noroeste Hispanico, *Revista de Guimarâes,* 71, 1961, pp. 140 ss.; J. M. Blázquez, *El sincretismo...*, p. 200.

11 Cf. J.A. Abásolo, *Epigrafía romana de la región de Lara de los Infantes,* Burgos 1974; J.A. Abásolo - M.L. Albertos - J.C. Elorza, *Los monumentos funerarios de época romana, en forma de casas, de la región de Poza de la Sal (Bureba, Burgos),* Burgos 1975.

Cf. *IRC* I, 33-38, pp. 76-84 et en plus *CIL* II, 6181. Pour une synthèse des divinités des eaux, voir J.M. Blázquez, *Imagen y mito, Estudios sobre religiones mediterráneas e ibéricas,* Madrid 1977, pp. 307 ss.; *id.*, *El sincretismo...*, pp. 200-201; *id.*, Le culte des eaux dans la Péninsule Ibérique, *Ogam*, 11, 1957, pp. 11 ss. Sur le nymphée de Santa Eulalia de Bóveda, voir M. Chamoso, Sobre el origen del monumento soterrado de Santa Eulalia de Bóveda (Lugo), *Cuadernos de Estudios Gallegos,* 7, 1952, pp. 231 ss., et plus recemment, L. Abad, Aportaciones al estudio de Santa Eulalia de Bóveda, *XV Congreso Nacional de Arqueologia, (Lugo, 1977),* Saragosse 1979, pp. 917 ss.

13 Pour les *Nymphae Caparenses,* cf. J.M. Blazquez, *Religiones primitivas de Hispania,* I, Madrid 1962, p. 199; *id.*, *Caparra*, Madrid 1966, pl. XXVII, 2-3; *id.*, *Diccionario...*, p. 52; J.M. Roldán, Las lápidas votivas de Baños de Montemayor, *Zephyrus,* 16, 1965, pp. 23 ss.

14 J.M. Blazquez, *Religiones...*, p. 175; *id.*, *Diccionario...*, p. 28.

15 S. Lambrino, Les cultes indigènes en Espagne sous Trajan et Hadrien, *Les Empereurs romains d'Espagne (Madrid-Itálica 1964)*, Paris 1965, pp. 225-239, et surtout, Le dieu lusitanien Endovellicus, *Bulletin d'Etudes Portugaises*, XV, 1951, pp. 93-147. Voir aussi, J.M. Blázquez, *Religiones...*, pp. 141 ss; *id.*, *Diccionario...*, pp. 39-42; H. Balmori, Por los confines de Occidente, *Emerita*, 33, 1965, pp. 253 ss., J. D'Encarnaçao, *Divinidades indigenas sob o dominio romano em Portugal*, Lisbonne 1975, pp. 110-117 et 181-185.

16 Cf. F. Arias Vilas - P. Le Roux - A. Tranoy, *Inscriptions romaines de la province de Lugo*, Paris 1979, 11-14, pp. 38-40.

17 Cf. J.M. Blázquez, *Diccionario...*, pp. 45-47 et planche p. 44; *id.*, *El sincretismo...*, pp. 201-202; J. D'Encarnaçao, Banda, uma importante divindade indigena, *Conimbriga*, 12, 1973, pp. 209 ss.

18 Cf. A. García y Bellido, *Esculturas romanas de España y Portugal*, Madrid 1949, pp. 467-470. Pour les exemples épigraphiques, cf. J. Vives, *Inscripciones latinas de la España romana*, Barcelona 1971 (=*ILER*), nos. 468-480 et 699. Voir en plus J.M. Blázquez, *Diccionario...*, p. 146.

19 J.M. Blázquez, *Diccionario...*, p. 80 (cf. p. 81).

20 J.M. Blázquez, *Diccionario...*, p. 95.

21 M. Bendala, La religiones mistéricas en la España romana, *La religión romana...* pp. 285-299. Cf. en plus *IRC I*, nos. 36, et 85-86, pp. 80-82, 129-132, et aussi p. 81 note 40.

22 Cf. A. Blanco Freijeiro, Documentos metróacos de Hispania, *Archivo Español de Arqueología*, 41, 1968, pp. 91-100; M. Bendala, *Las religiones mistéricas...*, pp. 287-290. Sur la Cybèle de Reus, très important car il s'agit d'un témoignage près de la côte méditerranéenne, voir G. Munilla, Una estatua repsesentando a la diosa Cibeles hallada en la villa romana de "Els Antigons", *Pyrenae* 15-16, 1979-80, pp. 277-286, et aussi sa Tesis de Licenciatura, inèdite et deposée à l'Université de Barcelone, 1981: *El culto a Cibeles y Atis en la provincia romana de la Tarraconense*.

23 *ILER*, 373-382 et A. Blanco Freijerio *Documentos...*.

24 Voir en plus des travaux cités dans les notes précedentes, E. Sanmartí, Dos asas con representación metróaca del Museo Arqueológico de Barcelona, *Ampurias*, 31-32, 1969-1970, pp. 285-289 où l'auteur publie les anses de Segisamon. Au Musée Archéologique de Barcelone on conserve un naiskos avec l'iconographie traditionelle de la déesse, de provenance inconnue (voir une photo dans *Pere Bosch Gimpera* i el Museu Arqueologic de Barcelona. 50 Aniversari, Barcelone 1986, p. 72). Finalement, J. Alvar, Un posible testimonio de culto a Cibeles en Cascais (Portugal) *Archivo Español de Arqueología*, 56, 1983, pp. 123-130.

25 Voir I. Rodà, Las dedicatorias a divinidades en la Barcelona romana, *La religión romana...*, p. 130, esp. bibliographie citée dans la note 46 dont on peut signaler, A. García y Bellido, *Les religions orientales...*, p. 147; J. Vermaseren, *Corpus Cultus Cybelae Attidisque (CCCA)* III, Leiden 1977, p. 40; A. Balil, Mosaicos circenses de Barcelona y Gerona, *Boletin de la Real Academia de la Historia* CLI, 1962, pp. 275-276; X. Barral, Unes pintures murales inèdites imel mosaic amb curses de circ de Barcelona, *Cuadernos de Arqueología e Historia de la Ciudad*, XV, 1973, pp. 33-34; *id.*, *Les mosaïques romaines et médievales de la Regio Laietana*, Barcelone 1978, pp. 32-33.

26 Cf. A. García y Bellido *Les religions orientales...*, pp. 56-63; aux représentations mentionnées dans ce travail, on pourrait ajouter par exemple l'Attis funéraire de la muraille de *Barcino* A. Balil, *Esculturas romanas de la Península Ibérica II* (Studia Archaeologica, 54), Valladolid 1979 (extrait de *BSAA*), no. 33, pp. 18-19, et *id.*, *Esculturas romanas de la Península Ibérica* (Studia Archaeologica 73) Valladolid 1983, nos. 122-130, pp. 26-29). Voir en plus la bibliographie qu'on a cité dans la note 22.

27 A. García y Bellido, *Les religions orientales...*, pp. 1-17.

28 A. García y Bellido, *Les religions orientales...*, pp. 140-151, esp. pp. 142-145, et aussi, C. Fernández Chicarro - F. Fernández, *Catálogo del Museo Arqueológico de Sevilla*, (II), Madrid 1980, (3ème ed.), pp. 76-79.

29 M. Tarradell - M. Font de Tarradell, *Eivissa cartaginesa*, Barcelone 1965. Sur les terrecuites, cf. M.E. Aubet, *El santuario de Es Cuiram*, (Trabajos del Museo Arqueológico de Ibiza), Ibisse 1982; M.P. San Nicolas Pedraz, *Las terracotas figuradas de la Ibiza púnica*, Thèse inèdite, Université Autonome de Barcelone, 1981; *id.*, Notas sobre la tipologia del santuario de Es Cuieram (Ibiza), *Archivo Español de Arqueología*, 56, 1983, pp. 239-241; *id.*, Testimonio

de culto a Demeter-Persephone en Ibiza, *ibidem*, 54, 1981, pp. 27-33 où l'on essaye de distinguer les cultes de Demeter et de Tanit; A.García y Bellido *Hispania Graeca*, t. II, Barcelona 1948, pp. 198-205; M. Bendala, *Las religiones mistéricas*... p. 290.

[30] Pour Tajo Montero voir note 8; A. García y Bellido, *Les religions orientales*..., pp. 146-157.

[31] Voir principalement les travaux de M. Bendala et M.P. San Nicolas Pedraz cités dans la note 29.

[32] Pour les dérivations du caractère primitif d'Astarté comme divinité féconde et créatrice, voir principalement, A. García y Bellido, *Les religions orientales*... pp. 12-13, et J.M. Blázquez, *Diccionario*..., pp. 30-39.

[33] A. García y Bellido, *Les religions orientales*...., pp. 105-124 et 166; J. Alvar, El culto a Isis en Hispania, *La religión romana*..., pp. 311-319. Voir note suivante.

[34] J. Alvar, *El culto a Isis*..., p. 311 dit ouvertement qu'il y a exclusivement des documents d'époque romaine. J. Padró, Las divinidades egipcies en la Hispania romana y sus precedentes, *La religión romana*....pp. 337 ss., pense que la pénetration du culte d'Isis est bien antérieur d'après le vase de l'Aliseda; voir aussi ce dernier travail (pp. 342-343) pour la séquence Isis-Hathor-Astarté. Au Musée de Barcelone il y a d'autre part une petite statuette de bronze répresentant Isis-Fortuna (cf. J. Padró - E. Sanmartí, Monuments relatifs aux cultes égyptiens à l'époque romaine du Musée Archéologique de Barcelone, *Hommages à Maarten J. Vermaseren* t. II, Leiden 1978, no. 4, pp. 917-918.

[35] Aux travaux cités dans la note 5 on pourrait ajouter qu'il y a le témoignage à Portugal, provenant de Beringel mais convervée au Musée de Beja, d'une sculpture fragmentaire de l'Aphrodite d'Aphrodisias, divinité pareille de fécondité de celle de l'Artemis éphesienne. Voir A. García y Bellido, El culto a Aphrodite de Aphrodisias en la Península Ibérica, *Archivo de Prehistoria Levantina* IV, 1953, pp. 219-222 qui l'avait publiée avec antériorité comme "tronco de una Artemis ephesia" (*id., Esculturas romanas*..., no. 160, pp. 150-151, pl. 121).

[36] Cf. *ILER*, 327. Pour la statue du théatre de Mérida, A. García y Bellido, *Esculturas romanas*..., no. 164, pp. 153-154, pl. 124, qu'on a trouvé avec une statue de Pluton et de Proserpine (*ibid.*, pp. 154-155).

[37] À Mérida comme Proserpina, *CIL*, II 462. Cf. en plus J.M. Blázquez, *El sincretismo*..., pp. 199-200; *id., Diccionario*..., pp. 39-42; J. D'Encarnaçao, *Divindades indigenas*..., pp. 110-117 qui pense avec reserve à son caractère agraire et médicale. Voir aussi A. García y Bellido, *Esculturas romanas*, p. 156.

[38] A. García y Bellido, Parerga de arqueología y epigrafía hispano-romanas II. Exvoto a Hecate, *Archivo Español de Arqueología* 26, 1963, pp. 196-197. La pièce est conversée au Musée de l'Armée de Madrid.

[39] C. Fernández Chicarro, Altar der *Matres Aufaniae* aus Carmona. Spanien, *Epigraphische Studien* V, Düsseldorf 1968-1969, pp. 149-150. Cf. J.M. Blázquez, *Diccionario*..., p. 42 et p. 124 pour les *Matres* indigènes.

THE REPRESENTATION OF THE SERPENT IN ANCIENT IBERIA

Margarita Bru Romo — Ana Vazquez-Hoys

In Ancient Iberia, the use of the serpent as a symbol began before the settlements of the Phoenicians, Greeks and Carthaginians and before the first waves of the Indoeuropean peoples. There is no doubt that it had the same sacred character as it did in most ancient cultures. We intend to give a summary of these representations from this early age to the Roman Period.

As we said, we find a cult to the serpent in Iberian Prehistory and Protohistory. Serpentine lines similar to those found in megalithic dolmens of Bretagne and Ireland appear in Spain and Portugal (Shee 1974: 105-123), but the representation of the snake is clearer from the Final Bronze Age onwards.

At that time two parallel events took place in Iberia: the coming of Indoeuropean Cultures from Europe and the first contacts with historic peoples from the Eastern Mediterranean. Both events, together with the peninsular substratum, generated a number of cultures in which either Celtic or oriental elements predominated. The Celtic influence can be seen especially in the North West. The oriental one produced Tartessic culture and Iberian Art, the first in Western and the second in Eastern Andalucia and along the Eastern Coast (Almagro Bachs — Almagro Gorbea 1976: 177). Anyhow, in all these cultures the serpent is present, either as a symbol of Life and Fertility or of Death and Immortality.

First, we shall draw attention to some pieces coming from the North West of Spain. In the Citania of Troia (Pericot 1953: 3) there is a serpent engraved on a previously levelled face of a rock. This serpent allows López Cuevillas (López Cuevillas - Bouza Brey 1920: 168) to affirm, on commenting Avienos' *Ora Maritima,* that there was a similarity between Celtic beliefs and those of an earlier, probably autochthonous people.

The ex-voto from Castelo de Moreira (Galicia) represents a sacrificial scene: a pig, a goat and two sheep walking on a line formed by four twisted bronze strings. On the reverse there is a basket or vase, a human torso and the front part of a serpent which can be either an apotropaic element or the Divinity to whom the sacrifice is dedicated

(López Cuevillas 1958: 160). Another ex-voto similar in shape in the National Archaeological Museum presents the snake in relation to the bull.

A bronze serpent with a triangular head and well defined eyes and mouth has been found at "El Palao" (Teruel). It can also be an ex-voto coming from a nearby sanctuary. Some stelae were also found; they are framed with serpentine lines similar to those in megalithic tombs. Some of these lines are more like floral stylizations but some of the decorative elements of the stelae (such as the hand, the animals and the rider's spear) are in an inverted position. This seems to point to some kind of magic ritual a part of which would be the serpent.

Serpents represented by broken lines like those mentioned above, also appear in some other stelae from Navarra and Burgos (Marco 1976: 76; 1978: 44; 1980: 149). In others the serpent frames a round graphic campus, now and then becoming a floral stylization or a twisted cord which ends in horses' heads. Nevertheless, it is evident that the element is the same.

The serpent represented as a vegetal stylization can be seen as well in the cup from Tivissa (Raddatz 1969: 90). According to some interpretations (Neumann 1955: 39) this time it might be a masculine sexual symbol.

The symbol of the serpent in the Phoenician world and its relationship with fertility and survival is obvious. In Ancient Iberia we find metal jars — Niebla, Siruela, Metropolitan Museum, Lazaro Galdeano's Museum, Villanueva de la Vera, La Joya, etc — of Phoenician type also decorated with serpents. J.M. Blázquez and J.P. Garrido believe that these jars come from Spanish workshops having strong Phoenician influence (Garrido Roig 1970).

Among Tartessian jewellery, most remarkable is a golden necklace with two pendants in the shape of a snake's head. The necklace comes from the tomb of a woman and belongs to the Aliseda treasure. The decoration is quite oriental but no exact parallel is known (Blanco Frejeiro 1956: 3). Two other pendants are spheres which may represent pomegranates; these together with the serpent's head would point to fertility symbolism.

The belt buckles of the so-called "Celtic belts", because some were found on sites of Celtiberian influence, have an oriental origin. The plaques of the belts have stylized feminine forms similar to megalithic idols; they hook into metallic serpentine terminals or into others truly like serpents, with clearly defined heads and tails (Pl. 37). The union of both elements, woman or goddess and snake, is an obvious reference to fertility. The pieces from La Joya (Huelva), Cerro de Huerta Ripoll (Córdoba), and Acebuchal (Sevilla) are well known items (Morán Cabré 1973: 597; 1977: 611).

Torques and bracelets with snake-like terminals are common not only in the Mediterranean but also in central Europe. Among the first we should remember the necklace from Chao de Lamas, in Portugal. Raddatz relates two bracelets from Villanueva de Córdoba (Jaén) with others found in South Germany and Italy, dated in an advanced La Téne Period. Bracelets and necklaces with snake-like terminals might be just a fashion in Mediterranean cultures.

We have already met snakes related to the bull-cult. At Reillo (Cuenca) it appears related to the ram (Maderuelo - Pastor 1981: 161-183). There is an andiron in the shape of a ram with four snakes on its back which, along with some pottery also with serpentine decoration, might point towards a fertility cult among cattle-breeding people at this site.

In some ceramic pieces of the Iberian culture the snake can be seen in association with the Tree of Life, the deer (instead of the Mesopotamian goat), the frog, fish or with astral symbols. In Azaila (Teruel) it appears near a very stylized Tree of Life running after a frog (Pl. 38). Nearby another frog is eating a snake. It should be noticed that both are aquatic creatures (Lucas 1979: 241).

At the Museum of Jaen there are two anthropomorphic figures with snakes on their backs which lean their heads on the figures' chest. Another one has a serpent along its left arm which is not visible when the figure is seen from the front (Ruano 1983: 54). The famous Iberian sanctuaries of Despeñaperros are near the area in which the statuettes have been found. There also are plenty of thermal springs, so the figures might be easily related either to fertility or health, or might belong to a funeral monument (Blázquez 1983: 426) similar to that of Pozo Moro. At Pozo Moro we also find the serpent, this time forming the end of the tail of a chimaera (Almagro Gorbea 1975: 671).

In Ancient Iberia, the representation of the serpent is rare in works connected with the Greek world. Apart from the Asklepios in the Archaeological Museum of Barcelona and the ex-voto from Mallorca (Garcia Bellido 1948: 127-130) there is little to be mentioned.

In connection with the Roman world the serpent appears in objects of a very different type. There is, of course, the traditional

Esculapius' serpent; we have some *arae* dedicated to him. In the small votive *arae* found in Italica (Martínez Munilla 1950: 208), now in the Museum of Seville, Esculapius' serpent appears together with a pine-cone, another of his attributes; there are two other *arae* in Barcelona, a beautiful one coming from Carthago-Nova(Beltrán 1947: 213) and the painted *ara* from Ampurias (Nieto Prieto 1971: 385). There is also the traditional Mithras' serpent: we should mention the two pieces in the Mithraeum of Merida, the Aion and the beautiful figure which has been recently identified as *Mithra saxigenus* (Bendala Galán 1979: 285). There are some golden rings, two in the Museum of Córdoba and one in the Museum of Huelva. The serpent also accompanies the headless Minerva and the beautiful *pondus* of the National Archaeological Museum. Obviously, it also appears in Mercury's *caduceus* (García Bellido 1949: 137, 180 and 452).

In other pieces the meaning of the serpent is not so clear. In the *ara* of Altea it is shown together with a pigeon and a pomegranate (Pl. 39) (Fita 1908: 375); in a piece of entablature it can be seen pursuing a frog as it does in the ceramics from Azaila already mentioned; as the symbol of Tellus, the fertile Earth, the serpent appears in the *trulla* of Castulo (Blanco Frejeiro 1961: 93); the feminine figure of the so-called *Casa de Pilatos* in Seville may represent Hygias though it seems to have been very badly restored; in the Voconios' stela from Mérida the two serpents may allude to the bracelets given as rewards to soldiers Bendala Galán 1972: 240). The bracelets might also have an apotropaic quality suggested by their serpent-like shape.

The last piece we would like to mention comes from the Roman city of Ercavica and it is in the Museum of Cuenca. It is a headless torso with a small serpent advancing along the body and a bigger serpent which seems to hang around the neck with its head and tail on the torso's back. It is known as the *Aion* of Ercavica but it is evident that the figure has two serpents and their position is peculiar enough to question such identification.

It seems that the most popular divinities in Ancient Iberia during the Roman period were those related to Fertility cults. Judging by the remains (inscriptions, coins, monuments), Diana and Venus were especially venerated in the East part of the Peninsula, while other deities were worshipped in the rest of the country. Some gravestones dedicated to Venus have been found in the Mediterranean coast; in these, Venus might be identified either with a chthonic aspect of the goddess or with some other goddess such as Demeter, Tanit, etc (Vázquez Hoys 1983: 311).

The already mentioned *ara* of Altea shows a pigeon, a serpent and a pomegranate in its decoration. This seems to point to an identification between funeral and fertility deities. Fita assumes that the pigeon — *Columba* — is the name of the dead woman; we suggest that its association with the serpent and the pomegranate rather points to a chthonic-fertility goddess. On the other hand the cult of Adonis and that of the Magna Mater continue in Sevilla up to the 3rd century and the cult of Hercules in Cádiz up to the 4th.

This might lead one to think that in Ancient Iberia pre-Roman people remained rather resilient to Roman cults. Because of their being so deeply rooted in the Punic and oriental worlds they seem to have a preference for those deities who could incarnate, above all, the old oriental goddesses.

It is evident that the serpent as a symbol has been used by cultures all over the world. Its persistence throughout the ages is impressive.

In Mesopotamia and in pre-Arian India, even in the magnificent bowls from Susa of the Vth millennium, the snake appears related to Water as a source of Life and Fertility. It also appears related to Death as part of the vital cycle of reproduction. Later on its symbolism becomes more complex and the snake can be found as guardian of the Dead, of Homes and of treasures. Nilsson (Nilsson 1941: 184) contemplates the possibility of its identification with the dead person turned into a hero. What is its meaning when it appears coiled around the Tree of Life advancing its head towards the Thracian horseman? In the Roman period according to Plinius, Ovidius and Elienus the spine of the dead person changed into a snake. Besides its funeral character the snake appears as founder of cities and begetter of heroes (Cumont 1949: 17). The serpent also has guessing and healing powers (Dumezil 1966: 496). It appears also with Mithra, as symbol of the generative power of Earth.

If we compare different proverbs, legends and tales, we can see that serpents appear either as kind and propitious animals, fiercely loyal to their masters, or as carriers of sorrow and death. Aristoteles (Bodson 1978: 78) in his *History of Animals* proposes to classify them by the different types of their psychology. According to him, the serpent seems to be a repulsive, evil and terrible creature. Moreover, not only in Greece but in most other countries people have always had ambivalent and contradictory experiences with snakes. This characteristic ambiguity has precisely been the one that has made possible the identification of the serpent with the *numinous* and the *sacred* since ancient times: as gods they inspire awe and can also be good and propitious; as gods serpents eat honey because of its youth-restoring qualities; serpents as gods have an aura of immortality (Vázquez Hoys 1981: 33).

The exact meaning of every single representation of the serpent in Ancient Iberia is difficult to determine. The meaning might be different or there might not be any meaning at all: the goldsmith or the sculptor may have just intended to copy a motif which was fashionable at the time. Nevertheless if we think that up to a few years ago, in some villages of the North-West of Spain, the skin of a snake was put on the womb of women in labour to propitiate the birth, it seems likely that in spite of its apparent ambivalence and in spite of the cultivated myths of the Classical Era, the serpent has maintained through the centuries its original association with Water and Fertility Goddesses.

Summary

We find a cult to the serpent in Iberian Prehistory and Protohistory. Indoeuropean and Mediterranean cultures adopted this cult which had similarities with the beliefs of an earlier people, probably autochthonous. Different *ex-votos*, Phoenician metal jars, the so-called "Celtic belts", Tartessian jewellery, Iberian pottery, etc., decorated with snakes prove this assertion.

In the Roman period the serpent appears in objects of a very different type and, most times, though it may seem just a fashionable decoration it also has an apotropaic or fertility meaning, as in the case of the *ara* of Altea or Voconio's stela. This meaning is still present in the beliefs of some peasant villages.

Résumé

Il existe un culte au serpent dans la préhistoire et protohistoire de l'ancienne Ibérie. Les cultures indo-européennes et méditerranéennes introduisirent ce culte qui était semblable aux croyances des peuples précédents, probablement autochtones. Il y a de différents *ex-votos*, des brocs phéniciens en métal, les dites "ceintures celtiques", l'orfèvrerie de l'ancienne Tartesse, la céramique Ibère, etc., tous décorés de serpents qui prouvent cette affirmation.

Dans la période romaine, le serpent apparaît sur des pièces d'un type très different et la plupart du temps, même s'il semble être tout simplement une décoration à la mode, il présente aussi un aspect apotropaique ou de fertilité qui apparaît aussi sur l'autel d'Altea et sur la stèle des *Voconios*. Cet aspect est encore présent dans les croyances de quelques peuples de l'Espagne agricole.

Bibliography

ALMAGRO BACHS, M. - ALMAGRO GORBEA, M.

1975 — Pozo Moro y el origen del Arte Ibérico *CAN* XIII, 671.

1976 — Resistencia y asimilación de elementos culturales del Mediterráneo oriental en Iberia prerromana. *Assimilation et résistence à la culture gréco-romaine dans le monde ancien préromain,* Paris.

ALMAGRO GORBEA, M.

1977 — *El Bronce final y el período orientalizante en Extremadura,* Madrid.

BELTRAN, A.

1947 — El ara del Museo de Barcelona y su relación con el culto de la Salud y Esculapio en Cartagonova, *Ampurias* IX-X, 49.

BENDALA GALAN, M.

1972 — Los llamados columbarios de Mérida, *Habis* 3, p. 240 lám 5 fig. 12

1979 — Las religiones mistéricas en la Espana romana, *Symposio sobre la Religión romana en Hispana,* Madrid.

BLANCO FREJEIRO, A.

1956 — Orientalia. Estudio de los objetos fenicios y orientalizantes en la Península, *AEA* XXXIX.

1961 — Un interesante fragmento cerámico del Museo arqueológico de Linares, *Oretania* 8-9.

BLAZQUEZ, J.Ma.

1975 — *Tartessos II,* Universidad de Salamanca.

BODSON, L.

1978 — *Contribution à l'etude de la place de l'animal dans la religion grecque ancienne,* Bruxelles.

CUMONT, F.

1942 — *Recherches sur le symbolisme funéraire des romains,* Paris.

1949 — *Lux Perpetua*, Paris.

DUMEZIL, G.

1966 — *La Religion romaine archaïque,* Paris.

FITA, F.

1908 — El ara de Altea, *BAH* 52.

GARCIA BELLIDO, A.

1948 — *Hispana Graeca II,* Barcelona.

1949 — *Esculturas romanas de Espana y Portugal,* Madrid.

GARRIDO ROIG, J.

1970 — Excavaciones en la Necrópolis de La Joya, *AEA* LXXI.

GOMEZ MORENO, M. - SANCHEZ PIJOAN, J.
1912 — *Materiales de Arqueología espanola*, Madrid.

LOPEZ CUEVILLAS, F. - BOUZA BREY, F.
1920 — Os Oestrimnios, os Saefes e a Ofiolatria en Galiza, *Arquivo de Seminario de Estudos Galegos*, II.

LOPEZ CUEVILLAS, F.
1958 — *La civilización céltica en Galicia,* Santiago de Compostela.

LUCAS, R.
1979 — La decoración figurada en la pintura vascular, *Actas Mesa Redonda sobre la Baja Epoca Ibérica*, Madrid.

MADERUELO, M.
1981 — Excavaciones en Reillo (Cuenca), *NAH* 12.

MARCO, F.
1976 — Nuevas estelas ibéricas en Alcaniz, *Pyrenae* XII, 1976, pp. 76 ss.
1978 — Estelas decoradas de los Conventos Cesaraugustano y Cluniense, *Caesaraugusta* 43-44.
1980 — Excavaciones en "El Palao" (Alcaniz, Teruel), *Caesaraugusta* 51-52.

MARTINEZ MUNILLA, C.
1950 — Sobre un ara de Itálica, *AEA* 23.

MORAN CABRE, J.
1973 — Sobre el carácter votivo y apotropaico de los broches de cinturón en la Edad del Hierro Peninsular, XIII *CAN,* Huelva.
1977 — La exponencia femenina y la signografía ofídica en broches de cinturón del Hierro hispánico, XIV *CAN*, Zaragoza.

NEUMANN, E.
1955 — *The Great Mother. Analysis of the Archetype,* Princeton.

NIETO PRIETO, F.J.
1971-1972 — Ara pintada de Ampurias dedicada a Esculapio, *Ampurias* XXXIII-XXXIV.

NILSSON, H.P.
1941 — *Geschichte der Griechischen Religion*, Munich.

PERICOT, L.
1953 — La representación serpentiforme de la citania de Troia, *AEA* XXVI.

RADDATZ, K.
1969 — *Die Schatzfunde der Iberischen Halbinsel,* Berlin, Madrider Forschungen. Band 5. Deutsches Archäologisches Institut Abteilung. Madrid, pls. 1 n. 1; 3 n. 3, 5; 6 n. 9, 12, 13, 14; 25 n. 3 y 6; 27 n. 3; 28 n. 1; 32 n. 5; 36 n. 4, 5, 6; 38 n. 3 y 4; 39 n. 1; 40 n. 3; 44 n. 3; 52 n. 1, 3, 8, 9, 10; 53 n. 4; 56 n. 1; 60 n. 2; 63-63; 72 n. 5, 7; 83 n. 2 y 3; 93 n. 2. Also pl. 90.

RUANO, E.
1983 — Panorama de la escultura ibérica en Andalucïa, *Bol. Asoc. Amigos Arqueología* 17.

SHEE, E.
1974 — Painted Megalithic Art in Western Iberia, *Actas III Congreso Arqueológico Nacional*, vol. I.

VAZQUEZ HOYS, A. Ma.
1981 — La serpiente en el mundo antiguo I. La serpiente en las religiones mediterráneas, *Bol. Asoc. Arqueología* 14.
1983 — Sobre la Diana de Segóbriga, *Homenaje al Profesor D. Martín Almagro Bachs* III, Madrid.

JUNO AND FERTILITY AT THE SANCTUARY OF TAS-SILĠ, MALTA

Horatio C.R. Vella

The attribution of the temple at Tas-Silġ in Malta to the divinity of Juno was established by 1963 when the *Missione Archeologica Italiana* excavated the site which had been known for some centuries to have been a temple of some sort.[1] The remains of the temple itself and the inscriptions leave no doubt that it was goddess Juno who was venerated there.

To put it briefly, three main conclusions were reached by the archaeologists: that a neolithic temple whose remains can still be seen had preceded in existence the Roman one; that goddess Juno was originally venerated as the neolithic Mother Goddess at the same site, transformed intermediately into Astarte by the Phoenicians and the Carthaginians; and that a male but subordinate divinity was venerated along with the Mother Goddess/ Astarte/ Juno. In my view, this last point was not fully developed, and is very important in throwing more light on the question of the fertility cult in Juno.

M. Cagiano de Azevedo, writing for the *Missione* in 1968, reported on the finding of a *baetylus* (a precious, round stone) and a large basin, both approximately thirty metres away from the prehistoric altar.[2] The *baetylus* was described as one metre thirty in height, standing by the basin, originally of a single block, of a diameter of less than five metres. *Baetyli* were formerly discovered both at Ġgantija in Gozo and at Tarxien in Malta, as well as elsewhere in Mediterranean countries. As in the case of other *baetyli*, the one from Tas-Silġ represented a male divinity, a fact confirmed by its complementary position to the temple of the Great Goddess. In this case the god is connected with the basin which served for rites of ablution. Both the Phoenicians and the Romans respected this *baetylus* and left it in its original position from neolithic times. It is obvious that they recognised in it the male divinity that essentially went together with the Great Goddess.

It is necessary now to establish our facts clearly both on the relationship of Juno with the Great Goddess, and on the identification of the male divinity represented by the *baetylus* also in Phoenician and Roman times at Tas-Silġ.

It is of interest to note that of all the neolithic temples in Malta and Gozo, the one at Tas-Silġ is unique in the islands in that a female divinity was venerated with a certain amount of continuity from neolithic times down to the Christian era. In the same place we have neolithic, Phoenician, Classical, Byzantine and Arab traces, and only a few yards from the site a shrine dedicated to "Our Lady of the Snow" gives both witness to the veneration of a female divinity in the locality and the meaning of the place-name of Tas-Silġ. Also, the name Dellimara, the peninsula which starts from Tas-Silġ south-eastwards, has been interpreted as deriving from "Dejr il-mara", meaning "the temple of the Lady".[3] This continual holy tradition is not found to have existed in the other neolithic temples in these islands.

The transformation of the Great Goddess divinity at Tas-Silġ into Astarte, and Juno later, is not only a marvellous event in the history of religions, but also symbolical of the general pattern in which the veneration of the "Great Goddess", "the Mother Earth", "the Goddess of Fertility", spread from the east through Asia Minor and Palestine to Crete, Greece, Malta, Sicily, Sardinia, Spain and the north as far as England.[4] In this missionary journey to the west, the cult of the fertile goddess, even if it had to lose some of its pristine characteristics and acquire new ones as a result of new contacts in strange lands, remained essentially the same. I would even add that the spread of this cult went hand-in-hand with the spread of the culture of the people who from time to time emigrated to the west, taking with them their gods, customs and language. It is probable, therefore, that where the same religion was practised in neolithic times, the same language was spoken, for which may I suggest pre-Phoenician words in the Maltese language as possibly applicable to this one common Mediterranean language in neolithic times?

To come back to the Great Goddess, it is a greater problem to differentiate between the Great Goddess herself and the Phrygian and Anatolian Cybele, the Syrian Ma, the Cretan Rhea, Britomartis, Dictunna and Aphaea, the Egyptian Isis, the Sumerian Inanna, the Akkadian Ishtar, the semitic Asherah or Astaroth (called by the Greeks Astarte), the Greek Demeter, Hera, Athena, Aphrodite, Artemis and Hecate, and the Roman Magna Mater and goddesses derived from the Greek ones, than to assume that all these goddesses were essentially different from each other but accidentally bearing similar characteristics.

The case with the Cretan and Greek goddesses is obvious. The emblems which the Minoan Great Goddess bears — for example, the double-axe (Greek λάβρυς, which gives the name to λαβυρίνθος), the dove and the snakes — were to be found both in the ancient Middle East in the Chalcolithic period, a thousand years before the Minoan period and, later on, with the Greek Athena in the case of the snakes. Most of the Greek goddesses, and their Roman counterparts, share their associations and concerns with birth, marriage, maternity, the moon and its supposed influence on the life of women, fertility, love, sex, and vegetation. Sometimes the roles of some goddesses have been confused exactly because they were so similar, especially in the case of Hecate and Artemis.[5]

As a result of her marriage with Zeus — originally, therefore, a chthonic goddess — Hera enjoyed the titles of "queen of heaven" and "the goddess of the stars". Though she and the rest of the goddesses are in essence reminiscences of the Cretan Rhea (who bore Zeus), Hera, of all the Greek pantheon, comes closest to the equivalence of Rhea, Cybele and the Great Goddess, and so does her Roman counterpart, Juno. We remind ourselves here that at Tas-Silġ the Great Goddess became Juno after having been intermediately Astarte, the supreme semitic goddess and the equivalent of the Great Goddess in the Near East.[6] It is true that we often take Aphrodite as the Greek counterpart of the semitic Astarte; but, as we have already established, most of the goddesses in the Greek pantheon were multiple forms of the same Great Goddess and, what is more important, Hera, and not Aphrodite, was supreme like Astarte.

Most of the ancient goddesses had two important and inseparable qualities in common: a supremacy over male divinities, and a relationship with a subordinate male god.

In Paleolithic times, the male divinity hardly played any part in the Mother Goddess cult for the reason that the male's part was less obvious than the more apparent conception and birth by the goddess. As his function was better understood in later ages, his role was firmly established though never more emphasised than that of the goddess. Such is the case with the Goddess in Minoan Crete and the Aegean, where the god was known simply as the Master of Animals, or Zeus. This god was to change tremendously when the Indo-Europeans came to Greece from the north and introduced their Sky-god and called him by the same name of the primitive, vegetation-god in Crete, Zeus. This change also removed the goddess from the chair of supremacy in Greece, and now Zeus (later on, Jupiter) and not Hera or Juno, becomes the god of heaven or Olympus. In Egypt, because the Pharaoh represented god on earth, and he was generally a king not a queen, the supreme deity was consequently a male. But at Tas-Silġ, as we have seen, the male god was represented only by the *baetylus* as from neolithic times, while the temple was dedicated to the female divinity, and not to himself.

The relationship between the Great Goddess and the male divinity was essentially an expression of the fertility cult. The increasing awareness of the essential role of the male divinity in the cult developed a myth of an aetiological nature. When in the northern hemisphere in summer all the vegetation went dry, the ancient peoples attributed this phenomenon to the annual death and absence of the male divinity. The coming of the rains towards the end of summer was then explained as the rebirth or resurrection of the same male god and the resumption of a relationship with the Great Goddess of fertility.

In the Babylonian myth, Tammuz was the male divinity associated with goddess Ishtar, and was the embodiment of the creative powers of spring and the personification of the autumnal decline in the seasonal cycle. When King Marduk replaced Enlil as head of the pantheon in about 1728 B.C., he assumed a Tammuz role as the reborn male divinity and the return of a prosperous season. (The assumption of a divine role applied also to the Egyptian pharaoh representing god on earth, and to the wearing of the mask representing a divinity in Greek Comedy). The Sumerian Dumuzi played a similar role to goddess Inanna, and so did the Egyptian Osiris to Isis and the Phrygian/ Anatolian Attis to Cybele.[7]

The death and resurrection theme was also celebrated annually at Byblos on the coast of Syria with a period of mourning followed by rejoicing at the restoration of Adonis, the youthful vegetation-god, in the spring. The same Adonis appears again as Aphrodite's subordinate male divinity in Greek mythology. One story describes him as a young hunter killed by a boar, another as an infant entrusted in a chest to Persephone in Hades, where he stayed for half a year, symbolising the absence of fertility on earth for that period.

The association of the Great Goddess with the dead god and her attempts to bring him back from the underworld earned her and her representations in Crete and Greece titles connected with the underworld. For example, the Minoan Great Goddess was also the guardian of the dead. At Hagia Triada in Crete, in a Late Minoan chamber-tomb, the Great Goddess is represented as receiving the life-giving blood of a victim conveyed in ritual jars by her priestesses, in order for her to give new life to the deceased. Of the Greek goddesses, Aphrodite, Artemis and Hecate were goddesses of the underworld. Hecate also ruled over ghosts and demons, and as a result of this she was recognised as the goddess of the cross-roads who drove away the evil influences from these dangerous spots. Even the Egyptian Isis, venerated in Greece and Rome, was believed that she could restore the dead beyond the grave.

These goddesses, therefore, through their similar characteristics (supremacies, association with a male god and the underworld) were various representations of an earlier supreme female divinity who was closely attached to a subordinate male god in the fertility cult. At Tas-Silġ, the Great Goddess was later on represented by Astarte and Juno, and was also attached to the male divinity represented by the *baetylus*, whose identification problem I now come to.

Until the excavations got started at Tas-Silġ by the *Missione* in 1963, it was believed, practically by all the historians concerned with Malta, that two big temples of the classical era had existed in Malta: one dedicated to Juno near Vittoriosa, and another dedicated to Hercules at Tas-Silġ.[8] This tradition originated from J. Quintin's description of Malta in Latin in 1533, himself relying merely on archaeological remains (without any inscriptions mentioned) and on Ptolemy's wrong bearings.[9] That a temple of some sort existed near Vittoriosa (where now a ditch separates Fort St. Angelo from the town) is credible and, in fact, a temple dedicated to Hercules had been suggested to have possibly once stood at that site.[10] More recently, a new suggestion that Hercules was venerated not on his own, but along with goddess Juno at Tas-Silġ can add light to our investigation.[11]

Ptolemy may have been wrong with the bearings, but his remark that both Juno and Hercules were venerated in Malta in the classical era must not escape our notice. The fact is that if Hercules had a temple for his own cult in classical times, Cicero would have written something about it as he did with the temple of Juno in connection with the Verrine case in Rome.[12] Maybe he was just interested with the one of Juno, which Verres actually robbed; but what about Pliny, Strabo and the others who mentioned Malta in their works?

The problem is really solved if we see the *baetylus* at Tas-Silġ as symbolically the equivalent of Attis, Adonis, the Cretan Zeus, Dumuzi, Tammuz, Osiris and Baal. When the Phoenicians and the Romans came to Malta, they recognised the male divinity in the *baetylus* as sacred and essentially important to the whole complex of the cult to the extent that even when the neolithic temple was turned into a Punico-Classical one, that stone remained in position up to this day.

Now the Canaanites in general worshipped Astarte, the goddess of fecundity, and represented her by wooden poles, and along with her Baal, whom they represented by altars or stone pillars. We should not be surprised, therefore, if the Phoenicians, who seemed to have worshipped Baal in most of their colonies, accepted the *baetylus* as their own deity. Furthermore, Baal means "Lord", as the name of Adonis does, which fact further suggests that Baal, Adonis, Attis, Tammuz and the rest were essentially one god. Again, the Canaanites called Baal also by the name of Melqart, meaning "King of the City". If, therefore, the Phoenicians, and the Carthaginians after them, named the male divinity at the temple of the Great Goddess at Tas-Silġ as Baal Melqart, the Romans would then have called him Hercules, the equivalent of Melqart. (The Straits of Gibraltar were known to the wandering Phoenicians "the Pillars of Melqart", to the Romans, "the Pillars of Hercules").

Now we find in Greco-Roman mythology that Hera/Juno was always the greatest enemy and the cause of the greatest obstacles to Heracles/Hercules. When he was born of Alcmene and Zeus, Hera was furious with her husband because of the affair, and did everything in her power to kill the child. Before his birth, she robbed him of his true inheritance, which had been promised by Zeus when he swore that he would be lord of the surrounding peoples. She contrived that Eurystheus instead would be born earlier through the intervention of the Eileithyae who delayed Heracles' birth. Hera then sent two serpents to attack Heracles and his twin-brother Iphicles in their cradle, but Heracles killed them both! Later on she sent on him a fit of furious homicidal madness, in which he killed his wife Megara and his children. So, then, how can we explain that Hercules was venerated along with Juno at Tas-Silġ?

We must, of course, not forget that there were more than one Heracles in the ancient world. Diodorus Siculus speaks of three Heracles, the first and most ancient of whom was the Egyptian, the second a Cretan, and third a Greek whom we know better. Cicero counts six heroes of this name, while according to Herodotus the Egyptians (and, with them, the Libyans) referred him to Phoenicia as the original source of their traditions on him.[13] It was this one who gave his name (Melqart) to the male divinity in Malta at Tas-Silġ through the coming of the Phoenicians.

The Greeks, if ever they came to Malta as settlers, and that before the Phoenicians, would not have venerated the *baetylus* as Heracles, but as Adonis who was associated with Aphrodite, the Greek goddess of love and fertility. The Romans, then, who also venerated Adonis, would have accepted him as their own with the same name. As things took place, however, the Romans found the Phoenician Melqart already in worship, and supposing he had nothing to do with Hera or the Greek legends, just translated him into Hercules and worshipped him along with Juno in the same way as they worshipped Adonis along with Venus (Aphrodite) elsewhere. This is how Hercules comes to be connected with goddess Juno and the fertility cult at Tas-Silġ in Malta.

CONCLUSION

Juno, therefore, a translation of the Greek Hera, chief of the goddesses in the Greco-Roman pantheon, was the Roman equivalent of the Phoenician supreme goddess Astaroth, known to us by the Greek name of Astarte, the goddess of fertility for the semitic peoples. As the neolithic Maltese Great Goddess was worshipped in relationship to her male divinity within her own temple, where he was represented by the *baetylus*, so was the Phoenician Astarte worshipped with Melqart, and Juno with Hercules in Roman times. The veneration of the Great Goddess with her subordinate male deity at Tas-Silġ down to Roman times may not have been continuous; yet the tradition was kept, the temple was re-utilised and the gods were re-named. If later peoples (the Phoenicians and the Romans) recognised the neolithic structure at Tas-Silġ as a temple and the Great Goddess as their own goddess of fertility, one concludes that the other neolithic temples in Malta and Gozo were *real* temples, while the Great Goddess of Fertility was not just a "fat lady" or a "Venus", but a *real* ancient deity whose fat propensities symbolise "Plenty".

Notes

I would like to thank the University of Zimbabwe for paying for the costs of my attendance to this Conference, and Dr. A. Bonanno for inviting me to it. I would like to add also that as a classicist I have discussed the subject more widely than an archaeologist would normally do.

1 See *Missione archeologica italiana a Malta 1963*, Roma, 1964.

2 The 1968 campaign, *Missione archeologica italiana a Malta 1968*, Roma, 1969: 117-9. See also S. Moscati, Un santuario a Malta, *Tra Cartagine e Roma*, Milano 1971: 42-3.

3 E. Coleiro, Malta nelle letterature classiche, *Missione archeologica italiana a Malta 1963*, Roma, 1964, 30. G. Wettinger, Early Maltese and Gozitan place-names, *Civilization: an encyclopaedia on Maltese civilization, history and contemporary arts* 24, 91-2, interprets "Dellimara" as deriving from "Dejr Limara", possibly meaning "Calimera's monastery-like building, Calimera being a surname current in Malta in the 15th c."

4 For the veneration of the Great Goddess in England, see, for example, M. Dames, *The Silbury treasure: the Great Goddess rediscovered*, London, 1976. On the identification of Astarte and Tanit through Juno at Tas-Silġ, see F.O. Hvidberg-Hansen, *La Déesse TNT – une étude sur la religion canaanéo-punique*, Copenhagen, 1979, 60-4.

5 Artemis "of the many breasts" of Ephesus, though not exactly the same as the Maltese Great Mother, shares with her the fertility aspect particularly symbolised by the many breasts. Some of the information here has been derived from E.O. James, *The cult of the Mother Goddess*, London 1959.

6 Most probably the Greeks in southern Italy and eastern Sicily traded with Phoenician Malta as they did with Carthage, but it is highly unlikely that they ever settled in Malta. The relics that that we have in Malta from the Greeks have been brought here by the Romans. See A. Bonanno, The tradition of an ancient Greek colony in Malta", *Hyphen* [**Malta**] IV, 1, 1983, pp. 1-17.

7 The severing of the genitals by the priests of Cybele has been interpreted either as an offering of the male fertility exclusively to the service of the goddess, or the retention of the fertility itself within the priests (J. Ferguson, *Greek and Roman religion: a source book*, New Jersey, U.S.A., 1980, 167).

8 For authors referring the temple of Juno to Vittoriosa and the temple of Hercules to Tas-Silġ, see H.C.R. Vella, "Quintinus (1536), and the temples of Juno and Hercules in Malta", *Athenaeum* 60, 1982, 274, n. 7 and 275 n. 15 respectively.

9 Quintinus A4v.: *Iunonis templum non solum inter magna, sed etiam inter magnifica numerari potuisse arbitror ex his quae pauca durant, medio fere loco inter oppidum et castellum. Ruina sparsa apparet in multa iugera, fundamentis et substructionibus templi bonam portus eius partem occupantibus, longe etiam in mari, in quo inaedificatum erat infra cliuum promontorii, in planitie undique a uentis et praealtis rupibus defensa; ibid.* A4v.: *Iunonem Ptolemaeus in ea insulae parte posuit, quae Orientem spectat, Herculem ad Austrum; ibid.* A4v.: *Herculani templi (si modo uera e Ptolemaeo diuino) immensae adhuc reliquiae patent; circuitu in passus ter mille et ultra, in eo insulae angulo quem ab argumento loci, patria lingua Euri Portum nominant. Ima pars extat in plerisque, lapidum longitudinis crassitudinisque stupendae.* All quotations on Quintinus here are taken from H.R.C. Vella, *The earliest description of Malta: Lyons, 1536*, Malta, 1980. See also PTOL. *Geog*. 4.3.13.

10 A. Bonanno, "L'habitat maltese in età romana", *Kokalos* 22-23, 1976-7, 391. But see also *id*., "Quintinus and the location of the temple of Hercules at Marsaxlokk", *Melita historica* 8, 1982, 191-204.

11 See Vella, *"Quintinus (1536)....., 275-6.*

12 CIC. *Ver*. 4. 103: *Insula est Melita, iudices, satis lato a Sicilia mari periculosoque diiuncta; in qua est eodem nomine oppidum, quo iste numquam accessit, quod tamen isti textrinum per triennium ad muliebrem uestem conficiendam fuit. Ab eo oppido non longe in promunturio fanum est Iunonis antiquum, quod tanta religione semper fuit ut non modo illis Punicis bellis quae in his fere locis nauali copia gesta atque uersata sunt, sed etiam hac praedonum multitudine semper inuiolatum sanctumque fuerit.*

13 DIOD. 3. 74; CIC. *N.D.* 3. 16; HER. 2. 44.

FIGURES

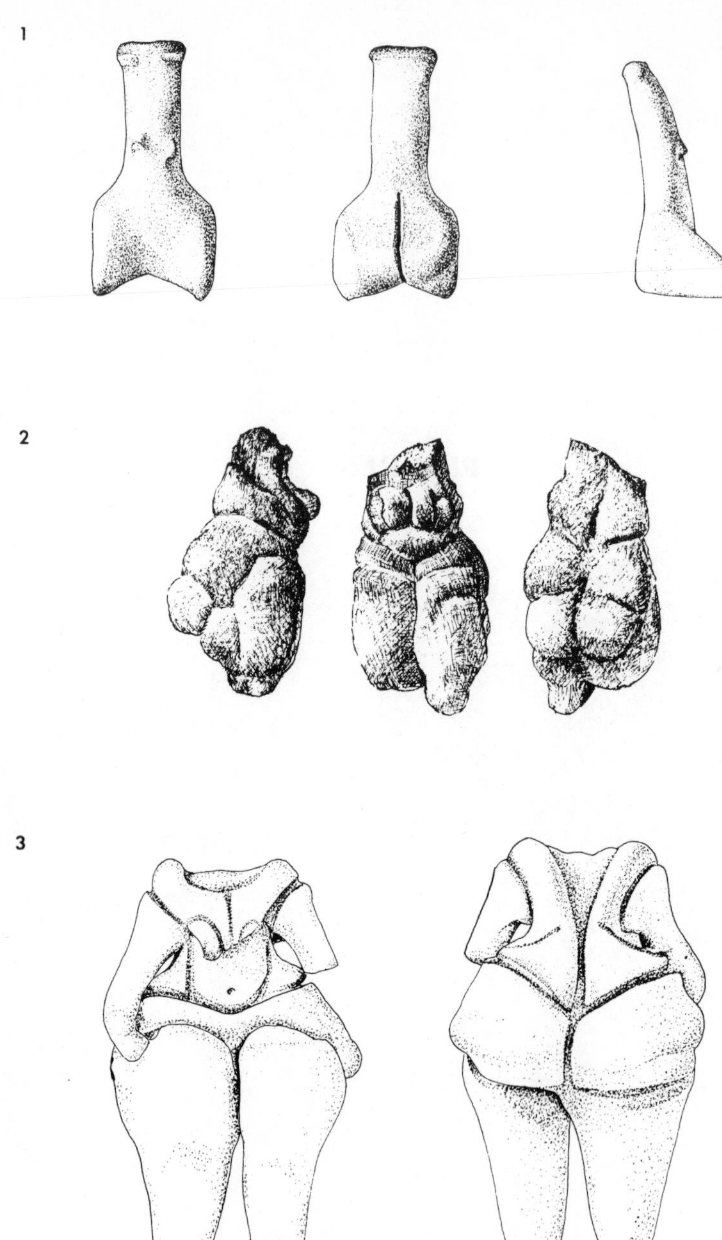
1
2
3

4

5

6

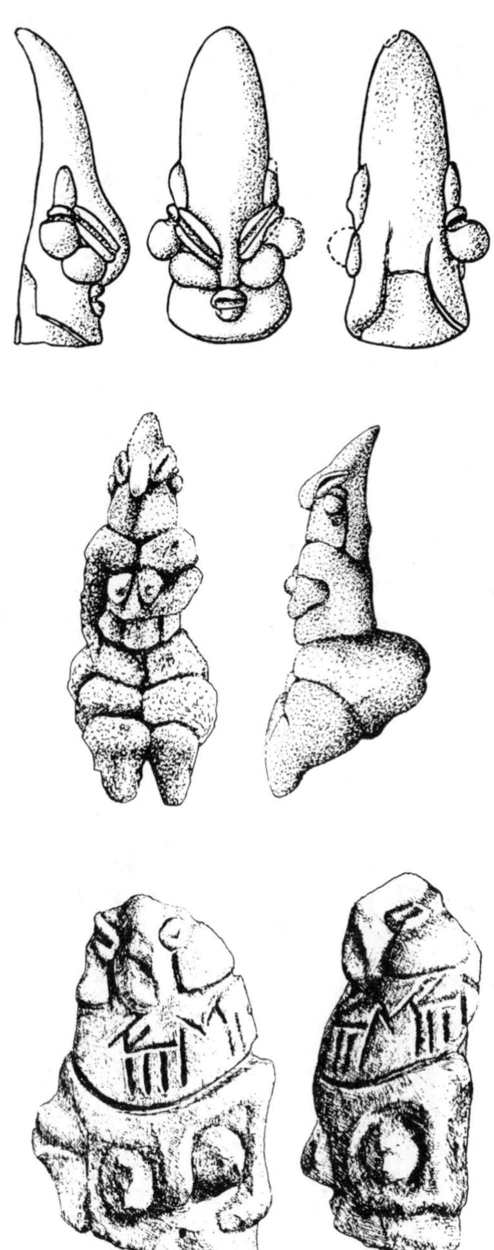

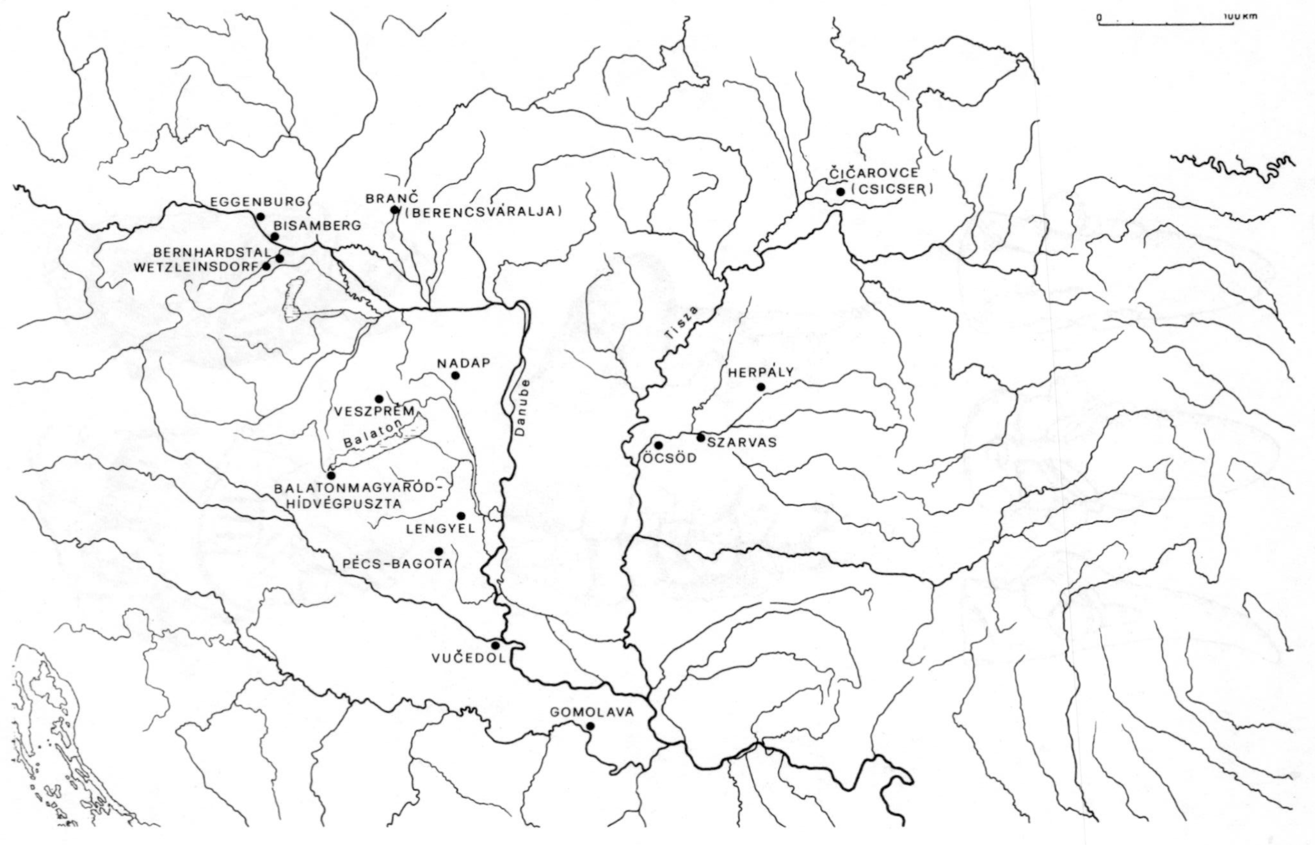
0
100 km
EGGENBURG
BISAMBERG
BERNHARDSTAL
WETZLEINSDORF
BRANČ
(BERENCSVÁRALJA)
ČIČAROVCE
(CSICSER)
NADAP
VESZPRÉM
Balaton
BALATONMAGYARÓD-
HÍDVÉGPUSZTA
LENGYEL
PÉCS-BAGOTA
VUČEDOL
GOMOLAVA
Danube
Tisza
HERPÁLY
SZARVAS
ÖCSÖD

8

N

-135

A

-130

-103

A'

-78

-100

-140

0 1 M

A – A'

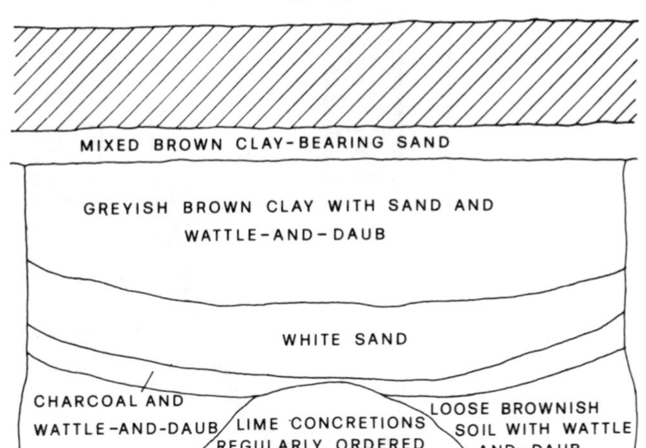

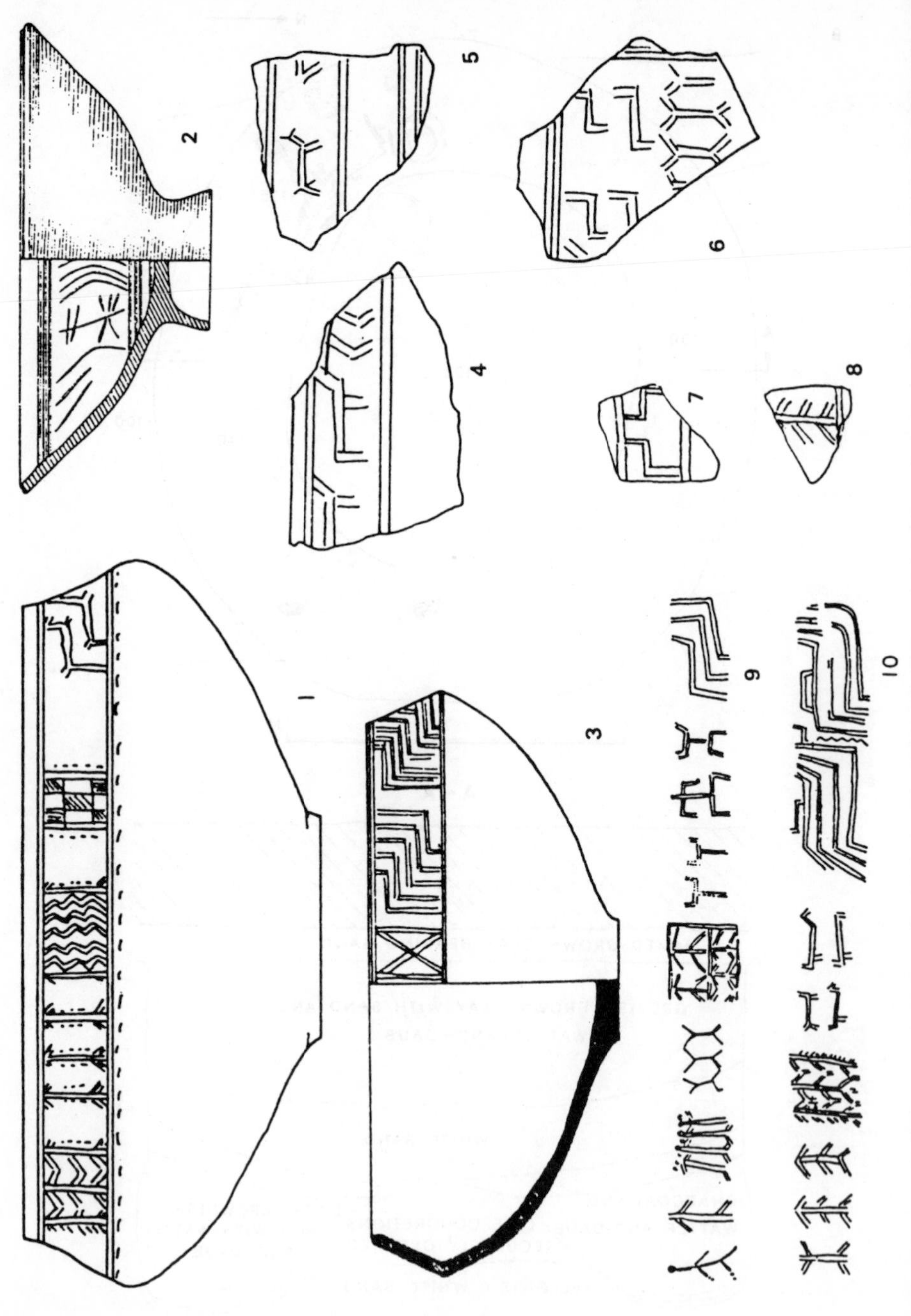
9a
1
2
3
4
5
6
7
8
9
10

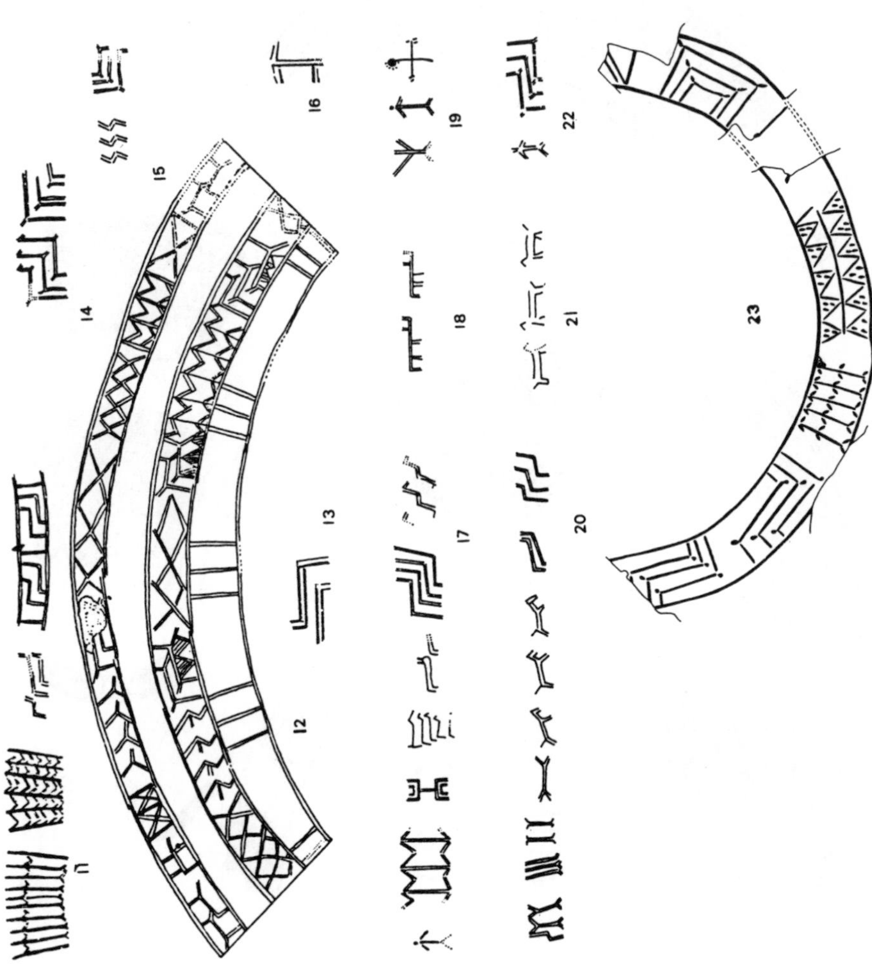
9b
11
12
13
14
15
16
17
18
19
20
21
22
23

10

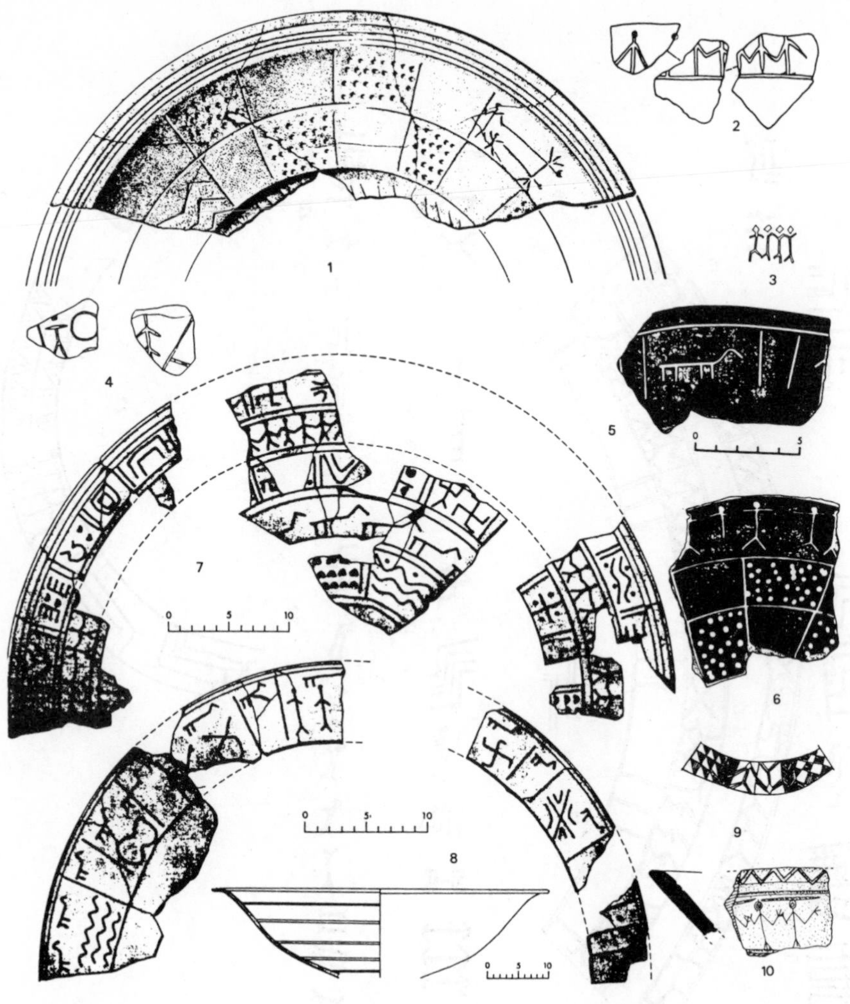

11

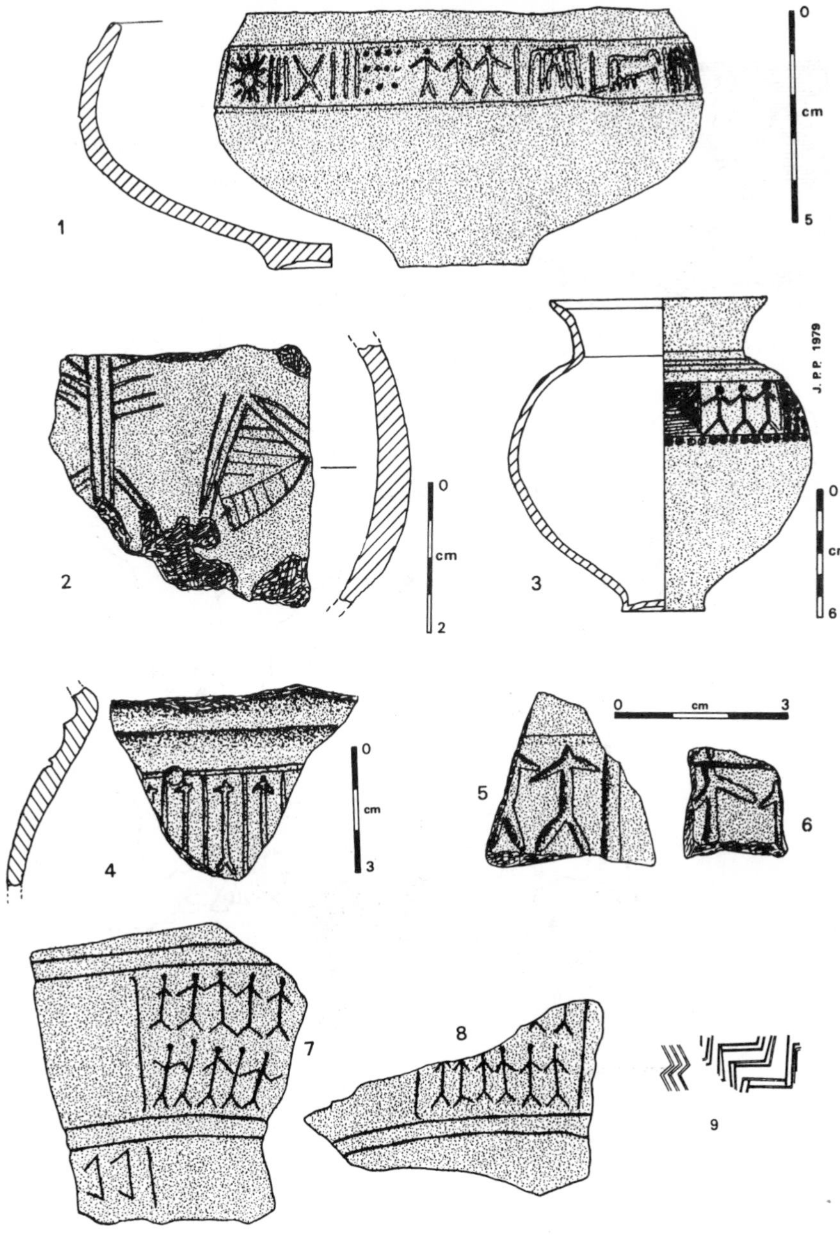

12

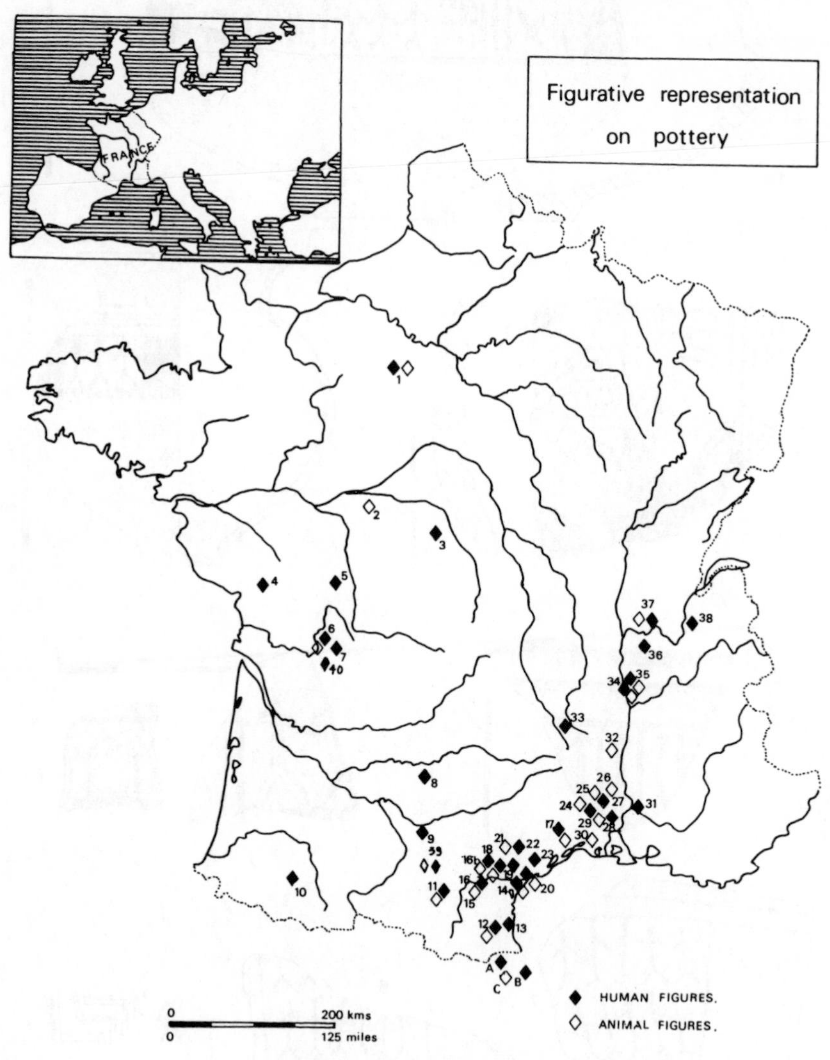
Figurative representation on pottery
FRANCE
HUMAN FIGURES.
ANIMAL FIGURES.
0
200 kms
0
125 miles

13

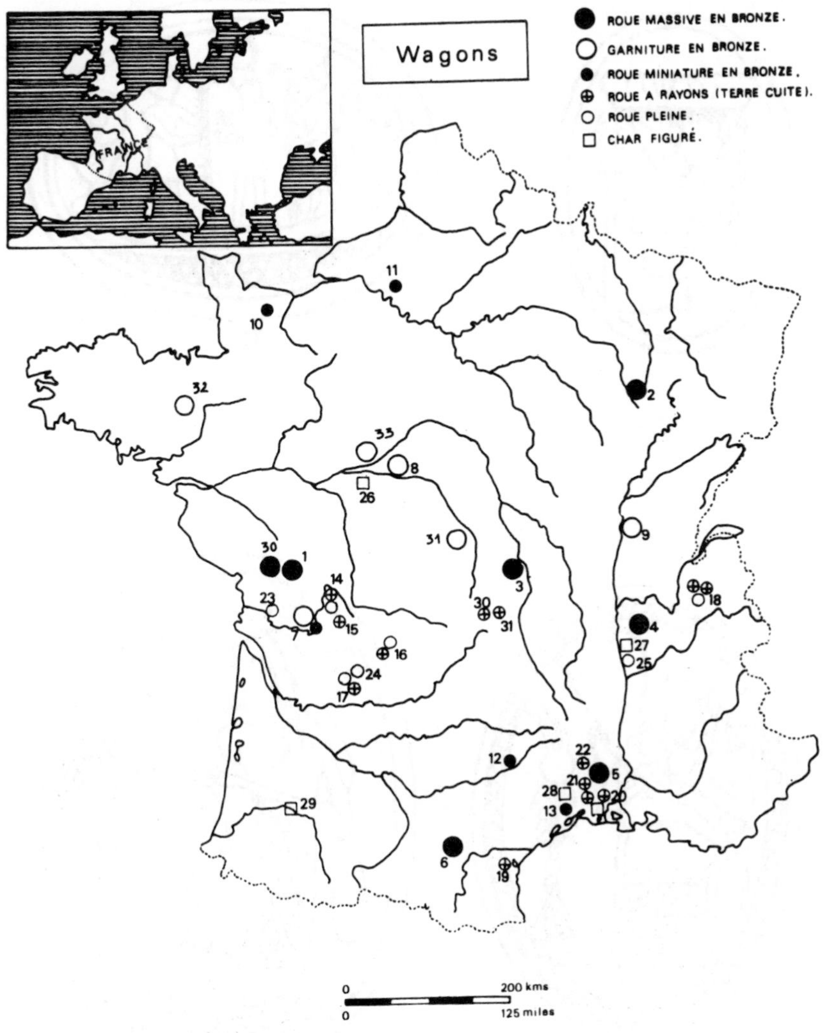

Wagons
ROUE MASSIVE EN BRONZE.
GARNITURE EN BRONZE.
ROUE MINIATURE EN BRONZE.
ROUE A RAYONS (TERRE CUITE).
ROUE PLEINE.
CHAR FIGURÉ.
FRANCE
0 200 kms
0 125 miles

14

15

16

17

18

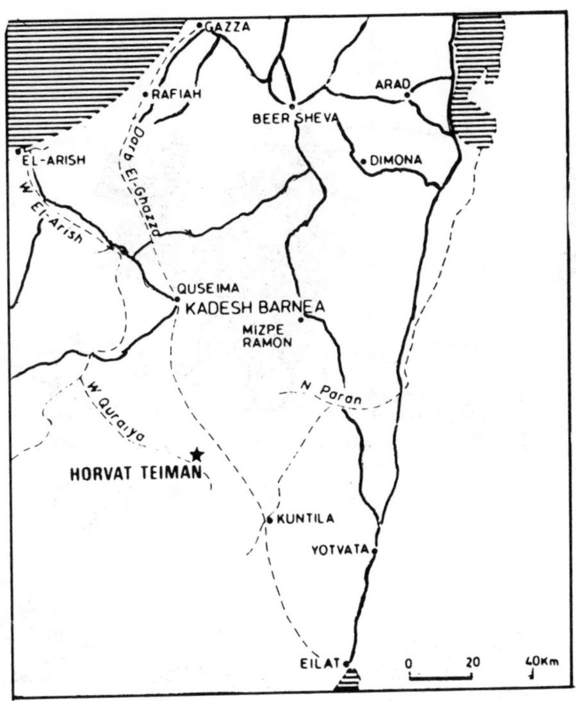
GAZZA
RAFIAH
ARAD
BEER SHEVA
EL-ARISH
Darb El-Ghazza
DIMONA
W. El-Arish
QUSEIMA
KADESH BARNEA
MIZPE
RAMON
N Paran
W. Quraiya
HORVAT TEIMAN
KUNTILA
YOTVATA
EILAT
0
20
40Km

19

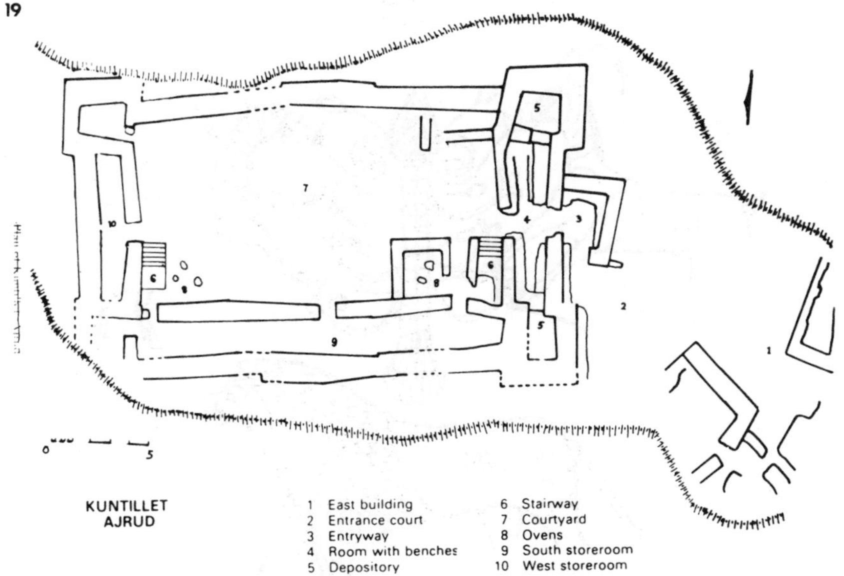
KUNTILLET
AJRUD
1 East building
2 Entrance court
3 Entryway
4 Room with benches
5 Depository
6 Stairway
7 Courtyard
8 Ovens
9 South storeroom
10 West storeroom
0
5

20

21

PLATES

1

2

3

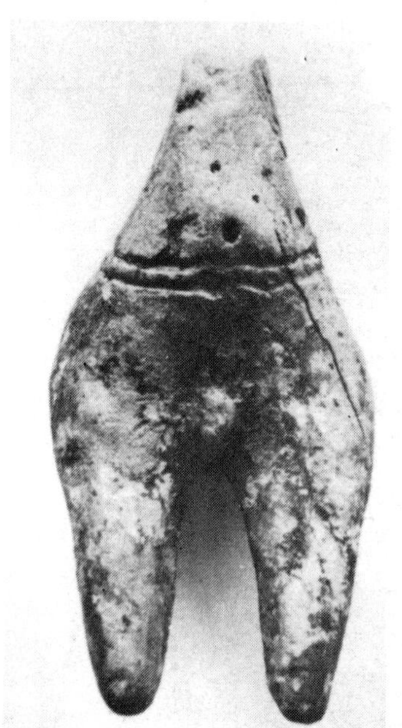

4

5

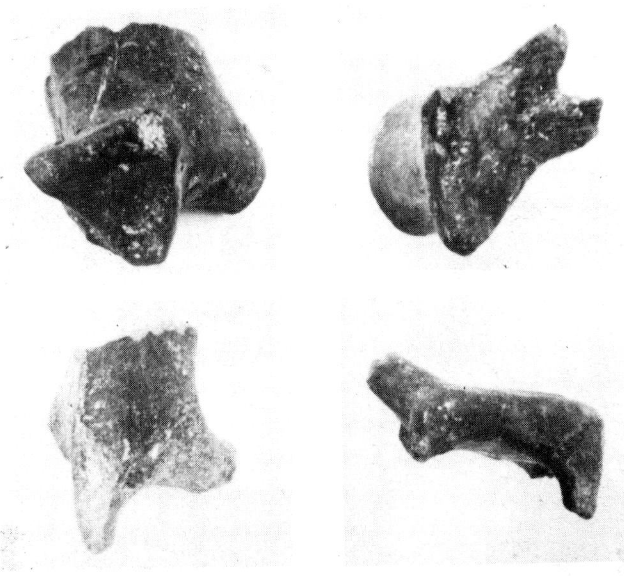

6

8

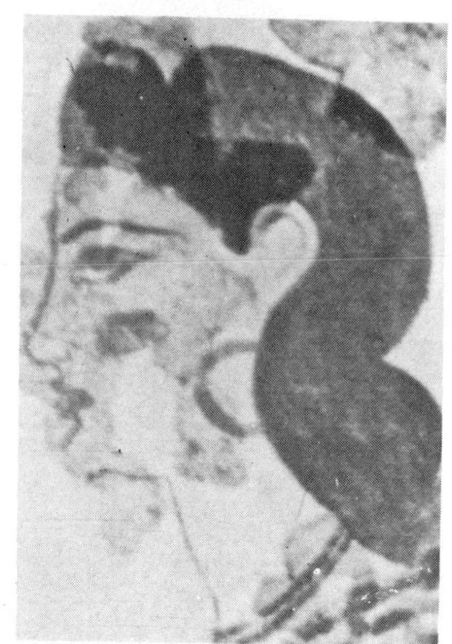

10

12

13

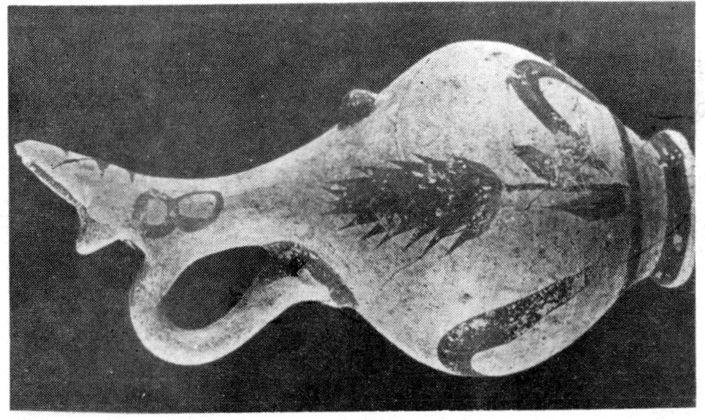

11

14

15

16

17

18

19

20

21

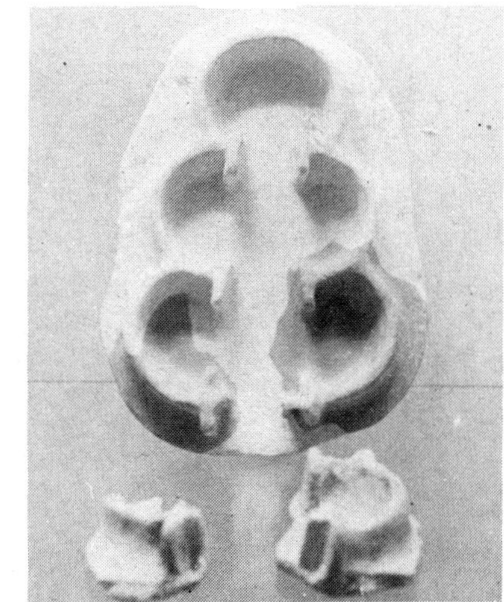

22

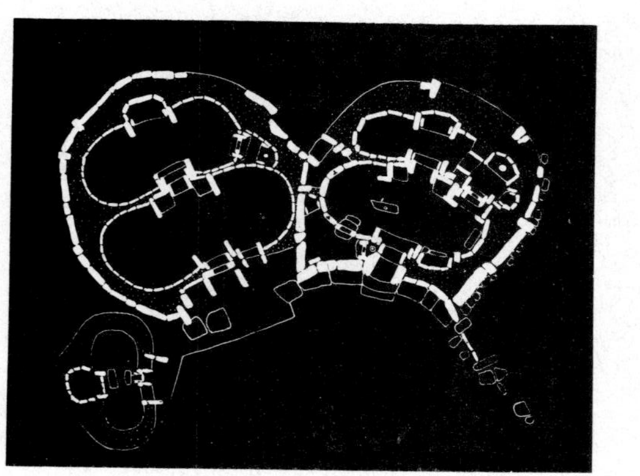

23

24

25

26a

26b

27

28

29a

30a

30b

29b

31a

31b

33a

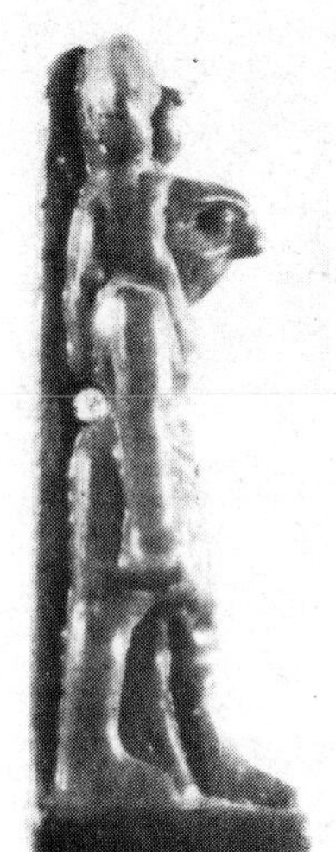

33b

32a

32b

34

35a

35b

36a

36b

37

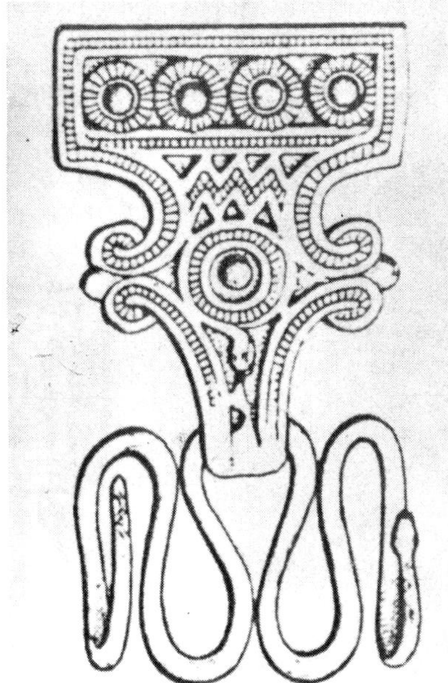

38

39

40

C VOCONIO C F PAP PATRI
CAECILIAE A N VI MATRI
VOCONIAE C F MARIAE SORORI
C VOCONIVS C F PROCVLVS FECIT

NOTES ON FIGURES

1. Stylized seated human figurine from Netiv Hagedud (Lower Jordan Valley). Sultanian phase of the Pre-Pottery Neolithic A. Height 0.42m.
2. Seated human figurine from Kefar Giladi. Yarmukian culture (sixth millennium B.C.E.).
3. Seated human figurine from Sha'ar Hagolan, Jordan Valley.
4. Head of human figurine from Sha'ar Hagolan, Jordan Valley.
5. Seated human figurine from H. Minha (Munhata), Jordan Valley. Height 0.10m.
6. Human figurine with animals incised on head, from Tel Aviv.
7. Neolithic and Chalcolithic cultural groups of western Hungary. Distribution map.
8. Plan and section of circular pit discovered in Balatonmagyarod-Homok, Hungary.
9. Représentations anthropomorphes et zoomorphes sur céramique dans l'aire mailacienne et ses marges.
   1- Le Canet (Pyrénées Orientales)
   2- Tumulus 1 de Bougarber (Pyrénées Atlantiques), d'après Mohen.
   3-4-5-6- Rouque-de-Viou à St. Dionisy (Gard), d'après Garmy.
   7-8- Grand Ranc à Boucoiran (Gard), d'après Dedet.
   9- Le Cayla à Mailhac (Aude), d'après Taffanel.
   10- Las Fados aà Pépieux (Aude), d'après Taffanel.
   11- Le Moulin à Mailhac (Aude), d'après Taffanel.
   12- Site AM 95-99 à Vendres (Hérault), d'après Abauzit.
   13- Grézac à Lodève (Hérault).
   14- Montpeyroux à Causses-et-Veyran (Hérault) d'après Louis-Taffanel.
   15- Grande Grotte à Montredon (Aude), d'après Louis-Taffanel.
   16- La Madeleine à Villeneuve-les-Maguelone (Hérault).
   17- Sextantio à Castelnau-le-Lez (Hérault) d'après Arnal, Majurel et Prades.
   18- Languissel à Nîmes-Caissargues (Gard).
   19- Cessero à St. Thibéry (Hérault), d'après Aris et Jully.
   20- Les Canals à Millas (Pyrénées Orientales).
   21- Camp Redon à Lansargues (Hérault), d'après Prades.
   22- En-Bonnes à Fanjeaux (Aude), d'après Louis-Taffanel.
   23- L'Estrade à Mireval-Lauragais (Aude), d'après Passelac.
10. Représentations anthropomorphes et zoomorphes du Bas-Dauphiné, de la Haute vallée du Rhône et de leurs marges.
   1- Virignin (Ain), d'après Bocquet.
   2- Pain-de-Sucre à Sérézin du Rhône (Isère), d'après Combier.
   3- Grésine à Brison-St. Innocent (Savoie), d'après Combier.
   4- Saint-Uze (Drôme), d'après Thivolle.
   5-6-7-8- Moras-en-Valloire (Drôme), d'après Nicolas et Martin.
   9- La Ferté-Hauterive (Allier), d'après Abauzit.
   10- Polignac (Haute-Loire), d'après Delporte.

11. Représentations anthropomorphes et zoomorphes sur céramique du Centre-Ouest et de l'Ouest.

 1- Vase orné d'une frise de pictogrammes du Quéroy à Chazelles (Charente) d'après Gomez.

 2- Tesson incisé de l'Ilot-les-Vases (Vendée), d'après Gendron.

 3- Urne à décor anthropomorphe de Rancogne (Charente), d'après Gruet.

 4- Anthropomorphes longilignes du Camp Allaric à Aslonnes (Vienne), d'après Pautreau.

 5-6- Anthropomorphes se donnant la main, urne à panneaux du Camp Allaric à Aslonnes (Vienne), d'après Pautreau.

 7-8- Anthropomorphes et signes de Villement à St. Aoustrille (Indre), d'après des Méloizes.

 9- Fort Harrouard à Sorel-Moussel (Eure-et-Loir), d'après Philippe.

12. Carte de répartition des figurations anthropomorphes et zoomorphes de la période de transition "Bronze-Fer", Céramiques.

 1- Fort-Harrouard à Sorel-Moussel (Eure).
 2- Danges à Sublaines (Indre-et-Loire).
 3- Villement à Ste Aoustrille (Indre).
 4- Ilôt-les-Vases à Nalliers (Vendée).
 5- Camp Allaric à Aslonnes (Vienne).
 6- Quéroy à Chazelles (Charante).
 7- Rancogne (Charente).
 8- Saillac (Lot).
 9- St. Sulpice-la-Pointe (Tarn).
 10- La Serre à Bougarber (Pyrénées Atlantiques).
 11- En-Bonnes à Fanjeaux (Aude).
 12- Les Canals à Millas (Pyrénées Orientales).
 13- Les Hospices à Canet (Pyrénées Orientales).
 14- Grande Grotte à Montredon (Aude).
 15- Las Fados à Pépieux (Aude).
 16- Le Cayla à Mailhac (Aude).
 16 bis- Le Moulin à Mailhac (Aude).
 17- Sextentio à Castelnau-le-Lez (Hérault).
 18- Grézec à Lodève (Hérault).
 19- Portal-Vielh à Vendres (Hérault).
 20- Site AM 95-99 à Vendres (Hérault).
 21- Servillonnette à Servian (Hérault).
 22- Cesser à St. Thibéry (Hérault).
 23- Montpeyroux à Caussas-et-Veyran (Hérault).
 24- Roque-de-Viou à St. Dionisy (Gard).
 25- La Font du Coucou à Calvisson (Gard).
 26- Grand-Ranc à Boucoiran (Gard).
 27- Languissel à Nîmes (Gard).
 28- Triple-Levée à Beaucaire (Gard).
 29- Camp Redon à Lansargues (Hérault).
 30- La Madeleine à Villeneuve-les-Magdelonna (Hérault).
 31- Vidauque à Cheval-Blanc (Vaucluse).
 32- Ranc-Pointu à St. Martin d'Ardèche (Ardèche).
 33- Polignac (Haute-Loire).
 34- St. Uzé (Drôme).

35- Moras-en-Valloire (Drôme).
36- Sérézin du Rhône (Isère).
37- Virignin (Ain).
38- Grésine à Brisson-St. Innocent (Savoie).
39- Mireval-Lauragais (Aude).
40- Agris (Charente).

A- Agullana. Girona (Espagne).
B- Punta del Pi. Girona (Espagne).
C- La Verna à Espolla. Girona (Espagne).

13. Carte des chars de la période de transition "Bronze-Fer". Roues fonctionnelles, modèles réduits, figurations.

Roue massive en bronze
1- Triou à Mougon (Deux-Sèvres).
2- Langres (Haute-Marne).
3- Jenzat (Allier).
4- La Côte-St. Andé (Isère).
5- Nîmes (Gard).
6- Fâ à Rennes-les-Baines (Aude).
30- Le Meréchal à Coulon (Deux-Sèvres).

Garniture de bronze pour roue en bois
7- Vénat à St. Yriex (Charente).
8- Choussy (Loir-et-Cher).
9- Ouroux-sur-Saône (Saône-et-Loire).
31- Petit-Villatte à Neuvy-sur-Barangeon (Cher).
32- St. Marc-le-Blanc (Ille et Vilaine).
33- Amboise (Indre-et-Loire).

Roue miniature en bronze
7- Vénat à St. Yriex (Charente).
10- Longueville (Calvados).
11- Deville-lès-Rouen (Seine-Maritime).
12- Landric à Saint-Baulize (Aveyron).
13- Environs de Montpellier (Hérault).

Roue miniature en terre cuite (avec rayon)
14- Bois du Roc à Vilhonneur (Charente).
15- Quéroy à Chazelles (Charente).
16- Chalucet à St. Jean-Ligoure (Haute-Vienne).
17- Puypinson à St. Léon-sur-l'Isle (Dordogne).
18- Grésine au lac du Bourget (Savoie).
19- Ilôt Louisset à Sigean (Aude).
20- Camp Redon à Lansargues (Hérault).
21- Roque de Viou à Saint-Dionisy (Gard).
22- Grand-Ranc à Boucoiran (Gard).
30- Busséol (Puy-de-Dôme).
31- Corrent (Puy-de-Dôme).

Roue miniature en terre cuite (pleine)
14- Bois du Roc à Vilhonneur (Charente).
16- Chalucet à St. Jean-Ligoure (Haute-Vienne).
17- Puypinsou à St. Léon-sur-l'Isle (Dordogne).

18- Grésine au lac du Bourget (Savoie).
23- Camp de Merpins (Charente).
24- Ecorneboeuf à Coulouniex-Chaniers (Dordogne).
25- Saint Uzé (Drôme).

Figurations de chars
20- Camp Redon à Lansargues (Hérault).
26- Sublaines (Indre-et-Loire).
27- Moras-en-Valloire (Drôme).
28- Substention à Castelnau-le-Lez (Hérault).
29- Larrivières (Landes).

14. Jasper scarab from Tharros: child god with royal crown. After V. Crespi, *Catalogo della raccolta di antichità sarde del Sig. R. Chessa,* Cagliari 1868, pl. II, 3.
15. Jasper scarab from Tharros (3:1): within a barque child god with royal crown, to whom infinite years of reign are assigned by means of palm-branches. Length: c. 14mm. After A. Della Marmora, *Memoria sopra alcune antichità sarde...*, Torino 1855, pl. A, 25.
16. Jasper scarab from Tharros (3:1): Egyptianizing mother goddess with child god as king, thymiaterion in front. Length: c. 15mm. After Della Marmora (see fig. 15), pl. A, 32.
17. Jasper scarab from Tharros (?) (3:1): standing Egyptianizing mother goddess (with strange pointed beard) who gives her breast to the child god provided with royal insignia; above her shoulder the fenestrated axe of Asiatic divinities. Length: 17mm. Sketch after A. Parrot *et al., Die Phönizier,* München 1977, p. 232, fig. 260.
18. Location of the site of Kuntillet' Ajrud (Horvat Teiman).
19. Plan of Kuntillet 'Ajrud.
20. Part of a drawing on one of the pithoi found at Kuntillet 'Ajrud.
21. Part of a drawing on one of the pithoi found at Kuntillet 'Ajrud.

NOTES ON PLATES

1. Figurine humaine de Dikili Tash (hauteur maximale conservée 0.057m.).
2. Figurine humaine de Dikili Tash (hauteur maximale conservée 0.096m.).
3. Figurine humaine de Dikili Tash (masculine; hauteur maximale conservée 0.062m.).
4. Figurine zoomorphe de Dikili Tash appartenant au type A (dimensions maximales conservées: hauteur 0.115m.; longueur 0.203m.; largeur 0.093m.).
5. Figurines zoomorphes de Dikili Tash appartenant au type B (dimensions maximales conservées: entre 0.02 et 0.055m.).
6. Seated human figurine from H. Minha (Munhata), Jordan Valley. Height 0.10m.
7. West House. Detail of the young priestess. Akrotiri, Santorini. After S. Marinatos.

8-9. Two women from the House of the Ladies. Akrotiri, Santorini. After S. Marinatos.

10. One of the Crocus-gatherers. Xesté 3. Akrotiri, Santorini. After S. Marinatos.
11. Nippled-ewer from Akrotiri. Athens, National Museum. After S. Marintos.
12. The spring fresco. Akrotiri, Santorini. After S. Marinatos.
13. Representation of a swallow on an amphora. Akrotiri, Santorini. After Ch. Doumas.
14. Standing human figure from Ħaġar Qim. Globigerina limestone. Height 0.382m.
15. Seated human figure from Ħaġar Qim, Malta, legs to the right. Globigerina limestone. Height 0.212m.
16. Seated human figure from Ħaġar Qim, Malta, legs to the left. Globigerina limestone. Height 0.194m.
17. Seated clothed figure from Ħaġar Qim, Malta, with necklace and deep holes on left side. Traces of red ochre. Globigerina limestone. Height 0.235m.
18. Seated clothed figure from Ħaġar Qim, Malta, with rope-holes in front, pigtail on back and traces of red ochre. Globigerina limestone. Height 0.192m.
19. Seated colossal statue from Tarxien, Malta. Globigerina limestone. Preserved height 1m.
20. Seated figure from Ħaġar Qim, Malta, seen from the back. Head missing. Globigerina limestone. Approx. height 0.24m.
21. Terracotta temple model from Ħaġar Qim, Malta. Original fragments and reconstructed model. Approx. length of model 0.28m.
22. Plan of the Mnajdra temple complex, Malta.
23. Three querns from the Tarxien temples, Malta. Tarxien Temples Museum.
24. Base of the seated colossal statue from Tarxien, Malta. National Museum of Archaeology, Valletta.
25. Animal carved in relief on the wall of a small room between the third and middle temples at Tarxien, Malta: sow or heifer? *In situ*.

26a-b. Plaquette of whitish steatite from Sardinia (3:1): cow with suckling calf, lotus behind // udjat. Cagliari Museum. 19,7 × 16,4 × 6,8mm. Hölbl 1986: pl. 87,1.

27. Plaquette of whitish steatite from Sardinia (3:1): divine child with curl and hand in mouth, protected by two winged goddesses carrying sun disc on head // udjat. Cagliari Museum. 18 × 14,3 × 5,4mm. Hölbl 1986: pl. 88,2b.

28. Plaquette of pale yellow, fine faience with vestiges of colourless glaze from Sardinia (3:1): divine child kneeling above lotus, hand on mouth, with debased Egyptian crown, protected by two winged goddesses (the left one with Hathor horns and sun disc, on head) // motif. Cagliari Museum. 20,3 × 17,3 × 6mm. Hölbl 1986: pl. 85,3b.
29. Plaquette of fine, light brown faience from Carthage (3:1): Hathor cow with sun disc between horns and gold sign above ridge, lotus (?) in front // udjat. with foot and feather of hawk. Louvre, AO 3051. 15,2 × 12,2 × 12,2 × 4,9mm. Unpublished.
30. Ram figurine of whitish steatite from Sardinia (4:1): hieroglyphic inscription on base: "every life". Cagliari Museum. Height 8mm., base 10,5 × 6,3mm. Hölbl 1986: pl. 77,10.
31. Amulet in the shape of sitting Isis with Horus child; light blue paste (2:1). Found in Cagliari, S. Avendrace. Cagliari Museum. Height 33,8mm. Hölbl 1986: pl. 29,3.
32. Late Egyptian Bes figurine with double face; faience with sea-green glaze (2:1). From Rabat, Malta. Valletta Museum. 42 × 24 × 11,3mm. Unpublished.
33. Falcon-headed divinity with sun disc on head (Re-Harakhty), clothed with kilt; faience with green glaze (2:1). From Rabat, Malta. Valletta Musuem. 32 × 11,6 × 6,5mm. Unpublished.
34. Aerial view of Kuntillet 'Ajrud.
35. Marble altar with bucrania and inscription from Sardis. Manisa Museum, Inv. no. 244.
36. Marble altar with bucrania and inscription from Ephesos. Selçuk Museum, Inv. no. 1728.
37. Belt buckle from "La Joya". Huelva Archaeological Museum.
38. Drawings on pottery from Azaila (Teruel). C.V.H. no. 55.
39. Ara from Altea (Alicante). Madrid, National Archaeological Museum.
40. The Voconios stela from Mérida. Mérida, Museo de Arte Romano.